Lenin Selected Writings: On Imperialist War

On Imperialist War

VI Lenin

Selected Writings: 1

Wellred Books
London

On Imperialist War
Selected Writings: 1
VI Lenin

First edition
Wellred Books, May 2024

UK distribution: Wellred Books Britain, wellredbooks.co.uk
124 City Road
London
EC1V 2NX
contact@wellredbooks.co.uk

USA distribution: Marxist Books, marxistbooks.com
WR Books
250 44th Street #208
Brooklyn
New York
NY 11232
sales@marxistbooks.com

DK distribution: Forlaget Marx, forlagetmarx.dk
Degnestavnen 19, st. tv.
2400 København NV
forlag@forlagetmarx.dk

Cover image: *Image of the Future from the 'Gas War'*
by Rudolf Eberle, 1916

Cover design by Jesse Murray-Dean

Layout by Wellred Books

ISBN: 978 1 916936 05 8

Printed in Great Britain by Bell and Bain Ltd, Glasgow

Contents

Appendices

Note on Dates

Until 14 February 1918, Russia used the Old Style (Julian) calendar, which is currently thirteen days behind the New Style (Gregorian) used in the West and which is standard today.

Only dates of articles written in Russia, or dates referring to events that happened in Russia, are given in the Old Style, with the New Style date also provided in brackets.

The articles in this volume are ordered chronologically according to the New Style calendar.

Introduction

This volume is a collection of Lenin's writings on the crucial question of the position of revolutionary Marxists towards war, specifically in relation to the First World War. The study of these texts is important today, when the question of war is again on the agenda and, disgracefully, many in the workers' movement, including some who call themselves 'communists' have taken a social-chauvinist position of support for their own ruling class.

The Marxist position on war was developed by Marx and Engels, at a time when capitalism still played a relatively progressive role and the bourgeoisie had conducted a series of progressive and even revolutionary wars. Lenin explained how, in the period between the Great French Revolution of 1789 and the Paris Commune of 1871, most wars in Europe were "wars of a bourgeois-progressive, national-liberating character" and as a consequence:

> ... all honest and revolutionary democrats, as well as all socialists, always wished success to that country (i.e. that bourgeoisie) which had helped to overthrow or undermine the most baneful foundations of feudalism, absolutism and the oppression of other nations.*

---

* VI Lenin, *Socialism and War*, in this volume, p. 64.

The twentieth century announced the beginning of a completely different period, that of imperialism. This had implications for the position of Marxists. By this time, Europe was dominated by imperialist powers and the idea of 'national defence' or of a just 'national war' no longer applied. Rather, wars were now being fought by different sets of slave-owners fighting each other "for a more 'just' redistribution of slaves", as Lenin put it.*

The Second International, which formally based itself on Marxism, had discussed the coming outbreak of war between imperialist powers and had taken a clear position against it. The Stuttgart Conference of the Socialist International in 1907 had adopted a resolution explaining clearly that wars "are part of the very nature of capitalism; they will cease only when the capitalist system is abolished".**

The main body of the resolution had been drafted by August Bebel, and it reflected the Marxist view on war in general terms, but lacked any concrete detail about action the workers must take against war and militarism. The Russian delegation (Lenin and Martov) drafted a number of amendments together with Rosa Luxemburg. These were put to the committee on 'Militarism and International Conflicts', which accepted them. Lenin explained:

> These amendments (1) stated that militarism is the chief weapon of class oppression; (2) pointed out the need for propaganda among the youth; (3) stressed that Social-Democrats should not only try to prevent war from breaking out or to secure the speediest termination of wars that have already begun, but should utilise the crisis created by the war to hasten the overthrow of the bourgeoisie.***

---

*   Ibid., p. 65.
**   'Resolution of the Seventh International Socialist Congress at Stuttgart', in this volume, p. 368.
*** Lenin, 'The International Socialist Congress in Stuttgart', in this volume, p. 7.
      The term 'Social-Democracy' at this time meant revolutionary socialist. All the revolutionary Marxists were called Social Democrats before 1914. It was in 1919, with the creation of the Communist Third International that they began to call themselves Communists.

In the committee discussing war and militarism at the Stuttgart Congress, Lenin and Luxemburg were also able to answer the semi-anarchist ideas of the French ultra-left Gustave Hervé, and in doing so they stressed the basic Marxist position on war:

> The notorious Hervé, who has made such a noise in France and Europe, advocated a semi-anarchist view by naively suggesting that every war be 'answered' by a strike and an uprising. He did not understand, on the one hand, that *war is a necessary product of capitalism*, and that *the proletariat cannot renounce participation in revolutionary wars*, for such wars are possible, and have indeed occurred in capitalist societies. He did not understand, on the other hand, that the possibility of 'answering' a war depends on the nature of the crisis created by that war. The choice of the means of struggle depends on these conditions; moreover, the struggle must consist (and here we have the third misconception, or shallow thinking of Hervéism) *not simply in replacing war by peace, but in replacing capitalism by socialism*. The essential thing is not merely to prevent war, but to utilise the crisis created by war in order to hasten the overthrow of the bourgeoisie.*

Ironically, Hervé, who did not base himself on a materialist understanding of the question, and who was obsessed with the struggle against militarism and war *in general*, swung violently in the opposite direction and joined the chauvinist 'national defence' camp in 1914.

A similar resolution to that of Stuttgart was approved by the Copenhagen Congress of the Socialist International in 1910 and at the Basel Congress in 1912. The Socialist International had clearly declared that the forthcoming war was an imperialist one, and that the duty of the Socialist parties was to oppose it by all means at their disposal.

The betrayal of 1914

However, when the war broke out in 1914, the Socialist International betrayed its own resolutions and gave wholehearted

---

* Ibid., p. 6, emphasis added.

support to the imperialist slaughter. One after another, in Germany, France, Belgium and Britain, the same socialist parties which had voted for the resolutions against the imperialist war now voted for war credits, declared a truce in the class struggle between labour and capital, entered governments of national unity with the ruling class, and succumbed to social-chauvinism.

This came as a big shock, including to Lenin, who initially thought that the issue of the German Social Democratic Party's (SPD) paper, *Vorwärts*, which announced support for war credits was a forgery by the general staff of the German army. In fact, while nominally still defending Marxist ideas and programme, the main parties of the Second International, including the large and influential SPD, had become thoroughly infected with reformism. Having developed in a period of prolonged economic upswing of capitalism, the top layers of the socialist organisations had been co-opted by capitalism. In *Imperialism, the Highest Stage of Capitalism* (1916), Lenin explained the social roots of chauvinism and revisionism, which he linked to the rise of imperialism. The super-profits derived from the exploitation of the colonies allowed the ruling class in the imperialist countries to buy off the top layer of the working class and its organisations, creating a labour aristocracy. They had become nothing more than "labour lieutenants of the capitalist class", as Lenin put it.*

Those who remained loyal to the internationalist, anti-imperialist principles of the movement were in a small minority, chiefly amongst them the Russian Bolsheviks and the Serbian party, which were the only ones not to vote for war credits, as well as prominent but initially isolated individuals, such as Karl Liebknecht and Rosa Luxemburg in Germany, James Connolly in Ireland, John Maclean in Scotland, Eugene V Debs in the US, and the great Balkan Marxist Christian Rakovsky. Others who opposed the war did so from a hopeless pacifist or neutral position, such as the British Independent Labour Party and the Italian Socialist Party.

---

* Lenin, *Imperialism, the Highest Stage of Capitalism*, Wellred Books, 2019, p. 8.

In this initial period, Lenin was isolated in exile (originally in Austrian-occupied Galicia, then in the safer neutral Switzerland), with very few means to maintain contact and correspondence with Bolsheviks inside Russia. He launched himself into a decisive battle to defend the principles of Marxism on the all-important question of the war. He saw as his main task that of establishing firm theoretical clarity and a clear line of demarcation, not only between the revolutionaries and the social-patriots, but also between the revolutionaries and the wavering elements (represented by Karl Kautsky), and with anyone who was not prepared to carry out a clean break with them.

The main ideas he fought for were that the war was an imperialist war and had to be opposed by the working class in all countries; that the leaders of the Social-Democracy had betrayed the movement; that the Second International was dead and a new international had to be built; and that the only way to end the war was through revolution. He also took a firm position against pacifism, explaining that an imperialist peace would be just the prelude to a new imperialist war.

Zimmerwald

Over a period of time, as the war – which everyone thought was only going to last a few months at most – became prolonged and more deadly, the voices within the labour movement opposed to the imperialist slaughter started to get a bigger echo. A conference of socialists opposed to the war was formally called by the Swiss and Italian parties. It took place in Zimmerwald, Switzerland, from 5-8 September 1915.

In preparation for the conference, Lenin wrote a pamphlet spelling out the position of the Bolsheviks regarding all important aspects of the opposition to the imperialist war. The pamphlet *Socialism and War*, which was co-signed by Zinoviev, was printed in German and given out to all Zimmerwald attendees.*

---

* In this volume, p. 57.

The document was a summary of the main ideas Lenin had been defending since the beginning of the war. He explained that Marxists are not pacifists. The Marxist approach to war starts from the understanding that war is the continuation of politics by other means, and therefore it must also be approached from the point of view of the interests of the working class. Marxists do not oppose all wars, but start from an analysis of the character of each war. Their attitude towards a war is not determined by who fired the first shot or who is 'the aggressor', as imperialist powers will always find or fabricate an excuse to justify a war. There are reactionary imperialist wars, which Marxists oppose, but there are also progressive wars. Revolutionaries are in favour of wars of national liberation and wars against imperialism by oppressed nations. Revolutionaries are also in favour of class war of the oppressed classes against the ruling class.

As Lenin later added, commenting on the position of German *Internationale* group of Luxemburg, Liebknecht and Zetkin, Marxists are also in favour of wars waged by a victorious proletarian state against attempts by the bourgeoisie to crush it.*

Marxists are opposed to the idea of 'national defence' in an imperialist war, as what this really means is the right of one group of robbers to plunder the colonial countries at the expense of an opposing group of robbers. The rights of small nations are used as an excuse by the imperialist powers.

In fact, in regards to the First World War, Lenin argued that the only instance in which the war could be considered to have a 'national' character, and therefore to be progressive, was in the case of Serbia, which had been attacked by Austria-Hungary. But even here, the national considerations were superseded by the general imperialist character of the war, and the fact that behind Serbia stood the interests of Russian imperialism. Most interestingly, Lenin's appraisal was emphatically shared by the Serbian Marxists – their understanding of the revolutionary

---

* See Lenin, 'The Military Programme of the Proletarian Revolution' on p. 199 and 'The Junius Pamphlet' on p. 173.

position towards war in the imperialist epoch was sharpened by the Balkan Wars that preceded the First World War, and they therefore took a principled position.*

In times of war, as in times of peace, the working class must maintain its class independence in defence of its own interests and not enter into any coalitions or agreements with the capitalist class. Marxists oppose 'national unity' or a 'social truce' in the name of 'national defence'.

Lenin reserved some of his strongest language for his attacks on the opportunists, chiefly represented by Kautsky. They 'in general' and 'in principle' opposed the war, but then made excuses for those who had voted for the war credits and succumbed to social-chauvinism. Opposing the war in words, they refused to struggle *in practice* against it. They also wavered on the question of the need for a clean break with the social-chauvinists.

For Lenin, this too was a crucial point. The Second International had betrayed the cause of the working class and a new international was needed.

How was the struggle against the imperialist war to be conducted? Lenin's starting point was that the only way to put an end to the war was by turning it into a civil war, a revolutionary war to overthrow the capitalist system. An imperialist peace would be merely the continuation of imperialist war, and would prepare for new predatory wars of conquest. The only consistent struggle against war was the struggle to bring the working class to power.

Additionally, Lenin highlighted cases of fraternisation between soldiers of different countries and stressed the need to carry out systematic work in that direction. In the conditions of curtailment of democratic rights in all the belligerent countries, he argued for the supplementing of legal and parliamentary work with underground and illegal work. More generally, he advocated support for all kinds of revolutionary mass action by the proletariat.

---

* See 'The position of Serbian socialists during WWI', *In Defence of Marxism*, 2023, available online at marxist.com/the-position-of-serbian-socialists-during-wwi.htm

The participants in the Zimmerwald Conference fell mostly into three groups. The right wing opposed the war, but mostly from a pacifist, not a revolutionary, position, and were against a clear break with the social-chauvinists. The Left wing around Lenin and the Bolsheviks, in addition to opposing the war, insisted that those socialists who had supported the war must be denounced; they demanded that socialist deputies should vote against war credits; they explained that the war could only be ended by revolutionary means; and they put forward the need for a clean break and the formation of a new international. Between these two groups stood a centre grouping, which sided with the Left on several key questions, but not completely.

It soon became clear that the Left was in a minority. One of the German delegates, Georg Ledebour, threatened to walk out if a call for socialist deputies to vote against the war credits was included in the final resolution.

In the end, a joint statement, including the most important ideas proposed by the Left, was agreed. It had been drafted by Trotsky, who, while not formally part of the Zimmerwald Left, sided with it on all the fundamental questions.

The Zimmerwald Manifesto declared that the war was imperialist and had to be opposed. It argued that the International and the parties which had voted for the war credits, which had joined national unity governments and had advocated social peace, had failed the working class. Finally, it reminded workers that war had to be opposed by the methods outlined in resolutions at previous socialist conferences.

However, it was clear that a number of crucial questions were left out, and therefore two additional statements were made at the conference by the Left, pointing out the shortcomings of the main manifesto.* The first statement explained that the manifesto did not contain any criticism of the opportunists. The second statement protested that the inclusion of the demand that socialist deputies

---

* See 'Two Declarations of the Zimmerwald Left', in this volume, p. 395.

should vote against war credits was blocked by the threat of a walkout by some German delegates.

The Left therefore made it clear that, while the manifesto was a step forward, there were a number of points which should have been made more clearly or more forcefully. They had therefore made a partial compromise on political clarity for the sake of maintaining unity with the centre, while preserving their freedom to explain their position fully and agitate for it publicly.

As we can see, even amongst those opposing the war, there was still confusion, and many had not drawn all the necessary conclusions, particularly in regards to the need for a clean break with opportunism and the need to found a new international.

Seven months after the Zimmerwald Conference, a follow up meeting was held in Kienthal, Switzerland, on 24-30 April 1916, with the participation of forty-three delegates. Of those, twelve supported the Zimmerwald Left led by Lenin, an increase of four since the previous conference. Working-class public opinion on the war had shifted even further, giving the Left a stronger position at Kienthal. On some issues, the Left managed to get twenty votes. Even the right wing of the anti-war socialists was coming under pressure from below to adopt a more radical stance, at least in words. The approved manifesto was thus a step forward in relation to Zimmerwald in two important aspects: it included an explicit criticism of the social-patriotic leaders of the Socialist International, and it openly called for socialist deputies to vote against war credits and break with governments of national unity.*

The main debate at Kienthal centred on the question of how the crisis of the socialist movement was to be resolved. The Zimmerwald Left openly called on workers "to create the theoretical and organisational preconditions for preparing the launching of a new International", while the Right and the Centre wanted the International to reconvene its leading body, the International Socialist Bureau, so as to wage a struggle there.

---

* The 'Kienthal Manifesto' is reproduced in this volume, p. 397.

Revolutionary defeatism

It is in this context that Lenin adopted a position of 'revolutionary defeatism':

> ... to us Russian Social-Democrats there cannot be the slightest doubt that, *from the standpoint of the working class and of the toiling masses of all the nations of Russia*, the defeat of the tsarist monarchy, the most reactionary and barbarous of governments, which is oppressing the largest number of nations and the greatest mass of the population of Europe and Asia, would be the lesser evil.*

Here Lenin stressed that the defeat of the tsarist monarchy was the lesser evil *from the point of view of the Russian workers*. The German social-chauvinists justified support for *their own* ruling class on the basis of the war aims of Germany being somehow 'progressive', as it was fighting the most reactionary force in Europe: Russian autocracy. But, of course, Lenin insisted that the German workers' main task was that of fighting *their own* ruling class.

In raising the idea that the defeat of one's own government is the lesser evil, Lenin was addressing the cadres, the most advanced layers of revolutionary Social-Democracy, and in so doing he used the sharpest formulations in order to straighten out any vacillation and to draw a line which excluded the confused elements. On important occasions, Lenin would 'bend the stick' in the opposite direction to his opponents to emphasise a point. This was a clear instance of that. As a result, the slogan of revolutionary defeatism is perhaps one of the most misunderstood and misinterpreted of Lenin's formulations.

First of all, Lenin clarified that this did not mean carrying out of acts of sabotage or adventurist actions:

> ... this does not mean 'blowing up bridges', organising unsuccessful strikes in the war industries, and in general helping the government defeat the revolutionaries.**

---

* Lenin, 'The War and Russian Social-Democracy', in this volume, p. 16.
** Lenin, 'The Defeat of One's Own Government in the Imperialist War', in this volume, p. 43.

Secondly, the slogan was used mainly between 1914 and 1916 in the context of polemics against the waverers and the centrists. In fact, the slogan was not used in any of the agitation carried out by the Bolsheviks in Russia during that period. In the classic work, *St. Petersburg Between the Revolutions*, Robert B McKean says:

> A textual analysis of forty-seven leaflets and appeals published illegally by Bolshevik militants between January 1915 and 22 February 1917 is most illuminating. Not a single leaflet mentioned the essential Leninist slogan of the defeat of Russia being the lesser evil...*

Most of the Bolshevik agitation before the revolution was centred on attacking the policies of the government against the working class, and advocating for revolutionary struggle against it as the only way to end the war, stressing the slogans of a democratic republic, the eight-hour day and the distribution of the land. This was the concrete practical meaning of 'the defeat of one's own government' – the continuation of the revolutionary agitation against the government, even during wartime, regardless of the fact that such agitation was bound to weaken that government in relation to the war effort.

That can also be seen in the draft resolution of the Left delegates to the Zimmerwald Conference, written by Karl Radek, but presented jointly with Lenin, with whom he collaborated closely in Switzerland. The resolution insisted on the need for revolutionary struggle against the capitalist governments, the need to use:

> ... all the struggles, all the reforms demanded by our minimum programme for the purpose of *sharpening this war crisis* as well as every social and political crisis of capitalism of extending them to an attack upon its very foundations.**

It concludes by quoting the words of Liebknecht's letter to the conference: "'Civil *war*, not "*civil peace*"' – that is the slogan!"***

---

* Robert B McKean, *St. Petersburg Between the Revolutions*, Yale, 1990, p. 361.
** 'Draft Resolution and Manifesto Submitted by the Left Wing Delegates at Zimmerwald', in this volume, p. 389, emphasis in original.
*** Ibid., p. 390, emphasis in original.

The resolution did not, however, contain any mention of the defeat of one's own government being the lesser evil.

Lenin also drafted his own resolution for the Left delegates. In it he explained that socialists should use "the masses' growing desire for peace" in order to intensify their revolutionary agitation and should not be "shying away in that agitation from considerations of the defeat of their 'own' country". It should also be noted here how, in this resolution, Lenin – who had energetically rejected pacifist illusions and even the use of the 'peace' slogan – made a point of recognising the need to base revolutionary agitation on the desire for peace *amongst the masses*. He explained that this was an expression of their rejection "of the bourgeois lie regarding the defence of the fatherland, and the awakening of their revolutionary consciousness".* Again, in Lenin's text there is no mention of the defeat of one's government being the lesser evil.

Lenin was taking aim at the opportunists, who everywhere capitulated to their own government and attempted to put a halt to the class struggle, to create 'social peace', in order to help the war effort. Lenin therefore posed the question in the negative: revolutionary agitation *should not be constrained* by the fact that it might lead to the weakening and defeat of the government. Quite the contrary.

After the February Revolution

Once the revolution broke out in Russia in February 1917, and Lenin was able to return to the country in April, he completely dropped the idea that the defeat of one's own government would be the lesser evil, *because he was now addressing the masses in the context of a revolution*. In all his writings and speeches after the February Revolution, we can see how he recognised the difference between the 'honest defencist' mood which existed amongst the mass of workers and peasants who had carried out the revolution, and the reactionary defencism of the ruling class, echoed by the social-chauvinists. As a result, he stressed the need to patiently explain the

---

* Lenin, 'The Draft Resolution of the Left Wing at Zimmerwald', in this volume, p. 112, both quotes.

programme of the Bolsheviks using slogans which serve to raise the level of understanding of these layers.

> The masses take a practical and not a theoretical approach to the question. We make the mistake of taking the theoretical approach. […]
>
> In view of the undoubted existence of a defencist mood among the masses, who recognise the war *only of necessity* and not for the sake of conquest, we must explain to them most circumstantially, persistently and patiently that the war cannot be ended in a non-rapacious peace unless capital is overthrown. […] The soldiers want a concrete answer: how to end the war. […] We must base ourselves only on the political consciousness of the masses. […] When the masses say they don't want conquest, I believe them. When Guchkov and Lvov say they don't want conquest, they are swindlers. When the worker says that he wants to defend the country, he voices the oppressed man's instinct.*

Here we can see Lenin's consistent revolutionary method. The conclusion he drew from this was *not to fall into defencism*, but rather to explain that *only when the workers take powe*r can a genuine defencist position be adopted.

In fact, on a number of occasions between February and October 1917, the Bolsheviks were at pains to defend themselves against the slanderous allegations of the Provisional Government that they were for the disorganisation of the army, or for a separate peace with Germany.

> This war cannot be ended by a refusal of the soldiers of one side only to continue the war, by a simple cessation of hostilities by one of the belligerents.
>
> The Conference reiterates its protest against the base slander spread by the capitalists against our Party to the effect that we are in favour of a separate peace with Germany. We consider the German capitalists to be as predatory as the Russian, British, French and other capitalists,

---

* Lenin, 'Report at a Meeting of Bolshevik Delegates to the All-Russia Conference of Soviets of Workers' and Soldiers' Deputies', in this volume, from p. 271, emphasis in original.

and Emperor Wilhelm as bad a crowned brigand as Nicholas II or the British, Italian, Romanian and all other monarchs.*

In June 1917, Lenin reproduced a leaflet distributed by Bolshevik agitators in the army:

> ... beware of those who, posing as Bolsheviks, will try to provoke you to riots and disturbances as a screen for their own cowardice! [...]
>
> The real Bolsheviks call you to conscious revolutionary struggle, and not to riots.**

In fact, there was a period just before the October Revolution in which the army high command and sections of the ruling class were openly working for a military defeat of Russia in order to drown the revolution in blood. In effect, they were putting their class interests before the national interest. At this point, Lenin developed his arguments further, explaining the measures that would be necessary to turn the capitalist imperialist war into a just war:

> The defence potential, the military might, of a country whose banks have been nationalised is *superior* to that of a country whose banks remain in private hands. The military might of a peasant country whose land is in the hands of peasant committees is *superior* to that of a country whose land is in the hands of landowners.***

The fundamental argument is the same: the workers must take power. But the way the argument is presented is different, taking into account the audience the Bolsheviks were addressing and the concrete mood of the masses at the time.

During a debate at the Extraordinary Fourth All-Russia Congress of Soviets about the ratification of the Brest-Litovsk peace treaty with Germany in March 1918, Lenin spelled out the change:

---

*   'Resolution on the War at the Seventh (April) All-Russia Conference of the RSDLP(B)', in this volume, p. 295.
** Lenin, 'Bolshevism and 'Demoralisation' of the Army', in this volume, p. 313.
*** Lenin, 'The Struggle Against Economic Chaos – and the War', from *The Impending Catastrophe and How to Combat It*, in this volume, p. 327.

We were defeatists at the time of the tsar, but at the time of Tsereteli and Chernov we were not defeatists.*

That is, while the tsarist autocracy was in power, the Bolsheviks were revolutionary defeatists, but they ceased to be so when tsarism was overthrown and the Provisional Government was established. Lenin himself explained the meaning of this change in a discussion during the Third Congress of the Comintern in 1921:

> At the beginning of the war we Bolsheviks adhered to a single slogan – that of civil war, and a ruthless one at that. We branded as a traitor everyone who did not support the idea of civil war. But when we came back to Russia in March 1917 we changed our position entirely. When we returned to Russia and spoke to the peasants and workers, we saw that they all stood for defence of the homeland, of course in quite a different sense from the Mensheviks, and we could not call these ordinary workers and peasants scoundrels and traitors. We described this as 'honest defencism'. [...] Our original stand at the beginning of the war was correct: it was important then to form a definite and resolute core. Our subsequent stand was correct too. It proceeded from the assumption that the masses had to be won over.**

Here we see the extraordinary skill of Lenin. First, he waged an implacable struggle for principles, not just against the open betrayers, but also against those who were willing to make compromises or were not prepared to draw all the necessary conclusions from the political break that had taken place.

He not only struggled against those to his right, but also against those who made left-wing, or more precisely 'ultra-left', mistakes. This was the case for instance in his criticism of the *Junius*

---

* Lenin, 'Reply to the Debate on the Report on Ratification of the Peace Treaty', *Extraordinary Fourth All-Russia Congress Of Soviets*, 14-16 March 1918, *Lenin Collected Works*, Vol. 27, Progress Publishers, 1960, p. 193.
  Irakli Tseretelli and Viktor Chernov were respectively Menshevik and Socialist-Revolutionary ministers in Kerensky's Provisional Government.
** Lenin, 'Speeches at a Meeting of Members of the German, Polish, Czechoslovak, Hungarian and Italian Delegations, 11 July', ibid., Vol. 42, p. 325.

Pamphlet.* He praised the text as an important breakthrough, as it showed the existence of an internationalist and revolutionary wing in the German Social-Democracy, where the betrayal had been most damaging. But at the same time, he insisted on pointing out certain shortcomings of the document, which unbeknownst to him had been written by Rosa Luxemburg (under the pseudonym Junius), and subjecting them to detailed criticism. One of those mistakes was related to the national question and the possibility of national wars in the epoch of imperialism, on which Luxemburg had a different position to Lenin.

Having thus established a principled position through an implacable struggle with other trends, and having won over the vanguard to a correct position, Lenin then, without changing his principles one iota, undertook the second part of the task: that of winning over the masses to that position. And that required being able to explain those same ideas in a way that the mass of workers and peasants would be able to understand, and which connected with their experiences and consciousness.

It is in this context that Lenin's criticism of Trotsky in 'The Defeat of One's Own Government in the Imperialist War', written in 1915, needs to be understood.**

Trotsky was at the time editing a daily anti-war newspaper in Paris, *Nashe Slovo*, and therefore his audience was different from that which Lenin was addressing. The slogan of the 'defeat of one's country being the lesser evil' could not be used in a paper which aimed to reach wider layers.

There was general political agreement between Lenin and Trotsky regarding the struggle against the imperialist war, as witnessed by their close collaboration at Zimmerwald and Kienthal, but Trotsky had illusions in the possibility of re-establishing the unity of the party, which Lenin adamantly opposed. On this question, Lenin was right.

---

*   See Lenin, 'The Junius Pamphlet', this volume, p. 173.
** See this volume, p. 43.

The Bolsheviks in power

One last observation. The Russian Revolution, as is known, was fought on the basis of the slogan 'Peace, Bread and Land', which the Bolsheviks argued could only be achieved through the workers and peasants coming to power, hence the slogan 'All Power to the Soviets'. Upon coming to power after the October Revolution, the Decree on Peace was one of the first passed by the Soviet Government.* In it, the Bolsheviks fulfilled their promises, offering a genuine democratic peace, without annexations, to all belligerent countries.

In addition, the Bolsheviks in power repudiated all secret treaties, which they made public, to the great embarrassment of the imperialist powers. These included, for instance, the Treaty of London, by which Britain, France and Russia promised territorial concessions to Italy to be carved out of Austria-Hungary in exchange for Italian support in the war; and the Constantinople and Sykes-Picot agreements between Britain, France and Russia for the division of the Ottoman Empire, even though they had promised the Arabs self-rule in exchange for rising up against the Turks.

Lenin put forward the idea that, if this proposal for a democratic peace were to be rejected, then Soviet power would wage a genuine defensive war, a revolutionary war against Germany and other imperialist powers that threatened the new workers' state. This was not to be. In fact, such was the state of demoralisation in the Russian Army that a strong tendency towards disintegration set in as the revolution triumphed.

During the peace negotiations at Brest-Litovsk in early 1918 between the Soviets, led by Trotsky, and the Central Powers, the Bolsheviks were barely able to hold the line at the front. They were stalling and hoping that revolution would break out in Germany. Revolution did break out in Germany, although not until November of that year. The German high command was fully aware of the

---

* See 'Second All-Russia Congress of Soviets of Workers' and Soldiers' Deputies', in this volume, p. 351.

dire situation of the Russian Army and extracted an onerous peace from the Soviets. Starting in February 1918, a whole new army had to be created, the Red Army of Workers and Peasants, tasked with defending the Revolution and Soviet power. But that falls beyond the scope of this volume.

Lenin's writings on the struggle against the imperialist war are a treasure trove for revolutionaries today. Much can be learned from a detailed study of the principles he defended – which were a development of those outlined by Marx and Engels, in new conditions – and also of the way he then applied those principles in his practical agitation aimed at winning over the masses. We hope that this selection, though by no means exhaustive, will help revolutionary communists today in that endeavour.

Jorge Martín,
April 2024

The International Socialist Congress in Stuttgart

20 October 1907

Editors note:

The International Socialist Congress in Stuttgart, Germany (the Seventh Congress of the Second International) was held from 18-24 August 1907 (New Style).

The Russian Social Democratic Party (RSDLP) was represented at it by thirty-seven delegates. Among the Bolshevik delegates attending the Congress were Lenin, Lunacharsky, and Litvinov.

The Congress considered the following questions: (1) Militarism and international conflicts; (2) Relations between the political parties and the trade unions; (3) The colonial question; (4) Immigration and emigration of workers; and (5) Women's suffrage.

The main work of the Congress was in the committees, where resolutions were drafted for the plenary sessions. Lenin was on the 'Militarism and International Conflicts' Committee.

The resolution adopted by the Congress is reproduced in this volume, p. 367.

* * *

A feature of the International Socialist Congress held in Stuttgart this August was its large and representative composition: the total of 886 delegates came from all the five continents. Besides providing an impressive demonstration of international unity in the proletarian struggle, the Congress played an outstanding part in defining the tactics of the socialist parties. It adopted general resolutions on a number of questions, the decision of which had hitherto been left solely to the discretion of the individual socialist parties. And the fact that more and more problems require uniform, principled decisions in different countries is striking proof that socialism is being welded into a single international force.

The full text of the Stuttgart resolutions will be found elsewhere in this issue.* We shall deal briefly with each of them in order to bring out the chief controversial points and the character of the debate at the Congress.

This is not the first time the colonial question has figured at international congresses. Up till now their decisions have always been an unqualified condemnation of bourgeois colonial policy as a policy of plunder and violence. This time, however, the Congress Commission was so composed that opportunist elements, headed by Van Kol of Holland, predominated in it. A sentence was inserted in the draft resolution to the effect that the Congress did not in principle condemn all colonial policy, for under socialism colonial policy could play a civilising role. The minority in the Commission (Ledebour of Germany, the Polish and Russian Social-Democrats, and many others) vigorously protested against any such idea being entertained. The matter was referred to Congress, where the forces of the two trends were found to be so nearly equal that there was an extremely heated debate.

The opportunists rallied behind Van Kol. Speaking for the majority of the German delegation, Bernstein and David urged acceptance of a 'socialist colonial policy' and fulminated against

---

*   The issue of *Proletary* (No. 17) which published this article also contained the
     resolution of the International Socialist Congress in Stuttgart, reproduced in
     this volume on p. 367.

the radicals for their barren, negative attitude, their failure to appreciate the importance of reforms, their lack of a practical colonial programme, etc. Incidentally, they were opposed by Kautsky, who felt compelled to ask the Congress to pronounce *against* the majority of the German delegation. He rightly pointed out that there was no question of rejecting the struggle for reforms; that was explicitly stated in other sections of the resolution, which had evoked no dispute. The point at issue was whether we should make concessions to the modern regime of bourgeois plunder and violence. The Congress was to discuss present-day colonial policy, which was based on the downright enslavement of primitive populations. The bourgeoisie was actually introducing slavery in the colonies and subjecting the native populations to unprecedented outrages and acts of violence, 'civilising' them by the spread of liquor and syphilis. And in that situation socialists were expected to utter evasive phrases about the possibility of accepting colonial policy in principle! That would be an outright desertion to the bourgeois point of view. It would be a decisive step towards subordinating the proletariat to bourgeois ideology, to bourgeois imperialism, which is now arrogantly raising its head.

The Congress defeated the Commission's motion by 128 votes to 108, with ten abstentions (Switzerland). It should be noted that at Stuttgart, for the first time, each nation was allotted a definite number of votes, varying from twenty (for the big nations, Russia included) to two (Luxembourg). The combined vote of the small nations, which either do not pursue a colonial policy, or which suffer from it, outweighed the vote of nations where even the proletariat has been somewhat infected with the lust of conquest.

This vote on the colonial question is of very great importance. First, it strikingly showed up socialist opportunism, which succumbs to bourgeois blandishments. Secondly, it revealed a negative feature in the European labour movement, one that can do no little harm to the proletarian cause, and for that reason should receive serious attention. Marx frequently quoted a very significant saying of Sismondi. The proletarians of the ancient world, this saying runs, lived at the expense of society; modern society lives at the expense of the proletarians.*

The non-propertied, but non-working, class is incapable of overthrowing the exploiters. Only the proletarian class, which maintains the whole of society, can bring about the social revolution. However, as a result of the extensive colonial policy, the European proletarian *partly* finds himself in a position when it is *not* his labour, but the labour of the practically enslaved natives in the colonies, that maintains the whole of society. The British bourgeoisie, for example, derives more profit from the many millions of the population of India and other colonies than from the British workers. In certain countries this provides the material and economic basis for infecting the proletariat with colonial chauvinism. Of course, this may be only a temporary phenomenon, but the evil must nonetheless be clearly realised and its causes understood in order to be able to rally the proletariat of all countries for the struggle against such opportunism. This struggle is bound to be victorious, since the 'privileged' nations are a diminishing faction of the capitalist nations.

There were practically no differences at the Congress on the question of women's suffrage. The only one who tried to make out a case for a socialist campaign in favour of a limited women's suffrage (qualified as opposed to universal suffrage) was a woman delegate from the extremely opportunist British Fabian Society. No one supported her. Her motives were simple enough: British bourgeois ladies hope to obtain the franchise for themselves, without its extension to women workers in Britain.

The First International Socialist Women's Conference was held concurrently with the Congress in the same building. Both at this Conference and in the Congress Commission there was an interesting dispute between the German and Austrian Social-Democrats on the draft resolution. In their campaign for universal suffrage, the Austrians tended to play down the demand for equal

---

*   See Karl Marx, *Capital*, Vol. 1, in *Marx and Engels Collected Works* (henceforth referred to as *MECW*), Lawrence & Wishart, 1975, p. 591, footnote.

rights of men and women; on practical grounds they placed the main emphasis on male suffrage. Clara Zetkin and other German Social-Democrats rightly pointed out to the Austrians that they were acting incorrectly, and that by failing to press the demand that the vote be granted to women as well as men, they were weakening the mass movement. The concluding words of the Stuttgart resolution ("the demand for universal suffrage should be put forward *simultaneously* for both men and women") undoubtedly relate to this episode of excessive 'practicalism' in the history of the Austrian labour movement.

The resolution on the relations between the socialist parties and the trade unions is of especial importance to us Russians. The Stockholm RSDLP Congress went on record for *non-Party* unions, thus endorsing the neutrality standpoint, which has always been upheld by our non-Party democrats, Bernsteinians and Socialist-Revolutionaries. The London Congress, on the other hand, put forward a different principle, namely, closer alignment of the unions with the Party, even including, under certain conditions, their recognition as Party unions. At Stuttgart, in the Social-Democratic subsection of the Russian section (the socialists of each country form a separate section at international congresses) opinion was divided on this issue (there was no split on other issues). Plekhanov upheld the neutrality principle. Voinov,* a Bolshevik, defended the anti-neutralist viewpoint of the London Congress and of the Belgian resolution (published in the Congress materials with de Brouckère's report, which will soon appear in Russian). Clara Zetkin rightly remarked in her journal *Die Gleichheit* that Plekhanov's arguments for neutrality were just as lame as those of the French. And the Stuttgart resolution – as Kautsky rightly observed and as anyone who takes the trouble to read it carefully will see – puts an end to recognition of the 'neutrality' principle. There is not a word in it about neutrality or non-party principles. On the contrary, it definitely recognises the

---

* Pseudonym of Anatoly Lunacharsky.

need for closer and stronger connections between the unions and the socialist parties.

The resolution of the London RSDLP Congress on the trade unions has thus been placed on a firm theoretical basis in the form of the Stuttgart resolution. The Stuttgart resolution lays down the general principle that in every country the unions must be brought into permanent and close contact with the socialist party. The London resolution says that in Russia this should take the form, under favourable conditions, of party unions, and party members must work towards that goal.

We note that the harmful aspects of the neutrality principle were revealed in Stuttgart by the fact that the trade-union half of the German delegation were the most adamant supporters of opportunist views. That is why in Essen, for example, the Germans were against Van Kol (the trade unions were not represented in Essen, which was a Congress solely of the Party), while in Stuttgart they supported him. By playing into the hands of the opportunists in the Social-Democratic movement the advocacy of neutrality in Germany has *actually* had harmful results. This is a fact that should not be overlooked, especially in Russia, where the bourgeois-democratic counsellors of the proletariat, who urge it to keep the trade-union movement 'neutral', are so numerous.

A few words about the resolution on emigration and immigration. Here, too, in the Commission there was an attempt to defend narrow, craft interests, to ban the immigration of workers from backward countries (coolies – from China, etc.). This is the same spirit of aristocratism that one finds among workers in some of the 'civilised' countries, who derive certain advantages from their privileged position, and are, therefore, inclined to forget the need for international class solidarity. But no one at the Congress defended this craft and petty-bourgeois narrow-mindedness. The resolution fully meets the demands of revolutionary Social-Democracy.

We pass now to the last, and perhaps the most important, resolution of the Congress – that on anti-militarism. The notorious

Hervé, who has made such a noise in France and Europe, advocated a semi-anarchist view by naively suggesting that every war be 'answered' by a strike and an uprising. He did not understand, on the one hand, that war is a necessary product of capitalism, and that the proletariat cannot renounce participation in revolutionary wars, for such wars are possible, and have indeed occurred in capitalist societies. He did not understand, on the other hand, that the possibility of 'answering' a war depends on the nature of the crisis created by that war. The choice of the means of struggle depends on these conditions; moreover, the struggle must consist (and here we have the third misconception, or shallow thinking of Hervéism) not simply in replacing war by peace, but in replacing capitalism by socialism. The essential thing is not merely to prevent war, but to utilise the crisis created by war in order to hasten the overthrow of the bourgeoisie. However, underlying all these semi-anarchist absurdities of Hervéism there was one sound and practical purpose: to spur the socialist movement so that it will not be restricted to parliamentary methods of struggle alone, so that the masses will realise the need for revolutionary action in connection with the crises which war inevitably involves, so that, lastly, a more lively understanding of international labour solidarity and of the falsity of bourgeois patriotism will be spread among the masses.

Bebel's resolution (moved by the Germans and coinciding in all essentials with Guesde's resolution) had one shortcoming – it failed to indicate the active tasks of the proletariat. This made it possible to read Bebel's orthodox propositions through opportunist spectacles, and Vollmar was quick to turn this possibility into a reality.

That is why Rosa Luxemburg and the Russian Social-Democratic delegates moved their amendments to Bebel's resolution. These amendments (1) stated that militarism is the chief weapon of class oppression; (2) pointed out the need for propaganda among the youth; (3) stressed that Social-Democrats should not only try to prevent war from breaking out or to secure the speediest termination of wars that have already begun, but should utilise the crisis created by the war to hasten the overthrow of the bourgeoisie.

The subcommission (elected by the Anti-Militarism Commission) incorporated all these amendments in Bebel's resolution. In addition, Jaurès made this happy suggestion: instead of enumerating the methods of struggle (strikes, uprisings) the resolution should cite historical examples of proletarian action against war, from the demonstrations in Europe to the revolution in Russia. The result of all this redrafting was a resolution which, it is true, is unduly long, but is rich in thought and precisely formulates the tasks of the proletariat. It combines the stringency of orthodox – i.e. the only scientific – Marxist analysis with recommendations for the most resolute and revolutionary action by the workers' parties. This resolution cannot be interpreted *à la* Vollmar, nor can it be fitted into the narrow framework of naïve Hervéism.

On the whole, the Stuttgart Congress brought into sharp contrast the opportunist and revolutionary wings of the international Social-Democratic movement on a number of cardinal issues and decided these issues in the spirit of revolutionary Marxism. Its resolutions and the report of the debates should become a handbook for every propagandist. The work done at Stuttgart will greatly promote the unity of tactics and unity of revolutionary struggle of the proletarians of all countries.

The War and Russian Social-Democracy

Written prior to 28 September (11 October) 1914

The European war, which the governments and the bourgeois parties of all countries have been preparing for decades, has broken out. The growth of armaments, the extreme intensification of the struggle for markets in the latest – the imperialist – stage of capitalist development in the advanced countries, and the dynastic interests of the more backward East-European monarchies were inevitably bound to bring about this war, and have done so. Seizure of territory and subjugation of other nations, the ruining of competing nations and the plunder of their wealth, distracting the attention of the working masses from the internal political crises in Russia, Germany, Britain and other countries, disuniting and nationalist stultification of the workers, and the extermination of their vanguard so as to weaken the revolutionary movement of the proletariat – these comprise the sole actual content, importance and significance of the present war.

It is primarily on Social-Democracy that the duty rests of revealing the true meaning of the war, and of ruthlessly exposing the falsehood, sophistry and 'patriotic' phrasemongering spread by the ruling classes, the landowners and the bourgeoisie, in defence of the war.

One group of belligerent nations is headed by the German bourgeoisie. It is hoodwinking the working class and the toiling masses by asserting that this is a war in defence of the fatherland, freedom and civilisation, for the liberation of the peoples oppressed by tsarism, and for the destruction of reactionary tsarism. In actual fact, however, this bourgeoisie, which servilely grovels to the Prussian Junkers, headed by Wilhelm II, has always been a most faithful ally of tsarism, and an enemy of the revolutionary movement of Russia's workers and peasants. In fact, whatever the outcome of the war, this bourgeoisie will, together with the Junkers, exert every effort to support the tsarist monarchy against a revolution in Russia.

In fact, the German bourgeoisie has launched a robber campaign against Serbia, with the object of subjugating her and throttling the national revolution of the Southern Slavs, at the same time sending the bulk of its military forces against the freer countries, Belgium and France, so as to plunder richer competitors. In fact, the German bourgeoisie, which has been spreading the fable that it is waging a war of defence, chose the moment it thought most favourable for war, making use of its latest improvements in military matériel and forestalling the rearmament already planned and decided upon by Russia and France.

The other group of belligerent nations is headed by the British and the French bourgeoisie, who are hoodwinking the working class and the toiling masses by asserting that they are waging a war for the defence of their countries, for freedom and civilisation, and against German militarism and despotism. In actual fact, this bourgeoisie has long been spending thousands of millions to hire the troops of Russian tsarism, the most reactionary and barbarous monarchy in Europe, and prepare them for an attack on Germany.

In fact, the struggle of the British and the French bourgeoisie is aimed at the seizure of the German colonies, and the ruining of a rival nation, whose economic development has been more rapid. In pursuit of this noble aim, the 'advanced' 'democratic' nations are helping the savage tsarist regime to still more throttle Poland, the Ukraine, etc., and more thoroughly crush the revolution in Russia.

Neither group of belligerents is inferior to the other in spoliation, atrocities and the boundless brutality of war; however, to hoodwink the proletariat and distract its attention from the only genuine war of liberation, namely, a civil war against the bourgeoisie both of its 'own' and of 'foreign' countries – to achieve so lofty an aim – the bourgeoisie of each country is trying, with the help of false phrases about patriotism, to extol the significance of its 'own' national war, asserting that it is out to defeat the enemy, not for plunder and the seizure of territory, but for the 'liberation' of all other peoples except its own.

But the harder the governments and the bourgeoisie of all countries try to disunite the workers and pit them against one another, and the more savagely they enforce, for this lofty aim, martial law and the military censorship (measures which even now, in wartime, are applied against the 'internal' foe more harshly than against the external), the more pressingly is it the duty of the class-conscious proletariat to defend its class solidarity, its internationalism, and its socialist convictions against the unbridled chauvinism of the 'patriotic' bourgeois cliques in all countries. If class-conscious workers were to give up this aim, this would mean renunciation of their aspirations for freedom and democracy, to say nothing of their socialist aspirations.

It is with a feeling of the most bitter disappointment that we have to record that the socialist parties of the leading European countries have failed to discharge this duty, the behaviour of these parties' leaders, particularly in Germany, bordering on downright betrayal of the cause of socialism. At this time of supreme and historic importance, most of the leaders of the present Socialist International, the Second (1889-1914), are trying to substitute nationalism for socialism. As a result of their behaviour, the workers' parties of these countries did not oppose the governments' criminal conduct, but called upon the working class to *identify* its position with that of the imperialist governments. The leaders of the International committed an act of treachery against socialism by voting for war credits, by reiterating the chauvinist ('patriotic') slogans of the bourgeoisie of their 'own' countries, by justifying and defending the war, by joining the bourgeois governments of the belligerent countries, and so on and so forth. The most influential socialist leaders and the most influential organs of the socialist press of present-day Europe hold views that are chauvinist, bourgeois and liberal, and in no way socialist. The responsibility for thus disgracing socialism falls primarily on the German Social-Democrats, who were the strongest and most influential party in the Second International. But neither can one justify the French socialists, who have accepted ministerial posts in the government of that very bourgeoisie which betrayed its country and allied itself with Bismarck so as to crush the Commune.

The German and the Austrian Social-Democrats are attempting to justify their support for the war by arguing that they are thereby fighting against Russian tsarism. We Russian Social-Democrats declare that we consider such justification sheer sophistry. In our country the revolutionary movement against tsarism has again assumed tremendous proportions during the past few years. This movement has always been headed by the working class of Russia. The political strikes of the last few years, which have involved millions of workers, have had as their slogan the overthrow of tsarism and the establishment of a democratic republic. During his visit to Nicholas II on the very eve of the war, Poincaré, President of the French Republic, could see for himself, in the streets of St. Petersburg, barricades put up by Russian workers. The Russian proletariat has not flinched from any sacrifice to rid humanity of the disgrace of the tsarist monarchy. We must, however, say that if there is anything that, under certain conditions, can delay the downfall of tsarism, anything that can help tsarism in its struggle against the whole of Russia's democracy, then that is the present war, which has placed the purses of the British, the French and the Russian bourgeois at the disposal of tsarism, to further the latter's reactionary aims. If there is anything that can hinder the revolutionary struggle of Russia's working class against tsarism, then that is the behaviour of the German and the Austrian Social-Democratic leaders, which the chauvinist press of Russia is continually holding up to us as an example.

Even assuming that German Social-Democracy was so weak that it was compelled to refrain from all revolutionary action, it should not have joined the chauvinist camp, or taken steps which gave the Italian socialists reason to say that the German Social-Democratic leaders were dishonouring the banner of the proletarian International.

Our Party, the Russian Social-Democratic Labour Party, has made, and will continue to make, great sacrifices in connection with the war. The whole of our working-class legal press has been suppressed. Most working-class associations have been disbanded, and a large number of our comrades have been arrested and exiled. Yet our parliamentary representatives – the Russian Social-Democratic Labour group in the Duma – considered it their imperative socialist duty not to vote for the war credits, and even to walk out of the Duma, so as to express their protest the more energetically; they considered it their duty to brand the European governments' policy as imperialist. Though the tsar's government has increased its tyranny tenfold, the Social-Democratic workers of Russia are already publishing their first illegal manifestos against the war, thus doing their duty to democracy and to the International.

While the collapse of the Second International has given rise to a sense of burning shame in revolutionary Social-Democrats – as represented by the minority of German Social-Democrats and the finest Social-Democrats in the neutral countries; while socialists in both Britain and France have been speaking up against the chauvinism of most Social-Democratic parties; while the opportunists, as represented, for instance, by the German *Sozialistische Monatshefte*, which have long held a national-liberal stand, are with good reason celebrating their victory over European socialism – the worst possible service is being rendered to the proletariat by those who vacillate between opportunism and revolutionary Social-Democracy (like the 'Centre' in the German Social-Democratic Party), by those who are trying to hush up the collapse of the Second International or to disguise it with diplomatic phrases.

On the contrary, this collapse must be frankly recognised and its causes understood, so as to make it possible to build up a new and more lasting socialist unity of the workers of all countries.

The opportunists have wrecked the decisions of the Stuttgart, Copenhagen and Basel congresses, which made it binding on socialists of all countries to combat chauvinism in all and any conditions, made it binding on socialists to reply to any war begun by the bourgeoisie and governments, with intensified propaganda of civil war and social revolution.* The collapse of the Second International is the collapse of opportunism, which developed from the features of a now bygone (and so-called 'peaceful') period of history, and in recent years has come practically to dominate the International. The opportunists have long been preparing the ground for this collapse by denying the socialist revolution and substituting bourgeois reformism in its stead; by rejecting the class struggle with its inevitable conversion at certain moments into civil

---

*   The Copenhagen Congress of the Second International was held between 28 August and 3 September 1910, the RSDLP being represented by Lenin, Plekhanov, Lunacharsky, Kollontai, Pokrovsky and others. The Congress appointed several committees for preliminary discussion and drafting of resolutions on the agenda items. Lenin worked on the cooperative committee.

The Congress' resolution 'The Struggle Against Militarism and War' confirmed the Stuttgart Congress' resolution on 'Militarism and International Conflicts' and listed the demands to be advanced by the socialist parliamentary deputies: (a) all conflicts between states to be unfailingly submitted for settlement by international courts of arbitration; (b) general disarmament; (c) abolition of secret diplomacy; (d) autonomy for all nations and their protection against military attacks and oppression.

The Basel Congress of the Second International was held on 24-25 November 1912. It was the extraordinary congress called in connection with the Balkan War and the imminent European war. The Congress adopted a manifesto emphasising the imperialist nature of the approaching world war, and called on the socialists of all countries to wage a vigorous struggle against war (reproduced in this volume on p. 371).

war, and by preaching class collaboration; by preaching bourgeois chauvinism under the guise of patriotism and the defence of the fatherland, and ignoring or rejecting the fundamental truth of socialism, long ago set forth in *The Communist Manifesto*, that the workingmen have no country; by confining themselves, in the struggle against militarism, to a sentimental, philistine point of view, instead of recognising the need for a revolutionary war by the proletarians of all countries, against the bourgeoisie of all countries; by making a fetish of the necessary utilisation of bourgeois parliamentarianism and bourgeois legality, and forgetting that illegal forms of organisation and propaganda are imperative at times of crises. The natural 'appendage' to opportunism – one that is just as bourgeois and hostile to the proletarian, i.e. the Marxist, point of view – namely, the anarcho-syndicalist trend, has been marked by a no less shamefully smug reiteration of the slogans of chauvinism, during the present crisis.

The aims of socialism at the present time cannot be fulfilled, and real international unity of the workers cannot be achieved, without a decisive break with opportunism, and without explaining its inevitable fiasco to the masses.

It must be the primary task of Social-Democrats in every country to combat that country's chauvinism. In Russia, this chauvinism has overcome the bourgeois liberals (the 'Constitutional-Democrats'), and part of the Narodniks – down to the Socialist-Revolutionaries and the 'Right' Social-Democrats.* (In particular, the chauvinist utterances of E Smirnov, P Maslov and G Plekhanov, for example,

---

* Socialist-Revolutionaries – a peasant-based party in Russia, founded at the end of 1901 and the beginning of 1902 as a result of the union of various Narodnik groups and circles. The Socialist-Revolutionaries did not recognise the class differences between the proletariat and the petty proprietors, glossed over the class contradictions within the peasantry, and rejected the proletariat's leading role in the revolution. The Socialist-Revolutionaries' views were an eclectic mixture of the ideas of Narodism and revisionism.

In the period of reaction between 1907 and 1910, the Socialist-Revolutionary Party suffered a complete ideological and organisational breakdown. During the First World War most of its members took a social-chauvinist position.

should be branded; they have been taken up and widely used by the bourgeois 'patriotic' press.)

In the present situation, it is impossible to determine, from the standpoint of the international proletariat, the defeat of which of the two groups of belligerent nations would be the lesser evil for socialism. But to us Russian Social-Democrats there cannot be the slightest doubt that, from the standpoint of the working class and of the toiling masses of all the nations of Russia, the defeat of the tsarist monarchy, the most reactionary and barbarous of governments, which is oppressing the largest number of nations and the greatest mass of the population of Europe and Asia, would be the lesser evil.

The formation of a republican United States of Europe should be the immediate political slogan of Europe's Social-Democrats. In contrast with the bourgeoisie, which is ready to 'promise' anything in order to draw the proletariat into the mainstream of chauvinism, the Social-Democrats will explain that this slogan is absolutely false and meaningless without the revolutionary overthrow of the German, the Austrian and the Russian monarchies.

Since Russia is most backward and has not yet completed its bourgeois revolution, it still remains the task of Social-Democrats in that country to achieve the three fundamental conditions for consistent democratic reform, viz. a democratic republic (with complete equality and self-determination for all nations), confiscation of the landed estates, and an eight-hour working day. But in all the advanced countries the war has placed on the order of the day the slogan of socialist revolution, a slogan that is the more urgent the more heavily the burden of war presses upon the shoulders of the proletariat, and the more active its future role must become in the re-creation of Europe, after the horrors of the present 'patriotic' barbarism in conditions of the tremendous technological progress of large-scale capitalism. The bourgeoisie's use of wartime laws to gag the proletariat makes it imperative for the latter to create illegal forms of agitation and organisation. Let the opportunists 'preserve' the legal organisations at the price of treachery to their convictions – revolutionary Social-Democrats will utilise the organisational experience and links of the working class so as to create illegal forms of struggle for socialism, forms appropriate to a period of crisis, and to unite the workers, not with the chauvinist bourgeoisie of their respective countries, but with the workers of all countries. The proletarian International has not gone under and will not go under. Notwithstanding all obstacles, the masses of the workers will create a new International. Opportunism's present triumph will be short-lived. The greater the sacrifices imposed by the war, the clearer will it become to the mass of the workers that the opportunists have betrayed the workers' cause and that the weapons must be turned against the government and the bourgeoisie of each country.

The conversion of the present imperialist war into a civil war is the only correct proletarian slogan, one that follows from the experience of the Commune, and outlined in the Basel Resolution (1912); it has been dictated by all the conditions of an imperialist war between highly developed bourgeois countries.* However difficult that transformation may seem at any given moment, socialists will never relinquish systematic, persistent and undeviating preparatory work in this direction now that war has become a fact.

It is only along this path that the proletariat will be able to shake off its dependence on the chauvinist bourgeoisie, and, in one form or another and more or less rapidly, take decisive steps towards genuine freedom for the nations and towards socialism.

Long live the international fraternity of the workers against the chauvinism and patriotism of the bourgeoisie of all countries!

Long live a proletarian International, freed from opportunism!

Central Committee of the
Russian Social-Democratic Labour Party

---

* See this volume, p. 371.

Dead Chauvinism and Living Socialism

How the International Can Be Restored

12 December 1914

For decades, German Social-Democracy was a model to the Social-Democrats of Russia, even somewhat more than to the Social-Democrats of the whole world. It is therefore clear that there can be no intelligent, i.e. critical, attitude towards the now prevalent social-patriotism or 'socialist' chauvinism, without a most precise definition of one's attitude towards German Social-Democracy. What was it in the past? What is it today? What will it be in the future?

A reply to the first of these questions may be found in *Der Weg zur Macht*, a pamphlet written by K Kautsky in 1909 and translated into many European languages. Containing a most complete exposition of the tasks of our times, it was most advantageous to the German Social-Democrats (in the sense of the promise they held out), and moreover came from the pen of the most eminent writer of the Second International. We shall recall the pamphlet in some detail – this will be the more useful now since those forgotten ideals are so often barefacedly cast aside.

Social-Democracy is a "revolutionary party" (as stated in the opening sentence of the pamphlet), not only in the sense that a steam engine is revolutionary, but "also in another sense". It wants conquest of political power by the proletariat, the dictatorship of the proletariat. Heaping ridicule on "doubters of the revolution", Kautsky writes:

> In any important movement and uprising we must, of course, reckon with the possibility of defeat. Prior to the struggle, only a fool can consider himself quite certain of victory.

However, to refuse to consider the possibility of victory would be "a direct betrayal of our cause". A revolution in connection with a war, he says, is possible both during and after a war. It is impossible to determine at which particular moment the sharpening of class antagonisms will lead to revolution, but, the author continues, "I can quite definitely assert that a revolution that war brings in its wake, will break out either during or immediately after the war"; nothing is more vulgar, we read further, than the theory of "the peaceful growing into socialism".

> Nothing is more erroneous [he continues] than the opinion that a cognition of economic necessity means a weakening of the will... The will, as a desire for struggle [he says] is determined, first, by the price of the struggle, secondly, by a sense of power, and thirdly, by actual power.

When an attempt was made, incidentally by *Vorwärts,* to interpret Engels' famous preface to *The Class Struggles in France* in the meaning of opportunism, Engels became indignant, and called shameful any assumption that he was a "peace-loving advocate for adherence to law no matter what".* "We have every reason to

---

*   In its issue of 30 March 1895, *Vorwärts* published a summary and several extracts from Friedrich Engels' introduction to Marx's *The Class Struggles in France, 1848-1850,* omitting very important propositions on the revolutionary role of the proletariat, which evoked vehement opposition from Engels. In his

believe", Kautsky goes on to say, "that we are entering upon a period of struggle for state power." That struggle may last for decades; that is something we do not know, but

> ... it will in all probability bring about, in the near future, a considerable strengthening of the proletariat, if not its dictatorship, in Western Europe.

The revolutionary elements are growing, Kautsky declares: out of 10 million voters in Germany in 1895, there were 6 million proletarians and 3.5 million people interested in private property; in 1907 the latter grew by 0.03 million, and the former by 1.6 million! "The rate of the advance becomes very rapid as soon as a time of revolutionary ferment comes." Class antagonisms are not blunted but, on the contrary, grow acute; prices rise, and imperialist rivalry and militarism are rampant. "A new era of revolution" is drawing near. The monstrous growth of taxes would

> ... long ago have led to war as the only alternative to revolution... had not that very alternative of revolution stood closer after a war than after a period of armed peace...

"A world war is ominously imminent", Kautsky continues, "and war means also revolution." In 1891, Engels had reason to fear a premature revolution in Germany; since then, however, "the situation has greatly changed". The proletariat "can no longer speak of a *premature* revolution" (Kautsky's italics). The petty bourgeoisie

---

letter to Kautsky of 1 April 1895, he protested that he was being presented as a "peace-loving advocate for adherence to law no matter what".

Engels insisted on the introduction being published in full. In 1895 it was published in the journal *Die Neue Zeit*, but with considerable deletions at the insistence of the German Social-Democratic Party leadership. Seeking to justify their reformist tactics, the leaders of German Social-Democracy subsequently began to interpret their version of the introduction as Engels' renunciation of revolution, armed uprisings and barricade fighting.

The original text was first published in 1955, and is reproduced in full in the Wellred Books edition of *The Class Struggles in France, 1848-1850*, published in 2021.

is downright unreliable and is ever more hostile to the proletariat, but in a time of crisis it is "capable of coming over to our side in masses". The main thing is that Social-Democracy "should remain unshakable, consistent, and irreconcilable". We have undoubtedly entered a revolutionary period.

This is how Kautsky wrote in times long, long past, fully five years ago. This is what German Social-Democracy was, or, more correctly, what it promised to be. This was the kind of Social-Democracy that could and had to be respected.

See what the selfsame Kautsky writes today. Here are the most important statements in his article 'Social-Democracy in Wartime' (*Die Neue Zeit*, No. 1, 2 October 1914):

> Our Party has far more rarely discussed the question of how to behave in wartime than how to prevent war... Never is government so strong, never are parties so weak, as at the outbreak of war... Wartime is least of all favourable to peaceful discussion... Today the practical question is: victory or defeat for one's own country.

Can there be an understanding among the parties of the belligerent countries regarding anti-war action? "That kind of thing has never been tested in practice. We have always disputed that possibility..." The difference between the French and German socialists is "not one of principle" (as both defend their fatherlands)...

> Social-Democrats of all countries have an equal right or an equal obligation to take part in the defence of the fatherland: no nation should blame the other for doing so...

"Has the International turned bankrupt?" "Has the Party rejected direct defence of its party principles in wartime?" (Mehring's questions in the same issue.)

> That is an erroneous conception... There are no grounds at all for such pessimism... The differences are not fundamental... Unity of principles remains... To disobey wartime laws would simply lead to suppression of our press.

Obedience to these laws

> … implies rejection of defence of party principles just as little as similar behaviour of our party press under that sword of Damocles – the Anti-Socialist Law.

We have purposely quoted from the original because it is hard to believe that such things could have been written. It is hard to find in literature (except in that coming from downright renegades) such smug vulgarity, such shameful departure from the truth, such unsavoury subterfuge to cover up the most patent renunciation both of socialism in general and of precise international decisions unanimously adopted (as, for instance, in Stuttgart and particularly in Basel) precisely in view of the possibility of a European war just like the present! It would be disrespectful towards the reader were we to treat Kautsky's arguments in earnest and try to analyse them: if the European war differs in many respects from a simple 'little' anti-Jewish pogrom, the 'socialist' arguments in favour of participation in such a war *fully* resemble the 'democratic' arguments in favour of participation in an anti-Jewish pogrom. One does not analyse arguments in favour of a pogrom; one only points them out so as to put their authors to shame in the sight of all class-conscious workers.

But how *could* it have come to pass, the reader will ask, that the leading authority in the Second International, a writer who once defended the views quoted at the beginning of this article, has sunk to something that is worse than being a renegade? That will not be understood, we answer, only by those who, perhaps unconsciously, consider that nothing out of the ordinary has happened, and that it is not difficult to 'forgive and forget', etc., i.e. by those who regard the matter from the renegade's point of view. Those, however, who have earnestly and sincerely professed socialist convictions and have held the views set forth in the beginning of this article will not be surprised to learn that "*Vorwärts* is dead" (Martov's expression in the Paris *Golos*) and that Kautsky is "dead". The political bankruptcy of individuals is not a rarity at turning points in history. Despite the tremendous services he has rendered, Kautsky has never been among those who, at great crises, immediately take a militant Marxist stand (recall his vacillations on the issue of Millerandism).*

It is such times that we are passing through. "You shoot first, Messieurs the Bourgeoisie!", Engels wrote in 1891, advocating, most correctly, the use of bourgeois legality by us, revolutionaries, in the period of so-called peaceful constitutional development.** Engels' idea was crystal clear: we class-conscious workers, he said, will be the next to shoot; it is to our advantage to exchange ballots for bullets (to go over to civil war) at the moment the bourgeoisie itself has broken the legal foundation it has laid down. In 1909 Kautsky voiced the undisputed opinion held by all revolutionary Social-Democrats when he said that revolution in Europe cannot now be *premature* and that war means revolution.

'Peaceful' decades, however, have not passed without leaving their mark. They have of necessity given rise to opportunism in all countries, and made it prevalent among parliamentarian, trade union, journalistic and other 'leaders'. There is no country in Europe where, in one form or another, a long and stubborn struggle has not been conducted against opportunism, the latter being supported in a host of ways by the entire bourgeoisie, which is striving to corrupt and weaken the revolutionary proletariat. Fifteen years ago, at the outset of the Bernstein controversy, the selfsame Kautsky wrote that should opportunism turn from a sentiment into

---

* Millerandism (or 'ministerial socialism', or else Ministerialism) refers to the opportunist tactic of socialists' participation in reactionary bourgeois governments. The term appeared when, in 1899, the French socialist Alexandre Millerand joined the bourgeois government of Waldeck-Rousseau.

The admissibility of socialists' participation in bourgeois governments was discussed at the Paris Congress of the Second International in 1900. The Congress adopted Kautsky's conciliatory resolution condemning socialists' participation in bourgeois governments but permitting it in certain 'exceptional' cases. The French socialists used this proviso to justify their joining the bourgeois government at the beginning of the First World War.

** See Friedrich Engels, 'Socialism in Germany', in *MECW*, Vol. 27, p. 241.

a trend, a split would be imminent. In Russia, the old *Iskra*,* which created the Social-Democratic Party of the working class, declared, in an article which appeared in its second issue early in 1901, under the title of 'On the Threshold of the Twentieth Century', that the revolutionary class of the twentieth century, like the revolutionary class of the eighteenth century – the bourgeoisie – had its own *Gironde* and its own *Mountain*.**

The European war is a tremendous historical crisis, the beginning of a new epoch. Like any crisis, the war has aggravated deep-seated antagonisms and brought them to the surface, tearing asunder all veils of hypocrisy, rejecting all conventions and deflating all corrupt or rotting authorities. (This, incidentally, is the salutary and progressive effect of all crises, which only the dull-witted adherents of 'peaceful evolution' fail to realise.) The Second International, which in its twenty-five or forty-five years of existence (according to whether the reckoning is from 1870 or 1889) was able to perform the highly important and useful work of expanding the influence of socialism and giving the socialist forces preparatory, initial and elementary organisation, has played its historical role and has passed away, overcome, not so much by the von Klucks as by

---

*   *Iskra* (*The Spark*) – the first all-Russian illegal Marxist newspaper, founded by Lenin in 1900. It played a decisive part in the establishment of the revolutionary Marxist party of the working class. Soon after the Second Congress of the RSDLP in 1903, the Mensheviks, helped by Plekhanov, gained control of *Iskra* from issue No. 52 onwards.

** The Mountain (Montagne) and the Gironde – the two political groups of the bourgeoisie during the French bourgeois revolution of 1789. The Montagnards, or Jacobins, was the name given to the more resolute representatives of the bourgeoisie, the revolutionary class of the time, who stood for the abolition of absolutism and the feudal system. Unlike the Jacobins, the Girondists vacillated between revolution and counter-revolution, and sought agreement with the monarchy.

Lenin called the opportunist trend in Social-Democracy the 'socialist Gironde', and the revolutionary Social-Democrats the 'proletarian Jacobins', 'the Mountain'. After the RSDLP split into Bolsheviks and Mensheviks, Lenin frequently stressed that the Mensheviks represented the Girondist trend in the working-class movement.

opportunism.* Let the dead bury their dead. Let the empty-headed busy-bodies (if not the intriguing lackeys of the chauvinists and the opportunists) labour at the task of bringing together Vandervelde and Sembat with Kautsky and Haase, as though we had another Ivan Ivanovich, who has called Ivan Nikiforovich a "gander", and has to be urged by his friends to make it up with his enemy.** An International does not mean sitting at the same table and having hypocritical and pettifogging resolutions written by people who think that genuine internationalism consists in German socialists justifying the German bourgeoisie's call to shoot down French workers, and in French socialists justifying the French bourgeoisie's call to shoot down German workers in the name of the 'defence of the fatherland'! The International consists in the coming together (first ideologically, then in due time organisationally as well) of people who, in these grave days, are capable of defending socialist internationalism in deed, i.e. of mustering their forces and 'being the next to shoot' at the governments and the ruling classes of their *own respective* 'fatherlands'. This is no easy task; it calls for much preparation and great sacrifices and will be accompanied by reverses. However, for the very reason that it is no easy task, it must be accomplished only together with those who *wish* to perform it and are not afraid of a complete break with the chauvinists and with the defenders of social-chauvinism.

Such people as Pannekoek are doing more than anyone else for the sincere, not hypocritical restoration of a socialist, not a chauvinist, International. In an article entitled 'The Collapse of the International', Pannekoek said:

> If the leaders get together in an attempt to patch up their differences, that will be of no significance at all.

---

* Alexander von Kluck – German general during the First World War.
** Ivan Ivanovich and Ivan Nikiforovich – characters in Nikolai Gogol's *The Tale of How Ivan Ivanovich Quarreled with Ivan Nikiforovich*, also known as *The Squabble*. The quarrel between these two provincial landowners, whose names have become proverbial, started on a most insignificant pretext, and dragged on endlessly.

Let us frankly state the facts; in any case the war will *compel* us to do so, if not tomorrow, then the day after. Three currents exist in international socialism:

1. The chauvinists, who are consistently pursuing a policy of opportunism;

2. The consistent opponents of opportunism, who in all countries have already begun to make themselves heard (the opportunists have routed most of them, but 'defeated armies learn fast'), and are capable of conducting revolutionary work directed towards civil war;

3. Confused and vacillating people, who at present are following in the wake of the opportunists and are causing the proletariat most harm by their hypocritical attempts to justify opportunism, something that they do almost scientifically and using the Marxist (*sic!*) method.

Some of those who are engulfed in the latter current can be saved and restored to socialism, but only through a policy of a most decisive break and split with the former current, with all those who are capable of justifying the war credits vote, 'the defence of the fatherland', 'submission to wartime laws', a willingness to be satisfied with legal means only, and the rejection of civil war. Only those who pursue a policy like *this* are really building up a socialist International. For our part, we, who have established links with the Russian Collegium of the Central Committee and with the leading elements of the working-class movement in St. Petersburg, have exchanged opinions with them and become convinced that we are agreed on the main points, are in a position, as editors of the Central Organ, to declare in the name of our Party that only work conducted in this direction is Party work and Social-Democratic work.

The idea of a split in the German Social-Democratic movement may seem alarming to many in its 'unusualness'. The objective situation, however, goes to show that either the unusual will come to pass (after all, Adler and Kautsky did declare, at the last session of the International Socialist Bureau* in July 1914, that they did not believe in miracles, and therefore did not believe in a European war!), or we shall witness the painful decomposition of what was once German Social-Democracy. In conclusion, we would like to remind those who are too prone to 'trust' the (former) German Social-Democrats that people who have been our opponents on a number of issues have arrived at the idea of such a split. Thus Martov has written in *Golos*:

> *Vorwärts* is dead... A Social-Democracy which publicly renounces the class struggle would do better to recognise the facts as they are, temporarily disband its organisation, and close down its organs.

Thus Plekhanov is quoted by *Golos* as having said in a report:

> I am very much against splits, but if principles are sacrificed for the integrity of the organisation, then better a split than false unity.

Plekhanov was referring to the German radicals: he sees a mote in the eye of the Germans, but not the beam in his own eye. This is an individual feature in him; over the past ten years we have all grown quite used to Plekhanov's radicalism in theory and opportunism in practice. However, if even persons with *such* 'oddities' begin to talk of a split among the Germans, it is a sign of the times.

---

* The International Socialist Bureau (ISB) – the executive body of the Second International, established by decision of the Paris Congress of 1900. Lenin was the RSDLP representative on the ISB from 1905 until June 1914, after which MM Litvinov represented the RSDLP, on Lenin's proposal. When the First World War broke out, the ISB became a pliable tool in the hands of the social-chauvinists.

To the Editors of 'Nashe Slovo'

9 February 1915

Editors note:

Nashe Slovo (*Our Word*) was a Russian language socialist internationalist paper published daily in Paris from January 1915 to September 1916, after the military authorities banned *Golos*. One of the main editors of the paper was Trotsky, who attended the Zimmerwald conference as its representative. Other editors were Martov (who broke with it in 1915), Manuilsky, Lozovski, Uritski, Chicherin and Antonov-Ovseyenko. The Bulgarian Christian Rakovsky helped finance the paper.

Lenin's letter to the newspaper was written in reply to the *Nashe Slovo* editors' proposal for joint action against social patriotism, in connection with the forthcoming London Conference of Entente Socialists. Lenin agreed to the proposal and submitted a draft declaration addressed to the London Conference. He criticised the social-chauvinist position of the Menshevik Organising Committee and the Bund, whom the *Nashe Slovo* editors had approached with the same proposal. *Nashe Slovo*'s editors did not accept Lenin's declaration, but drew up one of their own.

Following the London Conference, the *Nashe Slovo* editors
again proposed to the Central Committee of the RSDLP that
a joint conference of 'internationalists' be held, so as to define
the attitude towards the war and the social-chauvinists. In his
reply to the *Nashe Slovo* editors dated 10 (23) March 1915,
Lenin laid down a number of fundamental conditions for a
union of genuine internationalists. (See *Lenin Collected Works*
(henceforth referred to as *LCW*), Vol. 21, Progress Publishers,
1960, p. 165.) Since the *Nashe Slovo* editors came out in
defence of the Organising Committee and the Bund, Lenin
discontinued the talks.

Nashe Slovo's attempts at unification ended in an "ideological-
political fiasco", as Lenin put it. Lenin discussed this question
in *Socialism and War*, reproduced in this volume, p. 57, as
well as in the following articles included in *LCW*, Vol. 21:
'On the London Conference', p. 178; 'The Question of the
Unity of Internationalists', p. 188; 'The Collapse of Platonic
Internationalism', p. 194; 'The State of Affairs in Russian
Social-Democracy', p. 281.

* * *

Bern, 9 February 1915

Dear Comrades:

In your letter of 6 February you proposed to us a plan of struggle
against "official social-patriotism", in connection with the proposed
London Conference of socialists of the 'allied countries' of the
Triple Entente.* As you have, of course, seen from our newspaper

---

*   The London Conference of Socialists of the 'allied countries' of the Triple
Entente met on 14 February 1915. Its delegates represented the social-
chauvinists and the pacifist groups of the Socialist parties of Britain, France,
Belgium, as well as the Russian Mensheviks and Socialist-Revolutionaries.

Though the Bolsheviks were not invited to the Conference, Litvinov
(Maximovich) presented to the Conference the declaration of the Central
Committee of the RSDLP, which was based on Lenin's draft. The declaration
demanded the withdrawal of socialists from bourgeois governments and a
complete rupture with the imperialists; it called for an end to cooperation with the
imperialist governments, a resolute struggle against the latter, and condemnation
of voting for war credits. The chairman interrupted Litvinov as he was reading

Sotsial-Demokrat, we support that struggle in general, and are conducting it. That is why we are very glad to have received your message, and accept with pleasure your proposal for a discussion of a plan of joint action.

The conference, which is said to have been planned for 15 February (we have not yet received a single document regarding it), will perhaps be postponed until 25 February or later (judging from a letter from Huysmans, who wrote of the sitting of the Executive Commission for 20 February and of the plan for personal talks between members (the Secretary) of the Executive Commission and socialists of France, Britain and Russia). The conference may possibly be contemplated as one, not of official members of the International Socialist Bureau, but as *private* meetings between individual 'prominent' socialists.

That is why the contraposition to "official social-patriotism" of a "clear, revolutionary and internationalist" point of view, a contraposition which you write of and which has our full sympathy, should be prepared *for all possible contingencies* (both for a conference of the official representatives of parties and for a private meeting in all its forms, both for 15 February and for any later date).

For our part and in view of the desire you have expressed, we propose the following draft declaration, which contains such a contraposition (so that the declaration may be read and printed):

> The undersigned representatives of the Social-Democratic organisations of Russia (Britain, etc.) proceed from the conviction:
>
> That the present war is, on the part, not only of Germany and Austro-Hungary, but of Britain and France (acting in alliance with tsarism), an imperialist war, i.e. a war of the epoch of the final stage in the development of capitalism, an epoch in which bourgeois states, with their national boundaries, have outlived themselves; a war aimed exclusively at the grabbing of colonies, the plundering of rival countries,

---

the declaration, and deprived him of the right to speak. The latter handed the declaration over to the presidium and left the Conference hall.

and the weakening of the proletarian movement by setting the proletarians of one country against those of another.

Consequently it is the absolute duty of the socialists of all belligerent countries immediately and resolutely to carry out the *Basel Resolution*, viz.:

1. The break-up of all national blocs and the *Burgfrieden* [class truce] in all countries;

2. A call to the workers of all the belligerent countries to wage an energetic class struggle, both economic and political, against the bourgeoisie of their country, a bourgeoisie that is amassing unparalleled profits from war deliveries and makes use of the military authorities' backing so as to gag the workers and intensify oppression of the latter;

3. Decisive condemnation of any voting for war credits;

4. Withdrawal from the bourgeois governments of Belgium and France, and recognition that entry into governments and voting for war credits are the same kind of treachery to the cause of socialism as is the entire behaviour of the German and Austrian Social-Democrats;

5. That the hand be stretched out to internationalist elements in German Social-Democracy that refuse to vote for war credits, and that an international committee be set up, together with them, for the conduct of agitation for the cessation of the war, not in the spirit of the pacifists, the Christians, and the petty-bourgeois democrats, but in inseparable connection with the propaganda and organisation of mass revolutionary action by the proletarians of each country, against the governments and the bourgeoisie of that country;

6. Support for any attempts by the socialists of the belligerent countries to bring about contacts and fraternisation in the fighting forces and the trenches, despite the bans imposed by the military authorities of Britain, Germany, etc.;

7. A call to women socialists of the belligerent countries to intensify agitation in the direction indicated above;

8. A call for support by the entire world proletariat of the struggle against tsarism, and for support for those Social-Democrats of Russia who have not only refused to vote for credits, but have shown disregard of the danger of persecution and are conducting socialist work in the spirit of internationalist and revolutionary Social-Democracy.

* * *

As for certain Social-Democratic men of letters in Russia who have come out in defence of the official social-patriotism (as, for instance, Plekhanov, Alexinsky, Maslov, and others), the undersigned disclaim all responsibility for any action or statements by them, energetically protest against the latter, and declare that, according to all available information, the Social-Democratic workers of Russia do not hold that point of view.

It goes without saying that Comrade Litvinov, our Central Committee's official representative in the International Socialist Bureau (his address: We are sending him your letter and a copy of our reply to you. Please address him directly on all urgent matters), as he has been authorised to use his own judgement in the matter of all particular amendments, special steps in negotiations, etc.; we can merely state our *complete* solidarity with this comrade on *all* essential points.

As for the Organising Committee and the Bund, who are both represented in the International Socialist Bureau, we have grounds for apprehension that they stand *for* 'official social-patriotism' (in its Francophile or Germanophile form, or in any other that would reconcile these two tendencies). At any rate we would appreciate your kindness in sending us both your reply (your amendments, your counter-draft of the resolution, etc.) and the reply of those organisations (the Organising Committee, the Bund, etc.) that you have already addressed or intend doing so.

With comradely greetings,
Lenin

The Conference of the RSDLP Groups Abroad

Written no later than 19 February (4 March) 1915

Editors note:

Convened on Lenin's initiative, this conference was held in Bern on 27 February – 4 March 1915, and is also referred to as the Bern Conference. It was in fact a general conference of the Party, since neither a party congress nor an all-Russia conference could be convened during the war.

The Conference was attended by representatives of the RSDLP Central Committee, the RSDLP Central Organ, *Sotsial-Demokrat*, and delegates from RSDLP (Bolshevik) groups in Paris, Zürich, Geneva, Bern, Lausanne and from the Baugy group. Lenin was delegated by the Central Committee and the Central Organ, directed the work of the Conference, and made a report on the main item on the agenda, 'The War and the Tasks of the Party'. The Conference adopted resolutions on war as drafted by Lenin.

* * *

Held in Switzerland, a conference of the RSDLP groups whose members are resident abroad concluded its work several days ago. Besides discussing purely foreign affairs, which we shall try briefly to comment on in the next issues of the Central Organ, the conference framed resolutions on the important and burning question of the war. We are publishing these resolutions forthwith, in the hope that they will prove of use to all Social-Democrats who are earnestly seeking the way towards live work from the present-day welter of opinions which boil down to an acknowledgement of internationalism in word, and an urge to come to terms at any cost with social-chauvinism in deed. We might add that, on the question of the 'United States of Europe' slogan, the discussion was purely political, it being decided that the question be deferred pending a discussion, in the press, of the *economic* aspect of the matter.

The Conference's Resolutions

The conference, which stands on the basis of the Central Committee's manifesto, as published in No. 33, lays down the following principles designed to bring system into propaganda:*

On the character of the war

The present war is imperialist in character. This war is the outcome of conditions in an epoch in which capitalism has reached the highest stage in its development; in which the greatest significance attaches, not only to the export of commodities, but also to the export of capital; an epoch in which the cartelisation of production and the internationalisation of economic life have assumed impressive proportions, colonial policies have brought about the almost complete partition of the globe, world capitalism's productive forces have outgrown the limited boundaries of national and state divisions, and the objective conditions are perfectly ripe for socialism to be achieved.

The 'Defence of the Fatherland' slogan

The present war is, in substance, a struggle between Britain, France and Germany for the partition of colonies and for the plunder of rival countries; on the part of tsarism and the ruling classes of Russia, it is an attempt to seize Persia, Mongolia, Turkey in Asia,

---

* See VI Lenin, 'The War and Russian Social-Democracy', in this volume, p. 9.

Constantinople, Galicia, etc. The national element in the Austro-Serbian war is an entirely secondary consideration and does not affect the general imperialist character of the war.

The entire economic and diplomatic history of the last few decades shows that both groups of belligerent nations were systematically preparing the very kind of war such as the present. The question of which group dealt the first military blow or first declared war is immaterial in any determination of the tactics of socialists. Both sides' phrases on the defence of the fatherland, resistance to enemy invasion, a war of defence, etc. are nothing but deception of the people.

At the bottom of genuinely national wars, such as took place especially between 1789 and 1871, was a long process of mass national movements, of a struggle against absolutism and feudalism, the overthrow of national oppression, and the formation of states on a national basis, as a prerequisite of capitalist development.

The national ideology created by that epoch left a deep impress on the mass of the petty bourgeoisie and a section of the proletariat. This is now being utilised in a totally different and imperialist epoch by the sophists of the bourgeoisie, and by the traitors to socialism who are following in their wake, so as to split the workers, and divert them from their class aims and from the revolutionary struggle against the bourgeoisie.

The words in *The Communist Manifesto* that "the working men have no country" are today truer than ever before. Only the proletariat's international struggle against the bourgeoisie can preserve what it has won, and open to the oppressed masses the road to a better future.

The slogans of the revolutionary Social-Democrats

The conversion of the present imperialist war into a civil war is the only correct proletarian slogan, one that follows from the experience of the Commune, and outlined in the Basel Resolution (1912); it has been dictated by all the conditions of an imperialist war between highly developed bourgeois countries.*

---

* Ibid., p. 17.

Civil war, for which revolutionary Social-Democracy today calls, is an armed struggle of the proletariat against the bourgeoisie, for the expropriation of the capitalist class in the advanced capitalist countries, and for a democratic revolution in Russia (a democratic republic, an eight-hour working day, the confiscation of the landowners' estates), for a republic to be formed in the backward monarchist countries in general, etc.

The appalling misery of the masses, which has been created by the war, cannot fail to evoke revolutionary sentiments and movements. The civil war slogan must serve to coordinate and direct such sentiments and movements.

The organisation of the working class has been badly damaged. Nevertheless, a revolutionary crisis is maturing. After the war, the ruling classes of all countries will make a still greater effort to throw the proletariat's emancipation movement back for decades. The task of the revolutionary Social-Democrats – both in the event of a rapid revolutionary development and in that of a protracted crisis, will not consist in renouncing lengthy and day-by-day work, or in discarding any of the old methods of the class struggle. To direct both the parliamentary and the economic struggle against opportunism, in the spirit of revolutionary struggle of the masses – such will be the task.

The following should be indicated as the first steps towards converting the present imperialist war into a civil war:

1. An absolute refusal to vote for war credits, and resignation from bourgeois governments;

2. A complete break with the policy of a class truce (*bloc national*, *Burgfrieden*);

3. Formation of an underground organisation wherever the governments and the bourgeoisie abolish constitutional liberties by introducing martial law;

4. Support for fraternisation between soldiers of the belligerent nations, in the trenches and on battlefields in general;

5. Support for every kind of revolutionary mass action by the
   proletariat in general.

Opportunism and the collapse of the Second International

The collapse of the Second International is the collapse of socialist
opportunism. The latter has grown as a product of the preceding
'peaceful' period in the development of the labour movement. That
period taught the working class to utilise such important means of
struggle as parliamentarianism and all legal opportunities, create
mass economic and political organisations, a widespread labour
press, etc.; on the other hand, the period engendered a tendency
to repudiate the class struggle and to preach a class truce, repudiate
the socialist revolution, repudiate the very principle of illegal
organisations, recognise bourgeois patriotism, etc. Certain strata
of the working class (the bureaucracy of the labour movement and
the labour aristocracy, who get a fraction of the profits from the
exploitation of the colonies and from the privileged position of
their 'fatherlands' in the world market), as well as petty-bourgeois
sympathisers within the socialist parties, have proved the social
mainstay of these tendencies and channels of bourgeois influence
over the proletariat.

The baneful influence of opportunism has made itself felt most
strongly in the policies of most of the official Social-Democratic
parties of the Second International during the war. Voting for
war credits, participation in governments, the policy of a class
truce, the repudiation of an illegal organisation when legality has
been rescinded – all this is a violation of the International's most
important decisions, and a downright betrayal of socialism.

The Third International

The crisis created by war has exposed the real essence of opportunism
as the bourgeoisie's accomplice against the proletariat. The so-called
Social-Democratic 'Centre', headed by Kautsky, has in practice
completely slid into opportunism, behind a cover of exceedingly

harmful and hypocritical phrases and a Marxism falsified to
resemble imperialism. Experience shows that in Germany, for
instance, a defence of the socialist standpoint has been possible
only by resolute opposition to the will of the majority of the Party
leadership. It would be a harmful illusion to hope that a genuinely
socialist International can be restored without a full organisational
severance from the opportunists.

The Russian Social-Democratic Labour Party must support
all and every international and revolutionary mass action by the
proletariat, and strive to bring together all anti-chauvinist elements
in the International.

Pacifism and the 'Peace' slogan

Pacifism, the preaching of peace in the abstract, is one of the means
of duping the working class. Under capitalism, particularly in its
imperialist stage, wars are inevitable. On the other hand, however,
Social-Democrats cannot overlook the positive significance of
revolutionary wars, i.e. not imperialist wars, but such as were fought,
for instance, between 1789 and 1871, with the aim of doing away
with national oppression, and creating national capitalist states out
of the feudal decentralised states, or such wars that may be waged
to defend the conquests of the proletariat victorious in its struggle
against the bourgeoisie.

At the present time, the propaganda of peace unaccompanied
by a call for revolutionary mass action can only sow illusions and
demoralise the proletariat, for it makes the proletariat believe that
the bourgeoisie is humane, and turns it into a plaything in the hands
of the secret diplomacy of the belligerent countries. In particular,
the idea of a so-called democratic peace being possible without a
series of revolutions is profoundly erroneous.

The defeat of the tsarist monarchy

In each country, the struggle against a government that is waging
an imperialist war should not falter at the possibility of that
country's defeat as a result of revolutionary propaganda. The defeat

of the government's army weakens the government, promotes the liberation of the nationalities it oppresses, and facilitates civil war against the ruling classes.

This holds particularly true in respect of Russia. A victory for Russia will bring in its train a strengthening of reaction, both throughout the world and within the country, and will be accompanied by the complete enslavement of the peoples living in areas already seized. In view of this, we consider the defeat of Russia the lesser evil in all conditions.

The attitude towards other parties and groups

The war, which has engendered a spate of chauvinism, has revealed that the democratic (Narodnik) intelligentsia, the party of the Socialist-Revolutionaries (with complete instability of the oppositional trend, which is centred in *Mysl*), and the main group of liquidators (*Nasha Zarya*) which is supported by Plekhanov, are all in the grip of chauvinism. In practice, the Organising Committee is also on the side of chauvinism, beginning with Larin and Martov's camouflaged support of chauvinism and ending with Axelrod's defence of the principle of patriotism; so is the Bund, in which a Germanophile chauvinism prevails. The Brussels bloc (of 3 July 1914) has disintegrated, while the elements that are grouped around *Nashe Slovo* are vacillating between a Platonic sympathy with internationalism and a striving for unity, at any price, with *Nasha Zarya* and the Organising Committee. The same vacillation is manifest in Chkheidze's Social-Democratic group. The latter has, on the one hand, expelled the Plekhanovite, i.e. the chauvinist, Mankov; on the other hand, it wishes to cover up, by all possible means, the chauvinism of Plekhanov, *Nasha Zarya*, Axelrod, the Bund, etc.

It is the task of the Social-Democratic Labour Party in Russia to consolidate the proletarian unity created in 1912-14, mainly by *Pravda*, and to re-establish the Social-Democratic Party organisations of the working class, on the basis of a decisive

organisational break with the social-chauvinists.* Temporary
agreements are possible only with those Social-Democrats who
stand for a decisive organisational rupture with the Organising
Committee, *Nasha Zarya* and the Bund.

---

* *Pravda* – a legal Bolshevik daily published in St. Petersburg, founded in April
1912. Lenin directed *Pravda* from exile abroad. He wrote for the paper almost
daily, gave instructions to the editorial board, and rallied the Party's best literary
forces around the newspaper.

Pravda was constantly persecuted by the police, eventually being closed down
on 8 (21) July 1914, on the eve of the First World War. Publication was not
resumed until after the February Revolution in 1917.

The Defeat of One's Own Government in the Imperialist War

26 July 1915

Editors note:

After the Bern conference the Bolsheviks decided to issue a magazine called *Kommunist* as an international organ of the Left anti-war Social-Democrats. Trotsky was invited as a contributor, showing that they considered him a principled internationalist. Trotsky refused, explaining that there were a number of differences, one of them being the use of the 'defeat of your own government is the lesser evil' slogan. (See 'Open Letter to the Editorial Board of *Kommunist*', June 1915, *Nashe Slovo*, No. 105, in *Lenin's Struggle for a Revolutionary International*, John Riddell (ed.), Pathfinder, 1986, p. 365.) This article is Lenin's reply.

We have already discussed in the Introduction (this volume p. ix) the context of the differences between Lenin and Trotsky on the question of slogans and the evolution of Lenin's use of 'revolutionary defeatism'.

Aside from this question, Lenin's main criticism of Trotsky in this whole period was that he entertained illusions that unity could be reached with the conciliators. In this, Lenin was absolutely correct and Trotsky admitted as much later on. In a letter to the Dutch Marxist Gorter, around the same time, Lenin says:

> I congratulate you on your splendid attacks on opportunism and Kautsky. Trotsky's principal mistake is that he does not attack this gang. (*LCW*, Vol. 43, pp. 453-4a)

For a full exposition of Trotsky's views see *The War and the International* (which was published after the Revolution by the Soviet publishing house) and *The Programme for Peace*, a series of articles written in 1915-16 and then published by the Bolshevik press in June 1917.

* * *

During a reactionary war a revolutionary class cannot but desire the defeat of its government.

This is axiomatic, and disputed only by conscious partisans or helpless satellites of the social-chauvinists. Among the former, for instance, is Semkovsky of the Organising Committee (No. 2 of its *Izvestia*), and among the latter, Trotsky and Bukvoyed,* and Kautsky in Germany. To desire Russia's defeat, Trotsky writes, is

> ... an uncalled-for and absolutely unjustifiable concession to the political methodology of social-patriotism, which would replace the revolutionary struggle against the war and the conditions causing it, with an orientation – highly arbitrary in the present conditions – towards the lesser evil. (*Nashe Slovo*, No. 105.)

This is an instance of high-flown phraseology with which Trotsky always justifies opportunism. A "revolutionary struggle against the war" is merely an empty and meaningless exclamation, something at which the heroes of the Second International excel, *unless* it means revolutionary action against *one's own government* even in wartime. One has only to do some thinking in order to understand this. Wartime revolutionary action against one's own government indubitably means, not only desiring its defeat, but really facilitating such a defeat. ('Discerning reader': note that this

---

*   Bukvoyed was a pseudonym of David Riazanov.

does not mean 'blowing up bridges', organising unsuccessful strikes in the war industries, and in general helping the government defeat the revolutionaries.)

The phrase-bandying Trotsky has completely lost his bearings on a simple issue. It seems to him that to desire Russia's defeat *means* desiring the victory of Germany. (Bukvoyed and Semkovsky give more direct expression to the 'thought', or rather want of thought, which they share with Trotsky.) But Trotsky regards this as the "methodology of social-patriotism"! To help people that are unable to think for themselves, the Bern resolution (*Sotsial Demokrat*, No. 40) made it clear, that in *all* imperialist countries the proletariat must now desire the defeat of its own government.* Bukvoyed and Trotsky preferred to avoid this truth, while Semkovsky (an opportunist who is more useful to the working class than all the others, thanks to his naively frank reiteration of bourgeois wisdom) blurted out the following: "This is nonsense, because either Germany or Russia can win." (*Izvestia*, No. 2.)

Take the example of the Paris Commune. France was defeated by Germany but the workers were defeated by Bismarck and Thiers! Had Bukvoyed and Trotsky done a little thinking, they would have realised that *they* have adopted the viewpoint on the war held by *governments and the bourgeoisie*, i.e. that they cringe to the "political methodology of social-patriotism", to use Trotsky's pretentious language.

A revolution in wartime means civil war; the *conversion* of a war between governments into a civil war is, on the one hand, facilitated by military reverses ('defeats') of governments; on the other hand, one *cannot* actually strive for such a conversion without thereby facilitating defeat.

The reason why the chauvinists (including the Organising Committee and the Chkheidze group) repudiate the defeat 'slogan' is that *this slogan alone* implies a consistent call for revolutionary action against one's own government in wartime. Without such

---

* See 'The Conference of the RSDLP Groups Abroad', in this volume, p. 40.

action, millions of ultra-revolutionary phrases such as a war against 'the war and the conditions, etc.' are not worth a brass farthing.

Anyone who would in all earnest refute the 'slogan' of defeat for one's own government in the imperialist war should prove one of three things: (1) that the war of 1914-15 is not reactionary, or (2) that a revolution stemming from that war is impossible, or (3) that coordination and mutual aid are possible between revolutionary movements in *all* the belligerent countries. The third point is particularly important to Russia, a most backward country, where an immediate socialist revolution is impossible. That is why the Russian Social-Democrats had to be the first to advance the 'theory and practice' of the defeat 'slogan'. The tsarist government was perfectly right in asserting that the agitation conducted by the Russian Social-Democratic Labour group in the Duma – the *sole* instance in the International, not only of parliamentary opposition but of genuine revolutionary anti-government agitation among the masses – that this agitation has weakened Russia's 'military might' and is likely to lead to its defeat. This is a fact to which it is foolish to close one's eyes.

The opponents of the defeat slogan are simply afraid of themselves when they refuse to recognise the very obvious fact of the inseparable link between revolutionary agitation against the government and helping bring about its defeat.

Are coordination and mutual aid possible between the Russian movement, which is revolutionary in the bourgeois-democratic sense, and the socialist movement in the West? No socialist who has publicly spoken on the matter during the last decade has doubted this, the movement among the Austrian proletariat after 17 October 1905, *actually* proving it possible.*

---

*   This refers to the tsar's manifesto promulgated on 17 (30) October 1905. It promised "civil liberties" and a "legislative Duma". The manifesto was a concession wrested from the tsarist regime by the revolution, but that concession by no means decided the fate of the revolution as the liberals and Mensheviks claimed. The Bolsheviks exposed the real meaning of the manifesto and called upon the masses to continue the struggle and overthrow the autocracy.

Ask any Social-Democrat who calls himself an internationalist whether or not he approves of an understanding between the Social-Democrats of the various belligerent countries on joint revolutionary action against all belligerent governments. Many of them will reply that it is impossible, as Kautsky has done (*Die Neue Zeit*, 2 October 1914), thereby *fully proving* his social-chauvinism. This, on the one hand, is a deliberate and vicious lie, which clashes with the generally known facts and the Basel Manifesto. On the other hand, if it were true, *the opportunists would be quite right in many respects!*

Many will voice their approval of such an understanding. To this we shall say: if this approval is not hypocritical, it is ridiculous to think that, in wartime and for the conduct of a war, some 'formal' understanding is necessary, such as the election of representatives, the arrangement of a meeting, the signing of an agreement, and the choice of the day and hour! Only the Semkovskys are capable of thinking so. An understanding on revolutionary action even in a *single* country, to say nothing of a number of countries, can be achieved *only* by the force of the *example* of serious revolutionary action, by *launching* such action and *developing* it. However, such action cannot be launched without desiring the defeat of the government, and without contributing to such a defeat. The conversion of the imperialist war into a civil war cannot be 'made', any more than a revolution can be 'made'. It *develops* out of a number of diverse phenomena, aspects, features, characteristics and consequences of the imperialist war. That development is *impossible* without a series of military reverses and defeats of governments that receive blows from their *own* oppressed classes.

The 1905 Russian Revolution exerted a great influence on the working-class movement in other countries, in particular in Austria-Hungary. Lenin pointed out that the news about the tsar's concession and his manifesto, with its promise of "liberties", "played a decisive part in the final victory of universal suffrage in Austria".

Mass demonstrations took place in Vienna and other industrial cities in Austria-Hungary. In Prague barricades were put up. As a result, universal suffrage was introduced in Austria.

To repudiate the defeat slogan means allowing one's revolutionary ardour to degenerate into an empty phrase, or sheer hypocrisy.

What is the substitute proposed for the defeat slogan? It is that of "neither victory nor defeat" (Semkovsky in *Izvestia*, No. 2; also the *entire* Organising Committee in No. 1).* This, however, is nothing but a paraphrase of the *'defence of the fatherland'* slogan. It means shifting the issue to the level of a war between governments (who, according to the content of this slogan, are to *keep* to their old stand, "retain their positions"), and not to the level of the *struggle* of the oppressed classes against their governments! It means justifying the chauvinism of *all* the imperialist nations, whose bourgeoisie are always ready to *say – and do say to the people – that* they are 'only' fighting 'against defeat'. "The significance of our 4 August vote was that we are not for war *but against defeat*", David, a leader of the opportunists, writes in his book. The Organising Committee, together with Bukvoyed and Trotsky, stand on *fully* the same ground as David when they defend the 'neither-victory nor-defeat' slogan.

On closer examination, this slogan will be found to mean a 'class truce', the renunciation of the class struggle by the oppressed classes in all belligerent countries, since the class struggle is impossible without dealing blows at one's 'own' bourgeoisie, one's 'own' government, whereas dealing a blow at one's own government in wartime *is* (for Bukvoyed's information) high treason, *means* contributing to the defeat of one's own country. Those who accept the 'neither victory-nor-defeat' slogan can only be hypocritically in favour of the class struggle, of 'disrupting the class truce'; *in practice*, such people are renouncing an independent proletarian policy because they subordinate the proletariat of all belligerent countries to the *absolutely bourgeois* task of safeguarding the imperialist governments against defeat. The only policy of actual, not verbal disruption of the 'class truce', of acceptance of the class struggle, is for the proletariat *to take advantage* of the *difficulties* experienced by its government and its bourgeoisie *in order to overthrow them.*

---

* Note that this was the position of the Menshevik Semkovsky, not Trotsky.

This, however, cannot be achieved or *striven for*, without desiring the defeat of one's own government and without contributing to that defeat.

When, before the war, the Italian Social-Democrats raised the question of a mass strike, the bourgeoisie replied, no doubt correctly from their *own* point of view, that this would be high treason, and that Social-Democrats would be dealt with as traitors. That is true, just as it is true that fraternisation in the trenches is high treason. Those who write against 'high treason', as Bukvoyed does, or against the 'disintegration of Russia', as Semkovsky does, are adopting the bourgeois, not the proletarian point of view. A proletarian *cannot* deal a class blow at his government or hold out (in fact) a hand to his brother, the proletarian of the 'foreign' country which is at war with 'our side', *without committing* 'high treason', *without contributing* to the defeat, to the *disintegration* of his 'own', imperialist 'Great' Power.

Whoever is in favour of the slogan of 'neither victory nor defeat' is consciously or unconsciously a chauvinist; at best he is a conciliatory petty bourgeois, but in any case he is an *enemy* to proletarian policy, a partisan of the existing governments, of the present-day ruling classes.

Let us look at the question from yet another angle. The war cannot but evoke among the masses the most turbulent sentiments, which upset the usual sluggish state of mass mentality. Revolutionary tactics are *impossible* if they are not adjusted to these new turbulent sentiments.

What are the main currents of these turbulent sentiments? They are: (1) Horror and despair. Hence, a growth of religious feeling. Again the churches are crowded, the reactionaries joyfully declare. "Wherever there is suffering there is religion", says the arch-reactionary Barres. He is right, too. (2) Hatred of the 'enemy', a sentiment that is carefully fostered by the bourgeoisie (not so much by the priests), and is of economic and political value *only to the bourgeoisie*. (3) Hatred of one's *own* government and one's *own* bourgeoisie – the sentiment of all class-conscious workers who understand, on the one hand, that war is a 'continuation of the politics' of imperialism, which they counter by a 'continuation' of their hatred of their class enemy, and, on the other hand, that 'a war against war' is a banal phrase unless it means a revolution against their *own* government. Hatred of one's own government and one's own bourgeoisie cannot be aroused unless their defeat is desired; one *cannot* be a sincere opponent of a civil (i.e. class) truce without arousing hatred of one's own government and bourgeoisie!

Those who stand for the 'neither-victory-nor-defeat' slogan are in fact on the side of the bourgeoisie and the opportunists, for they do not believe in the possibility of international revolutionary action by the working class against their own governments, and *do not wish* to help develop such action, which, though undoubtedly difficult, is the only task worthy of a proletarian, the only socialist task. It is the proletariat in the most backward of the belligerent Great Powers which, through the medium of their party, have had to adopt – especially in view of the shameful treachery of the German and French Social-Democrats – revolutionary tactics that are quite unfeasible unless they 'contribute to the defeat' of their own government, but which alone lead to a European revolution, to the permanent peace of socialism, to the liberation of humanity from the horrors, misery, savagery and brutality now prevailing.

The Question of Peace

Written July – August 1915

The question of peace as an immediate programme of action for the socialists, and in this connection the question of peace terms, presents a universal interest. One can only be grateful to *Berner Tagwacht* for its efforts to pose the question, not from the usual petty-bourgeois national angle, but from one that is genuinely proletarian and internationalist. The editorial note in No. 73 (*'Friedenssehnsucht'*), that the German Social-Democrats who wish for peace must break (*sich lossagen*) with the policies of the Junker government, was excellent. Also excellent was Comrade AP's [Anton Pannekoek's] attack (Nos. 73 and 75) on the "pompous airs of impotent phrase-mongers" (*Wichtigtuerei machtloser Schönredner*), who are vainly attempting to solve the peace question from the petty-bourgeois point of view.

Let us see how this question should be posed by socialists.

The peace slogan can be advanced either in connection with definite peace terms, or without any conditions at all, as a struggle, not for a definite kind of peace, but for peace in general (*Frieden ohne weiteres*). In the latter case, we obviously have a slogan that is not only non-socialist but entirely devoid of meaning and content. Most people are definitely in favour of peace in general, including even Kitchener, Joffre, Hindenburg, and Nicholas the Bloodstained, for *each* of them wants an end to the war. The trouble is that every one of them advances peace terms that are imperialist (i.e. predatory and oppressive, towards other peoples), and to the advantage of his 'own' nation. Slogans must be brought forward so as to enable the masses, through propaganda and agitation, to see the unbridgeable distinction between socialism and capitalism (imperialism), and *not* for the purpose of *reconciling two* hostile classes and two hostile political lines, with the aid of a formula that 'unites' the most different things.

To continue: can the socialists of different countries be united on definite *terms* of peace? If so, such terms must undoubtedly include the recognition of the right to self-determination for all nations, and also renunciation of all 'annexations', i.e. infringements of that right. If, however, that right is recognised only for *some* nations, then you are defending the *privileges* of certain nations, i.e. you are a nationalist and imperialist, not a socialist. If, however, that right is recognised for *all* nations, then you cannot single out Belgium alone, for instance; you must take all the oppressed peoples, both in Europe (the Irish in Britain, the Italians in Nice, the Danes in Germany, 57 per cent of Russia's population, etc.) and *outside of Europe,* i.e. all colonies. Comrade AP has done well to remind us of them. Britain, France, and Germany have a total population of some 150 million, whereas the populations they oppress in the colonies number over 400 million! The essence of the imperialist war, i.e. a war waged for the interests of the capitalists, consists, not only in the war being waged with the aim of oppressing new nations, of carving up the colonies, but also in its being waged primarily by the advanced nations, which oppress a number of other peoples comprising the *majority* of the Earth's population.

The German Social-Democrats, who justify the seizure of Belgium or reconcile themselves to it, are actually imperialists and nationalists, not Social-Democrats, since they defend the 'right' of the German bourgeoisie (partly also of the German workers) to oppress the Belgians, the Alsatians, the Danes, the Poles, the

Negroes in Africa, etc. They are not socialists, but *menials* to the German bourgeoisie, whom they are aiding to rob other nations. The Belgian socialists who demand the liberation and indemnification of Belgium *alone* are also actually defending a demand of the Belgian bourgeoisie, who would go on plundering the 15,000,000 Congolese population and obtaining concessions and privileges in other countries. The Belgian bourgeoisie's foreign investments amount to something like 3,000 million francs. Safeguarding the profits from these investments by using every kind of fraud and machinations is the real 'national interest' of 'gallant Belgium'. The same applies in a still greater degree to Russia, Britain, France and Japan.

It follows that if the demand for the freedom of nations is not to be a false phrase covering up the imperialism and the nationalism of *certain individual countries*, it must be extended to all peoples and to all colonies. Such a demand, however, is obviously meaningless *unless* it is accompanied by a series of revolutions in all the advanced countries. Moreover, it cannot be accomplished without a successful socialist revolution.

Should this be taken to mean that socialists can remain indifferent to the peace demand that is coming from ever greater masses of the people? By no means. The slogans of the workers' class-conscious vanguard are one thing, while the spontaneous demands of the masses are something quite different. The yearning for peace is one of the most important symptoms revealing the beginnings of *disappointment* in the bourgeois lie about a war of 'liberation', the 'defence of the fatherland', and similar falsehoods that the class of capitalists beguiles the mob with. This symptom should attract the closest attention from socialists. All efforts must be bent towards *utilising* the masses' desire for peace. But how is it to be utilised? To recognise the peace *slogan* and repeat it would mean encouraging "pompous airs of impotent [and frequently what is worse: *hypocritical*] phrase-mongers"; it would mean *deceiving* the people with illusion that the existing governments, the present-day master classes, are capable – without being 'taught' a lesson (or rather without being eliminated) by a series of revolutions – of granting a peace in any way satisfactory to democracy and the working class. Nothing is more harmful than such deception. Nothing throws more dust in the eyes of the workers, nothing imbues them with a more deceptive idea about the *absence of deep* contradictions between capitalism and socialism, nothing *embellishes* capitalist slavery more than this deception does. No, we must make use of the desire for peace so as to explain to the masses that the benefits they expect from peace cannot be obtained without a series of revolutions.

An end to wars, peace among the nations, the cessation of pillaging and violence – such is our ideal, but only bourgeois sophists can seduce the masses with this ideal, if the latter is divorced from a direct and immediate call for revolutionary action. The ground for such propaganda is prepared; to practice that propaganda, one need only break with the opportunists, those allies of the bourgeoisie, who are hampering revolutionary work both directly (even to the extent of passing information to the authorities) and indirectly.

The slogan of self-determination of nations should also be advanced *in connection* with the imperialist era of capitalism. We do not stand for the *status quo*, or for the philistine utopia of *standing aside* in great wars. We stand for a revolutionary struggle against imperialism, i.e. capitalism. Imperialism consists in a striving of nations that oppress a number of other nations to extend and increase that oppression and to repartition the colonies. That is why the question of self-determination of nations today *hinges* on the conduct of socialists of the *oppressor* nations. A socialist of any of the *oppressor* nations (Britain, France, Germany, Japan, Russia, the United States of America, etc.) who does not recognise and does not struggle for the right of oppressed nations to self-determination (i.e. the right to secession) is in reality a chauvinist, not a socialist.

Only this point of view can lead to a sincere and consistent struggle against imperialism, to a proletarian, not a philistine approach (today) to the national question. Only this point of view can lead to a consistent application of the principle of combating any form of the oppression of nations; it removes mistrust among the proletarians of the oppressor and oppressed nations, makes for a united international struggle for the socialist revolution (i.e. for the only accomplishable regime of complete national equality), as distinct from the philistine utopia of freedom for all small states in general, under capitalism.

This is the point of view adopted by our Party, i.e. by those Social-Democrats of Russia who have rallied around the Central Committee. This was the point of view adopted by Marx when he taught the proletariat that "no nation can be free if it oppresses other nations".* It was from this point of view that Marx demanded the separation of Ireland from Britain, this in the interests of the freedom movement, not only of the Irish, but especially of the *British* workers.

If the socialists of Britain do not recognise and uphold Ireland's right to secession, if the French do not do the same for Italian Nice; the Germans for Alsace-Lorraine, Danish Schleswig, and Poland; the Russians for Poland, Finland, the Ukraine, etc.; and the Poles for the Ukraine – if all the socialists of the 'Great' Powers, i.e. the great robber powers, do not uphold that right in respect of the colonies, it is solely because they are in fact imperialists, not socialists. It is ridiculous to cherish illusions that people who do not fight for 'the right to self-determination' of the oppressed nations, while they themselves belong to the oppressor nations, are capable of practising socialist policies.

Instead of leaving it to the hypocritical phrase-mongers to deceive the people by phrases and promises concerning the possibility of a democratic peace, socialists must explain to the masses the impossibility of anything resembling a democratic peace, unless there are a series of revolutions and unless a revolutionary struggle is waged in every country against the *respective* government. Instead of allowing the bourgeois politicians to deceive the peoples with talk about the freedom of nations, socialists must explain to the masses in the *oppressor* nations that they cannot hope for their liberation,

---

*   See Marx and Engels, 'On Poland', in *MECW*, Vol. 6, p. 389.

as long as they help oppress other nations, and do not recognise and uphold the right of those nations to self-determination, i.e. the freedom to secede. That is the socialist, as distinct from the imperialist, policy to be applied to all countries, on the question of peace and the national question. True, this line is in most cases incompatible with the laws punishing high treason – but so is the *Basel Resolution*, which has been so shamefully betrayed by almost all the socialists of the oppressor nations.

The choice is between socialism and submission to the laws of Joffre and Hindenburg, between revolutionary struggle and servility to imperialism. There is no middle course. The greatest harm is caused to the proletariat by the hypocritical (or obtuse) authors of the 'middle-course' policy.

Socialism and War

The Attitude of the Russian Social-Democratic Labour
Party Towards the War

Written July – August 1915

Editors note:

Lenin decided to write this pamphlet in connection with the preparations for the first International Socialist Conference. Zinoviev helped draft the pamphlet though Lenin edited the entire text.

The pamphlet was published in German in September 1915 and distributed among the delegates to the Zimmerwald Socialist Conference. In 1916 it was published in French.

Preface to the First (Foreign) Edition

The war has been in progress for already a year. At the very outset of the war, our Party's attitude towards it was defined in the Central Committee's manifesto drawn up in September 1914 and (after it had been sent to the members of the CC and to our Party's responsible representatives in Russia, and had received their consent) published on 1 November 1914, in No. 33 of *Sotsial-Demokrat*, our Party's Central Organ.* Later, in No. 40 (29 March 1915), the resolutions of the Bern Conference were published, in which our principles and tactics were set forth more precisely.**

At present there is an obvious growth of revolutionary temper among the masses. In other countries, symptoms of the same phenomenon are to be seen on all sides, despite the suppression of the revolutionary aspirations of the proletariat by most of the official Social-Democratic parties, which have taken sides with their governments and their bourgeoisie. This state of affairs makes particularly urgent the publication of a pamphlet that sums up Social-Democratic tactics in relation to the war. In reprinting in

---

* See Lenin, 'The War and Russian Social-Democracy', in this volume, p. 9.

Sotsial-Demokrat – central organ of the RSDLP, published as an underground newspaper from February 1908 to January 1917. It featured more than eighty articles and other items by Lenin, who became its editor in December 1911.

** See Lenin, 'The Conference of the RSDLP Groups Abroad', in this volume, p. 35.

full the above-mentioned Party documents, we have provided them with brief comment, endeavouring to take due stock of all the main arguments in favour of bourgeois and of proletarian tactics that have been expressed in the appropriate literature and at Party meetings.

Preface to the Second Edition

This pamphlet was written in the summer of 1915, just before the Zimmerwald Conference.* It also appeared in German and French, and was reprinted in full in Norwegian in the organ of the Norwegian Social-Democratic Youth League. The German edition of the pamphlet was secretly brought to Germany – Berlin, Leipzig, Bremen and other cities – where it was secretly distributed by supporters of the Zimmerwald Left and by the Karl Liebknecht group. The French edition was secretly printed in Paris and distributed there by the French Zimmerwaldists. The Russian-language edition reached Russia in a very limited number of copies, and in Moscow was copied out in handwriting by workers. We are now reprinting this pamphlet in full, as a document. The reader should all the time remember that the pamphlet was written in August 1915. This must be kept in view particularly in connection with those passages which refer to Russia: Russia at that time was still tsarist, Romanov Russia.

Lenin,
1918

---

* *Zimmerwald Conference* – the first conference of internationalist socialists, held in Zimmerwald, Switzerland, on 5-8 September 1915. A struggle flared up at the conference between the Kautskyite centrist majority and the revolutionary internationalists headed by Lenin. At the conference, Lenin organised the internationalists into the Zimmerwald Left group.

1. The Principles of Socialism and the War of 1914-1915

The attitude of socialists towards wars

Socialists have always condemned wars between nations as barbarous and brutal. Our attitude towards war, however, is fundamentally different from that of the bourgeois pacifists (supporters and advocates of peace) and of the anarchists. We differ from the former in that we understand the inevitable connection between wars and the class struggle within a country; we understand that wars cannot be abolished unless classes are abolished and socialism is created; we also differ in that we regard civil wars, i.e. wars waged by an oppressed class against the oppressor class, by slaves against slaveholders, by serfs against landowners, and by wage-workers against the bourgeoisie, as fully legitimate, progressive and necessary. We Marxists differ from both pacifists and anarchists in that we deem it necessary to study each war historically (from the standpoint of Marx's dialectical materialism) and separately. There have been in the past numerous wars which, despite all the horrors, atrocities, distress and suffering that inevitably accompany all wars, were progressive, i.e. benefited the development of mankind by helping to destroy most harmful and reactionary institutions (e.g. an autocracy or serfdom) and the most barbarous despotisms in Europe (the Turkish and the

Russian). That is why the features historically specific to the present war must come up for examination.

The historical types of wars in modern times

The Great French Revolution ushered in a new epoch in the history of mankind. From that time down to the Paris Commune, i.e. between 1789 and 1871, one type of war was of a bourgeois-progressive character, waged for national liberation. In other words, the overthrow of absolutism and feudalism, the undermining of these institutions, and the overthrow of alien oppression, formed the chief content and historical significance of *such* wars. These were therefore progressive wars; during such wars, all honest and revolutionary democrats, as well as all socialists, always wished success to that country (i.e. that bourgeoisie) which had helped to overthrow or undermine the most baneful foundations of feudalism, absolutism and the oppression of other nations. For example, the revolutionary wars waged by France contained an element of plunder and the conquest of foreign territory by the French, but this does not in the least alter the fundamental historical significance of those wars, which destroyed and shattered feudalism and absolutism in the whole of the old, serf-owning Europe. In the Franco-Prussian war, Germany plundered France, but this does not alter the fundamental historical significance of that war, which liberated tens of millions of German people from feudal disunity and from the oppression of two despots, the Russian tsar and Napoleon III.

The difference between wars of aggression and of defence

The period of 1789-1871 left behind it deep marks and revolutionary memories. There could be no development of the proletarian struggle for socialism prior to the overthrow of feudalism, absolutism and alien oppression. When, in stressing the legitimacy of 'defensive' wars in *such* periods, socialists always had these aims in mind, namely revolution against medievalism and serfdom. By a 'defensive' war socialists have always understood a '*just*' war in this particular sense (Wilhelm Liebknecht once expressed himself precisely in this way). It is only in this sense that socialists have always regarded wars 'for the defence of the fatherland', or 'defensive' wars, as legitimate, progressive and just. For example, if tomorrow Morocco were to declare war on France, or India on Britain, or Persia or China on Russia, and so on, these would be 'just', and 'defensive' wars, *irrespective* of who would be the first to attack; any socialist would wish the oppressed, dependent and unequal states victory over the oppressor, slaveholding and predatory 'Great' Powers.

But imagine a slaveholder who owns 100 slaves warring against another who owns 200 slaves, for a more 'just' redistribution of slaves. The use of the term of a 'defensive' war, or a war 'for the defence of the fatherland', would clearly be historically false in such a case and would in practice be sheer deception of the common people, philistines, and the ignorant, by the astute slave-holders. It is in this way that the peoples are being deceived with 'national' ideology and the term of 'defence of the fatherland', by the present-day imperialist bourgeoisie, in the war now being waged between slave-holders with the purpose of consolidating slavery.

The war of today is an imperialist war

It is almost universally admitted that this war is an imperialist war. In most cases, however, this term is distorted, or applied to one side, or else a loophole is left for the assertion that this war may, after all, be bourgeois-progressive, and of significance to the national-liberation movement. Imperialism is the highest stage in the development of capitalism, reached only in the twentieth century. Capitalism now finds that the old national states, without whose formation it could not have overthrown feudalism, are too cramped for it. Capitalism has developed concentration to such a degree that entire branches of industry are controlled by syndicates, trusts and associations of capitalist multimillionaires, and almost the entire globe has been divided up among the 'lords of capital', either in the form of colonies, or by entangling other countries in thousands of threads of financial exploitation. Free trade and competition have been superseded by a striving towards monopolies, the seizure of territory for the investment of capital and as sources of raw materials, and so on. From the liberator of nations, which it was in the struggle against feudalism, capitalism in its imperialist stage has turned into the greatest oppressor of nations. Formerly progressive, capitalism has become reactionary; it has developed the forces of production to such a degree that mankind is faced with the alternative of adopting socialism, or of experiencing years and even decades of armed struggle between the 'Great' Powers for the artificial preservation of capitalism by means of colonies, monopolies, privileges and national oppression of every kind.

A war between the biggest slave-holders for the maintenance and consolidation of slavery

To make the significance of imperialism clear, we will quote precise figures showing the partition of the world among the so-called 'Great' Powers (i.e. those successful in great plunder). Hence it will be seen that, since 1876, most of the nations which were foremost fighters for freedom in 1789-1871, have, on the basis of a highly developed and 'over-mature' capitalism, become oppressors and enslavers of most of the population and the nations of the globe. From 1876 to 1914, six 'Great' Powers grabbed 25 million square kilometres, i.e. an area two-and-a-half times that of Europe! Six Powers have enslaved *523 million* people in the colonies. For every four inhabitants in the 'Great' Powers there are five in 'their' colonies. It is common knowledge that colonies are conquered with fire and sword, that the population of the colonies are brutally treated, and that they are exploited in a thousand ways (by exporting capital, through concessions, etc., cheating in the sale of goods, subjugation by the authorities of the 'ruling' nation, and so on and so forth). The Anglo-French bourgeoisie are deceiving the people when they say that they are waging a war for the freedom of nations and of Belgium; in fact they are waging a war for the purpose of retaining the colonies they have grabbed and robbed.

Division of the world among the 'Great' slave-owning Powers

	Colonies 1876		Colonies 1914		Metropolises 1914		Total	
	Sq. km	Population	Sq. km	Population	Sq. km	Population	Sq. km	Population
	millions		millions		millions		millions	
England	22.5	251.9	33.5	393.5	0.3	46.5	33.8	440.0
Russia	17.0	15.9	17.4	33.2	5.4	136.2	22.8	169.4
France	0.9	6.0	10.6	55.5	0.5	36.9	11.1	95.1
Germany	–	–	2.9	12.3	0.5	64.9	3.4	77.2
Japan	–	–	0.3	19.2	0.4	53.0	0.7	72.2
US	–	–	0.3	9.7	9.4	97.0	9.7	106.7
Total for the six 'Great' Powers	40.4	273.8	65.0	523.4	16.5	437.2	81.5	960.6
Colonies belonging to other than Great Powers (Belgium, Holland and other states)			9.9	45.3	–	–	9.9	45.3

Three "semi-colonial" countries (Turkey, China and Persia) 15.5 361.2

Total 105.9 1,367.1

Other states and countries 28.0 289.9

Grand total of the entire globe (exclusive of Polar regions) 133.9 1,657.0

The German imperialists would free Belgium, etc., at once if the British and French would agree to 'fairly' share their colonies with them. A feature of the situation is that in this war, the fate of the colonies is being decided by a war on the Continent. From the standpoint of bourgeois justice and national freedom (or the right of nations to existence), Germany might be considered absolutely in the right as against Britain and France, for she has been 'done out' of colonies, her enemies are oppressing an immeasurably far larger number of nations than she is, and the Slavs that are being oppressed by her ally, Austria, undoubtedly enjoy far more freedom than those of tsarist Russia, that veritable 'prison of nations'. Germany, however, is fighting, not for the liberation of nations, but for their oppression. It is not the business of socialists to help the younger and stronger robber (Germany) to plunder the older and overgorged robbers. Socialists must take advantage of the struggle between the robbers to overthrow all of them. To be able to do this, socialists must first of all tell the people the truth, namely, that this war is, in three respects, a war between slaveholders with the aim of consolidating slavery. This is a war, firstly, to increase the enslavement of the colonies by means of a 'more equitable' distribution and subsequent more concerted exploitation of them; secondly, to increase the oppression of other nations within the 'Great' Powers, since *both* Austria *and* Russia (Russia in greater degree and with results far worse than Austria) maintain their rule only by such oppression, intensifying it by means of war; and thirdly, to increase and prolong wage slavery, since the proletariat is split up and suppressed, while the capitalists are the gainers, making fortunes out of the war, fanning national prejudices and intensifying reaction, which has raised its head in all countries, even in the freest and most republican.

War is the continuation of politics by other (i.e. violent) 'means'

This famous dictum was uttered by Clausewitz, one of the profoundest writers on the problems of war.* Marxists have always rightly regarded this thesis as the theoretical basis of views on the significance of any war. It was from this viewpoint that Marx and Engels always regarded the various wars.

Apply this view to the present war. You will see that for decades, for almost half a century, the governments and the ruling classes of Britain and France, Germany and Italy, Austria and Russia, have pursued a policy of plundering colonies, oppressing other nations and suppressing the working-class movement. It is this, and only

---

*   See Carl von Clausewitz, *On War*, Penguin Classics, 1983, p. 119.

this, policy that is being continued in the present war. In particular, the policy of both Austria and Russia, in peacetime as well as in wartime, is a policy of enslaving nations, not of liberating them. In China, Persia, India and other dependent countries, on the contrary, we have seen during the past decades a policy of rousing tens and hundreds of millions of people to a national life, of their liberation from the reactionary 'Great' Powers' oppression. A war waged on such a historical basis can even today be a bourgeois-progressive war of national liberation.

If the present war is regarded as a continuation of the politics of the 'Great' Powers and of the principal classes within them, a glance will immediately reveal the glaring anti-historicity, falseness and hypocrisy of the view that the 'defence of the fatherland' idea can be justified in the present war.

The case of Belgium

The favourite plea of the social-chauvinists of the Triple (now Quadruple)* Entente (in Russia, Plekhanov and co.) is the case of Belgium. This instance, however, speaks against them. The German imperialists have brazenly violated the neutrality of Belgium, as belligerent states have done always and everywhere, trampling upon *all* treaties and obligations if necessary. Let us suppose that all states interested in the observance of international treaties should declare war on Germany with the demand that Belgium be liberated and indemnified. In that case, the sympathies of socialists would, of course, be with Germany's enemies. But the whole point is that the Triple (and Quadruple) Entente is waging war, *not* over Belgium; this is common knowledge and only hypocrites will disguise the fact. Britain is grabbing at Germany's colonies and Turkey, Russia is grabbing at Galicia and Turkey, France wants Alsace-Lorraine and even the left bank of the Rhine; a treaty has been concluded with Italy for the division of the spoils (Albania and Asia Minor); bargaining is going on

---

*   Italy joined the imperialist alliance of Britain, France and Russia after breaking away from the Triple Alliance.

with Bulgaria and Romania, also for the division of the spoils. In the present war waged by the governments of today, it is *impossible* to help Belgium *otherwise* than by helping to throttle Austria or Turkey, etc.! Where does 'defence of the fatherland' come in here? Herein lies the specific feature of imperialist war, a war between reactionary-bourgeois and historically outmoded governments, waged for the purpose of oppressing other nations. Whoever justifies participation in the present war is perpetuating the imperialist oppression of nations. Whoever advocates taking advantage of the present embarrassments of the governments so as to fight for the social revolution is championing the real freedom of really all nations, which is possible only under socialism.

What Russia is fighting for

In Russia, capitalist imperialism of the latest type has fully revealed itself in the policy of tsarism towards Persia, Manchuria and Mongolia, but, in general, military and feudal imperialism is predominant in Russia. In no country in the world are the majority of the population oppressed so much as in Russia; Great Russians constitute only 43 per cent of the population, i.e. less than half; the non-Russians are denied all rights. Of the 170 million inhabitants of Russia, *about 100 million* are oppressed and denied their rights. Tsarism is waging a war to seize Galicia and finally crush the liberties of the Ukrainians, and to obtain possession of Armenia, Constantinople, etc. Tsarism regards the war as a means of diverting attention from the mounting discontent within the country and of suppressing the growing revolutionary movement. To every two Great Russians in Russia today there are two or three non-Russians without even elementary rights: tsarism is striving, by means of the war, to increase the number of nations oppressed by Russia, to perpetuate this oppression, and thereby undermine the struggle for freedom which the Great Russians themselves are waging. The possibility of oppressing and robbing other nations perpetuates economic stagnation, because, frequently, the source of income is not the development of productive forces, but the semi-feudal exploitation of non-Russians. Thus on the part of Russia, the war is marked by its profoundly reactionary character, its hostility to national liberation.

What social-chauvinism is

Social-chauvinism is advocacy of the idea of 'defence of the fatherland' in the present war. This idea logically leads to the abandonment of the class struggle during the war, to voting for war credits, etc. In fact, the social-chauvinists are pursuing an anti-proletarian bourgeois policy, for they are actually championing, not 'defence of the fatherland' in the sense of combating foreign oppression, but the 'right' of one or other of the 'Great' Powers to plunder colonies and to oppress other nations. The social-chauvinists reiterate the bourgeois deception of the people that the war is being waged to protect the freedom and existence of nations, thereby taking sides with the bourgeoisie against the proletariat. Among the social-chauvinists are those who justify and varnish the governments and bourgeoisie of *one* of the belligerent groups of powers, as well as those who, like Kautsky, argue that the socialists of *all* the belligerent powers are equally entitled to 'defend the fatherland'. Social-chauvinism, which is, in effect, defence of the privileges, the advantages, the right to pillage and plunder, of one's 'own' (or any) imperialist bourgeoisie, is the utter betrayal of all socialist convictions and of the decision of the Basel International Socialist Congress.

The 'Basel Manifesto'

The manifesto on war unanimously adopted in Basel in 1912 has in view the very kind of war between Britain and Germany and their present allies, which broke out in 1914.* The manifesto openly declares that no interests of the people can serve to justify such a war waged "for the sake of the profits of the capitalists" and "the ambitions of dynasties" on the basis of the imperialist, predatory

---

* Reproduced in this volume, p. 371.

policy of the Great Powers. The manifesto openly declares that war is dangerous to "governments" (all of them without exception), notes their fear of "a proletarian revolution", and very definitely points to the example set by the Commune of 1871, and by October-December 1905, i.e. *to the examples of revolution and civil war.* Thus, the Basel Manifesto lays down, precisely for the present war, the tactics of the workers' revolutionary struggle on an international scale against their governments, the tactics of proletarian revolution. The Basel Manifesto repeats the words in the Stuttgart Resolution* that, in the event of war, socialists must take advantage of the "economic and political crisis" it will cause so as to "hasten the downfall of capitalism", i.e., take advantage of the governments' wartime difficulties and the indignation of the masses, to advance the socialist revolution.

The social-chauvinists' policy, their justification of the war from the bourgeois-liberation standpoint, their sanctioning of 'defence of the fatherland', their voting for credits, membership in governments, and so on and so forth, are downright treachery to socialism, which can be explained only, as we will soon show, by the victory of opportunism and of the national liberal-labour policy in the majority of European parties.

False references to Marx and Engels

The Russian social-chauvinists (headed by Plekhanov) make references to Marx's tactics in the war of 1870; the German (of the type of Lensch, David and co.) – to Engels' statement in 1891 that, in the event of war against Russia and France combined, it would be the duty of the German socialists to defend their fatherland; finally, the social-chauvinists of the Kautsky type, who want to reconcile and legitimatise international chauvinism, refer to the fact that Marx and Engels, while condemning war, nevertheless, from 1854-55 to 1870-71 and 1876-77, always took the side of one belligerent state or another, once war had broken out.

---

* Reproduced in this volume, p. 367.

All these references are outrageous distortions of the views of Marx and Engels, in the interest of the bourgeoisie and the opportunists, in just the same way as the writings of the anarchists Guillaume and co. distort the views of Marx and Engels so as to justify anarchism. The war of 1870-71 was historically progressive on the part of Germany, until Napoleon III was defeated: the latter, together with the tsar, had oppressed Germany for years, keeping her in a state of feudal disunity. But as soon as the war developed into the plundering of France (the annexation of Alsace and Lorraine), Marx and Engels emphatically condemned the Germans. Even at the beginning of the war, Marx and Engels approved of the refusal of Bebel and Liebknecht to vote for war credits, and advised Social-Democrats not to merge with the bourgeoisie, but to uphold the independent class interests of the proletariat. To apply to the present imperialist war the appraisal of this bourgeois-progressive war of national liberation is a mockery of the truth. The same applies with still greater force to the war of 1854-55, and to all the wars of the nineteenth century, when there existed *no* modern imperialism, *no* mature objective conditions for socialism, and *no* mass socialist parties *in any* of the belligerent countries, i.e. none of the conditions from which the Basel Manifesto deduced the tactics of a "proletarian revolution" *in connection* with a war between Great Powers.

Anyone who today refers to Marx's attitude towards the wars of the epoch of the *progressive* bourgeoisie, and forgets Marx's statement that "the workingmen have no country"– a statement that applies *precisely* to the period of the reactionary and outmoded bourgeoisie, to the epoch of the socialist revolution, is shamelessly distorting Marx, and is substituting the bourgeois point of view for the socialist.*

The collapse of the Second International

Socialists of all the world solemnly declared in Basel, in 1912, that they regarded the impending war in Europe as the 'criminal' and

---

* See Marx and Engels, *Manifesto of the Communist Party*, *MECW*, Vol. 6, p. 502.

most reactionary deed of *all* the governments, which must hasten the downfall of capitalism by inevitably engendering a revolution against it. The war came, the crisis was there. Instead of revolutionary tactics, most of the Social-Democratic parties launched reactionary tactics, and went over to the side of their respective governments and bourgeoisie. This betrayal of socialism signifies the collapse of the Second (1889-1914) International, and we must realise what caused this collapse, what brought social-chauvinism into being and gave it strength.

Social-chauvinism is the acme of opportunism

Throughout the existence of the Second International, a struggle was raging within all the Social-Democratic parties, between their revolutionary and the opportunist wings. In a number of countries a split took place along this line (Britain, Italy, Holland, Bulgaria). Not one Marxist has ever doubted that opportunism expresses bourgeois policies within the working-class movement, expresses the interests of the petty bourgeoisie and the alliance of a tiny section of bourgeoisified workers with their '*own*' bourgeoisie, against the interests of the proletarian masses, the oppressed masses.

The objective conditions at the close of the nineteenth century greatly intensified opportunism, converted the utilisation of bourgeois legality into subservience to the latter, created a thin crust of a working-class officialdom and aristocracy and attracted numerous petty-bourgeois 'fellow travellers' to the Social-Democratic parties.

The war has accelerated this development and transformed opportunism into social-chauvinism, transformed the secret alliance between the opportunists and the bourgeoisie into an open one. Simultaneously, the military authorities have everywhere instituted martial law and have muzzled the mass of the workers, whose old leaders have nearly all gone over to the bourgeoisie.

Opportunism and social-chauvinism stand on a common economic basis – the interests of a thin crust of privileged workers and of the petty bourgeoisie, who are defending their privileged position, their 'right' to some modicum of the profits that their 'own' national bourgeoisie obtain from robbing other nations, from the advantages of their 'Great' Power status, etc.

Opportunism and social-chauvinism have the same politico-ideological content – class collaboration instead of the class struggle, renunciation of revolutionary methods of struggle, helping one's 'own' government in its embarrassed situation, instead of taking advantage of these embarrassments so as to advance the revolution. If we take Europe as a whole and if we pay attention, not to individuals (even the most authoritative), we will find that it is the opportunist *trend* that has become the bulwark of social-chauvinism, whereas from the camp of the revolutionaries, more or less consistent protests against it are heard from almost all sides. And if we take, for example, the grouping of trends at the Stuttgart International Socialist Congress in 1907, we shall find that international Marxism was opposed to imperialism, while international opportunism was already in favour of it at the time.*

Unity with the opportunists means an alliance between the workers and their 'own' national bourgeoisie, and splitting the international revolutionary working class

In the past, before the war, opportunism was often looked upon as a legitimate, though 'deviationist' and 'extremist', component of the Social-Democratic Party. The war has shown the impossibility of this in the future. Opportunism has 'matured', and is now playing to the full its role as emissary of the bourgeoisie in the working-class movement. Unity with the opportunists has become sheer hypocrisy, exemplified by the German Social-Democratic Party. On every important occasion (e.g. the 4 August vote), the opportunists present an ultimatum, to which they give effect through their numerous links with the bourgeoisie, their majority on the executives of the trade unions, etc. Today, *unity* with the opportunists *actually* means subordinating the working class to their

---

* See the 'Stuttgart Resolution', in this volume, p. 367.

'own' national bourgeoisie, and an alliance with the latter for the purpose of oppressing other nations and of fighting for dominant-nation privileges; it means *splitting* the revolutionary proletariat of all countries.

No matter how hard, in individual instances, the struggle may be against the opportunists, who predominate in many organisations, whatever the specific nature of the purging of the workers' parties of opportunists in individual countries, this process is inevitable and fruitful. Reformist socialism is dying; regenerated socialism "will be revolutionary, uncompromising and insurrectionary", to use the apt expression of the French Socialist Paul Golay.

'Kautskyism'

Kautsky, the leading authority in the Second International, is a most typical and striking example of how a verbal recognition of Marxism has led in practice to its conversion into 'Struvism' or into 'Brentanoism'.* Another example is Plekhanov. By means of patent sophistry, Marxism is stripped of its revolutionary living spirit; *everything* is recognised in Marxism *except* the revolutionary methods of struggle, the propaganda and preparation of those methods, and the education of the masses in this direction. Kautsky 'reconciles' in an unprincipled way the fundamental idea of social-chauvinism, recognition of defence of the fatherland in the present war, with a diplomatic sham concession to the Lefts – his abstention from voting for war credits, his verbal claim to be in the opposition, etc. Kautsky, who in 1909 wrote a book on the approaching epoch of revolutions and on the connection between war and revolution, Kautsky, who in 1912 signed the Basel Manifesto on taking revolutionary advantage of

---

*　Struvism, or 'Legal Marxism', will be explained by Lenin later in the present pamphlet, p. 100.

　Brentanoism – A reformist theory by bourgeois economist Lujo Brentano. He tried to prove that it was possible to achieve social equality within the capitalist system by means of reforms and the conciliation of the interests of the capitalists and the workers. Under the cloak of Marxist phraseology, Brentano and his followers tried to subordinate the working-class movement to the interests of the bourgeoisie.

the impending war, is outdoing himself in justifying and embellishing social-chauvinism and, like Plekhanov, joins the bourgeoisie in ridiculing any thought of revolution and all steps towards the immediate revolutionary struggle.

The working class cannot play its world-revolutionary role unless it wages a ruthless struggle against this backsliding, spinelessness, subservience to opportunism, and unparalleled vulgarisation of the theories of Marxism. Kautskyism is not fortuitous; it is the social product of the contradictions within the Second International, a blend of loyalty to Marxism in word, and subordination to opportunism in deed.

This fundamental falseness of 'Kautskyism' manifests itself in different ways in different countries. In Holland, Roland Holst, while rejecting the idea of defending the fatherland, defends unity with the opportunists' party. In Russia, Trotsky, while rejecting this idea, also defends unity with the opportunist and chauvinist *Nasha Zarya* group. In Romania, Rakovsky, while declaring war on opportunism as being responsible for the collapse of the International, is at the same time ready to recognise the legitimacy of the idea of defending the fatherland. All this is a manifestation of the evil which the Dutch Marxists (Gorter and Pannekoek) have called 'passive radicalism', and which amounts to replacing revolutionary Marxism with eclecticism in theory, and servility to, or impotence towards, opportunism in practice.

The Marxists' slogan is a slogan of revolutionary Social-Democracy

The war has undoubtedly created a most acute crisis and has immeasurably increased the distress of the masses. The reactionary nature of this war, and the unblushing lies told by the bourgeoisie of *all* countries to conceal their predatory aims with 'national' ideology are, on the basis of an objectively revolutionary situation, inevitably creating revolutionary moods among the masses. It is our duty to help the masses become conscious of these moods, deepen them and give them shape. This task finds correct expression only in the slogan: convert the imperialist war into a civil war; *all* consistently waged class struggles in wartime and all seriously conducted 'mass-action' tactics inevitably lead to this. It is impossible to foretell whether a powerful revolutionary movement will flare up during the first or the second imperialist war of the 'Great' Powers, whether during or after it; in any case, it is our bounden duty to work systematically and unswervingly in this direction.

The Basel Manifesto makes direct reference to the example set by the Paris Commune, i.e. the conversion of a war between governments into a civil war. Half a century ago, the proletariat was too weak; the objective conditions for socialism had not yet matured, there could be no coordination and cooperation between the revolutionary movements in all the belligerent countries; the 'national ideology' (the traditions of 1792), with which a section of the Parisian workers were imbued, was a petty-bourgeois weakness, which Marx noted at the time, and was one of the causes of the downfall of the Commune. Half a century since that time, the conditions that then weakened the revolution have ceased to operate, and today it is unpardonable for a socialist to resign himself to a renunciation of activities in the spirit of the Paris Communards.

The example set by the fraternisation in the trenches

Cases of fraternisation between the soldiers of the belligerent nations, even in the trenches, have been reported in the bourgeois newspapers of all the belligerent countries. The grave importance attached to the matter by the governments and the bourgeoisie is evidenced by the harsh orders against such fraternisation issued by the military authorities (of Germany and Britain). If such cases of fraternisation have proved possible even when opportunism reigns supreme in the top ranks of the Social-Democratic parties of Western Europe, and when social-chauvinism has the support of the entire Social-Democratic press and all the authorities of the Second International, then that shows us how possible it would be to shorten the present criminal, reactionary and slave-holders' war and to organise a revolutionary international movement, if systematic work were conducted in this direction, at least by the Left-wing socialists in all the belligerent countries.

The importance of an underground organisation

No less than the opportunists, leading anarchists all over the world have disgraced themselves with social-chauvinism (in the spirit of Plekhanov and Kautsky) in this war. One of the useful results of this war will undoubtedly be that it will kill both anarchism and opportunism.

While under no circumstances or conditions refraining from utilising all legal opportunities, however small, for organising the masses and for the propaganda of socialism, the Social-Democratic parties must break with subservience to legality. "You shoot first, Messieurs the Bourgeoisie", wrote Engels, hinting at civil war and at the necessity of our violating legality *after* the bourgeoisie had done so.* The crisis has shown that the bourgeoisie violate it in all countries, even the freest, and that it is impossible to lead the masses to a revolution unless an underground organisation is set up for the purpose of advocating, discussing, appraising and preparing revolutionary methods of struggle. In Germany, for example, all the *honest* things that socialists are doing, are being done despite despicable opportunism and hypocritical 'Kautskyism', and moreover are being done secretly. In Britain, people are being sentenced to penal servitude for printing appeals against joining up.

It is a betrayal of socialism to consider compatible with membership in the Social-Democratic Party any repudiation of underground methods of propaganda, and ridicule of those methods, in the legally published press.

On the defeat of one's 'own' government in the imperialist war

The standpoint of social-chauvinism is shared equally by both advocates of victory for their governments in the present war

---

* See Engels, 'Socialism in Germany', *MECW*, Vol. 27, p. 241.

and by advocates of the slogan of 'neither victory nor defeat'. A revolutionary class cannot but wish for the defeat of its government in a reactionary war, and cannot fail to see that the latter's military reverses must facilitate its overthrow. Only a bourgeois who believes that a war started by governments must necessarily end as a war between governments, and wants it to end as such, can regard as 'ridiculous' and 'absurd' the idea that the socialists of *all* the belligerent countries should express their wish that *all* their 'own' governments should be defeated. On the contrary, it is a statement of this kind that would be in keeping with the innermost thoughts of every class-conscious worker, and be in line with our activities for the conversion of the imperialist war into a civil war.

The serious anti-war agitation being conducted by a section of the British, German and Russian socialists has undoubtedly 'weakened the military might' of the respective governments, but that agitation stands to the credit of the socialists. The latter must explain to the masses that they have no other road of salvation except the revolutionary overthrow of their 'own' governments, whose difficulties in the present war must be taken advantage of precisely for that purpose.

Pacifism and the peace slogan

The temper of the masses in favour of peace often expresses the beginning of protest, anger and a realisation of the reactionary nature of the war. It is the duty of all Social-Democrats to utilise that temper. They will take a most ardent part in any movement and in any demonstration motivated by that sentiment, but they will not deceive the people with admitting the idea that a peace without annexations, without oppression of nations, without plunder, and without the embryo of new wars among the present governments and ruling classes, is possible in the absence of a revolutionary movement. Such deception of the people would merely mean playing into the hands of the secret diplomacy of the belligerent governments and facilitating their counter-revolutionary plans. Whoever wants a lasting and democratic peace must stand for civil war against the governments and the bourgeoisie.

The right of nations to self-determination

The most widespread deception of the people by the bourgeoisie in the present war consists in their using the ideology of 'national liberation' to cloak their predatory aims. The British have promised the liberation of Belgium, the Germans of Poland, etc. Actually, as we have seen, this is a war waged by the oppressors of most of the world's nations for the purpose of increasing and expanding that oppression.

Socialists cannot achieve their great aim without fighting against all oppression of nations. They must, therefore, unequivocally demand that the Social-Democratic parties of the *oppressor* countries (especially of the so-called 'Great' Powers) should recognise and champion the *oppressed* nation's right to self-determination, in the specifically political sense of the term, i.e. the right to political secession. The socialist of a ruling or a colonial nation who does not stand for that right is a chauvinist.

The championing of this right, far from encouraging the formation of petty states, leads, on the contrary, to the freer, fearless and therefore wider and more universal formation of large states and federations of states, which are more to the advantage of the masses and are more in keeping with economic development.

In their turn, the socialists of the oppressed nations must unfailingly fight for complete unity of the workers of the oppressed and oppressor nationalities (this including organisational unity). The idea of the juridical separation of one nation from another (the so-called 'cultural-national autonomy' advocated by Bauer and Renner) is reactionary.

Imperialism is the epoch of the constantly increasing oppression of the nations of the world by a handful of 'Great' Powers; it is therefore impossible to fight for the socialist international revolution against imperialism unless the right of nations to self-determination is recognised. "No nation can be free if it oppresses other nations" (Marx and Engels).* A proletariat that tolerates the slightest coercion of other nations by its 'own' nation cannot be a socialist proletariat.

---

* See Marx and Engels, 'On Poland', in *MECW*, Vol. 6, p. 389.

2. Classes and Parties in Russia

The bourgeoisie and the war

In one respect, the Russian Government has not lagged behind its European *confrères*; like them, it has succeeded in deceiving its 'own' people on a grand scale. A huge and monstrous machine of falsehood and cunning has been set going in Russia as well, to infect the masses with chauvinism, and create the impression that the tsarist government is waging a 'just' war, and is disinterestedly defending its 'Slav brothers', etc.

The landowning class and the upper stratum of the commercial and industrial bourgeoisie have ardently supported the tsarist government's bellicose policy. They are rightly expecting enormous material gains and privileges for themselves from the carving up of the Turkish and the Austrian legacy. A series of their congresses have already voiced anticipation of the profits that will flow into their pockets should the tsarist army be victorious. Moreover, the reactionaries are very well aware that if anything can stave off the downfall of the Romanov monarchy and delay the new revolution in Russia, it can only be a foreign war ending in victory for the tsar.

Broad strata of the urban 'middle' bourgeoisie, of the bourgeois intelligentsia, professional people, etc., have also been infected with chauvinism – at all events at the beginning of the war. The Cadets – the party of the Russian liberal bourgeoisie – have given the tsar's government full and unconditional support. In the sphere of foreign policy, the Cadets have long been a government party. Pan-Slavism – with the aid of which tsarist diplomacy has more than once carried out its grand political swindles – has become the official ideology of the Cadets. Russian liberalism has degenerated into *national* liberalism. It is vying in 'patriotism' with the Black Hundreds; it always willingly votes for militarism on land and at sea, etc. Approximately the same thing is to be seen in the camp of Russian liberalism as in Germany in the 'seventies of the last century, when 'free-thinking' liberalism decayed and from it arose a national-liberal party. The Russian liberal bourgeoisie has definitely taken to the path of counter-revolution. The RSDLP's point of view on this question has been fully confirmed. The facts have shattered the view held by our opportunists that Russian liberalism is still a motive force of a revolution in Russia.

The ruling clique has also succeeded, with the aid of the bourgeois press, the clergy, etc., in rousing chauvinist sentiments among the peasantry. With the return of the soldiers from the field of slaughter, however, sentiment in the rural areas will undoubtedly turn against the tsarist monarchy. The bourgeois-democratic parties that come into contact with the peasantry have failed to withstand the chauvinist wave. The Trudovik party in the Duma refused to vote for war credits, but through its leader Kerensky it made a 'patriotic' declaration which played into the hands of the monarchy. In general, the entire legally published Narodnik press followed the liberals' lead. Even the Left wing of bourgeois democracy – the so-called Socialist-Revolutionary Party, which is affiliated to the International Socialist Bureau – is swimming with the same tide. Mr. Rubanovich, that party's representative on the ISB, has come out as a self-confessed social-chauvinist. Half of the number of this party's delegates to the London Conference of Socialists of the Entente countries voted for a chauvinist resolution (while the other half abstained from voting). Chauvinists predominate in the illegally published press of the Socialist-Revolutionaries (the newspaper *Novosti* and others). The revolutionaries from 'bourgeois circles', i.e. bourgeois revolutionaries who are not connected with the working class, have come to a dead end in this war. The sad fate of Kropotkin, Burtsev and Rubanovich is highly significant.

The working class and the war

The proletariat is the only class in Russia that nobody has been able to infect with chauvinism. Only the most ignorant strata of the workers were involved in the few excesses that occurred in the early days of the war. The part played by workers in the Moscow anti-German riots has been greatly exaggerated. By and large, the working class of Russia has proved immune to chauvinism.

The explanation lies in the revolutionary situation in the country and in the Russian proletariat's general conditions of life.

The years 1912-14 marked the beginning of a great new revolutionary upswing in Russia. We again witnessed a great strike movement, the like of which the world has never known. The number involved in the mass revolutionary strike in 1913 was, at the very lowest estimate, 1.5 million, and in 1914 it rose to over 2 million, approaching the 1905 level. The first barricade battles took place in St. Petersburg, on the eve of the war.

The underground Russian Social-Democratic Labour Party has performed its duty to the International. The banner of internationalism has not wavered in its hands. Our Party long ago severed all organisational ties with the opportunist groups and elements; its feet were not weighed down with the fetters of opportunism and of 'legalism at any price', this circumstance helping it perform its revolutionary duty – just as the break with Bissolati's opportunist party has helped the Italian comrades.

The general situation in our country does not favour any efflorescence of 'socialist' opportunism among the masses of the workers. In Russia we see a series of shades of opportunism and reformism among the intelligentsia, the petty bourgeoisie, etc., but it has affected an insignificant minority among the politically active sections of the workers. The privileged stratum of factory workers and clerical staff is very thin in our country. The fetishism of legality could not appear here. Before the war, the liquidators (the party of the opportunists led by Axelrod, Potresov, Cherevanin, Maslov, and others) found no serious support among the masses of the workers. The elections to the Fourth Duma resulted in the return of *all* six of the anti-liquidationist working-class candidates. The circulation of the legally published workers' press in Petrograd and Moscow and the collection of funds for it have incontrovertibly proved that four-fifths of the class-conscious workers are opposed to opportunism and liquidationism.

Since the beginning of the war, the tsar's government has arrested and exiled thousands and thousands of advanced workers, members of our underground RSDLP. This circumstance, together with the establishment of martial law in the country, the suppression of our newspapers, and so forth, has retarded the movement. But for all that, our Party is continuing its underground revolutionary activities. In Petrograd, our Party Committee is publishing the underground newspaper *Proletarsky Golos*.

Articles from *Sotsial-Demokrat*, the Central Organ published abroad, are reprinted in Petrograd and sent out to the provinces. Leaflets are secretly printed, and are circulated even in army barracks. In various secluded places outside the city, secret workers' meetings are held. Of late, big strikes of metalworkers have begun in Petrograd. In connection with these strikes, our Petrograd Committee has issued several appeals to the workers.

The Russian Social-Democratic Labour Group in the Duma, and the war

In 1913 a split took place among the Social-Democratic deputies to the Duma. On one side were the seven supporters of opportunism, led by Chkheidze; they had been returned by seven non-proletarian gubernias [provinces], where the workers totalled 214,000. On the other side were six deputies, *all* from the workers' curia, elected for the most industrialised centres in Russia, in which the workers number 1,008,000.

The chief issue in the split was the *alternative* between the tactics of revolutionary Marxism and the tactics of opportunist reformism.

In practice, the disagreement manifested itself mainly in the sphere of *extra*-parliamentary work among the masses. In Russia this work had to be conducted secretly, if those conducting it wished to remain on a revolutionary basis. The Chkheidze group remained a faithful ally of the liquidators (who repudiated underground work) and defended them in all talks with workers and at all meetings. Hence the split. The six deputies formed the RSDL Duma group, which, as a year's work has incontrovertibly shown, has the support of the vast majority of Russian workers.

On the outbreak of the war the disagreement stood out in glaring relief. The Chkheidze group confined itself to parliamentary action. It did not vote for war credits, for that would have roused a storm of indignation among the workers (we have seen that in Russia even the petty-bourgeois Trudoviks did not vote for war credits); neither did it utter any protest against social-chauvinism.

Expressing the political line of our Party, the RSDL Duma group acted quite differently. It carried into the midst of the working class a protest against the war, and conducted anti-imperialist propaganda among the masses of the Russian proletarians.

It met with a very sympathetic response from the workers – which frightened the government, compelling it, in flagrant violation of its own laws, to arrest our deputy comrades and exile them to Siberia for life. In its very first official announcement of the arrest of our comrades, the tsarist government wrote:

> An entirely exceptional position in this respect was taken by some members of Social-Democratic societies, the object of whose activities was to shake the military might of Russia by agitating against the war, by means of underground appeals and verbal propaganda.

Only our Party, through its Central Committee, gave a negative reply to Vandervelde's well-known appeal for a 'temporary' cessation of the struggle against tsarism. Moreover, it has now become known, from the testimony of Prince Kudashev, the tsar's envoy to Belgium, that Vandervelde did not draw up this appeal alone, but in collaboration with the above-mentioned envoy. The guiding centre of the liquidators agreed with Vandervelde and officially stated in the press that "in its *activities it does not oppose the war*".

The principal accusation levelled by the tsar's government against our deputy comrades was that they distributed this negative reply to Vandervelde among the workers. At the trial, the Prosecutor for the Crown, Mr. Nenarokomov, set up the German and French socialists as examples to our comrades.

> The German Social-Democrats [he said] voted for war credits and proved to be friends of the government. That is how the German Social-Democrats acted, but the dismal knights of Russian Social-Democracy did not act in this way… The socialists of Belgium and France unanimously forgot their quarrels with the other classes, forgot party strife, and unhesitatingly rallied about the flag.

But the members of the RSDL group, on instructions from the Party's Central Committee, did not act in this way, he complained…

The trial revealed an imposing picture of the extensive underground anti-war agitation our Party was conducting among the masses of the proletariat. It goes without saying that the tsar's court 'uncovered' only a fraction of the activities our comrades were conducting in this field, but even what was revealed showed how much had been done within the brief span of a few months.

At the trial, the underground manifestos issued by our groups and committees, against the war and for international tactics, were read out. The members of the RSDL group were in touch with the class-conscious workers all over Russia and did everything in their power to help the workers appraise the war from the Marxist standpoint.

Comrade Muranov, the deputy of the workers of Kharkov Gubernia, stated at the trial:

> Realising that the people did not return me to the Duma just to warm my seat there, I travelled about the country to ascertain the mood of the working class.

He admitted that he had undertaken the functions of a secret agitator of our Party, that in the Urals he had organised workers' committees at the Verkhneisetsky Works and elsewhere. The trial showed that, after the outbreak of war, members of the RSDL Duma group travelled, for propaganda purposes, throughout almost the whole of Russia and that Muranov, Petrovsky, Badayev and others arranged numerous workers' meetings, at which anti-war resolutions were passed, and so on.

The tsar's government threatened the accused with capital punishment. That was why they did not all behave at the trial as courageously as Comrade Muranov. They tried to make it difficult for the Prosecutors to secure convictions. This is being unworthily utilised by the Russian social-chauvinists so as to obscure the crux of the issue, viz. the kind of parliamentarianism the working class needs.

Parliamentarianism is recognised by Südekum and Heine, Sembat and Vaillant, Bissolati and Mussolini,* Chkheidze and Plekhanov; it is also recognised by our comrades in the RSDL group, as well as by the Bulgarian and Italian comrades who have broken with the chauvinists. There are different kinds of parliamentarianism. Some utilise the parliamentary arena in order to curry favour with their governments, or, at best, to wash their hands of everything, as the Chkheidze group has done. Others utilise parliamentarianism in order to remain revolutionary to the end, to perform their duty as socialists and internationalists even under the most difficult circumstances. The parliamentary activities of some give them ministerial posts; the parliamentary activities of others take them to prison, exile and penal servitude. Some serve the bourgeoisie, others – the proletariat. Some are social-imperialists. Others are revolutionary Marxists.

---

* Benito Mussolini was initially a prominent socialist, and an editor of the Italian Socialist Party's (PSI) Central Organ, *Avanti!*. He began to express an increasingly confused position after 1912, and took a social-chauvinist position soon after the start of the war. For this, he was expelled by the PSI. He began his own paper, campaigning for the war and 'revolutionary nationalism'. He went on to enlist in the army, before being wounded in action, returning to Italy and founding the Fascist movement in 1919.

3. *The Restoration of the International*

How should the International be restored? But first, a few words about how the International *should not* be restored.

The method of the social-chauvinists and of the 'centre'

Of course, the social-chauvinists of all countries are great 'internationalists'! Since the very beginning of the war they have been weighed down with concern over the International. On the one hand, they assure us that the talk about the *collapse* of the International is 'exaggerated'. Actually, nothing out of the common has happened. Listen to Kautsky: the International is simply a "peacetime instrument"; naturally, this instrument has not proved quite up to the mark in wartime. On the other hand, the social-chauvinists of all countries have found a very simple, and, what is most important, an international way out of the situation that has arisen. The solution is simple: it is only necessary to wait till the war ends, but until then the socialists of each country must defend their 'fatherland' and support their 'own' government. When the war ends, there will be a mutual 'amnesty', the admission that *everybody* was right and that in peacetime we live like brothers; in wartime, however, we stick to such-and-such resolutions, and call upon the German workers to exterminate their French brothers, and vice versa.

Kautsky, Plekhanov, Victor Adler and Heine are all equally agreed on this. Victor Adler writes that:

> … when we have passed through this difficult time, our first duty will be to refrain from pointing to the mote in each other's eye.

Kautsky asserts that "till now no serious socialists from any side have spoken in a way to arouse apprehension" concerning the fate of the International. "It is unpleasant to grasp hands [of the German Social-Democrats] that reek of the blood of the innocently slaughtered", Plekhanov says, but at once goes on to propose an "amnesty".

> It will here be quite appropriate [he writes] to subordinate *the heart to the mind*. For the sake of the great cause, the International will have to take into consideration even belated remorse.

In *Sozialistische Monatshefte*, Heine describes Vandervelde's behaviour as "courageous and dignified", and sets him up as an example to the German Lefts.

In short, when the war ends, appoint a commission consisting of Kautsky and Plekhanov, Vandervelde and Adler, and a 'unanimous' resolution in the spirit of a mutual amnesty will be drawn up in a trice. The dispute will be nicely hushed up. Instead of being helped to understand what has taken place, the workers will be deceived with a sham and paper 'unity'. A union of the social-chauvinists and hypocrites of all countries will be described as restoration of the International.

We must not close our eyes to the great danger inherent in such a 'restoration'. The social-chauvinists of all countries are equally interested in that outcome. All of them are equally unwilling that the masses of the workers of their respective countries should themselves try to understand the issue: socialism *or* nationalism? All of them are equally interested in concealing one other's sins. None of them are able to propose anything except what has already been proposed by Kautsky, that past master of 'international' hypocrisy.

Yet this danger has scarcely been realised. During a year of war, we have seen a number of attempts to restore international ties. We shall not speak of the London and Vienna conferences, at which outspoken chauvinists got together to help the General Staffs and the bourgeoisie of their 'fatherlands'. We are referring to the Lugano and Copenhagen conferences, the International Women's Conference, and the International Youth Conference. These assemblies were animated by the best intentions, but they wholly failed to discern the above-mentioned danger. They neither laid down a militant internationalist line, nor indicated to the proletariat the danger threatening it from the social-chauvinists' method of 'restoring' the International. At best, they confined themselves to repeating the old resolutions, without telling the workers that the cause of socialism is lost unless a struggle is waged against the social-chauvinists. At best they were *marking time*.

The state of affairs among the opposition

There cannot be the least doubt that what interests all internationalists most is the state of affairs among the German Social-Democratic opposition. The official German Social-Democratic Party, the strongest and the foremost in the Second International, has dealt the international workers' organisation the most telling blow. At the same time, however, it was among the German Social-Democrats that the strongest opposition arose. Of all the big European parties, it is in the German party that a loud voice of protest was first raised by comrades who have remained loyal to the banner of socialism. We were delighted to read the journals *Lichtstrahlen* and *Die Internationale*. It gave us still greater pleasure to learn of the distribution in Germany of secretly printed revolutionary manifestos, as for example the one entitled 'The Main Enemy is Within the Country'. This showed that the spirit of socialism is alive among the German workers, and that there are still people in Germany capable of upholding revolutionary Marxism.

The split in the present-day socialist movement has most strikingly revealed itself within the German Social-Democratic movement. Three trends can be clearly distinguished here: the opportunist chauvinists, who have nowhere sunk to such foul apostasy as in Germany; the Kautskian 'Centre', which have here proved totally incapable of playing any other role than that of menials to the opportunists; the Lefts, who are the only Social-Democrats in Germany.

Naturally, the state of affairs among the German Lefts is what interests us most. In them we see our comrades, the hope of all the internationalist elements. What is the state of affairs among them?

The journal *Die Internationale* was quite right in writing that the German Lefts are still in a state of ferment, that considerable regroupings still await them, and that within them some elements are more resolute and others less resolute.

Of course, we Russian internationalists do not in the least claim the right to interfere in the internal affairs of our comrades, the German Lefts. We understand that they alone are fully competent to determine their methods of combating the opportunists, according to the conditions of time and place. Only we consider it our right and our duty to express our frank opinion on the state of affairs.

We are convinced that the author of the leading article in the journal *Die Internationale* was perfectly right in stating that the Kautskian 'Centre' is doing more harm to Marxism than avowed social-chauvinism. Anyone who plays down differences, or, in the guise of Marxism, now teaches the workers that which Kautskyism is preaching, is in fact lulling the workers, and doing more harm than the Südekums and Heines, who are putting the issue squarely and are compelling the workers to try to make up their own minds.

The *Fronde* against the 'official bodies' which Kautsky and Haase have of late been permitting themselves should mislead nobody. The disagreements between them and the Scheidemanns are not on fundamentals. The former believe that Hindenburg and Mackensen are *already* victorious and that they can already permit themselves the luxury of protesting against annexations. The latter believe that Hindenburg and Mackensen are not *yet* victorious and that, therefore, it is necessary 'to hold out to the end'.

Kautskyism is waging only a sham struggle against the 'official bodies' just to be able, after the war, to conceal from the workers the clash of principles and to paper over the issue with a thousand and one padded resolutions drawn up in a vaguely 'Leftist' spirit, in the drafting of which the diplomats of the Second International are such experts.

It is quite understandable that, in their difficult struggle against the 'official bodies', the German opposition should also make use of this unprincipled Fronde raised by Kautskyism. However, to any internationalist, hostility towards neo-Kautskyism must remain the touchstone. Only he is a genuine internationalist who combats Kautskyism, and understands that, *even after* its leaders' pretended change of intention, the centre remains, on all fundamental issues, an *ally of the chauvinists and the opportunists*.

In general, our attitude towards wavering elements in the International is of tremendous importance. These elements – mainly socialists of a *pacifist* shade – are to be found both in the neutral countries and in some of the belligerent countries (in Britain, for example, the Independent Labour Party). Such elements can be our fellow-travellers. Ties with them for a struggle against the social-chauvinists are necessary. It should, however, be remembered that they are *merely* fellow-travellers, and that on all main and fundamental issues, these elements will march against us, not with us, when the International is being restored; they will side with Kautsky, Scheidemann, Vandervelde, and Sembat. At international conferences, we must not restrict our programme to what is acceptable to these elements. If we do, we shall fall captive to the wavering pacifists. This is what happened, for example, at the International Women's Conference in Bern. There the German delegation, which supported Comrade Clara Zetkin's point of view, actually played the part of the 'Centre'. The Women's Conference said only that which was acceptable to the delegates of the opportunist Dutch party led by Troelstra, and to the delegates of the Independent Labour Party; we shall always remember that, at the London conference of 'Entente' chauvinists, the ILP voted in favour of Vandervelde's resolution. We would like to express our greatest esteem for the ILP for the courageous struggle it has been waging against the British Government during the war. We know, however, that this party has never taken a Marxist stand. For our part, we hold that today it is the main task of the Social-Democratic opposition to raise the banner of revolutionary Marxism, to tell the workers firmly and definitely how we regard imperialist wars, and to advance a call for mass revolutionary action, i.e. convert the period of imperialist wars into the beginning of a period of civil wars.

Despite everything, revolutionary Social-Democratic elements exist in many countries. They are to be found in Germany, Russia, Scandinavia (where Comrade Höglund represents an influential trend), the Balkans (the party of the Bulgarian 'Tesnyaki'), Italy, Britain (part of the British Socialist Party), France (Vaillant himself has admitted in *l'Humanité* that he has received letters of protest from internationalists, but he has not published any one of them in full), Holland (the Tribunists), and so on. To rally these Marxist elements – however small their numbers may be at the outset – to reanimate, in their name, the now forgotten ideals of genuine socialism, and to call upon the workers of all lands to break with the chauvinists and rally about the old banner of Marxism – such is the task of the day.

Conferences with so-called programmes of 'action' have till now confined themselves to announcing a more or less outspoken programme of sheer pacifism. Marxism is not pacifism. Of course, the speediest possible termination of the war must be striven for. However, the 'peace' demand acquires a proletarian significance only if a *revolutionary* struggle is called for. Without a series of revolutions, what is called a democratic peace is a philistine Utopia. The purpose of a real programme of action can be served only by a *Marxist* programme which gives the masses a full and clear explanation of what has taken place, explains what imperialism is and how it should be combated, declares openly that the collapse of the Second International was brought about by opportunism, and openly calls for a Marxist International to be built up without and *against* the opportunists. Only a programme that shows that we have faith in ourselves and in Marxism, and that we have proclaimed a life-and-death struggle against opportunism, will sooner or later win us the sympathy of the genuinely proletarian masses.

The Russian Social-Democratic Labour Party and the Third International

The Russian Social-Democratic Labour Party has long parted company with its opportunists. Besides, the Russian opportunists have now become chauvinists. This only fortifies us in our opinion that a split with them is essential in the interests of socialism. We are convinced that the Social-Democrats' present differences with the social-chauvinists are in no way less marked than the socialists' differences with the anarchists when the Social-Democrats parted company with the latter. The opportunist Monitor was right when he wrote, in *Preussische Jahrbücher*, that the unity of today is to the advantage of the opportunists and the bourgeoisie, because it has compelled the Lefts to submit to the chauvinists and prevents the workers from understanding the controversy and forming their own genuinely working-class and genuinely socialist party. We are firmly convinced that, in the present state of affairs, a split with the opportunists and chauvinists is the prime duty of revolutionaries, just as a split with the yellow trade unions, the antisemites, the liberal workers' unions, etc., was essential in helping speed up the enlightenment of backward workers and draw them into the ranks of the Social-Democratic Party.

In our opinion, the Third International should be built up on that kind of revolutionary basis. To our Party, the question of the expediency of a break with the social-chauvinists does not exist, it has been answered with finality. The only question that exists for our Party is whether this can be achieved on an international scale in the immediate future.

It is perfectly obvious that to create an *international* Marxist organisation, there must be a readiness to form independent Marxist parties in the *various* countries. As a country with the oldest and strongest working-class movement, Germany is of decisive importance. The immediate future will show whether the conditions are mature for the formation of a new and Marxist International. If they are, our Party will gladly join such a Third International, purged of opportunism and chauvinism. If they are not, then that will show that a more or less protracted period of evolution is needed for that purging to be effected. Our Party will then form the extreme opposition within the old International, pending the time when the conditions in the various countries make possible the formation of an international workingmen's association standing on the basis of revolutionary Marxism.

We do not and cannot know what road world developments will take in the next few years. What we do know for certain and are unshakably convinced of is that *our* Party will work indefatigably in the above-mentioned direction, in *our* country and among *our* proletariat, and through its day-by-day activities will build up the Russian section of the *Marxist* International.

In Russia too there is no lack of avowed social-chauvinists and Centrist groups. These people will fight against the formation of a Marxist International. We know that, in principle, Plekhanov shares the standpoint of Südekum and is already holding out a hand to the latter. We know that, under Axelrod's leadership, the so-called Organising Committee is preaching Kautskyism on Russian soil. Under a cloak of working-class unity, these people are calling for unity with the opportunists and, through the latter, with the bourgeoisie. Everything we know about the present-day working-class movement in Russia, however, gives us full assurance that the class-conscious proletariat of Russia will, as hitherto, remain *with our Party.*

4. The History of the Split, and the Present State of the Social-Democracy in Russia

The tactics of the RSDLP in relation to the war, as outlined above, are the inevitable outcome of the thirty years' development of Social-Democracy in Russia. These tactics, as well as the present state of Social-Democracy in our country, cannot be properly understood without going deeper into the history of our Party. That is why here, too, we must remind the reader of the major facts in that history.

As an ideological trend, the Social-Democratic movement arose in 1883, when Social-Democratic views, as applied to Russia, were for the first time systematically expounded abroad by the Emancipation of Labour group. Until the early 'nineties, Social-Democracy was an ideological trend without links with the mass working-class movement in Russia. At the beginning of the 'nineties, the growth of public consciousness and the unrest and strike movement among the workers turned Social-Democracy into an active political force inseparably connected with the struggle (both economic and political) of the working class. It was from that time too that the split into Economists and Iskrists began in the Social-Democratic movement.

The Economists and the old 'Iskra' (1894-1903)

Economism was an opportunist trend in Russian Social-Democracy. Its political essence was summed up in the programme: "for the workers – the economic struggle; for the liberals – the political struggle." Its theoretical mainstay was so-called 'legal Marxism' or 'Struvism', which 'recognised' a 'Marxism' that was completely devoid of any revolutionary spirit and adapted to the needs of the liberal bourgeoisie. Pleading the backwardness of the mass of workers in Russia, and wishing to 'march with the masses', the Economists restricted the tasks and scope of the working-class movement to the economic struggle and to political support for liberalism; they set themselves no independent political or revolutionary tasks.

The old *Iskra* (1900-03) waged a victorious struggle against Economism, for the principles of revolutionary Social-Democracy. The finest elements in the class-conscious proletariat sided with *Iskra*. Several years before the Revolution, the Social-Democrats came out with a most consistent and uncompromising programme, whose correctness was borne out by the class struggle and by the action of the masses during the 1905 Revolution. Whereas the Economists adapted themselves to the backwardness of the masses, *Iskra* was educating the workers' vanguard that was capable of leading the masses onward. The present-day arguments of the social-chauvinists (i.e. the need to reckon with the masses; the progressiveness of imperialism; the 'illusions' harboured by the revolutionaries, etc.), were *all* advanced by the Economists. It was twenty years ago that the Russian Social-Democrats made their first acquaintance with the opportunist modification of Marxism into Struvism.

Menshevism and Bolshevism (1903-1908)

The period of bourgeois-democratic revolution gave rise to a fresh struggle between Social-Democratic trends; this was a direct continuation of the previous struggle. Economism developed into

Menshevism. The defence of the old *Iskra* revolutionary tactics gave rise to Bolshevism.

In the turbulent years of 1905-07, Menshevism was an opportunist trend backed by the bourgeois liberals, which brought liberal-bourgeois tendencies into the working-class movement. Its essence lay in an adaptation of the working-class struggle to suit liberalism. Bolshevism, on the contrary, set the Social-Democratic workers the task of rousing the democratic peasantry for the revolutionary struggle, despite the vacillation and treachery of the liberals. As the Mensheviks themselves admitted on more than one occasion, the mass of workers followed the Bolshevik lead in all the most important actions of the revolution.

The 1905 Revolution tested, developed and steeled the uncompromisingly revolutionary Social-Democratic tactics in Russia. The direct action of classes and parties repeatedly revealed the link between Social-Democratic opportunism (Menshevism) and liberalism.

Marxism and liquidationism (1908-1914)

The period of counter-revolution again placed on the order of the day – this time in an entirely new form – the question of the opportunist and revolutionary tactics of the Social-Democrats. The mainstream in Menshevism, regardless of protests from many of its finest representatives, brought forth the liquidationist trend, a renunciation of the struggle for another revolution in Russia, a renunciation of underground organisation and activities, contempt for and ridicule of the 'underground', of the slogan for a republic, etc. The group of legal contributors to the journal *Nasha Zarya* (Messrs. Potresov, Cherevanin, and others) formed a core – independent of the old Social-Democratic Party – which in a thousand ways has been supported, publicised and nurtured by the liberal bourgeoisie of Russia, who are out to win the workers away from the revolutionary struggle.

This group of opportunists was expelled from the Party by the January 1912 Conference of the RSDLP, which restored the Party, in the teeth of furious resistance from a number of groups and coteries abroad. For over two years (the beginning of 1912 until mid-1914) a stubborn struggle was in progress between the two Social-Democratic parties: the Central Committee, which was elected in January 1912, and the Organising Committee, which refused to recognise the January Conference and wanted to restore the Party in a different way, by maintaining unity with the *Nasha Zarya* group. A stubborn struggle raged between the two workers' dailies (*Pravda*, and *Luch* and their successors), and between the two Social-Democratic groups in the Fourth Duma (the RSDL group of Pravdists or Marxists, and the 'Social-Democratic group' of the liquidators led by Chkheidze).

The Pravdists, who championed loyalty to the Party's revolutionary principles, encouraged the incipient revival of the working-class movement (especially after the spring of 1912), combined underground and legal organisation, the press and agitation, and rallied about themselves the overwhelming majority of the class-conscious workers, whereas the liquidators – who as a political force operated exclusively through the *Nasha Zarya* group – banked on the all-round support of the liberal-bourgeois elements.

The open money contributions made by workers' groups to the newspapers of the two parties – a form of payment of Social-Democratic *membership dues* adapted to the Russian conditions of the time (and the only one legally possible and easily verifiable by the public) – strikingly confirmed the proletarian source of the strength and influence of the Pravdists (Marxists), and the bourgeois-liberal source of the liquidators (and their Organising Committee). Here are the brief figures of these contributions, which are given in full in the book *Marxism and Liquidationism* and summarised in the German Social-Democratic *Leipziger Volkszeitung* of 21 July 1914.

The number and sums of contributions to the St. Petersburg daily newspapers, Marxist (Pravdist) and liquidationist, from 1 January to 13 May 1914 were the following:

	Pravdists		Liquidators	
	No. of contributions	Sum in rubles	No. of contributions	Sum in rubles
From workers' groups	2,873	18,934	671	5,296
From non-workers' groups	713	2,650	453	6,760

Thus, by 1914 our Party had united four-fifths of the class-conscious workers of Russia around revolutionary Social-Democratic tactics. For the whole of 1913 the Pravdists received contributions from 2,181 workers' groups, the liquidators from 661. The figures from 1 January 1913 to 13 May 1914 were: 5,054 contributions from workers' groups for the Pravdists (i.e. for our Party), and 1,332, i.e. 20.8 per cent, for the liquidators.

Marxism and social-chauvinism (1914-1915)

The great European war of 1914-15 has given all the European Social-Democrats, as well as the Russian, an opportunity of putting their tactics to the test of a crisis of a world-wide scale. The reactionary and predatory nature of this war between slave-holders stands out in far more striking relief in the case of tsarism than it does in the case of the other governments. Yet the liquidators' main group (the only one which, besides ours, exerts serious influence in Russia, thanks to its liberal connections) has turned towards social-chauvinism! With its fairly lengthy monopoly of legality, this *Nasha Zarya* group has conducted propaganda among the masses, in favour of 'non-resistance to the war', and victory for the Triple (and now Quadruple) Entente; it has accused German imperialism of extraordinary sins, etc. Plekhanov, who, since 1903, has given numerous examples of his utter political spinelessness and his desertion to opportunism, has taken this stand even more emphatically (which has won him praise from the entire bourgeois press of Russia). Plekhanov has sunk so low as to declare that tsarism is waging a just war, and to grant interviews to Italian government newspapers, urging that country to enter the war!

The correctness of our appraisal of liquidationism and of the expulsion of the main group of liquidators from our Party has thus been fully confirmed. The liquidators' real programme and the real significance of their trend today consist, not only in opportunism in general, but in a defence of the dominant-nation privileges and advantages of the Great-Russian landowners and bourgeoisie. Liquidationism is a trend of *national liberal*-labour policy. It is an alliance of a section of the radical petty bourgeoisie and a tiny section of privileged workers, with their 'own' national bourgeoisie, against the mass of the proletariat.

The present state of affairs in the ranks of the Russian Social-Democrats

As we have already said, our January 1912 Conference has not been recognised by the liquidators, or by a number of groups abroad (those of Plekhanov, Alexinsky, Trotsky, and others), or by the so-called 'national' (i.e. non-Great Russian) Social-Democrats. Among the numberless epithets hurled against us, 'usurpers' and 'splitters' have been most frequently repeated. We have replied by quoting precise and objectively verifiable figures showing that our Party has united four-fifths of the class-conscious workers in Russia. This is no small figure, considering the difficulties of underground activities in a period of counter-revolution.

If 'unity' were possible in Russia on the basis of Social-Democratic tactics, without expelling the *Nasha Zarya* group, why have our numerous opponents not achieved it *even among themselves*? Three and a half years have elapsed since January 1912, and all this time our opponents, much as they have desired to do so, have failed to form a Social-Democratic party in opposition to us. This fact is our Party's best defence.

The entire history of the Social-Democratic groups that are fighting against our Party has been a history of collapse and disintegration. In March 1912, all of them, without exception, 'united' in reviling us. But already in August 1912, when the so-called August bloc was formed against us, disintegration set in among them. Some of the groups defected from them.* They were unable to form a party and a Central Committee; what they set up was only an Organising Committee "for the purpose of restoring unity". Actually, this Organising Committee proved an ineffective cover for the liquidationist group in Russia. Throughout the tremendous upswing of the working-class movement in Russia and the mass strikes of 1912-14, the only group in the entire August bloc to conduct work among the masses was the *Nasha Zarya* group, whose strength lay in its links with the liberals. Early in 1914, the Lettish Social-Democrats officially withdrew from the August bloc (the Polish Social-Democrats did not join it), while Trotsky, one of the leaders of the bloc, left it unofficially, again forming his own separate group. At the Brussels Conference of July 1914, at which the Executive Committee of the International Socialist Bureau, Kautsky and Vandervelde participated, the so-called Brussels bloc was formed against us, which the Letts did not join, and from which the Polish opposition Social-Democrats forthwith withdrew. On the outbreak of war, this bloc collapsed. *Nasha Zarya*, Plekhanov, Alexinsky and An [NN Jordania], leader of the Caucasian Social-Democrats, became open social-chauvinists, who came out for the desirability of Germany's defeat. The Organising Committee and the Bund defended the social-chauvinists and the principles of social-chauvinism. Although it voted against the war credits (in Russia, even the bourgeois democrats, the Trudoviks, voted against them), the Chkheidze Duma group remained *Nasha Zarya*'s faithful ally. Plekhanov, Alexinsky and co., our extreme social-chauvinists, were quite pleased with the Chkheidze group. In Paris, the newspaper *Nashe Slovo* (the former *Golos*) was launched, with the participation mainly of

---

* The Bolsheviks officially broke with the Mensheviks at their conference in Prague, May 1912. Hoping to reunite the two, Trotsky tried to convene a conference of all Social-Democrats at Vienna in August. But, as the Bolsheviks refused to attend, the initiative was stillborn. The so-called 'August bloc', as it was known, soon collapsed.

Martov and Trotsky, who wanted to combine a platonic defence of internationalism with an absolute demand for unity with *Nasha Zarya*, the Organising Committee or the Chkheidze group. After 250 issues, this newspaper was itself compelled to admit its disintegration: one section of the editorial board gravitated towards our Party, Martov remained faithful to the Organising Committee which publicly censured *Nashe Slovo* for its 'anarchism' (just as the opportunists in Germany, David and co., *Internationale Korrespondenz* and Legien and co. have accused Comrade Liebknecht of anarchism); Trotsky announced his rupture with the Organising Committee, but wanted to stand with the Chkheidze group. Here are the programme and the tactics of the Chkheidze group, as formulated by one of its leaders. In No. 5, 1915, of *Sovremenny Mir*, journal of the Plekhanov and Alexinsky trend, Chkhenkeli wrote:

> To say that German Social-Democracy was in a position to prevent its country from going to war and failed to do so would mean either secretly wishing that it should not only have breathed its last at the barricades, but also have the fatherland breathe its last, or looking at nearby things through an anarchist's telescope.*

These few lines express the sum and substance of social-chauvinism: both the justification, in principle, of the idea of 'defence of the fatherland' in the present war, and mockery – with the permission of the military censors – of the preachment of and preparation for revolution. It is not at all a question of whether the German Social-Democrats were or were not in a position to prevent war, or whether, in general, revolutionaries can guarantee the success of a revolution. The question is: shall socialists behave like socialists or really breathe their last in the embrace of the imperialist bourgeoisie?

---

*   *Sovremenny Mir*, No. 5, 1915, p. 148. Trotsky recently announced that he deemed it his task to enhance the prestige of the Chkheidze group in the International. No doubt Chkhenkeli will with equal energy enhance Trotsky's prestige in the International… – *Lenin*

Our Party's tasks

Social-Democracy in Russia arose before the bourgeois-democratic revolution (1905) in our country, and gained strength during the revolution and counter-revolution. The backwardness of Russia explains the extraordinary multiplicity of trends and shades of petty-bourgeois opportunism in our country; whereas the influence of Marxism in Europe and the stability of the legally existing Social-Democratic parties before the war converted our exemplary liberals into near-admirers of 'reasonable', 'European' (non-revolutionary), 'legal' 'Marxist' theory and Social-Democracy. The working class of Russia could not build up its party otherwise than in a resolute thirty-year struggle against all the varieties of opportunism. The experience of the world war, which has brought about the shameful collapse of European opportunism and has strengthened the alliance between our national-liberals and social-chauvinist liquidationism, has still further fortified our conviction that our Party must follow the same consistently revolutionary road.

The Draft Resolution of the Left Wing at Zimmerwald

Written prior to 20 August (2 September) 1915

Editors note:

On 4 September 1915, a meeting initiated by Russian and Polish left delegates to the Zimmerwald Conference took place. The meeting was attended by eight conference delegates and established the 'Zimmerwald Left'. Both Radek and Lenin had prepared draft resolutions for consideration. The Left delegates agreed to redraft Radek's proposal to include many of Lenin's points. We publish here Lenin's proposal and the Left's Resolution and Manifesto in the appendix on p. 387.

There are several differences between Lenin's draft and the one that was finally agreed by the left delegates, one of them being that the phrase about Socialists "not shying away in that agitation from considerations of the defeat of their 'own' country" is not included.

* * *

The present war has been engendered by imperialism. Capitalism has already achieved that highest stage. Society's productive forces and the magnitudes of capital have outgrown the narrow limits of the individual national states. Hence the striving on the part of the Great Powers to enslave other nations and to seize colonies as sources of raw material and spheres of investment of capital. The whole world is merging into a single economic organism; it has been carved up among a handful of Great Powers. The objective conditions for socialism have fully matured, and the present war is a war of the capitalists for privileges and monopolies that might delay the downfall of capitalism.

The socialists, who seek to liberate labour from the yoke of capital and who defend the world-wide solidarity of the workers, are struggling against any kind of oppression and inequality of nations. When the bourgeoisie was a progressive class, and the overthrow of feudalism, absolutism and oppression by other nations stood on the historical order of the day, the socialists, as invariably the most consistent and most resolute of democrats, recognised 'defence of the fatherland' in the meaning implied by those aims, and in that meaning alone. Today too, should a war of the oppressed nations against the oppressor Great Powers break out in the east of Europe or in the colonies, the socialists' sympathy would be wholly with the oppressed.

The war of today, however, has been engendered by an entirely different historical period, in which the bourgeoisie, from a progressive class, has turned reactionary. With both groups of belligerents, this war is a war of slaveholders, and is designed to preserve and extend slavery; it is a war for the repartitioning of colonies, for the 'right' to oppress other nations, for privileges and monopolies for Great-Power capital, and for the perpetuation of wage slavery by splitting up the workers of the different countries and crushing them through reaction. That is why, on the part of both warring groups, all talk about 'defence of the fatherland' is deception of the people by the bourgeoisie. Neither the victory of any one group nor a return to the *status quo* can do anything either to protect the freedom of most countries in the world from imperialist oppression by a handful of Great Powers, or to ensure that the working class keep even its present modest cultural gains. The period of a relatively peaceful capitalism has passed, never to return. Imperialism has brought the working class unparalleled intensification of the class struggle, want and unemployment, a higher cost of living, and the strengthening of oppression by the trusts, of militarism, and the political reactionaries, who are raising their heads in all countries, even the freest.

In reality, the 'defence of the fatherland' slogan in the present war is tantamount to a defence of the 'right' of one's 'own' national bourgeoisie to oppress other nations; it is in fact a national liberal-labour policy, an alliance between a negligible section of the workers and their 'own' national bourgeoisie, against the mass of the proletarians and the exploited. Socialists who pursue such a policy are in fact chauvinists, social-chauvinists. The policy of voting for war credits, of joining governments, of *Burgfrieden* [class truce] and the like, is a betrayal of socialism. Nurtured by the conditions of the 'peaceful' period, which has now come to an end, opportunism has now matured to a degree that calls for a break with socialism; it has become an open enemy to the proletariat's movement for liberation. The working class cannot achieve its historic aims without waging a most resolute struggle against both forthright opportunism and social-chauvinism (the majorities in the Social-Democratic parties of France, Germany and Austria; Hyndman, the Fabians and the trade unionists in Britain; Rubanovich, Plekhanov and *Nasha Zarya* in Russia, etc.) and the so-called Centre, which has surrendered the Marxist stand to the chauvinists.

Unanimously adopted by socialists of the entire world in anticipation of that very kind of war among the Great Powers which has now broken out, the Basel Manifesto of 1912 distinctly recognised the imperialist and reactionary nature of that war, declared it criminal for workers of one country to shoot at workers of another country, and proclaimed the approach of the *proletarian revolution* in connection with that very war. Indeed, the war is creating a revolutionary situation, is engendering revolutionary sentiments and unrest in the masses, is arousing in the finer part of the proletariat a realisation of the perniciousness of opportunism and is intensifying the struggle against it. The masses' growing desire for peace expresses their disappointment, the defeat of the bourgeois lie regarding the defence of the fatherland, and the awakening of their revolutionary consciousness. In utilising that temper for their revolutionary agitation, and not shying away in that agitation from considerations of the defeat of their 'own' country, the socialists will not deceive the people with the hope that, without the revolutionary overthrow of the present-day governments, a possibility exists of a speedy democratic peace, which will be durable in some degree and will preclude any oppression of nations, a possibility of disarmament, etc. Only the social revolution of the proletariat opens the way towards peace and freedom for the nations.

The imperialist war is ushering in the era of the social revolution. All the objective conditions of recent times have put the proletariat's revolutionary mass struggle on the order of the day. It is the duty of socialists, while making use of every means of the working class' legal struggle, to subordinate each and every of those means to this immediate and most important task, develop the workers' revolutionary consciousness, rally them in the international revolutionary struggle, promote and encourage any revolutionary action, and do everything possible to turn the imperialist war between the peoples into a civil war of the oppressed classes against their oppressors, a war for the expropriation of the class of capitalists, for the conquest of political power by the proletariat, and the realisation of socialism.

Appeal on the War

August 1915

Worker Comrades:

The European war has been in progress for over a year. All things considered, it will last for a long time, because, while Germany is best prepared and at present the strongest, the Quadruple Entente (Russia, Britain, France, and Italy) has more men and money, and besides, freely gets war material from the United States of America, the world's richest country.

What is this war being fought for, which is bringing mankind unparalleled suffering? The government and the bourgeoisie of each belligerent country are squandering millions of rubles on books and newspapers so as to lay the blame on the foe, arouse the people's furious hatred of the enemy, and stop at no lie so as to depict themselves as the side that has been unjustly attacked and is now 'defending' itself. In reality, this is a war between two groups of predatory Great Powers, and it is being fought for the partitioning of colonies, the enslavement of other nations, and advantages and privileges of the world market. This is a most reactionary war, a war of modern slaveholders aimed at preserving and consolidating capitalist slavery. Britain and France are lying when they assert that they are warring for Belgium's freedom. In reality, they have long been preparing the war, and are waging it with the purpose of robbing Germany and stripping her of her colonies; they have signed a treaty with Italy and Russia on the pillage and carving up of Turkey and Austria. The tsarist monarchy in Russia is waging a predatory war aimed at seizing Galicia, taking territory away from Turkey, enslaving Persia, Mongolia, etc. Germany is waging war with the purpose of grabbing British, Belgian and French colonies. Whether Germany or Russia wins, or whether there is a 'draw', the war will bring humanity fresh oppression of hundreds and hundreds of millions of people in the colonies, in Persia, Turkey and China, a fresh enslavement of nations, and new chains for the working class of all countries.

What are the tasks of the working class with regard to this war? The answer to this question is provided in a resolution unanimously adopted by the socialists of the whole world, at the Basel International Socialist Congress of 1912. This resolution was adopted in anticipation of a war of the very kind as started in 1914. This resolution says that the war is reactionary, that it is being prepared in the interests of "capitalist profits", that the workers consider it "a crime to shoot each other down", that the war will lead to "a proletarian revolution", that an example for the workers' tactics was set by the Paris Commune of 1871, and by October-December 1905, in Russia, i.e. by a revolution.

All class-conscious workers in Russia are on the side of the Russian Social-Democratic Labour group in the Duma, whose members (Petrovsky, Badayev, Muranov, Samoilov, and Shagov) have been exiled by the tsar to Siberia for revolutionary propaganda against the war and against the government. It is only in such revolutionary propaganda, and in revolutionary activities leading to a revolt of the masses, that the salvation of humanity from the horrors of the present and the future wars lies. Only the revolutionary overthrow of the bourgeois governments, in the first place of the most reactionary, brutal and barbarous tsarist government, will open the road to socialism and peace among nations.

The conscious or unwitting servants of the bourgeoisie are lying when they wish to persuade the people that the revolutionary overthrow of the tsarist monarchy can lead only to victories for and consolidation of the German reactionary monarchy and the German bourgeoisie. Although the leaders of the German socialists, like many leading socialists in Russia, have gone over to the side of their 'own' bourgeoisie and are helping to deceive the people with fables of a war of 'defence', there is mounting among the working masses of Germany an ever-stronger protest and indignation against their government. The German socialists who have not gone over to the side of the bourgeoisie have declared in the press that they consider the tactics of the Russian Social-Democratic Labour group in the Duma 'heroic'. In Germany, calls against the war and against the government are being published illegally. Tens and hundreds of the finest socialists of Germany, including Clara Zetkin, the well-known representative of the women's labour movement, have been thrown into prison by the German government for propaganda in a revolutionary spirit. In all the belligerent countries without exception, indignation is mounting in the working masses, and the example of revolutionary activities set by the Social-Democrats of Russia, and even more so any success of the revolution in Russia, will not fail to advance the great cause of socialism, of the victory of the proletariat over the bloodstained bourgeois exploiters.

The war is filling the pockets of the capitalists, into whose pockets gold is pouring from the treasuries of the Great Powers. The war is provoking a blind bitterness against the enemy, the bourgeoisie doing its best to direct the indignation of the people into such channels, to divert their attention from the *chief* enemy – the government and the ruling classes of their *own* country. However, the war which brings in its train endless misery and suffering for the toiling masses, enlightens and steels the finest representatives of the working class. If perish we must, let us perish in the struggle for our own cause, for the cause of the workers, for the socialist revolution, and not for the interests of the capitalists, the landowners and tsars – this is what every class-conscious worker sees and feels.

Revolutionary Social-Democratic work may be difficult at present, but it is possible. It is advancing throughout the world, and in this alone lies salvation.

Down with the tsarist monarchy, which has drawn Russia into a criminal war and which oppresses the peoples! Long live the world brotherhood of the workers, and the international revolution of the proletariat!

The Defeat of Russia and the Revolutionary Crisis

September 1915

The dissolution of the Fourth Duma in retaliation for the formation of an Opposition bloc consisting of liberals, Octobrists and nationalists, is one of the most vivid manifestations of the revolutionary crisis in Russia. The defeat of the armies of the tsarist monarchy; the growth of the strike movement and the revolutionary movement of the proletariat; the discontent of the masses and the formation of the liberal-Octobrist bloc for the purpose of reaching an understanding with the tsar on a programme of reforms and mobilising industry for the victory over Germany – such is the sequence and texture of events at the end of the first year of war.

There is obviously a revolutionary crisis in Russia, but its significance and the attendant tasks of the proletariat are not correctly understood by all.

History seems to be repeating itself: again there is a war, as in 1905, a war tsarism has dragged the country into with definite, patently annexationist, predatory and reactionary aims. Again there is military defeat, and a revolutionary crisis accelerated by it. Again the liberal bourgeoisie – in this case even in conjunction with large sections of the conservative bourgeoisie and the landowners – are advocating a programme of reform and of an understanding with the tsar. The situation is almost like that in the summer of 1905, prior to the Bulygin Duma, or in the summer of 1900, after the dissolution of the First Duma.

There is, however, actually a vast difference, viz. that this war has involved all Europe, all the most advanced countries with mass and powerful socialist movements. The imperialist war has *linked up* the Russian revolutionary crisis, which stems from a bourgeois-democratic revolution, with the growing crisis of the proletarian socialist revolution in the West. This link is so direct that no individual solution of revolutionary problems is possible in any single country – the Russian bourgeois-democratic revolution is now not only a prologue to, but an indivisible and integral part of, the socialist revolution in the West.

In 1905, it was the proletariat's task to consummate the bourgeois revolution in Russia so as to kindle the proletarian revolution in the West. In 1915, the second part of this task has acquired an urgency that puts it on a level with the first part. A new political division has arisen in Russia on the basis of new, higher, more developed and more complex international relations. This new division is between the chauvinist revolutionaries, who desire revolution so as to defeat Germany, and the proletarian internationalist revolutionaries, who desire a revolution in Russia *for the sake of* the proletarian revolution in the West, and simultaneously with that revolution. This new division is, in essence, one between the urban and the rural petty bourgeoisie in Russia, and the socialist proletariat. The new division must be clearly understood, for the impending revolution makes it the prime duty of a Marxist, i.e. of any class-conscious socialist, to realise the position of the *various classes*, and to interpret general differences over tactics and principles as differences in the positions of the various classes.

There is nothing more puerile, contemptible and harmful, than the idea current among revolutionary philistines, namely, that differences should be 'forgotten' 'in view' of the immediate common aim in the approaching revolution. People whom the experience of the 1905-14 decade has not taught the folly of this idea are hopeless from the revolutionary standpoint. Those who confine themselves, at this stage, to revolutionary exclamations, without analysing which classes have *proved* their ability to adopt, and have indeed adopted, a definite revolutionary programme, do not really differ from 'revolutionaries' like Khrustalyov, Aladin and Alexinsky.

We have before us the clear-cut stand of the monarchy and the feudal-minded landowners – 'no surrender' of Russia to the liberal bourgeoisie; better an understanding with the German monarchy. Equally clear is the liberal bourgeoisie's stand – exploit the defeat and the mounting revolution in order to wrest concessions from a frightened monarchy and compel it to share power with the bourgeoisie. Just as clear, too, is the stand of the revolutionary proletariat, which is striving to consummate the revolution by exploiting the vacillation and embarrassment of the government and the bourgeoisie. The petty bourgeoisie, however, i.e. the vast mass of the barely-awakening population of Russia, is groping blindly in the wake of the bourgeoisie, a captive to nationalist prejudices, on the one hand, prodded into the revolution by the unparalleled horror and misery of war, the high cost of living, impoverishment, ruin and starvation, but on the other hand, glancing *backward* at every step towards the idea of defence of the fatherland, towards the idea of Russia's state integrity, or towards the idea of small-peasant prosperity, to be achieved through a victory over tsarism and over Germany, but without a victory over capitalism.

This vacillation of the petty bourgeois, of the small peasant, is no accident, but the inevitable outcome of his economic position. It is foolish to shut one's eyes to this bitter but profound truth; it must be understood and traced back in the existing *political currents and groupings*, so as not to deceive ourselves and the people, and not to weaken and paralyse the revolutionary party of the Social-Democratic proletariat. The proletariat will debilitate itself if it permits its party to vacillate as the petty bourgeoisie does. The proletariat will accomplish its task only if it is able to march unfalteringly towards its great goal, pushing the petty bourgeoisie forward, letting the latter learn from its mistakes when it wavers to the right, and utilising all the petty bourgeoisie's forces to the utmost when life compels it to move to the left.

The Trudoviks, the SRs and the Organising Committee's liquidationist supporters – these are the political *trends* in Russia which have taken shape during the past decade, have proved their links with the various groups, elements and strata in the petty bourgeoisie, and shown vacillation from extreme revolutionism in word, to an alliance with the chauvinist Popular Socialists, or with *Nasha Zarya*, in deed. On 3 September 1915, for instance, the five secretaries of the Organising Committee abroad issued a manifesto on the tasks of the proletariat, which said not a word about opportunism and social-chauvinism, but called for a 'revolt' in the rear of the German army (this after a whole year of struggle against the slogan of civil war!) and proclaimed a slogan praised so highly in 1905 by the Cadets, viz. a "constituent assembly for the liquidation of the war and for the abolition of the autocratic [3 June] regime"!* People who have failed to understand the need for a cleavage between the party of the proletariat and these petty-bourgeois trends so that the revolution may be successful, have assumed the name of Social-Democrats in vain.

No, in the face of the revolutionary crisis in Russia, which is being accelerated by defeat – and this is what the motley opponents of 'defeatism' are afraid to admit – it will be the proletariat's duty to carry on the struggle against opportunism and chauvinism, or otherwise it will be impossible to develop the revolutionary consciousness of the masses, and to assist their movement by means of straightforward revolutionary slogans. Not a constituent assembly, but the overthrow of the monarchy, a republic, the confiscation of landed estates, and an eight-hour day will, as hitherto, be the slogans of the Social-Democratic proletariat, the slogans of our Party. In direct connection with this, and to make it possible really to single out the socialist tasks and contrast them with the tasks of bourgeois

---

*   On 3 June 1907 Minister of the Interior Pyotr Stolypin dissolved the Second
     Duma, marking the start of the period of reaction in tsarist Russia.

chauvinism (including the Plekhanov and the Kautsky brands) in all its propaganda and agitation, and in all working-class action, our Party will preserve the slogan of 'transform the imperialist war into a civil war', i.e. the slogan of the socialist revolution in the West.

The lessons of the war are compelling even our opponents to recognise in practice both the stand of 'defeatism' and the necessity of issuing – at first as a spirited phrase in a manifesto, but later more seriously and thoughtfully – the slogan of 'a revolt in the rear' of the German militarists, in other words, the slogan of a civil war. The lessons of the war, it appears, are knocking into their heads that which we have been insisting on since the very outset of the war. The defeat of Russia *has proved* the lesser evil, for it has tremendously enhanced the revolutionary crisis and has aroused millions, tens and hundreds of millions. Moreover, in conditions of an imperialist war, a revolutionary crisis in Russia could not but lead people's thoughts to the only salvation for the people – the idea of 'a revolt in the rear' of the German army, i.e. the idea of a civil war in *all* the belligerent countries.

Life teaches. Life is *advancing*, through the defeat of Russia, towards a revolution in Russia and, through that revolution and in connection with it, towards a civil war in Europe. Life has taken this direction. And, drawing fresh strength from these lessons of life, which have justified its position, the party of the revolutionary proletariat of Russia will, with ever greater energy, follow the path it has chosen.

The First Step

11 October 1915

The development of the international socialist movement is slow during the tremendous crisis created by the war. Yet it is moving towards a break with opportunism and social-chauvinism, as was clearly shown by the International Socialist Conference held at Zimmerwald, Switzerland, between 5-8 September 1915.

For a whole year, the socialists of the warring and the neutral countries vacillated and temporised. Afraid to admit to themselves the gravity of the crisis, they did not wish to look reality in the face, and kept deferring in a thousand ways the inevitable break with the opportunism and Kautskyism prevalent in the official parties of Western Europe.

However, the analysis of events which we gave a year ago in the manifesto of the Central Committee (*Sotsial-Demokrat*, No. 33)* has proved correct; the events have borne out its correctness. They *took* a course that resulted in the first International Socialist Conference being attended by representatives of the protesting elements of the minorities in Germany, France, Sweden and Norway, who acted *against* the decisions of the official parties, i.e. in fact acted schismatically.

---

* Lenin's 'The War and Russian Social-Democracy', in this volume, p. 9.

The work of the Conference was summed up in a manifesto and a resolution expressing sympathy with the arrested and the persecuted.* Both documents appear in this issue of *Sotsial-Demokrat*. By nineteen votes to twelve, the Conference refused to submit to a committee the draft resolution proposed by us and other revolutionary Marxists; our draft manifesto was passed on to the committee together with two others, for a joint manifesto to be drawn up. The reader will find elsewhere in this issue our two drafts; a comparison of the latter with the manifesto adopted clearly shows that a number of fundamental ideas of revolutionary Marxism were adopted.**

In practice, the manifesto signifies a step towards an ideological and practical break with opportunism and social-chauvinism. At the same time, the manifesto, as any analysis will show, contains inconsistencies, and does not say everything that should be said.

The manifesto calls the war imperialist and emphasises two features of imperialism: the striving of the capitalists of *every* nation for profits and the exploitation of others, and the striving of the Great Powers to partition the world and "enslave" weaker nations. The manifesto repeats the most essential things that should be said of the imperialist nature of the war, and were said in our resolution. In this respect, the manifesto merely *popularises* our resolution. Popularisation is undoubtedly a useful thing. However, if we want clear thinking in the working class and attach importance to systematic and unflagging propaganda, we must accurately and fully define the principles to be popularised. If that is not done, we risk repeating the error, the fault of the Second International which led to its collapse, viz. we shall be leaving room for ambiguity and misinterpretations. Is it, for instance, possible to deny the signal importance of the idea, expressed in our resolution, that the objective conditions are mature for socialism? The 'popular' exposition of the manifesto omitted this idea; failure has attended the attempt to combine, in one document, a clear and precise resolution based on principle, and an appeal.

---

*   Reproduced in this volume, p. 379 and p. 385 respectively.
** Both drafts are reproduced in this volume, p. 385.

"The capitalists of all countries … claim that the war serves to defend the fatherland … They are lying…", the manifesto continues. Here again, this forthright statement that the fundamental idea of opportunism in the present war – the 'defence of the fatherland' idea – is a lie, is a repetition of the kernel of the revolutionary Marxists' resolution. Again, the manifesto regrettably fails to say everything that should be said; it is half-hearted, afraid to speak the whole truth. After a year of war, who today is not aware of the actual damage caused to socialism, not only by the capitalist press *repeating and endorsing* the capitalists' *lies* (it is its business as a capitalist press to repeat the capitalists' lies), but also by the greater part of the socialist press doing so? Who does not know that European socialism's greatest crisis has been brought about not by the 'capitalists' lies', but by the *lies* of Guesde, Hyndman, Vandervelde, Plekhanov and *Kautsky*? Who does not know that the *lies* spoken by such leaders suddenly revealed all the strength of the opportunism that swept them away at the decisive moment?

Let us take a look at what has come about: to make the masses see things in a clearer light, the manifesto says that in the present war the defence of the fatherland idea is a capitalist lie. The European masses, however, are not illiterate, and almost all who have read the manifesto have heard, and still hear, *that same lie* from hundreds of socialist papers, journals and pamphlets, echoing them after Plekhanov, Hyndman, Kautsky and co. What will the readers of the manifesto think? What thoughts will arise in them after this display of timidity by the authors of the manifesto? Disregard the capitalists' lie about the defence of the fatherland, the manifesto tells the workers. Well and good. Practically all of them will say or think: the *capitalists'* lie has long stopped bothering us, but the lie of Kautsky and co…

The manifesto goes on to repeat another important idea in our resolution, viz. that the socialist parties and the workers' organisations of the various countries "have *flouted* obligations stemming from the decisions of the Stuttgart, Copenhagen and Basel congresses"; that the International Socialist Bureau too has *failed to do its duty*; that this failure to do its duty consisted in voting for war credits, joining governments, recognising "a class truce" (submission to which the manifesto calls *slavish*; in other words, it accuses Guesde, Plekhanov, Kautsky and co. of substituting for propaganda of socialism the propaganda of *slavish* ideas).

Is it consistent, we shall ask, to speak, in a 'popular' manifesto, of the failure of a number of parties to do their duty (it is common knowledge that the reference is to the strongest parties and the workers' organisations in the most advanced countries: Britain, France and Germany), without giving any explanation of this startling and unprecedented fact? The greater part of the socialist parties and the International Socialist Bureau itself have failed to do their duty! What is this – an accident and the failure of individuals, or the turning-point of an entire epoch? If it is the former, and *we* circulate that idea among the masses, it is tantamount to *our* renouncing the fundamentals of socialist doctrine. If it is the latter, how can we fail to say so forthright? We are facing a moment of historic significance – the collapse of the International as a whole, a turning point of an entire epoch – and yet we are *afraid* to tell the masses that the whole truth must be sought for and found, and that we must do our thinking to the very end. It is preposterous and ridiculous to suppose that the International Socialist Bureau and a number of parties could have collapsed, *without* linking up this event with the long history of the origin, the growth, the maturing and *over*-maturity of the general European opportunist movement, with its deep economic roots – deep, not in the sense that it is intimately linked with the masses, but in the sense that it is connected with a certain stratum of society.

Passing on to the 'struggle for peace', the manifesto states that: "This struggle is a struggle for freedom, the brotherhood of peoples, and socialism." It goes on to explain that in wartime the workers make sacrifices "in the service of the ruling classes", whereas they must learn to make sacrifices "*for their own cause*" (doubly underscored in the manifesto), "for the sacred aims of socialism". The resolution which expresses sympathy with arrested and persecuted fighters says that "the Conference solemnly undertakes

to honour the living and the dead by *emulating their example*"
and that its aim will be to "arouse the revolutionary spirit in the
international proletariat".

All these ideas are a reiteration of our resolution's fundamental
idea that a struggle for peace *without* a revolutionary struggle is
a hollow and false phrase, and that a revolutionary struggle for
socialism is the only way to put an end to the horror of war. But here
too we find inconsistency, timidity, and a failure to say everything
that ought to be said: it calls upon the masses to *emulate the example*
of the revolutionary fighters; it declares that the five members of
the Russian Social-Democratic Labour Duma group who have
been sentenced to exile in Siberia have carried on "the glorious
revolutionary tradition of Russia"; it proclaims the necessity of
"arousing the revolutionary spirit", but *it does not specify* forthright
and clearly the revolutionary methods of struggle.

Was our Central Committee right in signing this manifesto,
with all its inconsistency and timidity? We think it was. Our non-
agreement, the non-agreement, not only of our Central Committee
but of the entire *international* Left-wing section of the Conference,
which stands by the principles of *revolutionary Marxism*, is openly
expressed both in a special resolution, a separate draft manifesto,
and a separate declaration on the vote for a compromise manifesto.
We did not conceal a jot of our views, slogans, or tactics. A
German edition of our pamphlet, *Socialism and War*, was handed
out at the Conference.* We have spread, are spreading, and shall
continue to spread our views with no less energy than the manifesto
will. It is a fact that this manifesto is a *step forward* towards a real
struggle against opportunism, towards a rupture with it. It would
be sectarianism to refuse to take this step forward *together* with
the minority of German, French, Swedish, Norwegian and Swiss
socialists, when we retain full freedom and full opportunity to
criticise inconsistency and to work for greater things.** It would be

---

* In this volume, p. 57.

** We are not frightened by the fact that the Organising Committee and the
  Social-Revolutionaries signed the manifesto diplomatically, retaining all their

poor war tactics to refuse to adhere to the mounting international protest movement against social-chauvinism just because this movement is slow, because it takes 'only' a single step forward and because it is ready and willing to take a step backward tomorrow and make peace with the old International Socialist Bureau. Its readiness to make peace with the opportunists is so far merely wishful thinking. Will the opportunists agree to a peace? Is peace *objectively* possible between *trends* that are dividing more and more deeply – social-chauvinism and Kautskyism on the one hand, and on the other, revolutionary internationalist Marxism? We consider it impossible, and we shall continue our line, encouraged as we are by its *success* at the Conference of 5-8 September.

The success of our line is beyond doubt. Compare the facts: in September 1914, our Central Committee's manifesto seemed almost isolated. In March 1915, an international women's conference adopted a miserable pacifist resolution, which was blindly followed by the Organising Committee. In September 1915, we rallied in a whole group of the international Left wing. We came out with our own tactics, voiced a number of our fundamental ideas in a joint manifesto, and took part in the formation of an International Socialist Committee, i.e. a practically new International Socialist Bureau, against the wishes of the old one, and on the basis of a manifesto that openly condemns the tactics of the latter.

The workers of Russia, whose overwhelming majority followed our Party and its Central Committee even in the years 1912-14, will now, from the experience of the international socialist movement, see that our tactics are being confirmed in a wider area, and that our fundamental ideas are shared by an ever growing and finer part of the proletarian International.

---

links with – *and all their attachment to* – *Nasha Zarya*, Rubanovich, and the July 1915 Conference of the Popular Socialists and the Socialist-Revolutionaries in Russia. We have means enough to combat corrupt diplomacy and unmask it. It is more and more unmasking itself. *Nasha Zarya* and Chkheidze's group are *helping* us unmask Axelrod and co. – *Lenin*

Revolutionary Marxists at the International Socialist Conference, 5-8 September 1915

11 October 1915

The ideological struggle at the Conference was waged between a compact group of internationalists, revolutionary Marxists, and the vacillating near-Kautskyites, who formed the Right wing of the Conference. The unitedness of the former group is one of the most important facts and greatest achievements of the Conference. After a year of war, the trend represented by our Party proved the *only* trend in the International to adopt a fully definite resolution as well as a draft manifesto based on the latter, and to unite the consistent Marxists of Russia, Poland, the Lettish territory, Germany, Sweden, Norway, Switzerland and Holland.

What arguments did the vacillating elements advance against us? The Germans admitted that we were advancing towards revolutionary battles, but, they said, we do not have to proclaim from the house-tops such things as fraternisation in the trenches, political strikes, street demonstrations and civil war. Such things are done, they said, but not spoken of. Others added: this is childishness, verbal pyrotechnics.

The German semi-Kautskyites castigated themselves for these ridiculously, indecently contradictory and evasive speeches by passing a resolution of sympathy and a declaration on the need to "follow the example" of the members of the RSDL Duma group, who distributed *Sotsial-Demokrat*, our Central Organ, which proclaimed civil war from the housetops.

You are following the bad example set by Kautsky, we replied to the Germans; in word, you recognise the impending revolution; in deed, you refuse to tell the masses about it openly, to call for it, and indicate the most concrete means of struggle which the masses are to test and legitimise in the course of the revolution. In 1847, Marx and Engels, who were living *abroad* – the German philistines were horrified at revolutionary methods of struggle being spoken of from abroad! – called for revolution, in their celebrated 'Manifesto of the Communist Party'; they spoke forthright of the use of force, and branded as contemptible any attempt to conceal the revolutionary aims, tasks and methods of the struggle. The Revolution of 1848 proved that Marx and Engels *alone* had applied the correct tactics to the events. Several years prior to the 1905 Revolution in Russia, Plekhanov, who was then still a Marxist, wrote an unsigned article in the old *Iskra* of 1901, expressing the editorial board's views on the coming insurrection, on ways of preparing it, such as street demonstrations, and even on technical devices, such as using wire in combating cavalry. The Russian Revolution proved that the old Iskrists alone had approached the events with the correct tactics. We are now faced with the following alternative: either we are really and truly convinced that the war is creating a revolutionary situation in Europe, and that all the economic and socio-political circumstances of the imperialist period are leading up to a revolution of the proletariat – in which case we are in duty bound to explain to the masses the need for revolution, call for it, create the necessary organisations, and speak fearlessly and most concretely of the various methods of the forcible struggle and its 'technique'. This duty of ours does not depend upon whether the revolution will be strong enough, or whether it will arrive with a first or a second imperialist war, etc. Or else we are not convinced that the situation is revolutionary, in which case there is no sense in our just talking about a war against war. In that case, we are, in fact, national liberal-labour politicians of the Südekum-Plekhanov or Kautsky variety.

The French delegates also declared that the present situation in Europe, as they saw it, would lead to revolution. But, they said, first, "we have not come here to provide a formula for a Third international"; secondly, the French worker "believes nobody and nothing"; he is demoralised and satiated with anarchist and Hervéist phrases. The former argument is unreasonable, because the joint compromise manifesto *does* "provide a formula" for a Third International, though it is inconsistent, incomplete and not given sufficient thought. The latter argument is very important as a very serious factual argument, which takes the specific situation in France into account, not in the meaning of defence of the fatherland, or the enemy invasion, but in taking note of the 'sore points' in the French labour movement. The only thing that logically follows from this, however, is that the French socialists would perhaps join general European revolutionary action by the proletariat *more slowly* than others, and not that such action is unnecessary. The question as to *how rapidly*, in which way and in which particular forms the proletariat of the various countries are capable of taking revolutionary action was not raised at the Conference and could not have been. The conditions for this are not yet ripe. For the present it is our task to jointly *propagandise* the correct tactics and leave it to events to indicate the *tempo* of the movement, and the modifications in the mainstream (according to nation, locality and trade). If the French proletariat has been demoralised by anarchist phrases, it has been demoralised by Millerandism too, and it is not our business to *increase* this demoralisation by *leaving things unsaid in* the manifesto.

It was none other than Merrheim who uttered the characteristic and profoundly correct phrase: "The [Socialist] Party, Jouhaux [secretary of the General Confederation of Labour] and the government are three heads under one bonnet."* This is the truth, a fact proved by the experience of the year of struggle waged by the French internationalists against the Party and Messrs. Jouhaux. There is, however, only one conclusion to be drawn: the government cannot be fought unless the opportunist parties and the leaders of anarcho-syndicalism are fought against. Unlike our resolution, the joint manifesto merely indicated the tasks in the struggle but did not say everything that should have been said about them.

Arguing against our tactics, one of the Italians said:

> Your tactics come either too late [since the war has already begun] or too soon [because the war has not yet created the conditions for revolution]; besides, you propose to 'change the programme' of the International, since all our propaganda has always been conducted 'against violence'.

It was very easy for us to reply to this by quoting Jules Guesde in *En garde!* to the effect that not a single influential leader of the Second International ever rejected the use of violence and direct revolutionary methods of the struggle in general. It has always been argued that the legal struggle, parliamentarism and insurrection are interlinked, and *must inevitably* pass into each other according to the changes in the conditions of the movement. From the same book, *En garde!*, we quoted a passage in a speech delivered by Guesde in 1899, in which he spoke of the possibility of a war for markets, colonies, etc., and went on to say that if there were any French, German and British Millerands in such a war, then "what would become of international working-class solidarity?" In this speech Guesde condemned himself in advance. As for declaring propaganda of revolution 'inopportune', this objection rests on a confusion of concepts usual among socialists in the Romance countries: they confuse the beginning of a revolution with open

---

*   The French General Confederation of Labour (*Confédération Général du Travail*) (CGT) was founded in 1895 and was strongly influenced by anarcho-syndicalists and reformists. Its leaders recognised only the economic struggle, and opposed the proletarian party's leadership of the trade union movement. During the First World War, its leaders sided with the imperialist bourgeoisie.

and direct propaganda for revolution. In Russia, nobody places the beginning of the 1905 Revolution before January 1905, whereas revolutionary propaganda, in the very narrow sense of the word, the propaganda and the preparation of mass action, demonstrations, strikes, barricades, had been conducted *for years* prior to that.* The old *Iskra*, for instance, began to propagandise the matter at the end of 1900, as Marx did in 1847, when nobody thought as yet of the *beginning of a revolution* in Europe.

After a revolution has begun, it is 'recognised' even by the liberals and its other enemies; they often recognise it so as to deceive and betray it. *Before* the revolution, revolutionaries foresee it, realise its inevitability, make the masses understand its necessity, and explain its course and methods to the masses.

By the irony of history, Kautsky and his friends, who tried to take out of Grimm's hands the initiative of convening the Conference, and attempted to disrupt the Conference of the Left wing (Kautsky's closest friends even went *on a tour* for this purpose, as Grimm disclosed at the Conference), were *the very ones* who pushed the Conference *to the left*. By *their* deeds, the opportunists and the Kautskyites have proved the correctness of the stand taken by our Party.

---

*   On 9 (22) January 1905, tsarist troops opened fire on unarmed demonstrators outside the Winter Palace. Bloody Sunday, as it became known, served as the starting-point of the 1905 Russian Revolution.

Opportunism and the Collapse of the Second International

January 1916

Editors note:

This article was written by Lenin in German and published in January 1916 in the first issue of the theoretical magazine of the Zimmerwald Left, *Vorbote* (*Herald*). Earlier, Lenin had written an article in Russian in December 1915 under the same title.

* * *

I

Has the Second International really ceased to exist? This is being stubbornly denied by its most authoritative representatives, like Kautsky and Vandervelde. Their point of view is that, save for the rupture of relations, nothing has really happened; all is quite well.

To get at the truth of the matter, let us turn to the manifesto of the Basel Congress of 1912, which applies particularly to the present imperialist world war and which was accepted by all the socialist parties of the world.* No socialist, be it noted, will dare in

---

* Reproduced in this volume, p. 371.

theory deny the necessity of making a concrete, historical appraisal of every war.

Now that war has broken out, neither the avowed opportunists nor the Kautskyites dare repudiate the Basel Manifesto or compare its demands with the conduct of the socialist parties during the war. Why? Because the manifesto completely exposes both.

There is not a single word in the Basel Manifesto about the defence of the fatherland, or about the difference between a war of aggression and a war of defence; there is nothing in it at all about what the opportunists and Kautskyites* of Germany and of the Quadruple Alliance at all crossroads are now dinning into the ears of the world. Nor could it have said anything of the sort, because what it does say absolutely rules out the use of such concepts. It makes a highly concrete reference to the series of political and economic conflicts which had for decades been preparing the ground for the present war, had become quite apparent in 1912, and which brought about the war in 1914. The manifesto recalls the Russo-Austrian conflict for "hegemony in the Balkans"; the conflicts between Britain, France and Germany (between *all* these countries!) over their "policy of conquest in Asia Minor"; the Austro-Italian conflict over the "striving for domination" in Albania, etc. In short, the manifesto defines all these as conflicts emanating from "capitalist imperialism". Thus, the manifesto very clearly recognises the predatory, imperialist, reactionary, slave-driving character of the present war, i.e. a character which makes the idea of defending the fatherland theoretical nonsense and a practical absurdity. The big sharks are fighting each other to gobble up other peoples' 'fatherlands'. The manifesto draws the inevitable conclusions from undisputed historical facts: the war "cannot be justified on the slightest pretext of its being in the interest of the people"; it is being prepared "for the sake of the capitalists' profits and the ambitions of dynasties". It would be a

---

* This does not refer to the personalities of Kautsky's followers in Germany, but to the international type of pseudo-Marxist who vacillates between opportunism and radicalism, but is in reality only a fig-leaf for opportunism. – *Lenin*

"crime" for the workers to "shoot each other down". That is what the manifesto says.

The epoch of capitalist imperialism is one of ripe and rotten-ripe capitalism, which is about to collapse, and which is mature enough to make way for socialism. The period between 1789 and 1871 was one of progressive capitalism when the overthrow of feudalism and absolutism, and liberation from the foreign yoke were on history's agenda. 'Defence of the fatherland', i.e. defence against oppression, was permissible on these grounds, and on these *alone*. The term would be applicable even now in a war *against* the imperialist Great Powers, but it would be absurd to apply it to a war *between* the imperialist Great Powers, a war to decide who gets the biggest piece of the Balkan countries, Asia Minor, etc. It is not surprising, therefore, that the 'socialists' who advocate 'defence of the fatherland' in the present war shun the Basel Manifesto as a thief shuns the scene of his crime. For the manifesto proves them to be social-chauvinists, i.e. socialists in words, but chauvinists in deeds, who are helping 'their own' bourgeoisie to rob other countries and enslave other nations. That is the very substance of chauvinism – to defend one's 'own' fatherland even when its acts are aimed at enslaving other peoples' fatherlands.

Recognition that a war is being fought for national liberation implies one set of tactics; its recognition as an imperialist war, another. The manifesto clearly points to the latter. The war, it says, "will bring on an economic and political crisis", which must be "utilised", not to lessen the crisis, not to defend the fatherland, but, on the contrary, to "*rouse*" the masses and "hasten the downfall of capitalist rule". It is impossible to hasten something for which historical conditions are not yet mature. The manifesto declares that social revolution is *possible*, that the conditions for it *have matured*, and that it will break out precisely *in connection* with war. Referring to the examples of the *Paris Commune and the Revolution of 1905* in Russia, i.e. examples of mass strikes and of civil war, the manifesto declares that "the ruling classes" fear "a proletarian revolution". It is sheer falsehood to claim, as Kautsky does, that the socialist attitude to the *present* war has not been defined. This question was not merely discussed, but decided in Basel, where the tactics of revolutionary proletarian mass struggle were recognised.

It is downright hypocrisy to ignore the Basel Manifesto altogether, or in its most essential parts, and to quote instead the speeches of leaders, or the resolutions of various parties, which, in the first place, *antedate* the Basel Congress, secondly, were not decisions adopted by the parties of the whole world, and thirdly, applied to various *possible* wars, but never to the present war. The point is that the epoch of national wars between the big European powers has been superseded by an epoch of imperialist wars between them, and that the Basel Manifesto had to recognise this fact officially for the first time.

It would be a mistake to regard the Basel Manifesto as an empty threat, a collection of platitudes, as so much hot air. Those whom the manifesto exposes would like to have it that way. But it is not true. The manifesto is but the fruit of the great propaganda work carried on throughout the entire epoch of the Second International; it is but the summary of all that the socialists had disseminated among the masses in the hundreds of thousands of speeches, articles and manifestos in all languages. It merely reiterates what *Jules Guesde*, for example, wrote in 1899, when he castigated socialist ministerialism in the event of war: he wrote of war provoked by the "capitalist pirates" (*En Garde!*, p. 175); it merely repeats what *Kautsky* wrote in 1909 in his *Road to Power*, where he admitted that the "peaceful" epoch was over and that the epoch of wars and revolutions was on. To represent the Basel Manifesto as so much talk, or as a mistake, is to regard as mere talk, or as a mistake, everything the socialists have done in the last twenty-five years. The opportunists and the Kautskyites find the contradiction between the manifesto and its non-application so intolerable because it lays bare the profound contradictions in the work of the Second International. The relatively 'peaceful' character of the period between 1871 and 1914 served to foster opportunism first as a *mood*, then as a *trend*, until finally it formed a *group or stratum* among the labour bureaucracy and petty-bourgeois fellow-travellers. These elements were able to gain control of the labour movement only by paying lip-service to revolutionary aims and revolutionary tactics. They were able to win the confidence of the masses only by their protestations that all this 'peaceful' work served to *prepare* the proletarian revolution. This contradiction was a boil which just had to burst, and burst it has. Here is the question: is it worth trying, as Kautsky and co. are doing, to force the pus back into the body for the sake of 'unity' (with the pus), or should the pus be removed as quickly and as thoroughly as possible, regardless of the pang of pain caused by the process, to help bring about the complete recovery of the body of the labour movement?

Those who voted for war credits, entered cabinets and advocated 'defence of the fatherland' in 1914-15 have patently betrayed socialism. Only hypocrites will deny it. This betrayal must be explained.

II

It would be absurd to regard the whole question as one of personalities. What has opportunism to do with it when men like *Plekhanov* and *Guesde*, etc.? – asks Kautsky (*Die Neue Zeit*, 28 May 1915). What has opportunism to do with it when *Kautsky*, etc.? – replies *Axelrod* on behalf of the opportunists of the Quadruple Alliance (*Die Krise der Sozialdemokratie*, Zürich, 1915, p. 21). This is a complete farce. *If the crisis of the whole movement is to be explained, an examination must be made, firstly, of the economic significance of the present policy; secondly, its underlying ideas; and thirdly, its connection with the history of the various trends in the socialist movement.*

What is the economic substance of defencism in the war of 1914-15? The bourgeoisie of *all* the big powers are waging the war to divide and exploit the world, and oppress other nations. A few crumbs of the bourgeoisie's huge profits may come the way of the small group of labour bureaucrats, labour aristocrats and petty-bourgeois fellow-travellers. Social-chauvinism and opportunism have the same class basis, namely, the alliance of a small section of privileged workers with 'their' national bourgeoisie *against* the working-class masses; the alliance between the lackeys of the bourgeoisie and the bourgeoisie *against* the class the latter is exploiting.

Opportunism and social-chauvinism have the same political content, namely, class collaboration, repudiation of the dictatorship of the proletariat, repudiation of revolutionary action, unconditional acceptance of bourgeois legality, confidence in the bourgeoisie and lack of confidence in the proletariat. *Social-chauvinism is the direct continuation and consummation of British liberal-labour politics, of Millerandism and Bernsteinism.**

The struggle between the two main trends in the labour movement – revolutionary socialism and opportunist socialism – fills the entire period from 1889 to 1914. Even today there are two main trends on the attitude to war in every country. Let us drop the bourgeois and opportunist habit of referring to personalities. Let us take the *trends* in a number of countries. Let us take ten European countries: Germany, Britain, Russia, Italy, Holland, Sweden, Bulgaria, Switzerland, Belgium and France. In the first eight the division into opportunist and revolutionary trends corresponds to the division into social-chauvinists and internationalists. In Germany the strongholds of social-chauvinism are *Sozialistische Monatshefte*** and Legien and co.; in Britain the Fabians and the Labour Party (the ILP has always been allied with them and has supported their organ, and in this bloc it has always been weaker than the social-chauvinists, whereas three-sevenths of the BSP are internationalists);*** in Russia this trend is represented by *Nasha*

---

* Bernsteinism – an opportunist trend in German and International Social-Democracy hostile to Marxism. It emerged in Germany at the end of the nineteenth century, and got its name from Eduard Bernstein, a German Social-Democrat, who tried to revise Marx's revolutionary theory on the lines of bourgeois liberalism. Among his supporters in Russia were the legal Marxists, the Economists, the Bund and the Mensheviks.

** *Sozialistische Monatshefte* (*Socialist Monthly*) was the chief organ of the German Social-Democratic opportunists and an organ of international opportunism; during the First World War it took a social-chauvinist stand.

*** The Fabian Society is a British reformist organisation founded in 1884.

The Independent Labour Party (ILP) was a reformist organisation founded by the leaders of the 'new trade unions' in 1893.

*Zarya** (now *Nashe Dyelo*), by the Organising Committee,** and by the Duma group led by Chkheidze; in Italy it is represented by the reformists with Bissolati at their head; in Holland, by Troelstra's party; in Sweden, by the majority of the Party led by Branting; in Bulgaria, by the so-called 'Shiroki' socialists;*** in Switzerland by Greulich and co. In *all* these countries it is the revolutionary Social-Democrats who have voiced a more or less vigorous protest against social-chauvinism. France and Belgium are the two exceptions; there internationalism also exists, but is very weak.

Social-chauvinism is opportunism in its finished form. It is quite ripe for an open, frequently vulgar, alliance with the bourgeoisie and the general staffs. It is this alliance that gives it great power and a monopoly of the legal press and of deceiving the masses. *It is absurd to go on regarding opportunism as an inner-party phenomenon.* It is ridiculous to think of carrying out the Basel resolution together with David, Legien, Hyndman, Plekhanov and Webb. Unity with the social-chauvinists means unity with one's 'own' national bourgeoisie, which exploits other nations; it means splitting the international proletariat. This does not mean that an immediate break with the opportunists is possible everywhere; it means only that historically this break is imminent; that it is necessary and inevitable for the revolutionary struggle of the proletariat; that history, which has led us from 'peaceful' capitalism to imperialist capitalism, has paved the way for this break. *Volentem ducunt fata, nolentem trahunt.* [The fates lead the willing, drag the unwilling.]

III

This is very well understood by the shrewd representatives of the bourgeoisie. That is why they are so lavish in their praise

---

The British Socialist Party (BSP) was founded in Manchester in 1911 by a merger of the Social-Democratic Party with other socialist groups.

* *Nasha Zarya* (*Our Dawn*) was a legal monthly of the Menshevik liquidators.

** The Organising Committee (OC) was the Mensheviks' governing centre, formed at the August conference of Menshevik liquidators and all anti-Party groups and trends in 1912.

*** An opportunist trend within the Bulgarian Social-Democratic Party.

of the present socialist parties, headed by the 'defenders of the fatherland', i.e. the defenders of imperialist plunder. That is why the social-chauvinist leaders are rewarded by their governments either with ministerial posts (in France and Britain), or with a monopoly of unhindered legal existence (in Germany and Russia). That is why in Germany, where the Social-Democratic Party was strongest and where its transformation into a national-liberal *counter-revolutionary* labour party has been most obvious, things have got to the stage where the public prosecutor qualifies the struggle between the 'minority' and the 'majority' as 'incitement to class hatred'! That is why the greatest concern of the clever opportunists is to retain the former 'unity' of the old parties, which did the bourgeoisie so many good turns in 1914 and 1915. The views held by these opportunists in all countries of the world were expounded with commendable frankness by a German Social-Democrat in an article signed 'Monitor' which appeared in April 1915, in the reactionary magazine *Preussische Jahrbücher.** Monitor thinks that it would be very dangerous for the bourgeoisie if the Social-Democrats were to move *still further to the right*.

> It must preserve its character as a labour party with socialist ideals; for the day it gives this up a new party will arise and adopt the programme the old party had disavowed, giving it a still more radical formulation. (*Preussische Jahrbücher*, 1915, No. 4, pp. 50-1.)

Monitor hit the nail on the head. That is just what the British Liberals and the French Radicals have always wanted – phrases with a revolutionary ring to deceive the masses and induce them to place their trust in the Lloyd Georges, the Sembats, the Renaudels, the Legiens and the Kautskys, in the men capable of preaching 'defence of the fatherland' in a predatory war.

But Monitor represents only one variety of opportunism, the frank, crude, cynical variety. Others act with stealth, subtlety and

---

* *Preussische Jahrbücher* (*Prussian Yearbook*) – a conservative monthly of the German capitalists and landowners published in Berlin from 1858 to 1935.

'honesty'. Engels once said that for the working class 'honest' opportunists were the greatest danger.* Here is one example. *Kautsky* wrote in *Die Neue Zeit* (26 November 1915) as follows:

> The opposition against the majority is growing; the masses are in an opposition mood… After the war [only *after* the war? – *Lenin*] class antagonisms will become so sharp that radicalism will gain the upper hand among the masses… After the war [only *after* the war?] we shall be menaced with the desertion of the radical elements from the Party and their influx into the party of anti-parliamentary [?? meaning extra-parliamentary] mass action… Thus, our Party is splitting up into two extreme camps which have nothing in common.

To preserve unity, Kautsky tries to persuade the majority in the Reichstag to allow the minority to make a few radical parliamentary speeches. That means Kautsky wants to use a few radical parliamentary speeches to reconcile the revolutionary masses with the opportunists, who have "nothing in common" with revolution, who have long had the leadership of the trade unions, and now, relying on their close alliance with the bourgeoisie and the government, have also captured the leadership of the Party. What essential difference is there between this and Monitor's 'programme'? There is none, save for the sugary phrases which prostitute Marxism.

At a meeting of the Reichstag group on 18 March 1915, *Wurm*, a Kautskyite, "warned" against "pulling the strings too taut":

> There is growing opposition among the workers' masses to the majority of the group, we must keep to the Marxist [?! probably a misprint: this should read "the Monitor"] Centre.**

Thus we find that the revolutionary sentiment of the *masses* was admitted as a *fact* on behalf of *all* the Kautskyites (the so-called

---

* See Engels, 'A Critique of the Draft Social-Democratic Programme of 1891', in *MECW*, Vol. 27, p. 227.

** '*Klassenkampf gegen den Krieg! Material zum Fall Liebknecht*' ['The Class Struggle Against the War! Material on the Liebknecht Case']. Printed for private circulation only, p. 67. – *Lenin*

Centre) *as early as March 1915!!* But eight and a half months later, Kautsky again comes forward with the proposal to 'reconcile' the militant masses with the opportunist, counter-revolutionary party – and he wants to do this with a few revolutionary-sounding phrases!!

War is often useful in exposing what is rotten and discarding the conventionalities.

Let us compare the British Fabians with the German Kautskyites. Here is what a *real* Marxist, Frederick Engels, wrote about the former on 18 January 1893:

> … a band of careerists who have understanding enough to realise the inevitability of the social revolution, but who could not possibly entrust this gigantic task to the raw proletariat alone… Fear of the revolution is their fundamental principle. (Letters to Sorge, p. 390.)*

And on 11 November 1893, he wrote:

> … these haughty bourgeois who kindly condescend to emancipate the proletariat from above if only it would have sense enough to realise that such a raw, uneducated mass cannot liberate itself and can achieve nothing without the kindness of these clever lawyers, writers and sentimental old women. (ibid., p. 401.)**

In theory Kautsky looks down upon the Fabians with the contempt of a Pharisee for a poor sinner, for he swears by 'Marxism'. But what actual difference is there between the two? Both signed the Basel Manifesto, and both treated it as Wilhelm II treated Belgian neutrality. But Marx all his life castigated those who strove to quench the revolutionary spirit of the workers.

Kautsky has put forward his new theory of 'ultra-imperialism' in opposition to the revolutionary Marxists. By this he means that the "rivalries of national finance capitals" are to be superseded by the "joint exploitation of the world by international finance capital." (*Die Neue Zeit*, 30 April 1915.) But he adds: "We do not as yet have sufficient data to decide whether this new

---

* See Engels, 'Letter to A Sorge', 18 January 1893, in *MECW*, Vol. 50, p. 83.
** See Engels, 'Letter to A Sorge', 11 November 1893, ibid, pp. 229-30.

phase of capitalism is possible." On the grounds of the mere assumption of a "new phase", which he does not even dare declare definitely "possible", the inventor of this "phase" rejects his own revolutionary declarations as well as the revolutionary tasks and revolutionary tactics of the proletariat – rejects them *now*, in the "phase" of a crisis, which *has already broken out*, the phase of war and the unprecedented aggravation of class antagonisms! Is this not Fabianism at its most abominable?

Axelrod, the leader of the Russian Kautskyites, says:

> The centre of gravity of the problem of internationalising the proletarian movement for emancipation is the internationalisation of everyday practice, [for example] labour protection and insurance legislation must become the object of the workers' international organisation and action. (Axelrod, *The Crisis of Social-Democracy*, Zürich, 1915, pp. 39-40.)

Not only Legien, David and the Webbs, but even Lloyd George himself, and Naumann, Briand and Milyukov would quite obviously subscribe to such "internationalism". As in 1912, Axelrod is quite prepared to utter the most revolutionary phrases for the very distant future, if the future International "comes out [against the governments in the event of war] and raises a revolutionary storm". How brave we are! But when it comes to supporting and developing the incipient revolutionary ferment among the masses *now*, Axelrod says that these tactics of revolutionary mass action

> … would be justified to some extent if we were on the very eve of the social revolution, as was the case in Russia, for example, where the student demonstrations of 1901 heralded the approaching decisive battles against absolutism…

At the present moment, however, all that is "utopia", "Bakuninism", etc. This is fully in the spirit of Kolb, David, Südekum and Legien.

What dear old Axelrod forgets is that in 1901 nobody in Russia knew, or could have known, that the first 'decisive battle' would take place four years later – please note, *four* years later – and that it would be '*in*decisive'. Nevertheless, we revolutionary Marxists alone were right at that time: we ridiculed the Krichevskys and Martynovs, who called for an immediate assault. We merely advised the workers to kick out the opportunists everywhere and to exert every effort to support, sharpen and extend the demonstrations and other mass revolutionary action. The present situation in Europe is absolutely similar. It would be absurd to call for an 'immediate' assault; but it would be a shame to call oneself a Social-Democrat and not to advise the workers to break with the opportunists and exert all their efforts to strengthen, deepen, extend and sharpen the incipient revolutionary movement and demonstrations. Revolution never falls ready-made from the skies, and when revolutionary ferment starts no one can say whether and when it will lead to a 'real', 'genuine' revolution. Kautsky and Axelrod are giving the workers old, shop-worn, counter-revolutionary advice. Kautsky and Axelrod are feeding the masses with hopes that the *future* International will surely be revolutionary, but they are doing this for the sole purpose of protecting, camouflaging and prettifying the *present* domination of the counter-revolutionary elements – the Legiens, Davids, Vanderveldes and Hyndmans. Is it not obvious that 'unity' with Legien and co. is the best means of preparing the 'future' revolutionary International?

"It would be folly to strive to convert the world war into civil war", declares *David*, the leader of the German opportunists (*Die Sozialdemokratie und der Weltkrieg*, 1915, p. 172), in reply to the manifesto of the Central Committee of our Party, 1 November 1914. This manifesto says, *inter alia*:

> However difficult that transformation may seem at any given moment, socialists will never relinquish systematic, persistent and undeviating preparatory work in this direction now that war has become a fact.*

(This passage is also quoted by David, p. 171.) A month before David's book appeared, our Party published its resolutions defining

---

* Lenin, 'The War and Russian Social-Democracy', in this volume, p. 17.

"systematic preparation" as follows: (1) refusal to vote for credits; (2) disruption of the class truce; (3) formation of illegal organisations; (4) support for solidarity manifestations in the trenches; (5) support for all revolutionary mass action.*

David is almost as brave as Axelrod. In 1912, he did not think that reference to the Paris Commune in anticipation of the war was "folly".

Plekhanov, a typical representative of the Entente social-chauvinists, takes the same view of revolutionary tactics as David. He calls them a "farcical dream". But listen to *Kolb*, an avowed opportunist, who wrote:

> The consequence of the tactics of Liebknecht's followers would be that the struggle within the German nation would be brought up to boiling point. (*Die Sozialdemokratie am Scheidewege*, p. 50.)

But what is a struggle brought up to boiling point if not civil war?

If our Central Committee's tactics, which broadly coincide with those of the Zimmerwald Left, were "folly", "dreams", "adventurism", "Bakuninism" – as David, Plekhanov, Axelrod, Kautsky and others have asserted – they could never lead to a "struggle within a nation", let alone to a struggle brought up to boiling point. Nowhere in the world have anarchist phrases brought about a struggle within a nation. But the facts indicate that precisely in 1915, as a result of the crisis produced by the war, revolutionary ferment among the masses is on the increase, and there is a spread of strikes and political demonstrations in Russia, strikes in Italy and in Britain, and hunger demonstrations and political demonstrations in Germany. Are these not the beginnings of revolutionary mass struggles?

The sum and substance of Social-Democracy's practical programme in this war is to support, develop, extend and sharpen mass revolutionary action, and to set up illegal organisations, for without them there is no way of telling the truth to the masses of people even in the

---

* See Lenin, 'The Conference of the RSDLP Groups Abroad', in this volume, p. 35.

'free' countries. The rest is either lies or mere verbiage, whatever its trappings of opportunist or pacifist theory.*

When we are told that these "Russian tactics" (David's expression) are not suitable for Europe, we usually reply by pointing to the facts. On 30 October, a delegation of Berlin women comrades called on the Party's Presidium in Berlin, and stated that

> ... now that we have a large organising apparatus it is much easier to distribute illegal pamphlets and leaflets and to organise 'banned meetings' than it was under the Anti-Socialist Law... Ways and means are not lacking, but the will evidently is. (*Berner Tagwacht*, 1915, No. 271.)**

Had these bad comrades been led astray by the Russian 'sectarians', etc.? Is it these comrades who represent the real *masses*, or is it Legien and Kautsky? Legien, who in his report on 27 January 1915 fumed against the "anarchistic" idea of forming underground organisations; or Kautsky, who has become such a counter-revolutionary that on 26 November, *four* days before the 10,000-strong demonstration in Berlin, he denounced street demonstrations as "adventurism"!!

We've had enough of empty talk, and of prostituted 'Marxism' *à la* Kautsky! After twenty-five years of the Second International, after the Basel Manifesto, the workers will no longer believe fine words. Opportunism is rotten-ripe; it has been transformed into social-chauvinism and has definitely deserted to the bourgeois camp. It has severed its spiritual and political ties with Social-Democracy. It will also break off its organisational ties. The workers

---

* At the International Women's Congress held in Bern in March 1915, the representatives of the Central Committee of our Party urged that it was absolutely necessary to set up illegal organisations. This was rejected. The British women laughed at this proposal and praised British 'liberty'. But a few months later British newspapers, like the *Labour Leader*, reached us with blank spaces, and then came the news of police raids, confiscation of pamphlets, arrests and Draconian sentences imposed on comrades who had spoken in Britain about peace, nothing but peace! – *Lenin*

** *Berner Tagwacht* (*Berne Reveille*) – organ of the Social-Democratic Party of Switzerland, published in Bern from 1893.

are already demanding 'illegal' pamphlets and 'banned' meetings, i.e. underground organisations to support the revolutionary mass movement. Only when 'war against war' is conducted on these lines does it cease to be empty talk and becomes Social-Democratic work. In spite of all difficulties, setbacks, mistakes, delusions and interruptions, this work will lead humanity to the victorious proletarian revolution.

Speech Delivered at an International Meeting in Bern

8 February 1916

Editors note:

This speech was delivered at an international rally during the enlarged meeting of the executive of the Zimmerwald group in Bern.

* * *

Comrades! The European war has been raging for more than eighteen months. With every passing day, and month, it becomes clearer and clearer to the mass of the workers that the Zimmerwald Manifesto expressed the truth when it declared that talk about 'defence of the fatherland' and suchlike phrases are nothing but a capitalist fraud. It is becoming more evident every day that this is *a war between capitalists, between big robbers*, who are quarrelling over who is to get the largest slice, who is to plunder the greatest number of countries, and to suppress and enslave the greatest number of nations.

It may sound incredible, especially to Swiss comrades, but it is true, nevertheless, that *in Russia*, too, it is not only murderous tsarism, or the capitalists, but also a section of the so-called, or former, socialists who are saying that Russia is fighting a 'defensive war', that she is only fighting against the German invasion. But the whole world knows that for decades tsarism has been oppressing more than 100 million people belonging to other nationalities in Russia, and that for decades Russia has been pursuing a predatory policy towards China, Persia, Armenia and Galicia. *Neither Russia, nor Germany, nor any other Great Power for that matter has any right to claim that it is waging a 'defensive war'*; all the Great Powers are waging a capitalist imperialist war, a predatory war, a war for the oppression of small and foreign nations, a war for the profits of the capitalists, who have been converting proletarian blood and the horrible sufferings of the masses into the pure gold of their immense fortunes.

Four years ago, in November 1912, when it had become quite clear that war was in the offing, representatives of the socialist parties of the world met at the International Socialist Congress in Basel. Even at that time, there was no room for doubt that the impending war would be a war between the Great Powers, between these great plunderers and that the responsibility would fall upon the governments and the capitalist class of *all* the Great Powers. This truth was openly stated in the Basel Manifesto, which was adopted *unanimously* by the socialist parties of the world. *The Basel Manifesto says nothing at all about a 'defensive war' or 'defence of the fatherland'.* It castigates the governments and the bourgeoisie of *all* the Great Powers, without exception. It says openly that war would be the greatest of crimes, that the workers consider it a crime to shoot at each other, and that the horrors of war and the indignation these would rouse among the workers would inevitably lead to a *proletarian revolution.*

When the war actually broke out, it became evident that its character had been correctly defined at Basel. But the socialist and labour organisations were not unanimous in carrying out the Basel decisions; they split. We find that the socialist and labour organisations are now split into two big camps in all countries of the world. The smaller section, the leaders, functionaries and officials, have betrayed socialism and have sided with their governments. The other section, to which the mass of class-conscious workers belong, continues to gather its forces and to fight against the war and for the proletarian revolution.

The views of this latter section were expressed in the Zimmerwald Manifesto, to mention one document.

In Russia, from the very beginning of the war, the workers' *deputies* in the Duma waged a determined revolutionary struggle against the war and the tsarist monarchy. Five workers' deputies – Petrovsky, Badayev Muranov, Shagov and Samoilov – distributed revolutionary leaflets against the war and carried on persistent revolutionary agitation. The tsarist government ordered the arrest of these five deputies; they were tried and sentenced to exile in Siberia for life. The leaders of the working class of Russia have languished in Siberia for months, but their cause has not been defeated; their work is being continued along the same lines by the class-conscious workers of all Russia.

Comrades! You have heard speakers from various countries who have told you about the workers' revolutionary struggle against the war. I merely want to add another example, that of the United States of America, the biggest and richest country. Its capitalists are now making enormous profits out of the European war. And they are also campaigning for war. They are saying that America, too, must prepare to enter the war, and that hundreds of millions of the people's dollars must be siphoned off into new armaments, into armaments without end. A section of the socialists in America have also responded to this false, criminal call. Let me read a statement by Comrade *Eugene Debs*, a most popular leader of the American socialists, and the presidential candidate of the American Socialist Party.

In the 11 September 1915 issue of the American weekly, *Appeal to Reason*, No. 32, he says:

> I am not a capitalist soldier; I am a proletarian revolutionist. I do not belong to the regular army of the plutocracy, but to the irregular army of the people. I refuse to obey any command to fight from the ruling class... I am opposed to every war but one; I am for that war with heart

and soul, and that is the worldwide war of the social revolution. In that war I am prepared to fight in any way the ruling class may make necessary...

This is what *Eugene Debs*, the American Bebel, the beloved leader of the American workers, is telling them.

This goes to show once again, comrades, that *the rallying of the working-class forces is truly under way in all countries of the world*. War inflicts horrible sufferings on the people, but we must not, and we have no reason at all, to despair of the future.

The millions of victims who will fall in the war, and as a consequence of the war, will not have died in vain. The millions who are starving, the millions who are sacrificing their lives in the trenches, are not only suffering, they are also gathering strength; they are pondering over the real causes of the war; they are becoming more determined and are acquiring a clearer revolutionary understanding. In *all* countries of the world there is growing discontent among the masses and greater ferment; there are strikes, demonstrations and protests against the war. *This is an earnest of the proletarian revolution against capitalism that is bound to follow the European war.*

Proposals Submitted by the Central Committee of the RSDLP to the Second Socialist Conference at Kienthal

Written February – March 1916

Editors note:

A second Socialist Zimmerwald Conference took place during the war, on 24-30 April 1916, in the small town of Kienthal in neutral Switzerland. Forty-three delegates from ten countries attended. The Left was stronger at this conference than it had been at Zimmerwald. The Kienthal Manifesto is reproduced on p. 397.

* * *

Theses on points 5, 6, 7a, 7b, and 8 of the agenda: the struggle to end the war; the attitude towards the problems of peace, *parliamentary* action and mass struggles, and the convocation of the International Socialist Bureau.

The International Socialist Committee, in its notice convening the Second Conference, invited the affiliated organisations to discuss the above questions, and to send in their proposals. In reply to this invitation our Party submits the following theses.

* * *

1. Just as all war is but a continuation by violent means of the politics which the belligerent states and their ruling classes had been conducting for many years, sometimes for decades, before the outbreak of war, so the peace that ends any war can be nothing but a consideration and a record of the actual changes brought about in the relation of forces in the course of and as a result of the war.

2. As long as the foundations of present, i.e. bourgeois, social relations remain intact, an imperialist war can lead only to an imperialist peace, i.e. to greater, more extensive and more intense oppression of weak nations and countries by finance capital, which grew to gigantic proportions not only in the period prior to the war, but also during the war. The objective content of the policies pursued by the bourgeoisie and the governments of *both* groups of Great Powers before and during the war leads to intensified economic oppression, national enslavement and political reaction. Therefore, provided the bourgeois social system remains, the peace that follows upon the war, whatever its outcome, must perpetuate this worsening of the economic and political condition of the masses.

   To assume that a democratic peace may emerge from an imperialist war is, in theory, to substitute vulgar phrases for an historical study of the policies conducted before and during that war. In practice, it is to deceive the masses of the people by beclouding their political consciousness, by covering up and prettifying the real policies pursued by the ruling classes to prepare the ground for the coming peace, by concealing from the masses the main thing, namely, that a democratic peace is impossible without a whole series of revolutions.

3. Socialists do not refuse to fight for reform. Even now, for example, they must vote in parliament for improvements, however slight, in the condition of the masses, for increased relief to the inhabitants of the devastated areas, for the lessening

of national oppression, etc. But it is sheer bourgeois deception to preach reforms as a solution for problems for which history and the actual political situation demand revolutionary solutions. That is precisely the kind of problems the present war has brought to the fore. These are the fundamental questions of imperialism, i.e. the very existence of capitalist society, the questions of postponing the collapse of capitalism by a re-division of the world to correspond to the new relation of forces among the 'Great' Powers, which in the last few decades have developed, not only at fantastic speed, but – and this is particularly important – also with extreme unevenness. Real political activity working a change in the relation of social forces, and not merely deceiving the masses with words, is now possible only in one of two forms – either helping 'one's own' national bourgeoisie to rob other countries (and calling this 'defence of the fatherland' or 'saving the country'), or assisting the proletarian socialist revolution fostering and stirring up the ferment which is beginning among the masses in all the belligerent countries, aiding the incipient strikes and demonstrations, etc., extending and sharpening these as yet feeble expressions of revolutionary mass struggle into a general proletarian assault to overthrow the bourgeoisie.

Just as all the social-chauvinists are at present deceiving the people by covering up the real, i.e. imperialist, policy of the capitalists, which is being continued in the present war with hypocritical phrases about the 'dishonest' attack and 'honest' defence on the part of this or that group of predatory capitalists, so phrases about a 'democratic peace' serve only to deceive the people, as if the coming peace, which is already being prepared by the capitalists and diplomats, could 'simply' abolish 'dishonest' attacks and restore 'honest' relations, and as if it would not be a continuation, a development, and a perpetuation of this very imperialist policy, i.e. a policy of financial looting, colonial robbery, national oppression, political reaction and intensified capitalist exploitation in every form.

What the capitalists and their diplomats now need is 'socialist' servants of the bourgeoisie to deafen, dupe and drug the people with talk about a 'democratic peace' so as to cover up the real policy of the bourgeoisie, making it difficult for the masses to realise the real nature of this policy and diverting them from the revolutionary struggle.

4. The 'democratic' peace programme, in drafting which prominent representatives of the Second International are now engaged, is precisely such a piece of bourgeois deception and hypocrisy. For example, Huysmans at the Arnhem Congress and Kautsky in *Die Neue Zeit*, the most authoritative, official, and 'theoretical' spokesmen of this International, formulated this programme as suspension of the revolutionary struggle until the imperialist governments have concluded peace; in the meantime, there are verbal repudiation of annexations and indemnities, verbal recognition of the self-determination of nations, democratisation of foreign politics, courts of arbitration to examine international conflicts between states, disarmament, a United States of Europe, etc., etc. The real political significance of this 'peace programme' was revealed with particular force by Kautsky, when, to prove the "unanimity of the International" on this question, he cited the unanimous adoption by the London Conference (February 1915) and the Vienna Conference (April 1915) of the main point of this programme, namely, the "independence of nations". Kautsky, before the whole world, thus openly gave his sanction to the deliberate deception of the people perpetrated by the social-chauvinists, who combine verbal, hypocritical recognition of 'independence' or self-determination of nations, recognition that binds no one and leads nowhere, with support for 'their own' governments in the imperialist war, notwithstanding the fact that on *both* sides the war is *accompanied by* systematic violations of the 'independence' of weak nations and is being

waged *for the purpose* of consolidating and extending their oppression.

Objectively, this cheap 'peace programme' reinforces the subjection of the working class to the bourgeoisie by 'reconciling' the workers, who are beginning to develop a revolutionary struggle, with their chauvinist leaders, by underplaying the gravity of the crisis in the socialist movement to bring back the pre-war state of affairs in the socialist parties which led the majority of the leaders to desert to the bourgeoisie. The fact that this 'Kautskyite' policy is clothed in plausible phrases and that it is being conducted not only in Germany but in all countries, makes it all the more dangerous for the proletariat. In Britain, for instance, this policy is being pursued by the majority of the leaders; in France, by Longuet, Pressemane and others; in Russia, by Axelrod, Martov, Chkheidze and others; Chkheidze is screening the chauvinist idea of 'defence of the country' in the present war with the 'save the country' phrase, paying lip-service to Zimmerwald, on the one hand, and on the other, praising Huysmans' notorious Arnhem speech in an official declaration by his group; but neither from the floor of the Duma nor in the press has he actually opposed the participation of the workers in the war industries committees, and remains on the staff of newspapers advocating such participation. In Italy, a similar policy is being pursued by Treves: see the threat made by *Avanti!*, the Central Organ of the Italian Socialist Party, of 5 March 1916, to expose Treves and other 'reformist-possibilists', to expose those "who resorted to every means to prevent the Party Executive and Oddino Morgari from taking action to secure unity at Zimmerwald and to create a new International", etc., etc.

5. The chief of the 'peace questions' at the present time is that of annexations. It most strikingly reveals the now prevailing socialist hypocrisy and the tasks of real socialist propaganda and agitation.

It is necessary to explain the meaning of annexations, and why and how socialists must fight against them, Not *every* appropriation of 'foreign' territory can be described as an annexation, for, generally speaking, socialists favour the abolition of frontiers between nations and the formation of larger states; nor can every disturbance of the *status quo* be described as an annexation, for this would be extremely reactionary and a mockery of the fundamental concepts of the science of history; nor can every military seizure of territory be called annexation, for socialists cannot repudiate violence and wars in the interests of the majority of the population. Annexation must apply only to the appropriation of territory *against the will* of the population of that territory; in other words, the concept of annexation is inseparably bound up with the concept of self-determination of nations.

The present war, however – precisely because it is an imperialist war insofar as *both* groups of belligerent powers are concerned – inevitably had to and did give rise to the phenomenon of the bourgeoisie and the social-chauvinists 'fighting' violently against annexations when this is done by an enemy state. This kind of 'struggle against annexations' and this kind of 'unanimity' on the question of annexation is plainly sheer hypocrisy. Obviously, the French socialists who defend war over Alsace-Lorraine, and the German socialists who do not demand freedom for Alsace-Lorraine, for German Poland, etc., to separate from Germany, and the Russian socialists who describe the war being waged to return Poland to tsarist bondage as a war to 'save the country', and who demand that Polish territory be annexed to Russia in the name of 'peace without annexations' etc., etc., are *in fact annexationists.*

To prevent the struggle against annexations from being mere hypocrisy, or an empty phrase, to make it really educate the masses in the spirit of internationalism, the question must be presented in such a way as to open the eyes of the masses to the fraud in this matter of annexations, instead of covering it up.

It is not enough for the socialists of each country to pay lip-service to the equality of nations or to orate, swear and invoke the name of God to witness their opposition to annexations. The socialists of every country must demand immediate and unconditional *freedom to secede* for the colonies and nations oppressed by *their own* 'fatherland'.

Without this condition, recognition of the self-determination of nations and principles of internationalism would, even in the Zimmerwald Manifesto, remain a dead letter, at best.

6. The socialists' 'peace programme', and their programme of 'struggle to end the war', must proceed from the exposure of the lie of the 'democratic peace', the pacific intentions of the belligerents, etc., now being spread among the people by demagogic ministers, pacifist bourgeois, social-chauvinists and Kautskyites in all countries. Any 'peace programme' will deceive the people and be a piece of hypocrisy, unless its principal object is to explain to the masses the need for a revolution, and to support, aid and develop the mass revolutionary struggles breaking out everywhere (ferment among the masses, protests, fraternisation in the trenches, strikes, demonstrations, letters from the front to relatives – for example, in France – urging them not to subscribe to war loans, etc., etc.).

It is the duty of socialists to support, extend and intensify every popular movement to end the war. But it is actually being fulfilled only by those socialists who, like Liebknecht, in their parliamentary speeches, call upon the soldiers to lay down their arms, and preach revolution and transformation of the imperialist war into a civil war for socialism.

The positive slogan we muse put forward to draw the masses into revolutionary struggle and to explain the necessity for revolutionary measures to make a 'democratic' peace possible, is that of repudiation of debts incurred by states.

It is not enough to hint at revolution, as the Zimmerwald Manifesto does, by saying that the workers must make

sacrifices for their own and not for someone else's cause. The
masses must be shown their road clearly and definitely. They
must know where to go and why. That mass revolutionary
actions during the war, if successfully developed, can lead
only to the transformation of the imperialist war into a civil
war for socialism is obvious, and it is harmful to conceal this
from the masses. On the contrary, this aim must be indicated
clearly, no matter how difficult its attainment may appear
now, while we are still at the beginning of the road. It is not
enough to say, as the Zimmerwald Manifesto does, that "the
capitalists lie when they speak about defence of the fatherland"
in the present war, and that the workers in their revolutionary
struggle must ignore their country's military situation; it is
necessary to state clearly what is merely hinted at here, namely,
that not only the capitalists, but also the social-chauvinists and
the Kautskyites lie when they allow the term 'defence of the
fatherland' to be applied in the present, imperialist war and that
revolutionary action during the war is impossible unless 'one's
own' government is threatened with defeat; it must be stated
clearly that every defeat of the government in a reactionary
war facilitates revolution, which alone is capable of bringing
about a lasting and democratic peace. Finally, the masses must
be told that unless they themselves create illegal organisations
and a press that is free from military censorship, i.e. an illegal
press, it will be quite impossible to render serious support to the
incipient revolutionary struggle, to develop it, to criticise some
of its steps, to correct its errors and systematically to extend and
sharpen it.

7. On the question of socialist parliamentary action, it must
    be borne in mind that the Zimmerwald resolution not only
    expresses sympathy for the five Social-Democratic deputies in
    the State Duma, who belong to our Party, and who have been
    sentenced to exile to Siberia, but also expresses its solidarity
    with their tactics. It is impossible to recognise the revolutionary

struggle of the masses while resting content with exclusively legal socialist activity in parliament. This can only arouse legitimate dissatisfaction among the workers, cause them to desert Social-Democracy for anti-parliamentary anarchism or syndicalism. It must be stated clearly and publicly that Social-Democratic members of parliament must use their position not only to make speeches in parliament, but also to render all possible aid outside parliament to the underground organisation and the revolutionary struggle of the workers, and that the masses themselves, through their illegal organisation, must supervise these activities of their leaders.

8. The question of the convocation of the International Socialist Bureau boils down to a fundamental question of principle, i.e. whether the old parties and the Second International can be united. Every step forward taken by the international labour movement along the road mapped out by Zimmerwald shows more and more clearly the inconsistency of the position adopted by the Zimmerwald majority; for, on the one hand, it identifies the policy of the old parties and of the Second International with *bourgeois* policy in the labour movement, with a policy which does not pursue the interests of the proletariat, but of the bourgeoisie (for example, the statement in the Zimmerwald Manifesto that the "capitalists" lie when they speak of "defence of the fatherland" in the present war; also the still more definite statements contained in the circular of the International Socialist Committee of 10 February 1916);* on the other hand, the International Socialist Committee is afraid of a break with the International Socialist Bureau and has promised officially to dissolve when the Bureau reconvenes.

---

* The 'Appeal to All Affiliated Parties and Groups', adopted unanimously by the enlarged meeting of the ISC in Bern on 5-9 February 1916. The delegation of the RSDLP Central Committee, led by Lenin, stated that it regarded the 'Appeal' as a step forward as compared with the decisions of the First International Socialist Conference at Zimmerwald, but did not find it satisfactory on all points.

We state that not only was such a promise never voted on, but it was never even discussed in Zimmerwald.

The six months since Zimmerwald have proved that *actual* work in the spirit of Zimmerwald – not empty phrases but work – is bound up throughout the world with the split that is becoming deeper and wider. In Germany, illegal anti-war leaflets are being printed despite the Party's decisions, i.e. schismatically. When Deputy Otto Rühle, Karl Liebknecht's closest friend, said openly that there were actually two parties in existence, one helping the bourgeoisie and the other fighting against it, many, including the Kautskyites, reviled him, but no one refuted him. In France, Bourderon, a member of the Socialist Party, is a determined opponent of a split, but at the same time he submits a resolution to his Party disapproving of the Party's Central Committee and of the parliamentary group (*desapprouver Comm. Adm. Perm. et Gr. Parl.*), which, if adopted, would certainly have caused an immediate split. In Britain, T Russell Williams, a member of the ILP, writing in the moderate *Labour Leader*, openly admits that a split is inevitable and finds support in letters written by local functionaries. The example of America is perhaps still more instructive, because even there, in a neutral country, two irreconcilably hostile trends in the Socialist Party have become revealed: on the one hand, the adherents of so-called 'preparedness', i.e. war, militarism and navalism, and on the other, socialists like Eugene Debs, former presidential candidate from the Socialist Party, who openly preaches civil war for socialism, precisely in connection with the coming war.

Actually, there is already a split throughout the world; two entirely irreconcilable working-class policies in relation to the war have crystallised. We must not close our eyes to this fact; to do so would only result in confusing the masses of the workers, in befogging their minds, in hindering the revolutionary mass struggle with which all Zimmerwaldists officially sympathise, and in strengthening the influence over the masses of those leaders whom the International Socialist Committee, in its circular of 10 February 1916, openly accuses of "misleading" the masses and of hatching a "plot", (*Pakt*) *against* socialism.

It is the social-chauvinists and Kautskyites of all countries who will undertake the task of restoring the bankrupt International Socialist Bureau. The task of the socialists is to explain to the masses the inevitability of a split with those who pursue a bourgeois policy under the flag of socialism.

Peace Without Annexations and the Independence of Poland as Slogans of the Day in Russia

29 February 1916

The Bern resolution of our Party declared:

> Pacifism, the preaching of peace in the abstract is one of the means of duping the working class... At the present time, the propaganda of peace unaccompanied by a call for revolutionary mass action can only sow illusions and demoralise the proletariat, for it makes the proletariat believe that the bourgeoisie is humane and turns it into a plaything in the hands of the secret diplomacy of the belligerent countries. (See *Sotsial-Demokrat*, No. 40 and *Socialism and War*)*

The opponents of our point of view on the question of peace, who are numerous among Russian political *émigrés*, but not among the Russian workers, have never taken the trouble to analyse these propositions. Theoretically irrefutable, these propositions have now received striking and practical confirmation from the turn of events in our country.

---

* Both texts are included in this edition: 'The Conference of the RSDLP Groups Abroad', p. 35; *Socialism and War*, p. 57.

Rabocheye Utro, the organ of the Petersburg legalist-liquidators, which is ideologically supported by the Organising Committee, is known to have adopted a social-chauvinist, 'defencist' position from its very first issue. It published the 'defencist' manifestos of the Petersburg and Moscow social-chauvinists. Both manifestos express, *inter alia*, the idea of 'peace without annexations', and *Rabocheye Utro*, No. 2, which particularly stresses that slogan, prints it in italics and calls it "a line which provides the country with a way out of the impasse". It is calumny to call us chauvinists, the paper seems to say; we fully accept the most "democratic", even "truly socialist" slogan of "peace without annexations".

No doubt Nicholas the Bloody finds it to his advantage to have his loyal subjects put forward such a slogan at the present time. Tsarism, supported by the landowners and the bourgeoisie, led its armies to rob and enslave Galicia (not to mention the treaty to carve up Turkey, etc.). The armies of the no less predatory German imperialists repulsed the Russian robbers and expelled them, not only from Galicia, but also from 'Russian Poland'. (In this struggle for the interests of both these cliques, hundreds of thousands of Russian and German workers and peasants fell on the field of battle.) The 'peace without annexations' slogan thus turned out to be an excellent "plaything in the hands of the secret diplomacy" of tsarism; the latter can now say: "Look, we are the aggrieved; we have been robbed, deprived of Poland; we are opposed to annexations!"

How much the *Rabocheye Utro* social-chauvinists 'relish' the part of lackeys to tsarism is particularly evident from an article in the first issue of that paper, entitled 'Polish Emigration'.

> The months of the war [we read] have engendered in the minds of broad sections of the Polish people a strong urge to independence.

The implication is that there was no such thing before the war.

> The mass [this seems to be a misprint and ought to read "the idea, the thought", etc.] of Poland's national independence has triumphed in the social consciousness of broad sections of Polish democrats... The

Polish question looms relentlessly in all its magnitude before Russian democrats...

"The Russian liberals" refuse to give straightforward answers to the vexed questions "of Poland's independence".

Nicholas the Bloody, Khvostov, Chelnokov, Milyukov and co. are, of course, entirely in favour of Poland's independence – they are heart and soul in favour of it *now*, when this slogan, *put into practice*, means *victory* over Germany, the country which has deprived Russia of Poland. Let us not forget that before the war, the creators of 'the Stolypin labour party'* were wholly and unreservedly opposed to the slogan of the self-determination of nations and Poland's right to secede, putting up the opportunist Semkovsky for the noble purpose of defending the tsarist oppression of Poland. Now that Poland has been taken from Russia they are *in favour* of the 'independence' of Poland (from Germany; but on this point they maintain a discreet silence).

You social-chauvinist gentlemen will not deceive the class-conscious workers of Russia! Your *1915* 'Octobrist'** slogan on 'independence for Poland' and 'peace without annexations' is in practice servility to tsarism, which at the present time, in February 1916 to be precise, is sorely in need of camouflaging *its* war with fine words about 'peace without annexations' (driving Hindenburg out of Poland) and 'independence for Poland' (independence from Wilhelm, but dependence upon Nicholas II).

The Russian Social-Democrat who has not forgotten his Programme argues differently. Russian democracy, he will say, having Great-Russian democracy in mind first of all and most of all, for it alone in Russia has always enjoyed freedom of language – this democracy has undoubtedly *gained* from the fact that *at*

---

* A group of Mensheviks who adapted themselves to the Stolypin regime and tried to obtain the tsarist government's permission to set up a legal 'labour' party, with the price being abandonment of the programme of the RSDLP.

** The Octobrists or the League of October Seventeenth were a counter-revolutionary party of the big merchants and industrialists, and big landowners who ran their estates on capitalist lines.

present Russia does not oppress Poland and hold it by force. The
Russian proletariat has undoubtedly gained from the fact that it
no longer oppresses a people it had helped to oppress yesterday.
German democracy has undoubtedly lost, for as long as the German
proletariat tolerates Germany's oppression of Poland it will remain
in a position which is worse than that of a slave – it is the position
of a flunkey helping to keep others enslaved. Only the German
Junkers and the bourgeoisie have really gained.

Hence, Russian Social-Democrats must expose the *deception*
of the people by tsarism, *now that* the slogans of 'peace without
annexations' and 'independence for Poland' are being played up
in Russia, for in the present situation both these slogans express
and justify the desire to continue the war. We must say: No war
over Poland! The Russian people do not want to become Poland's
oppressor again!

But how can we help liberate Poland from Germany? Isn't it
our duty to do so? Of course it is, though never by supporting
the imperialist war waged by Russia, be it tsarist, or bourgeois, or
even bourgeois-republican, but by *supporting* the revolutionary
proletariat of Germany, by supporting those elements in the Social-
Democratic Party of Germany who are fighting against the *counter-
revolutionary* labour party of the Südekums, and Kautsky and co.
Kautsky very recently demonstrated his counter-revolutionary
nature in a most flagrant manner; on 26 November 1915, he
described street demonstrations as "*adventurism*" (just as Struve
said on the eve of 9 January 1905, that there were no revolutionary
people in Russia), and yet, on 30 November 1915, 10,000 working
women demonstrated in Berlin!

All those who do not want to back the freedom of nations,
the right of nations to self-determination, *hypocritically*, in the
Südekum, Plekhanov, Kautsky fashion, but want to do this *sincerely*,
must *oppose* the war over the oppression of Poland, they must
stand *for* the right of the nations Russia is *now* oppressing, namely,
the Ukraine, Finland, etc., to secede from Russia. Those who do
not wish to be social-chauvinists *in deed* must support only those

elements in the socialist parties of all countries which are working, directly, immediately, right now, for the proletarian revolution in their own countries.

Not 'peace without annexations', but peace to the cottages, war on the palaces; peace to the proletariat and the working people, war on the bourgeoisie!

The Junius Pamphlet

July 1916

At last there has appeared in Germany, illegally, without any adaptation to the despicable Junker censorship, a Social-Democratic pamphlet dealing with questions of the war! The author, who evidently belongs to the 'Left-radical' wing of the Party, takes the name of Junius (which in Latin means junior) and gives his pamphlet the title: *The Crisis of Social-Democracy*.* Appended are the 'Theses on the Tasks of International Social-Democracy', which have already been submitted to the Bern ISC (International Socialist Committee) and published in No. 3 of its *Bulletin*; the theses were drafted by the *Internationale* group, which in the spring of 1915 published one issue of a magazine under that title (with articles by Zetkin, Mehring, R Luxemburg, Thalheimer, Duncker, Ströbel and others), and which in the winter of 1915-16 convened a conference of Social-Democrats from all parts of Germany where these theses were adopted.**

The pamphlet, the author says in the introduction dated 2 January 1916, was written in April 1915, and published "without any alteration". "Outside circumstances" had prevented its earlier

---

* The anonymous author was in fact Rosa Luxemburg.
** The all-Germany conference of Left-wing Social-Democrats was held at Karl Liebknecht's home in Berlin on 1 January 1916.

publication. The pamphlet is devoted not so much to the "crisis of Social-Democracy" as to an analysis of the war, to refuting the legend of it being a war for national liberation, to proving that it is an imperialist war on the part of Germany as well as on the part of the other Great Powers, and to a revolutionary criticism of the behaviour of the official party. Written, in a very lively style, Junius' pamphlet has undoubtedly played and will continue to play an important role in the struggle against the ex-Social-Democratic Party of Germany, which has deserted to the bourgeoisie and the Junkers, and we extend our hearty greetings to the author.

To the Russian reader who is familiar with the Social-Democratic literature in Russian published abroad in 1914-16, the Junius pamphlet does not offer anything new in principle. In reading this pamphlet and comparing the arguments of this German revolutionary Marxist with what has been stated, for example, in the manifesto of the Central Committee of our Party (September-November 1914),[*] in the Bern resolutions (March 1915)[**] and in the numerous commentaries on them, it only becomes clear that Junius' arguments are very incomplete and that he makes two mistakes. Before proceeding with a criticism of Junius' faults and errors we must strongly emphasise that this is done for the sake of self-criticism, which is so necessary to Marxists, and of submitting to an all-round test the views which must serve as the ideological basis of the Third International. On the whole, the Junius pamphlet is a splendid Marxist work, and its defects are, in all probability, to a certain extent accidental.

The chief defect in Junius' pamphlet, and what marks a definite step backward compared with the legal (although immediately suppressed) magazine, *Internationale*, is its silence regarding the connection between social-chauvinism (the author uses neither this nor the less precise term social-patriotism) and opportunism. The author rightly speaks of the "capitulation" and collapse of the German Social-Democratic Party and of the "treachery" of its

---

[*] Lenin, 'The War and Russian Social-Democracy', in this volume, p. 9.
[**] Lenin, 'The Conference of the RSDLP Groups Abroad', in this volume, p. 35.

official leaders", but he goes no further. The *Internationale*, however, did criticise the 'Centre', i.e. Kautskyism, and quite properly poured ridicule on it for its spinelessness, its prostitution of Marxism and its servility to the opportunists. This same magazine *began* to expose the true role of the opportunists by revealing, for example, the very important fact that on 4 August 1914, the opportunists came out with an ultimatum, a ready-made decision to vote *for* war credits in *any* case. Neither the Junius pamphlet nor the theses say *anything* about opportunism or about Kautskyism! This is wrong from the standpoint of theory, for it is impossible to *account for* the "betrayal" without linking it up with opportunism as a *trend* with a long history behind it, the history of the whole Second International. It is a mistake from the practical political standpoint, for it is impossible either to understand the "crisis of Social-Democracy", or overcome it, without clarifying the meaning and the role of *two trends* – the openly opportunist trend (Legien, David, etc.) and the tacitly opportunist trend (Kautsky and co.). This is a step backward compared with the historic article by Otto Rühle in *Vorwärts* of 12 January 1916, in which he directly and openly pointed out that a split in the Social-Democratic Party of Germany was *inevitable* (the editors of *Vorwärts* replied by repeating honeyed and hypocritical Kautskyite phrases, for they were unable to advance a single material argument to disprove the assertion that there were *already* two parties in existence, and that these two parties could not be reconciled). It is astonishingly inconsistent, because the *Internationale*'s thesis No. 12 *directly* states that it is necessary to create a "new" International, owing to the "treachery" of the "official representatives of the socialist parties of the leading countries" and their "adoption of the principles of bourgeois imperialist policies". It is clearly quite absurd to suggest that the old Social-Democratic Party of Germany, or the party which tolerates Legien, David and co., would participate in a "new" International.

We do not know why the *Internationale* group took this step backward. A very great defect in revolutionary Marxism in Germany as a whole is its lack of a compact illegal organisation that would systematically pursue its own line and educate the masses in the spirit of the new tasks; such an organisation would also have to take a definite stand on opportunism and Kautskyism. This is all the more necessary now, since the German revolutionary Social-Democrats have been deprived of their last two daily papers; the one in Bremen (*Bremer Bürger-Zeitung*), and the one in Brunswick (*Volksfreund*), both of which have gone over to the Kautskyites. The International Socialists of Germany (ISD) group *alone* clearly and definitely remains at its post.

Some members of the *Internationale* group have evidently once again slid down into the morass of unprincipled Kautskyism. Ströbel, for instance, went so far as to drop a curtsey in *Die Neue Zeit* to Bernstein and Kautsky! And only the other day, on 15 July 1916, he had an article in the papers entitled 'Pacifism and Social-Democracy', in which he defends the most vulgar type of Kautskyite pacifism. As for Junius, he strongly opposes Kautsky's fantastic schemes like "disarmament", "abolition of secret diplomacy", etc. There may be two trends within the *Internationale* group: a revolutionary trend and a trend inclining to Kautskyism.

The first of Junius' erroneous propositions is embodied in the fifth thesis of the *Internationale* group.

> National wars are no longer possible in the epoch (era) of this unbridled imperialism. National interests serve only as an instrument of deception, in order to place the working masses at the service of their mortal enemy, imperialism.

The beginning of the fifth thesis, which concludes with the above statement, discusses the nature of the *present* war as an imperialist war. It may be that this negation of national wars generally is either an oversight, or an accidental overstatement in emphasising the perfectly correct idea that the *present* war is an imperialist war, not a national war. This is a mistake that must be examined, for various Social-Democrats, in view of the false assertions that the *present* war is a national war, have likewise mistakenly denied the possibility of *any* national war.

Junius is perfectly right in emphasising the decisive influence of the "imperialist atmosphere" of the *present* war, in maintaining that behind Serbia stands Russia, "behind Serbian nationalism stands Russian imperialism", and that the participation of, say, Holland in the war would *likewise* be imperialist, for, first, Holland would be defending her colonies and, second, would be allied with one of the *imperialist* coalitions. That is irrefutable in respect to the *present* war. And when Junius stresses what for him is most important, namely, the struggle against the "phantom of national war", "which at present holds sway over Social-Democratic policies" (p. 81), then it must be admitted that his views are both correct and fully to the point.

The only mistake, however, would be to exaggerate this truth, to depart from the Marxist requirement of concreteness, to apply the appraisal of this war to all wars possible under imperialism, to ignore the national movements *against* imperialism. The sole argument in defence of the thesis, "national wars are no longer possible", is that the world has been divided among a small group of 'great' imperialist powers and for that reason any war, even if it starts as a national war, is *transformed* into an imperialist war involving the interest of one of the imperialist powers or coalitions (Junius, p. 81).

The fallacy of this argument is obvious. That all dividing lines, both in nature and society, are conventional and dynamic, and that *every* phenomenon might, under certain conditions, be transformed into its opposite, is, of course, a basic proposition of Marxist dialectics. A national war *might* be transformed into an imperialist war *and vice versa*. Here is an example: the wars of the Great French Revolution began as national wars and indeed were such. They were revolutionary wars – the defence of the great revolution against a coalition of counter-revolutionary monarchies. But when Napoleon founded the French Empire and subjugated a number of big, viable and long-established national European states, these national wars of the French became imperialist wars and *in turn* led to wars of national liberation *against* Napoleonic imperialism.

Only a sophist can disregard the difference between an imperialist and a national war on the grounds that one *might* develop into the other. Not infrequently have dialectics served – and the history of Greek philosophy is an example – as a bridge to sophistry. But we remain dialecticians and we combat sophistry not by denying the possibility of all transformations in general, but by analysing the *given* phenomenon in its concrete setting and development.

Transformation of the present imperialist war of 1914-16 into a national war is highly improbable, for the class that represents *progressive* development is the proletariat which is objectively striving to transform it into a civil war against the bourgeoisie. Also this: there is no very considerable difference between the forces of the two coalitions, and international finance capital has created a reactionary bourgeoisie everywhere. But such a transformation should *not* be proclaimed *impossible*: *if* the *European* proletariat remains impotent, say, for twenty years; *if* the present war *ends* in victories like Napoleon's and in the subjugation of a number of viable national states; *if* the transition to socialism of non-European imperialism (primarily Japanese and American) is also held up for twenty years by a war between these two countries, for example, then a great national war in Europe would be possible. It would hurl Europe *back* several decades. That is improbable. But *not* impossible, for it is undialectical, unscientific and theoretically wrong to regard the course of world history as smooth and always in a forward direction, without occasional gigantic leaps back.

Further. National wars waged by colonies and semi-colonies in the imperialist era are not only probable but *inevitable*. About 1,000 million people, or *over half* of the world's population, live in the colonies and semi-colonies (China, Turkey, Persia). The national liberation movements there are either already very strong, or are growing and maturing. Every war is the continuation of politics by other means. The continuation of national liberation politics in the colonies will *inevitably* take the form of national wars *against* imperialism. Such wars *might* lead to an imperialist war of the present 'great' imperialist powers, but on the other hand they might not. It will depend on many factors.

Example: Britain and France fought the Seven Years' War for the possession of colonies. In other words, they waged an imperialist war (which is possible on the basis of slavery and primitive capitalism as well as on the basis of modern highly developed capitalism). France suffered defeat and lost some of her colonies. Several years later there began the national liberation war of the North American States against Britain alone. France and Spain, then in possession of some parts of the present United States, concluded a friendship treaty with the States in rebellion against Britain. This they did out of hostility to Britain, i.e. in their own imperialist interests. French troops fought the British on the side of the American forces. What we have here is a national liberation war in which imperialist rivalry is an auxiliary element, one that has no serious importance. This is the very opposite to what we see in the war of 1914-16 (the national element in the Austro-Serbian War is of no serious importance compared with the all-determining element of imperialist rivalry). It would be absurd, therefore, to apply the concept imperialism indiscriminately and conclude that national wars are "impossible". A national liberation war, waged, for example, by an alliance of Persia, India and China against one or more of the imperialist powers, is both possible and probable, for it would follow from the national liberation movements in these countries. The transformation of such a war into an imperialist war between the present-day imperialist powers would depend upon very many concrete factors, the emergence of which it would be ridiculous to guarantee.

Third, even in Europe, national wars in the imperialist epoch cannot be regarded as impossible. The 'epoch of imperialism' made the present war an imperialist one and it inevitably engenders new imperialist wars (until the triumph of socialism). This 'epoch' has made the policies of the present great powers thoroughly imperialist, but it by no means precludes national wars on the part of, say, small (annexed or nationally-oppressed) countries *against* the imperialist powers, just as it does not preclude large-scale national movements in Eastern Europe. Junius takes a very sober view of Austria, for example, giving due consideration not only to 'economic' factors, but to the peculiar political factors. He notes "Austria's intrinsic lack of cohesion" and recognises that the "Habsburg monarchy is not the political organisation of a bourgeois state, but only a loose syndicate of several cliques of social parasites", and that "the liquidation of Austria-Hungary is, from the historical standpoint, only the continuation of the disintegration of Turkey and, at the same time, a requirement of the historical process of development". Much the same applies to some of the Balkan countries and Russia. And if the 'great' powers are altogether exhausted in the present war, or if the revolution in Russia triumphs, national wars and even victorious national wars, are quite possible. Practical intervention by the imperialist powers is *not* always feasible. That is one point. Another is that the superficial view that the war of a small state against a giant is hopeless should be countered by the observation that even a hopeless war is a war just the same. Besides, certain factors operating within the 'giant' countries – the outbreak of revolution, for example – can turn a 'hopeless' war into a very 'hopeful' one.

We have dwelt in detail on the erroneous proposition that "national wars are no longer possible" not only because it is patently erroneous from the theoretical point of view – it would certainly be very lamentable if the 'Left' were to reveal a light-hearted attitude to Marxist theory at a time when the establishment of the Third International is possible only on the basis of unvulgarised Marxism. But the mistake is very harmful also from the standpoint of practical politics, for it gives rise to the absurd propaganda of 'disarmament', since it is alleged that there can be no wars except reactionary wars. It also gives rise to the even more ludicrous and downright reactionary attitude of indifference to national movements. And such an attitude becomes chauvinism when members of the 'great' European nations, that is, the nations which oppress the mass of small and colonial peoples, declare with a pseudo-scientific air:

"national wars are no longer possible"! National wars *against* the imperialist powers are not only possible and probable; they are inevitable, *progressive* and *revolutionary*, though of course, to be *successful*, they require either the concerted effort of huge numbers of people in the oppressed countries (hundreds of millions in our example of India and China), or a *particularly* favourable conjuncture of international conditions (e.g. the fact that the imperialist powers cannot interfere, being paralysed by exhaustion, by war, by their antagonism, etc.), or the *simultaneous* uprising of the proletariat against the bourgeoisie in one of the big powers (this latter eventuality holds first place as the most desirable and favourable for the victory of the proletariat).

It would be unfair, however, to accuse Junius of indifference to national movements. At any rate, he remarks that among the sins of the Social-Democratic parliamentary group was its silence on the death sentence passed on a native leader in the Cameroons on charges of 'treason' (evidently he attempted to organise an uprising against the war). Elsewhere Junius especially emphasises (for the benefit of the Legiens, Lensches and the other scoundrels who are still listed as 'Social-Democrats') that colonial peoples must be regarded as nations along with all the others. Junius clearly and explicitly states:

> Socialism recognised the right of every nation to independence and freedom, to independent mastery of its destinies [...] international socialism recognises the right of free, independent and equal nations, but it is only socialism that can create such nations, and only it can realise the right of nations to self-determination. And this socialist slogan [Junius justly remarks] serves, like all other socialist slogans, not to justify the existing order of things, but to indicate the way forward, and to stimulate the proletariat in its active revolutionary policy of transformation... (pp. 77-8.)

It would be a grave mistake indeed to believe that all the German Left Social-Democrats have succumbed to the narrow-mindedness and caricature of Marxism now espoused by certain Dutch and

Polish Social-Democrats who deny the right of nations to self-determination even under socialism. But the *specific*, Dutch-Polish, roots of *this* mistake we shall discuss elsewhere.

Another fallacious argument is advanced by Junius on the question of defence of the fatherland. This is a cardinal political question during an imperialist war. Junius has strengthened us in our conviction that our Party has indicated the only correct approach to this question; the proletariat is opposed to defence of the fatherland in this imperialist war *because* of its predatory, slave-owning, reactionary character, *because* it is possible and necessary to oppose to it (and to strive to convert it into) civil war for socialism. Junius, however, while brilliantly exposing the imperialist character of the present war as distinct from a national war, makes the very strange mistake of trying to drag a national programme into the *present*, *non*-national, war. It sounds almost incredible, but there it is.

The official Social-Democrats, both of the Legien and of the Kautsky stripe, in their servility to the bourgeoisie (who have been making the most noise about foreign 'invasion' in order to deceive the mass of the people as to the imperialist character of the war), have been particularly assiduous in repeating this 'invasion' argument. Kautsky, who now assures naive and credulous people (incidentally, through Spectator, a member of the Russian Organising Committee) that he joined the opposition at the end of 1914, continues to use this 'argument'! To refute it, Junius quotes extremely instructive examples from history, which prove that "invasion and class struggle are not contradictory in bourgeois history, as official legend has it, but that one is the means and the expression of the other". For example, the Bourbons in France invoked foreign invaders against the Jacobins; the bourgeoisie in 1871 invoked foreign invaders against the Commune. In his *Civil War in France*, Marx wrote:

> The highest heroic effort of which old society is still capable is national war; and this is now proved to be a mere governmental humbug,

intended to defer the struggle of classes, and to be thrown aside as soon as that class struggle bursts out into civil war.*

"The classical example for all times", says Junius, referring to 1793, "is the Great French Revolution." From all this, he draws the following conclusion:

> The century of experience thus proves that it is not a state of siege, but relentless class struggle, which rouses the self-respect, the heroism and the moral strength of the mass of the people, and serves as the country's best protection and defence against the external enemy.

Junius' practical conclusion is this:

> Yes, it is the duty of the Social-Democrats to defend their country during a great historical crisis. But the grave guilt that rests upon the Social-Democratic Reichstag group consists in their having given the lie to their own solemn declaration, made on 4 August 1914, "In the hour of danger we will not leave our fatherland unprotected". They *did* leave the fatherland unprotected in the hour of its greatest peril. For their first duty to the fatherland in that hour was to show the fatherland what was really behind the present imperialist war; to sweep away the web of patriotic and diplomatic lies covering up this encroachment on the fatherland; to proclaim loudly and clearly that both victory and defeat in the present war are equally fatal for the German people; to resist to the last the throttling of the fatherland due to the state of siege; to proclaim the necessity of immediately arming the people and of allowing the people to decide the question of war and peace; resolutely to demand a permanent session of the people's representatives for the whole duration of the war in order to guarantee vigilant control over the government by the people's representatives, and control over the people's representatives by the people; to demand the immediate abolition of all restrictions on political rights, for only a free people can successfully defend its country; and finally, to oppose the imperialist war programme, which is to preserve Austria and

---

* Marx, *The Civil War in France*, Wellred Books, 2021, p. 71.

Turkey, i.e. perpetuate reaction in Europe and in Germany, with the old, truly national programme of the patriots and democrats of 1848, the programme of Marx, Engels and Lassalle – the slogan of a united, Great German Republic.

This is the banner that should have been unfurled before the country, which would have been a truly national banner of liberation, which would have been in accord with the best traditions of Germany and with the international class policy of the proletariat. […]

Hence, the grave dilemma – the interests of the fatherland or the international solidarity of the proletariat – the tragic conflict which prompted our parliamentarians to side, "with a heavy heart", with the imperialist war, is purely imaginary, it is a bourgeois nationalist fiction. On the contrary, there is complete harmony between the interests of the country and the class interests of the proletarian International, both in time of war and in time of peace; both war and peace demand the most energetic development of the class struggle, the most determined fight for the Social-Democratic programme.

This is how Junius argues. The fallacy of his argument is strikingly evident, and since the tacit and avowed lackeys of tsarism, Plekhanov and Chkhenkeli, and perhaps even Martov and Chkheidze, may gloatingly seize upon Junius' words, not for the purpose of establishing theoretical truth, but for the purpose of wriggling, covering up their tracks and throwing dust into the eyes of the workers, we must in greater detail elucidate the *theoretical* source of Junius' error.

He suggests that the imperialist war should be "opposed" with a national programme. He urges the advanced class to turn its face to the past and not to the future! In France, in Germany and in the whole of Europe, it was a *bourgeois*-democratic revolution that, *objectively*, was on the order of the day in 1793 and 1848. Corresponding to this *objective* historical situation was the "truly national", i.e. the national *bourgeois* programme of the then existing democracy; in 1793, this programme was carried out by the most revolutionary elements of the bourgeoisie and the plebeians, and in 1848 it was proclaimed by Marx in the name of the whole of progressive democracy. *Objectively*, the feudal and dynastic wars were then opposed by revolutionary-democratic wars, by wars for national liberation. This was the content of the historical tasks of that epoch.

At the present time, the *objective* situation in the biggest advanced states of Europe is different. Progress, if we leave out for the moment the possibility of temporary steps backward, can be made only in the direction of *socialist* society, only in the direction of the *socialist revolution*. From the standpoint of progress, from the standpoint of the progressive class, the imperialist bourgeois war, the war of highly developed capitalism, can, *objectively*, be opposed only with a war *against* the bourgeoisie, i.e. primarily civil war for power between the proletariat and the bourgeoisie; for *unless* such a war is waged, serious progress is *impossible*; this may be followed – only under certain special conditions – by a war to defend the socialist state against bourgeois states. That is why the Bolsheviks (fortunately, very few, and quickly handed over by us to the *Prizyv* group) who were ready to adopt the point of view of conditional defence, i.e. defence of the fatherland on condition that there was a victorious revolution and the victory of a republic in Russia, were true to the *letter* of Bolshevism, but betrayed its *spirit*; for being drawn into the imperialist war of the leading European powers, Russia would *also* be waging an imperialist war, even under a republican form of government!

In saying that the class struggle is the best means of defence against invasion, Junius applies Marxist dialectics only half way, taking one step on the right road and immediately deviating from it. Marxist dialectics call for a concrete analysis of each specific historical situation. It is true that class struggle is the best means of defence against invasion *both* when the bourgeoisie is overthrowing feudalism, and when the proletariat is overthrowing the bourgeoisie. Precisely because it is true with regard to *every* form of class oppression, it is *too general*, and therefore, *inadequate* in the present *specific* case. Civil war against the bourgeoisie is *also* a form of class struggle, and only this form of class struggle would have saved Europe (the whole of Europe, not only one country) from the peril of invasion. The 'Great German Republic', had it existed in 1914-16, would *also* have waged an *imperialist* war.

Junius came very close to the correct solution of the problem and to the correct slogan: civil war against the bourgeoisie for socialism; but, as if afraid to speak the whole truth, he turned *back*, to the fantasy of a 'national war' in 1914, 1915 and 1916. If we examine the question not from the theoretical angle but from the purely practical one, Junius' error remains just as evident. The whole of bourgeois society, all classes in Germany, including the peasantry, were *in favour* of war (in all probability *the same* was the case in Russia – at least a majority of the well-to-do and middle peasantry and a very considerable portion of the poor peasants were evidently under the spell of bourgeois imperialism). The bourgeoisie was armed to the teeth. Under such circumstances, to 'proclaim' the programme of a republic, a permanent parliament, election of officers by the people (the 'armed nation'), etc., would have meant, *in practice, 'proclaiming' a revolution* (with the wrong revolutionary programme!).

In the same breath, Junius quite rightly says that a revolution cannot be 'made'. Revolution was on the order of the day in the 1914-16 period, it was hidden in the depths of the war, was *emerging* out of the war. This should have been *'proclaimed'* in the name of the revolutionary class, and *its* programme should have been fearlessly and fully announced – socialism is impossible in time of war without civil war against the arch-reactionary, criminal bourgeoisie, which condemns the people to untold disaster. Systematic, consistent, practical measures should have been planned, *which could be carried out no matter at what* pace the revolutionary crisis might develop, and which would be in line with the maturing revolution. These measures are indicated in our Party's resolution: (1) voting against war credits; (2) violation of the 'class truce'; (3) creation of an illegal organisation; (4) fraternisation among the soldiers; (5) support for all the revolutionary actions of the masses.* The success of *all* these steps *inevitably* leads to civil war.

The promulgation of a great historical programme was undoubtedly of tremendous significance; not the old national German programme, which became obsolete in 1914, 1915 and 1916, but the proletarian internationalist and socialist programme. "You, the bourgeoisie, are fighting for plunder; we, the workers of *all* the belligerent countries, declare war upon you for, socialism" – that's the sort of speech that should have been delivered in the parliaments on 4 August 1914, by socialists who had not betrayed the proletariat, as the Legiens, Davids, Kautskys, Plekhanovs, Guesdes, Sembats, etc., had done.

Evidently Junius' error is due to two kinds of mistakes in reasoning. There is no doubt that Junius is decidedly opposed to the imperialist war and is decidedly *in favour* of revolutionary tactics; and all the gloating of the Plekhanovs over Junius' 'defencism' cannot wipe out this *fact*. Possible and probable calumnies of this kind must be answered promptly and bluntly.

But, first, Junius has not completely rid himself of the 'environment' of the German Social-Democrats, even the Leftists, who are afraid of a split, who are afraid to follow revolutionary slogans to their logical conclusions.** This is a false fear, and the Left Social-Democrats of Germany must and *will* rid themselves of it. They *are sure to do so* in the course of their struggle against the social-chauvinists. The fact is that they are fighting against *their*

---

* See Lenin, 'The Conference of the RSDLP Groups Abroad', in this volume, p. 35.

** We find the same error in Junius' arguments about which is better, victory or defeat? His conclusion is that both are equally bad (ruin, growth of armaments, etc.). This is the point of view not of the revolutionary proletariat, but of the pacifist petty bourgeoisie. If one speaks about the 'revolutionary intervention' of the proletariat – of this both Junius and the theses of the *Internationale* group speak, although unfortunately in terms that are too general – one *must* raise the question from *another* point of view, namely: (1) Is 'revolutionary intervention' possible without the risk of defeat? (2) Is it possible to scourge the bourgeoisie and the government of one's *own* country without taking that risk? (3) Have we not always asserted, and does not the historical experience of reactionary wars prove, that defeats help the cause of the revolutionary class? – *Lenin*

own social-chauvinists resolutely, firmly and *sincerely*, and this is the tremendous, the fundamental difference in principle between them and the Martovs and Chkheidzes, who, with one hand (*à la* Skobelev) unfurl a banner bearing the greeting, "To the Liebknechts of All Countries", and with the other hand tenderly embrace Chkhenkeli and Potresov!

Secondly, Junius apparently wanted to achieve something in the nature of the Menshevik 'theory of stages', of sad memory; he wanted to *begin* to carry out the revolutionary programme from the end that is 'more suitable', 'more popular' and more acceptable to the *petty bourgeoisie*. It is something like a plan 'to outwit history', to outwit the philistines. He seems to say, surely, nobody would oppose a *better* way of defending the real fatherland; and the real fatherland is the Great German Republic, and the best defence *is* a militia, a permanent parliament, etc. Once it was accepted, that programme would automatically lead to the next stage – to the socialist revolution.

Probably, it was reasoning of this kind that consciously or semi-consciously determined Junius' tactics. Needless to say, such reasoning is fallacious. Junius' pamphlet conjures up in our mind the picture of a *lone* man who has no comrades in an illegal organisation accustomed to thinking out revolutionary slogans to their conclusion and systematically educating the masses in their spirit. But this shortcoming – it would be a grave error to forget this – is not Junius' personal failing, but the result of the weakness of *all* the German Leftists, who have become entangled in the vile net of Kautskyite hypocrisy, pedantry and 'friendliness' for the opportunists. Junius' adherents have managed, *in spite* of their isolation, to *begin* the publication of illegal leaflets and to start the war against Kautskyism. They will succeed in going further along the right road.

A Caricature of Marxism and Imperialist Economism (extract)

Written August – October 1916

"No one can discredit revolutionary Social-Democracy as long as it does not discredit itself." That maxim always comes to mind, and must always be borne in mind, when any major theoretical or tactical proposition of Marxism is victorious, or even placed on the order of the day, and when, *besides* outright and resolute opponents, it is assailed by friends who hopelessly discredit and disparage it and turn it into a caricature. That has happened time and again in the history of the Russian Social-Democratic movement. In the early 'nineties, the victory of Marxism in the revolutionary movement was attended by the emergence of a caricature of Marxism in the shape of Economism, or 'strikeism'. The Iskrists would not have been able to uphold the fundamentals of proletarian theory and policy, either against petty-bourgeois Narodism or bourgeois liberalism, without long years of struggle against Economism. It was the same with Bolshevism, which triumphed in the mass labour movement in 1905 due, among other things, to correct application of the boycott of the tsarist Duma slogan in the autumn of 1905, when the key battles of the

Russian revolution were being fought.* Bolshevism had to face –
and overcome by struggle – another caricature in 1908-10, when
Alexinsky and others noisily opposed participation in the Third
Duma.**

It is the same today too. Recognition of the *present* war as
imperialist and emphasis on *its* close connection with the imperialist
era of capitalism encounters not only resolute opponents, but also
irresolute friends, for whom the word 'imperialism' has become all
the rage. Having *memorised* the word, they are offering the workers
hopelessly confused theories and reviving many of the old mistakes
of the old Economism. Capitalism has triumphed – *therefore* there
is no need to bother with political problems, the old Economists
reasoned in 1894 – 1901, falling into rejection of the political
struggle in Russia. Imperialism has triumphed – *therefore* there is
no need to bother with the problems of political democracy, reason
the present-day imperialist Economists. Kievsky's article, printed
above, merits attention as a sample of these sentiments, as one such
caricature of Marxism, as the first attempt to provide anything
like an integral literary exposition of the vacillation that has been
apparent in certain circles of our Party abroad since early 1915.***

If imperialist Economism were to spread among the Marxists,
who in the present great crisis of socialism have resolutely come out
against social-chauvinism and for revolutionary internationalism,
that would be a very grave blow to our trend – and to our Party.
For it would discredit it from within, from its own ranks, would
make it a vehicle of caricaturised Marxism. It is therefore necessary

---

*   The Bulygin Duma, named after Alexander Bulygin, Minister of the Interior,
    had no legislative functions, permitted merely to discuss certain questions as a
    consultative body under the tsar.
** The reference is to the Otzovists and Ultimatumists. The Otzovists demanded
    the recall of the Social-Democratic deputies from the Third Duma and the
    cessation of activities in legal organisations such as the trade unions, the
    cooperatives, etc. Ultimatumism was a variant of Otzovism.
*** 'The Proletariat and the "Right of Nations to Self-Determination", in the Era of
    Finance Capital', published in August 1916 by the Bolshevik Georgy Pyatakov,
    whose pseudonym was 'P Kievsky'.

to thoroughly discuss at least the most important of Kievsky's numerous errors, regardless of how 'uninteresting' this may be, and regardless of the fact, also, that all too often we shall have to tediously explain elementary truths which the thoughtful and attentive reader has learned and understood long since from our literature of 1914 and 1915.

We shall begin with the 'central' point of Kievsky's disquisitions in order to immediately bring to the reader the very 'substance' of this new trend of imperialist Economism.

1. The Marxist Attitude Towards War and 'Defence of the Fatherland'

Kievsky is convinced, and wants to convince his reader, that he "disagrees" *only* with §9 of our Party Programme dealing with national self-determination. He is very angry and tries to refute the charge that on the question of democracy he is departing from the fundamentals of Marxism *in general*, that he has "betrayed" (the angry quotation marks are Kievsky's) Marxism on basic issues. But the point is that the moment our author begins to discuss his allegedly partial disagreement on an individual issue, the moment he adduces his arguments, considerations, etc., he immediately reveals that he is deviating from Marxism all along the line. Take §b (Section 2) of his article. "This demand [i.e. national self-determination] directly [!!] leads to social-patriotism", our author proclaims, explaining that the "treasonous" slogan of fatherland defence follows "quite [!] logically [!] from the right of nations to self-determination"... In his opinion, self-determination implies

> ... sanctioning the treason of the French and Belgian social-patriots, who are defending this independence [the national independence of France and Belgium] with arms in hand! They are *doing* what the supporters of 'self-determination' only advocate [...] Defence of the fatherland belongs to the arsenal of our worst enemies [...] We categorically refuse to understand how one can *simultaneously* be against defence of the fatherland and for self-determination, against the fatherland and for it.

That's Kievsky. He obviously has not understood our resolutions against the fatherland defence slogan in the present war. It is therefore necessary again to explain the meaning of what is so clearly set out in our resolutions.

The resolution our Party adopted at its Bern Conference in March 1915, 'On the Defence of the Fatherland Slogan', begins with the words: "*The present war is, in substance...*"*

That the resolution deals with the *present* war could not have been put more plainly. The words "in substance" indicate that we must distinguish between the apparent and the real, between appearance and substance, between the word and the deed. The purpose of all talk about defence of the fatherland in this war is mendaciously to present as national the imperialist war of 1914-16, waged for the division of colonies, the plunder of foreign lands, etc. And to obviate even the slightest possibility of distorting our views, we added to the resolution a special paragraph on "*genuinely* national wars", which "took place *especially* (especially does not mean exclusively!) between 1789 and 1871".

The resolution explains that the "basis" of these "genuinely" national wars was a "long process of mass national movements, of a struggle against absolutism and feudalism, the overthrow of national oppression..."

Clear, it would seem. The present imperialist war stems from the general conditions of the imperialist era and is not accidental, not an exception, not a deviation from the general and typical. Talk of defence of the fatherland is therefore a deception of the people, for this war is *not* a national war. In a *genuinely* national war the words 'defence of the fatherland' are *not* a deception and *we are not opposed to it*. Such (genuinely national) wars took place "especially" in 1789 – 1871, and our resolution, while not denying by a single word that they are possible now too, explains how we should distinguish a genuinely national from an imperialist war covered by deceptive national slogans. Specifically, in order to distinguish the two we must examine whether the "basis" of

---

* Lenin, 'The Conference of the RSDLP Groups Abroad', in this volume, p. 36.

the war is a "long process of mass national movements", the "overthrow of national oppression". The resolution on 'pacifism' expressly states:

> Social-Democrats cannot overlook the positive significance of revolutionary wars, i.e. not imperialist wars, but such as were conducted, for instance [note: "for instance"], between 1789 and 1871 with the aim of doing away with national oppression…

Could our 1915 Party resolution speak of the national wars waged from 1789 to 1871 and say that we do not deny the positive significance of such wars if they were not considered possible today too? Certainly not.

A commentary, or popular explanation, of our Party resolutions is given in the Lenin and Zinoviev pamphlet *Socialism and War*.* It plainly states, on page 5, that "socialists have regarded wars 'for the defence of the fatherland', or 'defensive' wars, as legitimate, progressive and just" *only* in the sense of "overthrowing alien oppression". It cites an example: Persia against Russia, "*etc.*", and says:

> These would be just, and defensive wars, irrespective of who would lie the first to attack; any socialist would wish the oppressed, dependent and unequal states victory over the oppressor, slave-holding and predatory 'Great' Powers.

The pamphlet appeared in August 1915 and there are German and French translations. Kievsky is fully aware of its contents. And never, on no occasion, has he or anyone else challenged the resolution on the defence of the fatherland slogan, or the resolution on pacifism, or their interpretation in the pamphlet. Never, not once! We are therefore entitled to ask: are we slandering Kievsky when we say that he has absolutely failed to understand Marxism if, beginning with March 1915, he has not challenged our Party's views on the war, whereas now, in August 1916, in an article on self-determination, i.e. on a supposedly partial issue, he reveals an amazing lack of understanding of a *general* issue?

---

*   In the present volume, p. 57.

Kievsky says that the fatherland defence slogan is "treasonous". We can confidently assure him that *every* slogan is and always will be "treasonous" *for those* who mechanically repeat it without understanding its meaning, without giving it proper thought, *for those* who merely memorise the words without analysing their implications.

What, generally speaking, is 'defence of the fatherland'? Is it a scientific concept relating to economics, politics, etc.? No. It is a much bandied about current expression, sometimes simply a philistine phrase, intended to *justify the war*. Nothing more. Absolutely nothing! The term 'treasonous' can apply only in the sense that the philistine is capable of justifying *any* war by pleading 'we are defending our fatherland', whereas Marxism, which does not degrade itself by stooping to the philistine's level, requires an historical analysis of each war in order to determine whether or not *that particular* war can be considered progressive, whether it serves the interests of democracy and the proletariat and, in *that sense*, is legitimate, just, etc.

The 'defence of the fatherland' slogan is all too often unconscious philistine justification of war and reveals inability to analyse the meaning and implications of a particular war and see it in historical perspective.

Marxism makes that analysis and says: *if* the 'substance' of a war is, *for example*, the overthrow of alien oppression (which was *especially* typical of Europe in 1789 – 1871), then such a war is progressive as far as the oppressed state or nation is concerned. *If*, however, the 'substance' of a war is redivision of colonies, division of booty, plunder of foreign lands (and such is the war of 1914-16), then all talk of defending the fatherland is 'sheer deception of the people'.

How, then, can we disclose and define the 'substance' of a war? War is the continuation of policy. Consequently, we must examine the policy pursued prior to the war, the policy that led to and brought about the war. If it was an imperialist policy, i.e. one designed to safeguard the interests of finance capital and rob and oppress colonies and foreign countries, then the war stemming from that policy is imperialist. If it was a national liberation policy, i.e. one expressive of the mass movement against national oppression, then the war stemming from that policy is a war of national liberation.

The philistine does not realise that war is 'the continuation of policy', and consequently limits himself to the formula that 'the enemy has attacked us', 'the enemy has invaded my country', without stopping to think *what issues* are at stake in the war, *which* classes are waging it, and with *what* political objects. Kievsky stoops right down to the level of such a philistine when he declares that Belgium has been occupied by the Germans, and hence, from the point of view of self-determination, the "Belgian social-patriots are right", or: the Germans have occupied part of France, hence, "Guesde can be satisfied", for "what is involved is territory populated by his nation" (and not by an alien nation).

For the philistine the important thing is *where* the armies stand, who is winning at *the moment*. For the Marxist the important thing is *what issues* are at stake in *this* war, during which first one, then the other army may be on top.

What is the present war being fought over? The answer is given in our resolution (based on the policy the belligerent powers pursued for decades prior to the war). England, France and Russia are fighting to keep the colonies they have seized, to be able to rob Turkey, etc. Germany is fighting to take over these colonies and to be able herself to rob Turkey, etc. Let us suppose even that the Germans take Paris or St. Petersburg. Would that change the nature of the present war? Not at all. The Germans' purpose – and more important, the policy that would bring it to realisation if they were to win – is to seize the colonies, establish domination over Turkey, annex areas populated by other nations, for instance, Poland, etc. It is definitely not to bring the French or the Russians under foreign domination. The real essence of the present war is not national but imperialist. In other words, it is not being fought to enable one side to overthrow national oppression, which the other side is trying to maintain. It is a war between two groups of oppressors, between two freebooters over the division of their booty, over who shall rob Turkey and the colonies.

In short: a war *between* imperialist Great Powers (i.e. powers that oppress a whole number of nations and enmesh them in dependence on finance capital, etc.), or *in alliance* with the Great Powers, is an imperialist war. Such is the war of 1914-16. And in *this* war 'defence of the fatherland' is a deception, an attempt to justify the war.

A war *against* imperialist, i.e. oppressing, powers by oppressed (for example, colonial) nations is a genuine national war. It is possible today too. 'Defence of the fatherland' in a war waged by an oppressed nation against a foreign oppressor is not a deception. Socialists are *not* opposed to 'defence of the fatherland' in *such* a war.

National self-determination is the same as the struggle for complete national liberation, for complete independence, against annexation, and socialists *cannot* – without ceasing to be socialists – reject *such* a struggle in whatever form, right down to an uprising or war.

Kievsky thinks he is arguing against Plekhanov: it was Plekhanov who pointed to the link between self-determination and 'defence of the fatherland'! Kievsky *believed* Plekhanov that the link was *really* of the kind Plekhanov made it out to be. And having believed him, Kievsky took fright and decided that he must reject self-determination so as not to fall into Plekhanov's conclusions… There is great trust in Plekhanov, and great fright, but there is no trace of *thought* about the substance of Plekhanov's mistake!

The social-chauvinists plead self-determination in order to present this war as a national war. There is only one correct way of combating them: we must show that the war is being fought not to liberate nations, but to determine which of the great robbers will oppress *more* nations. To fall into negation of wars *really* waged for liberating nations is to present the worst possible caricature of Marxism. Plekhanov and the French social-chauvinists harp on the republic in France in order to justify its 'defence' against the German monarchy. If we were to follow Kievsky's line of reasoning, we would have to oppose either the republic or a war *really* fought to preserve the republic!! The German social-chauvinists point to universal suffrage and compulsory primary education in their country to justify its 'defence' against tsarism. If we were to follow Kievsky's line of reasoning, we would have to oppose either universal suffrage and compulsory primary education or a war *really* fought to safe guard political freedom against attempts to abolish it!

Up to the 1914-16 war, Karl Kautsky was a Marxist, and many of his major writings and statements will always remain models of Marxism. On 26 August 1910, he wrote in *Die Neue Zeit*, in reference to the imminent war:

> In a war between Germany and England the issue is not democracy, but world domination, i.e. exploitation of the world. That is not an issue on which Social-Democrats can side with the exploiters of their nation. (*Neue Zeit*, 28. Jahrg., Bd. 2, S. 776.)

There you have an excellent Marxist formulation, one that fully coincides with our own and fully exposes the *present-day* Kautsky, who has turned from Marxism to defence of social-chauvinism. It is a formulation (we shall have occasion to revert to it in other articles) that clearly brings out the principles underlying the Marxist attitude towards war. War is the continuation of policy. Hence, once there is a struggle for democracy, a war for democracy is *possible*. National self-determination is but one of the democratic demands and does not, in principle, differ from other democratic demands. 'World domination' is, to put it briefly, the substance of imperialist policy, of which imperialist war is the continuation. Rejection of 'defence of the fatherland' in a democratic war, *i.e.* rejecting participation in such a war, is an absurdity that has nothing in common with Marxism. To embellish imperialist war by applying to it the concept of 'defence of the fatherland', i.e. by presenting it as a democratic war, is to deceive the workers and side with the reactionary bourgeoisie.

The Military Programme of the Proletarian Revolution

September 1916

Editors note:

The 'Military Programme of the Proletarian Revolution' (in a letter Lenin refers to it as 'On Disarmament') was written in German and meant for publication in the Swiss, Swedish and Norwegian Left Social-Democratic press. However, it was not published at the time. Lenin somewhat re-edited it for publication in Russian which appeared with the name 'The 'Disarmament' Slogan' in *Sbornik Sotsial-Demokrata*, No. 2, December 1916.

The original, German text appeared in *Jugend-Internationale*, organ of the International League of Socialist Youth Organisations, Nos. 9 and 10, September and October 1917 under the heading '*Das Militärprogramm der proletarischen Revolution*'. The article was printed with this editorial foreword:

> In our day, when Lenin is one of the most spoken-of leaders of the Russian revolution, the following article by this veteran revolutionary stalwart, in which he sets out a large part of his political programme, is of especial interest. We received it shortly before his departure from Zürich in April 1917.

The heading was apparently given by the editors of *Jugend-Internationale*.

* * *

Among the Dutch, Scandinavian and Swiss revolutionary Social-Democrats who are combating the social-chauvinist lies about 'defence of the fatherland' in the present imperialist war, there have been voices in favour of replacing the old Social-Democratic minimum-programme demand for a 'militia', or 'the armed nation', by a new demand: 'disarmament'. The *Jugend-Internationale* has inaugurated a discussion on this issue and published, in No. 3, an editorial supporting disarmament. There is also, we regret to note, a concession to the 'disarmament' idea in R Grimm's latest theses. Discussions have been started in the periodicals *Neues Leben* and *Vorbote*.

Let us take a closer look at the position of the disarmament advocates.

I

Their principal argument is that the disarmament demand is the clearest, most decisive, most consistent expression of the struggle against all militarism and against all war.

But in this principal argument lies the disarmament advocates' principal error. Socialists cannot, without ceasing to be socialists, be opposed to all war.

Firstly, socialists have never been, nor can they ever be, opposed to revolutionary wars. The bourgeoisie of the imperialist 'Great' Powers has become thoroughly reactionary, and the war *this* bourgeoisie is now waging we regard as a reactionary, slave-owners' and criminal war. But what about a war *against* this bourgeoisie? A war, for instance, waged by peoples oppressed by and dependent upon this bourgeoisie, or by colonial peoples, for liberation? In §5 of the *Internationale* group theses we read: "National wars are no longer possible in the era of this unbridled imperialism." That is obviously wrong.

The history of the twentieth century, this century of 'unbridled imperialism', is replete with colonial wars. But what we Europeans, the imperialist oppressors of the majority of the world's peoples, with our habitual, despicable European chauvinism, call 'colonial wars' are often national wars, or national rebellions of these oppressed peoples. One of the main features of imperialism is that it accelerates capitalist development in the most backward countries, and thereby extends and intensifies the struggle against national oppression. That is a fact, and from it inevitably follows that imperialism must often give rise to national wars. *Junius*, who defends the above-quoted 'theses' in his pamphlet, says that in the imperialist era every national war against an imperialist Great Power leads to intervention of a rival imperialist Great Power. Every national war is thus turned into an imperialist war. But that argument is wrong, too. This *can* happen, but does not always happen. Many colonial wars between 1900 and 1914 did not follow that course. And it would be simply ridiculous to declare, for instance, that after the present war, if it ends in the utter exhaustion of all the belligerents, "there can be no" national, progress, revolutionary wars "of any kind", waged, say, by China in alliance with India, Persia, Siam, etc., against the Great Powers.

To deny all possibility of national wars under imperialism is wrong in theory, obviously mistaken historically, and tantamount to European chauvinism in practice: we who belong to nations that oppress hundreds of millions in Europe, Africa, Asia, etc., are invited to tell the oppressed peoples that it is 'impossible' for them to wage war against 'our' nations!

Secondly, civil war is just as much a war as any other. He who accepts the class struggle cannot fail to accept civil wars, which in every class society are the natural, and under certain conditions inevitable, continuation, development and intensification of the class struggle. That has been confirmed by every great revolution. To repudiate civil war, or to forget about it, is to fall into extreme opportunism and renounce the socialist revolution.

Thirdly, the victory of socialism in one country does not at one stroke eliminate all wars in general. On the contrary, it presupposes wars. The development of capitalism proceeds extremely unevenly in different countries. It cannot be otherwise under commodity production. From this it follows irrefutably that socialism cannot achieve victory simultaneously *in all* countries. It will achieve victory first in one or several countries, while the others will for some time remain bourgeois or pre-bourgeois. This is bound to create not only friction, but a direct attempt on the part of the bourgeoisie of other countries to crush the socialist state's victorious proletariat. In such cases, a war on our part would be a legitimate and just war. It would be a war for socialism, for the liberation of other nations from the bourgeoisie. Engels was perfectly right when, in his letter to Kautsky of 12 September 1882, he clearly stated that it was possible for *already victorious* socialism to wage "defensive wars". What he had in mind was defence of the victorious proletariat against the bourgeoisie of other countries.

Only after we have overthrown, finally vanquished and expropriated the bourgeoisie of the whole world, and not merely in one country, will wars become impossible. And from a scientific point of view it would be utterly wrong – and utterly un-revolutionary – for us to evade or gloss over the most important thing: crushing the resistance of the bourgeoisie – the most difficult task, and one demanding the greatest amount of fighting, in the *transition* to socialism. The 'social' parsons and opportunists are always ready to build dreams of future peaceful socialism. But the very thing that distinguishes them from revolutionary Social-Democrats is that they refuse to think about and reflect on the fierce class struggle and class *wars* needed to achieve that beautiful future.

We must not allow ourselves to be led astray by words. The term 'defence of the fatherland', for instance, is hateful to many because both avowed opportunists and Kautskyites use it to cover up and gloss over the bourgeois lie about the *present* predatory war. This is a fact. But it does not follow that we must no longer see through to the meaning of political slogans. To accept 'defence of the fatherland' in the present war is no more nor less than to accept it as a 'just' war, a war in the interests of the proletariat – no more nor less, we repeat, because invasions may occur in any war. It would be sheer folly to repudiate 'defence of the fatherland' *on the part* of oppressed nations in their wars *against* the imperialist Great Powers, or on the part of a victorious proletariat in *its* war against some Galliffet of a bourgeois state.*

Theoretically, it would be absolutely wrong to forget that every war is but the continuation of policy by other means. The present imperialist war is the continuation of the imperialist policies of two groups of Great Powers, and these policies were engendered and fostered by the sum total of the relationships of the imperialist era. But this very era must also necessarily engender and foster policies of struggle against national oppression and of proletarian struggle against the bourgeoisie and, consequently, also the possibility and inevitability, first, of revolutionary national rebellions and wars; second, of proletarian wars and rebellions *against* the bourgeoisie; and, third, of a combination of both kinds of revolutionary war, etc.

II

To this must be added the following general consideration.

An oppressed class which does not strive to learn to use arms, to acquire arms, only deserves to be treated like slaves. We cannot, unless we have become bourgeois pacifists or opportunists, forget that we are living in a class society from which there is no way out, nor can there be, save through the class struggle. In every class society, whether based on slavery, serfdom, or, as at present, wage-labour, the oppressor class is always armed. Not only the modern standing army, but even the modern militia – and even in the most democratic bourgeois republics, Switzerland, for instance – represent the bourgeoisie armed *against* the proletariat. That is such an elementary truth that it is hardly necessary to dwell upon it.

---

* General Galliffet was a leading commander in the repression of the Paris Commune, noted for his brutality. He became Minister of War in Waldeck-Rousseau's government.

Suffice it to point to the use of troops against strikers in all capitalist countries.

A bourgeoisie armed against the proletariat is one of the biggest fundamental and cardinal facts of modern capitalist society. And in face of this fact, revolutionary Social-Democrats are urged to 'demand' 'disarmament'! That is tantamount of complete abandonment of the class-struggle point of view, to renunciation of all thought of revolution. Our slogan must be: arming of the proletariat to defeat, expropriate and disarm the bourgeoisie. These are the only tactics possible for a revolutionary class, tactics that follow logically from, and are dictated by, the whole *objective development* of capitalist militarism. Only *after* the proletariat has disarmed the bourgeoisie will it be able, without betraying its world-historic mission, to consign all armaments to the scrap-heap. And the proletariat will undoubtedly do this, but *only when this condition has been fulfilled, certainly not before.*

If the present war rouses among the reactionary Christian socialists, among the whimpering petty bourgeoisie, *only* horror and fright, only aversion to all use of arms, to bloodshed, death, etc., then we must say: capitalist society is and has always been *horror without end*. If this most reactionary of all wars is now preparing for that society an *end to horror*, we have no reason to fall into despair. But the disarmament 'demand', or more correctly, the dream of disarmament, is, objectively, nothing but an expression of despair at a time when, as everyone can see, the bourgeoisie itself is paving the way for the only legitimate and revolutionary war – civil war against the imperialist bourgeoisie.

A lifeless theory, some might say, but we would remind them of two world-historical facts: the role of the trusts and the employment of women in industry, on the one hand, and the Paris Commune of 1871 and the December 1905 uprising in Russia, on the other.

The bourgeoisie makes it its business to promote trusts, drive women and children into the factories, subject them to corruption and suffering, condemn them to extreme poverty. We do not 'demand' such development, we do not 'support' it. We fight it.

But *how* do we fight? We explain that trusts and the employment of women in industry are progressive. We do not want a return to the handicraft system, pre-monopoly capitalism, domestic drudgery for women. Forward through the trusts, etc., and beyond them to socialism!

With the necessary changes that argument is applicable also to the present militarisation of the population. Today the imperialist bourgeoisie militarises the youth as well as the adults; tomorrow, it may begin militarising the women. Our attitude should be: All the better! Full speed ahead! For the faster we move, the nearer shall we be to the armed uprising against capitalism. How can Social-Democrats give way to fear of the militarisation of the youth, etc., if they have not forgotten the example of the Paris Commune? This is not a 'lifeless theory' or a dream. It is a fact. And it would be a sorry state of affairs indeed if, all the economic and political facts notwithstanding, Social-Democrats began to doubt that the imperialist era and imperialist wars must inevitably bring about a repetition of such facts.

A certain bourgeois observer of the Paris Commune, writing to an English newspaper in May 1871, said: "If the French nation consisted entirely of women, what a terrible nation it would be!" Woman and teenage children fought in the Paris Commune side by side with the men. It will be no different in the coming battles for the overthrow of the bourgeoisie. Proletarian women will not look on passively as poorly armed or unarmed workers are shot down by the well-armed forces of the bourgeoisie. They will take to arms, as they did in 1871, and from the cowed nations of today – or more correctly, from the present-day labour movement, disorganised more by the opportunists than by the governments – there will undoubtedly arise, sooner or later, but with absolute certainty, an international league of the 'terrible nations' of the revolutionary proletariat.

The whole of social life is now being militarised. Imperialism is a fierce struggle of the Great Powers for the division and redivision of the world. It is therefore bound to lead to further militarisation in all countries, even in neutral and small ones. How will proletarian women oppose this? Only by cursing all war and everything military, only by demanding disarmament? The women of an oppressed and really revolutionary class will never accept that shameful role. They will say to their sons: "You will soon be grown up. You will be given a gun. Take it and learn the military art properly. The proletarians need this knowledge not to shoot your brothers, the workers of other countries, as is being done in the present war, and as the traitors to socialism are telling you to do. They need it to fight the bourgeoisie of their own country, to put an end to exploitation, poverty and war, and not by pious wishes, but by defeating and disarming the bourgeoisie."

If we are to shun such propaganda, precisely such propaganda, in connection with the present war, then we had better stop using fine words about international revolutionary Social-Democracy, the socialist revolution and war against war.

III

The disarmament advocates object to the 'armed nation' clause in the programme also because it more easily leads, they allege, to concessions to opportunism. The cardinal point, namely, the relation of disarmament to the class struggle and to the social revolution, we have examined above. We shall now examine the relation between the disarmament demand and opportunism. One of the chief reasons why it is unacceptable is precisely that, together with the illusions it creates, it inevitably weakens and devitalises our struggle against opportunism.

Undoubtedly, this struggle is the main, immediate question now confusing the International. Struggle against imperialism that is not closely linked with the struggle against opportunism is either an empty phrase or a fraud. One of the main defects of Zimmerwald and Kienthal – on the main reasons why these embryos of the Third International may possibly end in a fiasco – is that the question of fighting opportunism was not even raised openly, let alone solved in the sense of proclaiming the need to break with the opportunists. Opportunism has triumphed – temporarily – in the European labour movement. Its two main shades are apparent in all the big countries: first, the avowed, cynical, and therefore less dangerous social-imperialism of Messrs. Plekhanov, Scheidemann, Legien, Albert Thomas and Sembat, Vandervelde, Hyndman, Henderson, et al.; second, the concealed, Kautskyite opportunism: Kautsky-Haase and the Social-Democratic Labour Group in Germany; Longuet, Pressemane, Mayeras, et al., in France; Ramsay MacDonald and the other leaders of the Independent Labour Party in England; Martov, Chkheidze, et al., in Russia; Treves and the other so-called Left reformists in Italy.

Avowed opportunism is openly and directly opposed to revolution and to incipient revolutionary movements and outbursts. It is in direct alliance with the governments, varied as the forms of this alliance may be – from accepting ministerial posts to participation in the war industries committees (in Russia).* The masked opportunists, the Kautskyites, are much more harmful and dangerous to the labour movement, because they hide their advocacy of alliance with the former under a cloak of plausible, pseudo-'Marxist' catchwords and pacifist slogans. The fight against both these forms of prevailing opportunism must be conducted in *all* fields of proletarian politics: parliament, the trade unions, strikes, the armed forces, etc. The main distinguishing feature of *both* these forms of prevailing opportunism is the concrete question of the *connection between the present war and revolution*, and *the other concrete questions of revolution*, are hushed up, concealed, or

---

* The war industries committees were established in Russia in May 1915 by the imperialist bourgeoisie to help the tsarist government in the prosecution of the war. The Central War Industry Committee was headed by one of Russia's biggest capitalists, Alexander Guchkov, leader of the Octobrists. In an attempt to bring the workers under their influence and foster chauvinist sentiments, the bourgeoisie decided to organise 'workers' groups' in these committees, thereby creating the impression that a 'class peace' had been achieved in Russia between the bourgeoisie and the proletariat.

The Bolsheviks declared a boycott of the committees and successfully carried it out with the support of the majority of workers. As a result of Bolshevik propaganda, elections to the 'workers' groups' were held only in seventy out of a total of 239 regional and local committees, and workers' representatives were elected only in thirty-six of them.

treated with an eye to police prohibitions. And this despite the fact that before the war the connection between *this* impending war and the proletarian revolution was emphasised innumerable times, both unofficially and officially in the Basel Manifesto.* The main defect of the disarmament demand is its evasion of all the concrete questions of revolution. Or do the advocates of disarmament stand for an altogether new kind of revolution, unarmed revolution?

To proceed. We are by no means opposed to the fight for reforms. And we do not wish to ignore the sad possibility – if the worst comes to the worst – of mankind going through a second imperialist war, if revolution does not come out of the present war, in spite of our efforts. We favour a programme of reforms directed *also* against the opportunists. They would be only too glad if we left the struggle for reforms entirely to them and sought escape from sad reality in a nebulous 'disarmament' fantasy. 'Disarmament' means simply running away from unpleasant reality, not fighting it.

In such a programme, we would say something like this:

'To accept the "defence of the fatherland" slogan in the 1914-16 imperialist war is to corrupt the labour movement with the aid of a bourgeois lie.'

Such a concrete reply to a concrete question would be more correct theoretically, much more useful to the proletariat and more unbearable to the opportunists than the disarmament demand and repudiation of 'all and any' 'defence of the fatherland'. And we would add:

'The bourgeoisie of all the imperialist Great Powers – England, France, Germany, Austria, Russia, Japan, the United States – has become so reactionary and so intent on world domination, that *any* war waged by *the bourgeoisie of those* countries is bound to be reactionary. The proletariat must not only oppose all such wars, but must also wish for the defeat of its "own" government in such wars and utilise its defeat for revolutionary insurrection, if an insurrection to prevent the war proves unsuccessful.'

---

*   In this volume, p. 371.

On the question of a militia, we should say: We are not in favour of a bourgeois militia; we are in favour only of a proletarian militia. Therefore, 'not a penny, not a man', not only for a standing army, but even for a bourgeois militia, even in countries like the United States, or Switzerland, Norway, etc. The more so that in the freest republican countries (e.g. Switzerland) we see that the militia is being increasingly Prussianised, particularly in 1907 and 1911, and prostituted by being used against strikers. We can demand popular election of officers, abolition of all military law, equal rights for foreign and native-born workers (a point particularly important for those imperialist states which, like Switzerland, are more and more blatantly exploiting larger numbers of foreign workers, while denying them all rights). Further, we can demand the right of every hundred, say, inhabitants of a given country to form voluntary military-training associations, with free election of instructors paid by the state, etc. Only under these conditions could the proletariat acquire military training for *itself* and not for its slaveowners; and the need for such training is imperatively dictated by the interests of the proletariat. The Russian Revolution showed that every success of the revolutionary movement, even a partial success like the seizure of a certain city, a certain factory town, or winning over a certain section of the army, inevitably *compels* the victorious proletariat to carry out just such a programme.

Lastly, it stands to reason that opportunism can never be defeated by mere programmes; it can only be defeated by deeds. The greatest, and fatal, error of the bankrupt Second International was that its words did not correspond to its deeds, that it cultivated the habit of hypocritical and unscrupulous revolutionary phrase-mongering (note the present attitude of Kautsky and co. towards the Basel Manifesto). Disarmament as a social idea, i.e. an idea that springs from, and can affect, a certain social environment, and is not the invention of some crackpot, springs, evidently, from the peculiar 'tranquil' conditions prevailing, by way of exception, in certain small states, which have for a fairly long time stood aside from the world's path of war and bloodshed, and hope to remain in that way. To be convinced of this, we have only to consider the arguments advanced, for instance, by the Norwegian advocates of disarmament. "We are a small country", they say.

'Our army is small; there is nothing we can do against the Great Powers [and, consequently, nothing we can do to resist forcible involvement in an imperialist *alliance* with one or the other Great Power group]... We want to be left in peace in our backwoods and continue our backwoods politics, demand disarmament, compulsory arbitration, permanent neutrality, etc. ["permanent" after the Belgian fashion, no doubt?]'

The petty striving of petty states to hold aloof, the petty-bourgeois desire to keep as far away as possible from the great battles of world history, to take advantage of one's relatively monopolistic position in order to remain in hidebound passivity – this is the *objective* social environment which may ensure the disarmament idea a certain degree of success and a certain degree of popularity in some small states. That striving is, of course, reactionary and is based entirely on illusions, for, in one way or another, imperialism draws the small states into the vortex of world economy and world politics.

In Switzerland, for instance, the imperialist environment objectively prescribes *two* courses to the labour movement: the opportunists, in alliance with the bourgeoisie, are seeking to turn the country into a republican-democratic monopolistic federation that would thrive on profits from imperialist bourgeois tourists, and to make this 'tranquil' monopolistic position as profitable and as tranquil as possible.

The genuine Swiss Social-Democrats are striving to use Switzerland's relative freedom and her 'international' position to help the victory of the close alliance of the revolutionary elements in the European workers' parties. Switzerland, thank God, does not have 'a separate language of her own', but uses three world languages, the three languages spoken in the adjacent belligerent countries.

If 20,000 Swiss party members were to pay a weekly levy of 2 centimes as a sort of 'extra war tax', we would have 20,000 francs per annum, a sum more than sufficient periodically to publish in three languages and distribute among the workers and soldiers of the belligerent countries – in spite of the bans imposed by the general staffs – all the truthful evidence about the incipient revolt of the workers, their fraternising in the trenches, their hope that the weapons will be used for revolutionary struggle against the imperialist bourgeoisie of their 'own' countries, etc.

That is not new. It is being done by the best papers, like *La Sentinelle*, *Volksrecht*, and the *Berner Tagwacht*, although, unfortunately, on an inadequate scale.* Only through such activity can the splendid decision of the Aarau Party Congress become something more than merely a splendid decision.**

The question that interests us now is: Does the disarmament demand correspond to this revolutionary trend among the Swiss Social-Democrats? It obviously does not. Objectively, disarmament is an extremely national, a specifically national programme of small states. It is certainly not the international programme of international revolutionary Social-Democracy.

---

* *La Sentinelle* was produced by the Social-Democratic organisation of Neuchâtel Canton in western Switzerland.

 Volksrecht (*People's Right*) was the daily organ of the Swiss Social-Democratic Party founded in Zürich.

 Berner Tagwacht (*Bern Guardian*) was a Social-Democratic newspaper founded in Bern.

** The Aarau Congress of the Swiss Social-Democratic Party met on 20-21 November 1915. The central issue was the party's attitude towards the Zimmerwald internationalist groups, and the struggle developed between the three following trends: (1) anti-Zimmerwaldists; (2) supporters of the Zimmerwald Right; and (3) supporters of the Zimmerwald Left. Robert Grimm tabled a resolution urging the party to affiliate with the Zimmerwald group and endorse the political programme of the Zimmerwald Right.

 The Left forces, in an amendment moved by the Lausanne branch, called for mass revolutionary struggle against the war, declaring that only a victorious proletarian revolution could put an end to the imperialist war. Under Grimm's pressure, the amendment was withdrawn, but it was again proposed by MM Kharitonov, a Bolshevik with the right to vote delegated by one of the party's branches. Out of tactical considerations, Grimm and his supporters were obliged to approve the amendment and it was carried by 258 votes to 141.

A Separate Peace

6 November 1916

Russia and Germany are already negotiating a separate peace. The negotiations are official, and the two powers have already reached agreement on the main points.

A statement to that effect appeared recently in the Bern socialist paper and is based on information in its possession.* The Russian Embassy in Bern hastened to issue an official denial, and the French chauvinists ascribed these rumours to 'German dirty work', but the socialist paper refused to attach any importance whatsoever to these denials. In support of its statement it pointed to the presence in Switzerland of German (Billow) and Russian "statesmen" (Shturmer, Giers and a diplomat who arrived from Spain), and to the fact that Swiss commercial circles were in possession of similar reliable information obtained from Russian commercial circles.

Of course, deception on both sides is quite possible. Russia cannot very well admit that she is negotiating a separate peace, and

---

* Lenin is here referring to the *Berner Tagwacht*, which published the following articles on the Russo-German negotiations for a separate peace: '*Die Vorbereitung des Separatfriedens*' ('Preparation of a Separate Peace') in its issue No. 230, 11 October 1916; an editorial, '*Die Friedensgerüchte*' ('Peace Rumours'), in No. 241, 13 October; and '*Zum Separatfrieden*' ('On a Separate Peace') in No. 242, 14 October.

Germany cannot miss an opportunity to create discord between Russia and England, irrespective of whether or not there are negotiations, and if so, how successfully they are proceeding.

To understand the question of a separate peace we must proceed not from rumours and reports about what is taking place in Switzerland, which cannot be effectively verified, but from indisputably established *political facts* of the last few decades. Let Messrs. Plekhanov, Chkhenkeli, Potresov and co., now cast in the role of Marxist-liveried lackeys or jesters of Purishkevich and Milyukov, try as they will to prove 'Germany's war guilt' and that Russia is fighting a 'war of defence' – the class-conscious workers have not listened and will not listen to these clowns. The war was engendered by the Great Power imperialist relations, i.e. by their struggle for division of the loot, a struggle to decide which of them is to gobble up this or that colony or small state. *Two* conflicts are in the foreground in this war. First, between England and Germany. Second, between Germany and Russia. These three Great Powers, these three great freebooters, are the principal figures in the present war. The rest are dependent allies.

Both conflicts were prepared by the *whole* policy these powers pursued for *several decades* before the war. England is fighting to rob Germany of her colonies and to ruin her principal competitor, who has ruthlessly outrivalled England by her superior technique, organisation and commercial drive – and so thoroughly that England *could not* retain her world domination without war. Germany is fighting because her capitalists consider themselves – and rightly so – entitled to the 'sacred' bourgeois right to world supremacy in looting and plundering colonies and dependent countries. In particular, Germany is fighting to subjugate the Balkan countries and Turkey. Russia is fighting for possession of Galicia, which she needs, in particular, to throttle the Ukrainian people (for Galicia is the only place where the Ukrainians have, or can have, liberty – relatively speaking, of course), Armenia and Constantinople, and also to subjugate the Balkan countries.

Parallel with the Russo-German conflict of predatory 'interests' is another no less – if not more – profound conflict between Russia and England. The aim of Russia's imperialist policy, determined by the age-long rivalry and objective international strength-ratio of the Great Powers, may be briefly defined as follows: smash Germany's power in Europe with the aid of England and France in order to rob Austria (by annexing Galicia) and Turkey (by annexing Armenia and, especially, Constantinople); and, after that, smash England's power in Asia with the aid of Japan *and Germany* in order to seize the *whole* of Persia, complete the partition of China, etc.

For centuries tsarism has been striving to conquer Constantinople and a larger and larger part of Asia. It has systematically shaped its policy accordingly and has exploited every antagonism and conflict between the Great Powers. England has resisted these efforts longer, and with more persistence and vigour, than Germany. From 1878, when the Russian armies were approaching Constantinople and the English fleet appeared at the Dardanelles and threatened to bombard the Russians if they dared enter 'Tsargrad',* to 1885, when Russia was on the verge of war with England over division of the spoils in Central Asia (Afghanistan; the Russian army's advance into the heart of Central Asia threatened British rule in India), and down to 1902, when England concluded a treaty with Japan, in preparation for the latter's war against Russia – throughout all these years. England was the most resolute opponent of Russia's predatory policies, because Russia threatened to undermine British domination over a number of other nations.

And now? Just see what is happening in the present war. One loses patience with the 'socialists', who have deserted the proletariat to go over to the bourgeoisie and talk about Russia waging a 'war of defence', or to 'save the country' (Chkheidze). One loses patience with sentimental Kautsky and co. and their talk of a democratic peace, as if the present governments, or any bourgeois government for that matter, *could* conclude such a peace. As a matter of fact,

---

* Tsargrad is the old Russian name for Constantinople.

they are enmeshed in a net of *secret treaties* with each other, with their allies, and *against* their allies. And the content of these treaties is not accidental, it was not determined merely by 'malice', but by the whole course and development of imperialist foreign policy. Those 'socialists' who hoodwink the workers with banal phrases about nice things in general (defence of the fatherland, democratic peace) *without* exposing the *secret* treaties *their own* governments have concluded to rob foreign countries – such 'socialists' are downright traitors to socialism.

The German, the English and the Russian governments only stand to gain from speeches in the socialist camp about a nice little peace, because, firstly, they instil belief in the possibility of such a peace under the present governments, and, secondly, divert attention from these governments' predatory policies.

War is the continuation of policy. But policy also 'continues' *during* war! Germany has secret treaties with Bulgaria and Austria on the division of spoils and continues to conduct secret negotiations on the subject. Russia has secret treaties with England, France, etc., and *all* of them concern *plunder* and *robbery*, robbing Germany of her colonies, robbing Austria, partitioning Turkey, etc.

The 'socialist' who under such circumstances delivers speeches to the people and the governments about a nice little peace resembles the clergyman who, seeing before him in the front pews the mistress of a brothel and a police officer, who are working hand in glove, 'preaches' to them, and to the people, love of one's neighbour and observance of the Christian commandments.

There is undoubtedly a secret treaty between Russia and England, and among other things it concerns Constantinople. That Russia hopes to get Constantinople, and that England does not want to give it to her is well known. If England does give Russia Constantinople, she will either attempt to take it from her later, or else will make this 'concession' on terms directed against Russia. The text of the secret treaty is unknown, but that the struggle between England and Russia centres around precisely this question, that this struggle is going on even now, is not only known, but beyond the slightest doubt. It is also known that, in addition to the old treaties between Russia and Japan (the 1910 treaty, for instance, which allowed Japan to 'gobble up' Korea and Russia to gobble up Mongolia), a *new* secret treaty was concluded during the present war, directed not only against China, but, to a *certain extent, also against England*. That is beyond doubt, although the text of the treaty is unknown. In 1904-05 Japan defeated Russia with England's aid; now she is carefully preparing to defeat England with Russia's aid.

There is a pro-German party in Russian 'governing circles' – the Court gang of Nicholas the Bloody, the nobility, army, etc. In Germany, the bourgeoisie (followed by the socialist-chauvinists) has of late markedly turned towards a pro-Russian policy, towards a separate peace with Russia, towards placating Russia in order to strike with full force against England. As far as Germany is concerned, this plan is clear and leaves no room for doubt. As for Russia, the situation is that tsarism would, of course, prefer to smash Germany first in order to 'take' as much as possible – the whole of Galicia, the whole of Poland, Armenia, Constantinople – 'crush' Austria, etc. It would then be much easier, with the aid of Japan, to turn against England. But, apparently, Russia has not the strength for that. That's at the bottom of it.

Mr. Plekhanov, the ex-socialist, has tried to make out that the Russian reactionaries are generally in favour of peace with Germany, whereas the 'progressive bourgeoisie' are in favour of crushing 'Prussian militarism' and support friendship with 'democratic' England. That is a fairytale suitable to the mental level of political infants. The fact is that tsarism *and* all the Russian reactionaries *and* the 'progressive' bourgeoisie (Octobrists and Cadets) want the *same thing*: rob Germany, Austria and Turkey in Europe, and defeat England in Asia (so as to take the whole of Persia, Mongolia, Tibet, etc.). These 'dear friends' disagree only as to *when and how* to turn from a struggle against Germany to a struggle against England. Only about when and how!

This question, the only one on which the dear friends differ, will be determined by *military and diplomatic considerations* known in full *only* to the tsarist government; the Milyukovs and Guchkovs know only a quarter of them.

Take the whole of Poland from Germany and Austria! Tsarism is *in favour* of that, but has it the strength? And will England allow it?

Take Constantinople and the Straits! Crush and dismember Austria! Tsarism is entirely in favour of that. But has it the strength? And will England allow it?

Tsarism knows just how many millions of soldiers have been slaughtered and how many *more* may be drawn from the people; it knows just how many shells are being expended and how many more can be obtained (in the event of war with China, which is threatening, and which is quite possible, Japan will *not* supply any more ammunition!). Tsarism knows how its secret negotiations with England concerning Constantinople have been and are progressing; it knows the strength of the British forces in Salonika, Mesopotamia, etc. Tsarism knows all this. It has all the cards in its hands and is making exact calculations – insofar as exact calculations are possible in such matters where that very doubtful and elusive element, the 'fortune of war', plays so great a part.

As for the Milyukovs and Guchkovs, the less they know the more they talk. And the Plekhanovs, the Chkhenkelis, the Potresovs know nothing at all of tsarism's secret pacts; they are forgetting even what they knew before, do not study what can be learned from the foreign press, do not examine the course of tsarism's foreign policy before the war, do not trace its course during the war, and are consequently playing the part of socialist Simple Simons.

If tsarism has become convinced that even with all the aid of liberal society, with all the zeal of the war industries committees, with all the help the Plekhanovs, Gvozdyovs, Potresovs, Bulkins, Chirkins, Chkheidzes ('Save the country', don't laugh!), Kropotkins, and the whole of that menial crowd are giving to the noble cause of producing more shells – that even with all this help and with the present state of military strength (or military impotence) of all the allies it can possibly drag and has dragged into the war, it *cannot* achieve more, it cannot hit Germany *harder*, or that it can do so only at excessive cost (for example, the loss of 10 million *more* Russian soldiers, the recruiting, training and equipment of whom would cost so many more billions of rubles and so many more years of war), then tsarism *cannot but seek* a separate peace with Germany.

If 'we' go after too much booty in Europe, 'we' run the risk of utterly exhausting 'our' military resources, of gaining almost nothing in Europe and of losing the opportunity of getting 'our share' in Asia. This is how tsarism argues, and it argues *correctly* from the standpoint of imperialist interests. It argues *more correctly* than the bourgeois and opportunist chatterboxes, the Milyukovs, Plekhanovs, Guchkovs and Potresovs.

If no more can be obtained in Europe even after Romania and Greece (from which 'we' have taken all we could) have joined in, then let us take what can still be had! England *cannot* give us anything just now. Germany will perhaps return to us Courland and a part of Poland, certainly Eastern Galicia – which 'we' particularly need for the purpose of throttling the Ukrainian movement, the movement of historically hitherto dormant people numbering many millions, for freedom and the right to use their native language – and, very likely, Turkish Armenia also. If we take this *now*, we may emerge from the war *with increased strength*, and *tomorrow* we may, with the aid of Japan and Germany, with a wise policy and with the further aid of the Milyukovs, Plekhanovs and Potresovs in 'saving' the beloved 'fatherland', get a good slice of Asia in a war against England (the whole of Persia and the Persian Gulf with an outlet to the ocean much better than Constantinople, which is an outlet only to the Mediterranean and is guarded by islands which England can easily take and fortify, thus depriving 'us' of every outlet to the open sea), etc.

This is exactly how tsarism argues, and, we repeat, it argues correctly, not only from the narrow monarchist point of view, but also from the general imperialist point of view. It knows more and sees farther than the liberals, the Plekhanovs and the Potresovs.

It is quite possible, therefore, that tomorrow, or the day after we shall wake up and hear the three monarchs proclaim:

'Hearkening to the voices of our beloved peoples, we have resolved to endow them with the blessings of peace, to sign an armistice and to convene a general European Peace Congress.'

The three monarchs may even display their sense of humour by quoting fragments of the speeches of Vandervelde, Plekhanov and Kautsky, such as: we "promise" – promises are the only thing that is cheap, even in this period of soaring prices – "to discuss the question of reducing armaments and of a 'lasting' peace", etc. Vandervelde, Plekhanov and Kautsky will run along and arrange their 'socialist' congress in the same city as the Peace Congress; and there will be no end of pious wishes, sentimental phrases and talk of the need to 'defend the fatherland' in all languages. The stage will be well set for concealing the transition from an imperialist Anglo-Russian alliance against Germany to an imperialist Russo-German alliance against England!

But whether the war ends in this way in the very near future, or whether Russia 'holds out' a little longer in her effort to vanquish Germany and rob Austria more; whether the separate peace negotiations will prove a shrewd blackmailer's trick (tsarism showing England a draft of a treaty with Germany and saying: "Either so many billion rubles and such-and-such concessions or guarantees, or I sign this treaty tomorrow"), *in all cases* the imperialist war *cannot* end otherwise than in an imperialist peace, *unless* it is transformed into a civil war of the proletariat against the bourgeoisie for socialism. In all cases, unless this happens, the imperialist war will result in the strengthening of one or two of the three strongest imperialist powers – England, Germany and Russia – at the expense of the weak (Serbia, Turkey, Belgium, etc.), and it is quite possible that *all* three robbers will become stronger after the war, having divided the booty among themselves (the colonies, Belgium, Serbia, Armenia). The only argument will be over the share each should get.

In all cases, both the full-fledged and avowed social-chauvinists, i.e. the individuals who openly accept 'defence of the fatherland' in the present war, and the disguised, half-way social-chauvinists, i.e. the Kautskyites with their preachment of 'peace' *in general*, 'without victors or vanquished', etc., will inevitably, unavoidably and undoubtedly be fooled and discredited. For any peace concluded by the same, or similar, bourgeois governments that started the war will glaringly show the peoples what a servile role both these types of socialists played in relation to imperialism.

Whatever the outcome of the present war, those who maintained that the only possible socialist way out of it is through civil war by the proletariat for socialism, will have been proved correct. The Russian Social-Democrats who maintained that the defeat of tsarism, its complete military smash-up, is, 'in all cases', the lesser evil, will have been proved correct. For history never stands still; it continues its forward movement during this war too. And if the European proletariat cannot advance to socialism now, cannot cast off the social-chauvinist and Kautskyite yoke in the course of this first great imperialist war, then East Europe and Asia can advance to democracy with seven-league strides only if tsarism is utterly smashed and deprived of *all* possibility to pursue its semi-feudal type imperialist policy.

The war will kill and destroy everything weak, social-chauvinism and Kautskyism included. An imperialist peace would further accentuate *these* weaknesses, show them up in a still more despicable and abhorrent light.

Bourgeois Pacifism and Socialist Pacifism

1 January 1917

Editors note:

Lenin intended this series of articles for the newspaper *Novy Mir* (*New World*) published in New York by Russian socialist émigrés. They did not appear in *Novy Mir* and Lenin re-edited the first two articles, which were published in the last issue (No. 58) of *Sotsial-Demokrat*, on 31 January 1917, under the heading 'A Turn in World Politics'.

* * *

1. The turn in world politics

There are symptoms that such a turn has taken place, or is about to take place, namely, a turn from imperialist war to imperialist peace.

The following are the outstanding symptoms: both imperialist coalitions are undoubtedly severely exhausted; continuing the war has become difficult; the capitalists generally, and finance capital in particular, find it difficult to skin the people substantially more than they have done already in the form of outrageous 'war' profits; finance capital in the neutral countries, the United States, Holland, Switzerland, etc., which has made enormous profits out of the war, is satiated; the shortage of raw materials and food supplies makes it difficult for it to continue this 'profitable' business; Germany is making strenuous efforts to induce one or another ally of England, her principal imperialist rival, to desert her; the German government has made pacifist pronouncements, followed by similar pronouncements by a number of neutral governments.

Are there any chances for a speedy end to the war?

It is very hard to give a positive reply to this question. In our opinion, two possibilities present themselves rather definitely.

First, conclusion of a separate peace between Germany and Russia, though perhaps not in the usual form of a formal written treaty. Second, no such peace will be concluded; England and her allies are still in a position to hold out for another year or two, etc. If the first assumption is correct the war will come to an end, if not immediately, then in the very near future, and no important changes in its course can be expected. If the second assumption is correct, then the war may continue indefinitely.

Let us examine the first possibility.

That negotiations for a separate peace between Germany and Russia were conducted quite recently, that Nicholas II himself, or the top court clique, favour such a peace, that a turn has taken place in world politics from a Russo-British imperialist alliance against Germany to a no less imperialist Russo-German alliance against England – all that is beyond doubt.

The replacement of Shturmer by Trepov, the tsarist government's public declaration that Russia's 'right' to Constantinople has been recognised by all the Allies, and the setting up by Germany of a separate Polish state – these seem to indicate that the separate peace negotiations have ended in failure.* Perhaps tsarism entered into them *solely* to blackmail England, obtain formal and unambiguous recognition of Nicholas the Bloody's 'right' to Constantinople and certain 'weighty' guarantees of that right?

---

*   Boris Shturmer, Prime Minister of Russia from 2 February 1916, was dismissed and replaced with Alexander Trepov on 23 November 1916.

There is nothing improbable in that assumption, considering that the main, fundamental purpose of the present imperialist war is the division of the spoils among the three principal imperialist rivals, the three robbers, Russia, Germany and England.

On the other hand, the clearer it becomes to tsarism that there is no practical, military possibility of regaining Poland, winning Constantinople, breaking Germany's iron front, which she is magnificently straightening out, shortening and strengthening by her recent victories in Romania, the more tsarism is finding itself *compelled* to conclude a separate peace with Germany, *that is*, to abandon its imperialist alliance with England against Germany for an imperialist alliance with Germany against England. And why not? Was not Russia on the verge of war with England as a result of their imperialist rivalry over the division of the spoils in Central Asia? And did not England and Germany negotiate in 1898 for an alliance *against* Russia? They secretly agreed then to divide up the Portuguese colonies 'in the event' of Portugal failing to meet her financial obligations!

The growing trend among leading imperialist circles in Germany towards an alliance with Russia against England was already clearly defined several months ago. The basis of this alliance, apparently, is to be the partition of Galicia (it is very important for tsarism to strangle the centre of Ukrainian agitation and Ukrainian liberty), Armenia and *perhaps Romania!* In fact there was a 'hint' in a German newspaper that Romania might be divided among Austria, Bulgaria and Russia! Germany could agree to other minor concessions to tsarism if only she could achieve an alliance with Russia, and perhaps also with Japan, against England.

A separate peace between Nicholas II and Wilhelm II could have been concluded secretly. There have been instances in diplomatic history of treaties known only to two or three persons and kept secret from everyone else, even Cabinet Ministers. Diplomatic history knows instances of the 'Great Powers' gathering at 'European' congresses after the principal rivals had secretly decided the main questions among themselves (for example, the secret agreement between Russia and England to plunder Turkey, prior to the Berlin Congress of 1878). It would not be at all surprising if tsarism rejected a formal separate peace between the governments for the reason, among others, that the present situation in Russia might result in Milyukov and Guchkov, or Milyukov and Kerensky, taking over the government, while at the same time, it may have concluded a secret, informal, but none the less 'durable' treaty with Germany to the effect that the two 'high contracting parties' undertake jointly to pursue *such-and-such* a policy at the forthcoming peace congress!

It is impossible to say whether or not this assumption is correct. At any rate, it is a thousand times nearer the *truth*, is a far better description of *things as they actually are*, than are the pious phrases about peace between the present governments, or between any bourgeois governments for that matter, on the basis of no annexations, etc. These phrases either express innocent desires or are hypocrisy and lies meant to conceal the truth. And the truth of the present time, of the present war, of the present attempts to conclude peace, is the *division of the imperialist spoils*. That is at the bottom of it all; and to understand this truth, to express it, "to show things as they actually are", is the fundamental task of socialist policy as distinct from bourgeois policy, the principal aim of which is to conceal, to gloss over this truth.

Both imperialist coalitions have grabbed a certain amount of loot, and the two principal and most powerful of the robbers, Germany and England, have grabbed most. England has not lost an inch of her territory or of her colonies; but she has 'acquired' the German colonies and part of Turkey (Mesopotamia). Germany has lost nearly all her colonies, but has acquired immeasurably more valuable territory in Europe, having seized Belgium, Serbia, Romania, part of France, part of Russia, etc. The fight now is over the division of the loot, and the 'chieftain' of each of the robber gangs, i.e. England and Germany, must to some degree reward his allies, who, with the exception of Bulgaria and to a lesser extent Italy, have lost a great deal. The weakest of the allies have lost most: in the English coalition, Belgium, Serbia, Montenegro and

Romania have been crushed; in the German coalition, Turkey has lost Armenia and part of Mesopotamia.

So far Germany has secured undoubtedly far more loot than England. So far Germany has won; she has proved to be far stronger than anyone anticipated before the war. Naturally, therefore, it would be to Germany's advantage to conclude peace as speedily as possible, for her rival might still be able, given the most favourable opportunity conceivable (although not very probably), to mobilise a larger reserve of recruits, etc.

Such is the *objective* situation. Such is the present position in the struggle for the division of the imperialist loot. It is quite natural that *this* situation should give rise to pacifist strivings, declarations and pronouncements, mainly on the part of the bourgeoisie and governments of the German coalition and of the neutral countries. It is equally natural that the bourgeoisie and *its* governments are compelled to exert every effort to hoodwink the people, to cover up the hideous nakedness of an imperialist peace – the division of the loot – by phrases, utterly false phrases about a democratic peace, the liberty of small nations, armaments reduction, etc.

But while it is natural for the bourgeoisie to try to hoodwink the people, how are the socialists fulfilling their duty? This we shall deal with in the next article (or chapter).

2. The pacifism of Kautsky and Turati

Kautsky is the most authoritative theoretician of the Second International, the most prominent leader of the so-called 'Marxist centre' in Germany, the representative of the opposition which organised a separate group in the Reichstag, the Social-Democratic Labour Group (Haase, Ledebour and others). A number of Social-Democratic newspapers in Germany are now publishing articles by Kautsky on the terms of peace, which paraphrase the official Social-Democratic Labour Group declaration on the German government's well-known note proposing peace negotiations. The declaration, which calls on the German government to propose definite terms of peace, contains the following characteristic statement:

In order that this [German government] note may lead to peace, all countries must unequivocally renounce all thought of annexing foreign territory, of the political, economic or military subjection of any people whatsoever…

In paraphrasing and concretising this, Kautsky set out to 'prove' in his lengthy articles that Constantinople must not go to Russia and that Turkey must not be made a vassal state to anyone.

Let us take a closer look at these political slogans and arguments of Kautsky and his associates.

In a matter that affects Russia, i.e. Germany's imperialist rival, Kautsky advances, not abstract or 'general' demands, but a very concrete, precise and definite demand: Constantinople must not go to Russia. He thereby *exposes* the *real* imperialist designs… of Russia. In a matter that affects Germany, however, i.e. the country where the majority of the party, which regards Kautsky as its member (and appointed him editor of its principal, leading theoretical organ, *Die Neue Zeit*), is helping the bourgeoisie and the government to conduct an imperialist war, Kautsky does *not* expose the *concrete* imperialist designs of *his own* government, but confines himself to a 'general' desideratum or proposition: Turkey must not be made a vassal state to anyone!!

How, in substance, does Kautsky's policy differ from that of the militant, so to speak, social-chauvinists (i.e. socialists in words but chauvinists in deeds) of France and England? While frankly exposing the concrete imperialist actions of Germany, they make shift with 'general' desiderata or propositions when it is a matter of countries or nations conquered by England and Russia. They shout about the seizure of Belgium and Serbia, but are silent about the seizure of Galicia, Armenia, the African colonies.

Actually, both the policy of Kautsky and that of Sembat and Henderson help *their* respective imperialist governments by focusing attention on the wickedness of their rival and enemy, while throwing a veil of vague, general phrases and sentimental wishes around the *equally* imperialist conduct of '*their own*' bourgeoisie. We would cease to be Marxists, we would cease to be socialists in general, if we confined ourselves to the Christian, so to speak, contemplation of the benignity of benign general phrases and refrained from exposing their *real* political significance. Do we not constantly see the diplomacy of all the imperialist powers flaunting magnanimous 'general' phrases and 'democratic' declarations in order to *conceal* their robbery, violation and strangulation of small nations?

"Turkey must not be made a vassal state to anyone…" If I say no more than that, the impression is that I favour Turkey's complete freedom. As a matter of fact, I am merely repeating a phrase usually uttered by German diplomats who are *deliberately* lying and deceiving, and employ that phrase to conceal the *fact* that Germany *has already* converted Turkey into her financial *and* military vassal! And if I am a German socialist, my 'general' phrases can only be to the *advantage* of German diplomacy, for their real significance is that they put German imperialism *in a good light*.

"All countries must renounce all thought of annexations… of the economic subjection of any people whatsoever…" What magnanimity! A thousand times the imperialists have 'renounced all thought' of annexations and of the financial strangulation of weak nations. But should we not compare these renunciations with the *facts*, which show that any one of the big banks of Germany, England, France and the United States *does hold* small nations '*in subjection*'? Can the present bourgeois government of a wealthy country *really* renounce annexations and the economic subjugation of alien peoples when millions and millions have been invested in the railways and other enterprises of weak nations?

Who is really fighting annexations, etc.? Those who bandy magnanimous phrases, which, objectively, have the same significance as the Christian holy water sprinkled on the crowned and capitalist robbers? Or those who explain to the workers the impossibility of eliminating annexations and financial strangulation without overthrowing the imperialist bourgeoisie and its governments?

Here is an Italian illustration of the kind of pacifism Kautsky preaches.

Avanti!, the Central Organ of the Socialist Party of Italy, of 25 December 1916, contains an article by the well-known reformist, Filippo Turati, entitled 'Abracadabra'. On 22 November 1916, he writes, the socialist group tabled a peace resolution in the Italian Parliament. It declared that "the principles proclaimed by the representatives of England and Germany were identical, and these principles should be made the basis of a possible peace"; and it invited "the government to start peace negotiations through the mediation of the United States and other neutral countries". This is Turati's own account of the socialist proposal.

On 6 December 1916, the Chamber 'buries' the socialist resolution by 'adjourning' the debate on it. On 12 December, the German Chancellor proposes in the Reichstag the very thing the Italian socialists proposed. On 22 December, Wilson issues his Note which, in the words of Turati, "paraphrases and repeats the ideas and arguments of the socialist proposal". On 23 December, other neutral countries come on the scene and paraphrase Wilson's Note.

We are accused of having sold ourselves to the Germans, exclaims Turati. Have Wilson and the neutral countries also sold themselves to Germany?

On 17 December Turati delivered a speech in Parliament, one passage of which caused an unusual and deserved sensation. This is the passage, quoted from the report in *Avanti!*:

> Let us assume that a discussion similar to the one proposed by Germany is able, in the main, to settle such questions as the evacuation of Belgium and France, the restoration of Romania, Serbia and, if you will, Montenegro; I will add the rectification of the Italian frontiers in regard to what is indisputably Italian and corresponds to guarantees of a strategical character...

At this point the bourgeois and chauvinist Chamber interrupts Turati, and from all sides the shout goes up: "Excellent! So you too want all this! Long live Turati! Long live Turati!"

Apparently, Turati realised that there was something wrong about this bourgeois enthusiasm and tried to 'correct' himself and 'explain'.

> Gentlemen [he said], there is no occasion for irrelevant jesting. It is one thing to admit the relevance and right of national unity, which we have always recognised, but it is quite another thing to provoke, or justify, war for this aim.

But neither Turati's 'explanation', nor the articles in *Avanti!* in his defence, nor Turati's letter of 21 December, nor the article by a certain 'BB' in the Zürich *Volksrecht* can 'correct' or explain away the fact that *Turati gave himself away!* Or, more correct, not Turati, but the whole of socialist pacifism represented by Kautsky, and, as we shall see below, the French 'Kautskyites', gave itself away. The Italian bourgeois press was right in seizing upon and exulting over this passage in Turati's speech.

The above-mentioned 'BB' tried to defend Turati by arguing that the latter referred only to 'the right of nations to self-determination'.

Poor defence! What has this to do with 'the right of nations to self-determination', which, as everyone knows, the Marxist programme regards – and the programme of international democracy has always regarded – as referring to the defence of *oppressed* nations? What has it to do with the imperialist war, i.e. a war for the division of colonies, a war for the *oppression* of foreign countries, a war *among* predatory and oppressing powers to decide *which* of them shall oppress *more* foreign nations?

How does this argument about self-determination of nations, used to justify an imperialist, not national, war, differ from the speeches of Alexinsky, Hervé and Hyndman? They argue that *republican* France is opposed to monarchist Germany, though everyone knows that this war is not due to the conflict between republican and monarchist principles, but is a war between two imperialist coalitions for the division of colonies, etc.

Turati explained and pleaded that he does *not* 'justify' the war.

We will take the reformist, Kautskyite Turati's word for it that he did not *intend* to justify the war. But who does not know that in politics it is not intentions that count, but deeds, not good intentions, but facts, not the imaginary, but the real?

Let us assume that Turati did not want to justify the war and that Kautsky did not want to justify Germany's placing Turkey in the position of a vassal to German imperialism. But the *fact* remains that these two benign pacifists *did justify the war!* That is the point. Had Kautsky declared that "Constantinople must not go to Russia, Turkey must not be made a vassal state to anyone" not in a magazine which is so dull that nobody reads it, but in parliament, before a lively, impressionable bourgeois audience, full of southern temperament, it would not have been surprising if the witty bourgeois had exclaimed: "Excellent! Hear, hear! Long live Kautsky!"

Whether he intended to or not, deliberately or not, the fact is that Turati expressed the point of view of a bourgeois broker proposing a friendly deal between imperialist robbers. The 'liberation' of Italian areas belonging to Austria would, *in fact*, be a concealed reward to the Italian bourgeoisie for participating in the imperialist war of a gigantic imperialist coalition. It would be a small sop thrown in, in addition to the share of the African colonies and spheres of influence in Dalmatia and Albania. It is natural, perhaps, for the reformist Turati to adopt the bourgeois standpoint; but Kautsky really differs in no way from Turati.

In order not to embellish the imperialist war and help the bourgeoisie falsely represent it as a national war, as a war for the liberation of nations, in order to avoid sliding into the position of bourgeois reformism, one must speak not in the language of Kautsky and Turati, but in the language of Karl Liebknecht: tell *one's own* bourgeoisie that they are hypocrites when they talk about national liberation, that this war cannot result in a democratic peace unless the proletariat 'turns its guns' against *its own* governments.

That is the only possible position of a genuine Marxist, of a genuine socialist and not a bourgeois reformist. Those who repeat the general, meaningless, non-committal, goody-goody desires of pacifism are not really working for a democratic peace. Only he is working for such a peace who exposes the imperialist nature of the present war and of the imperialist peace that is being prepared, and calls upon the peoples to rise in revolt against the criminal governments.

At times some try to defend Kautsky and Turati by arguing that, legally, they could no more than 'hint' at their opposition to the government, and that the pacifists of this stripe do make such 'hints'. The answer to that is, first, that the impossibility of legally speaking the truth is an argument not in favour of concealing the truth, but in favour of setting up an illegal organisation and press that would be free of police surveillance and censorship. Second, that moments occur in history when a socialist *is called upon* to break with all legality. Third, that even in the days of serfdom in Russia, Dobrolyubov and Chernyshevsky managed to speak the truth, for example, by their silence on the Manifesto of 19 February 1861,* and their ridicule and castigation of the liberals, who made exactly the same kind of speeches as Turati and Kautsky.

In the next article we shall deal with French pacifism, which found expression in the resolutions passed by the two recently held congresses of French labour and socialist organisations.

3. The pacifism of the French socialists and syndicalists

The congresses of the French General Confederation of Labour (CGT) and of the French Socialist Party have just been held. The true significance and true role of socialist pacifism at the present moment were quite definitely revealed at these congresses.

This is the resolution passed *unanimously* at the trade union congress. The majority of the ardent chauvinists headed by the notorious Jouhaux, the anarchist Broutchoux and… the 'Zimmerwaldist' Merrheim all voted for it:

---

* The Manifesto of 19 February 1861 abolished serfdom in Russia.

This Conference of National Corporative Federations, trade unions and labour exchanges, having taken cognisance of the Note of the President of the United States which "invites all nations now at war with each other to publicly expound their views as to the terms upon which the war might be brought to an end":

- Requests the French Government to agree to this proposal;

- Invites the government to take the initiative in making a similar proposal to its allies in order to speed the hour of peace;

- Declares that the federation of nations, which is one of the guarantees of a final peace, can be secured only given the independence, territorial inviolability and political and economic liberty of all nations, big and small.

The organisations represented at this conference pledge themselves to support and spread this idea among the masses of the workers in order to put an end to the present indefinite and ambiguous situation, which can only benefit secret diplomacy, against which the working class has always protested.

There you have a sample of 'pure' pacifism, entirely in the spirit of Kautsky, a pacifism approved by an official labour organisation which has nothing in common with Marxism and is composed chiefly of chauvinists. We have before us an outstanding document, deserving the most serious attention, of the *political unity* of the chauvinists and the 'Kautskyites' on a platform of hollow pacifist phrases. In the preceding article we tried to explain the *theoretical* basis of the unity of ideas of the chauvinists and the pacifists, of the bourgeois and the socialist reformists. Now we see this unity achieved *in practice* in another imperialist country.

At the Zimmerwald Conference, 5-8 September 1915, Merrheim declared: "The party, the Jouhaux and the government are three heads under one bonnet", i.e. they are all one. At the CGT Conference, on 26 December 1916, Merrheim voted *together with Jouhaux* for a pacifist resolution. On 23 December 1916, one of the frankest and most extreme organs of the German social-imperialists, the Chemnitz *Volksstimme*, published a leading article entitled 'The Disintegration of the Bourgeois Parties and the Restoration of Social-Democratic Unity'. Needless to say, it praises peace-loving Südekum, Legien, Scheidemann and co., the whole German Social-Democratic Party majority and, also, the peace-loving German government. It proclaims:

> The first party congress convened after the war must restore party unity, with the exception of the few fanatics who refuse to pay party dues [i.e. the adherents of Karl Liebknecht!]; … Party unity based on the policy of the Party Executive, the Social-Democratic Reichstag group and the trade unions.

This is a supremely clear expression of the idea, and a supremely clear proclamation of the policy of 'unity' between the avowed German social-chauvinists on the one hand and Kautsky and co. and the Social-Democratic Labour Group on the other – unity on the basis of pacifist phrases – 'unity' as achieved in France on 26 December 1916, between Jouhaux and Merrheim!

The Central Organ of the Socialist Party of Italy, *Avanti!*, writes in a leading article in its issue of 28 December 1916:

> Although Bissolati and Südekum, Bonomi and Scheidemann, Sembat and David, Jouhaux and Legien have deserted to the camp of bourgeois nationalism and have betrayed internationalist ideological unity, which they promised to serve faithfully and loyally, we shall stay together with our German comrades, men like Liebknecht, Ledebour, Hoffmann, Meyer, and with our French comrades, men like Merrheim, Blanc, Brizon, Raffin-Dugens, who have not changed and have not vacillated.

Note the confusion expressed in that statement:

Bissolati and Bonomi were *expelled* from the Socialist Party of Italy as reformists and chauvinists before the war. *Avanti!* puts them on the same level as Südekum, and Legien, and quite rightly, of course. But Südekum, David and Legien are at the head of the alleged Social-Democratic Party of Germany, which, in fact, is a social-chauvinist party, and yet this very *Avanti!* is opposed to their expulsion, opposed to a rupture with them, and opposed to the formation of a Third International. *Avanti!* quite correctly describes Legien and Jouhaux as deserters to the camp of bourgeois nationalism and contrasts their conduct with that of Liebknecht, Ledebour, Merrheim and Brizon. But we have seen that Merrheim *votes on the same side as Jouhaux*, while Legien, in the Chemnitz *Volksstimme*, declares his confidence that party unity will be restored, with the *single* exception, however, of Liebknecht supporters, i.e. 'unity' *with* the Social-Democratic Labour Group (including Kautsky) to which Ledebour belongs!!

This confusion arises from the fact that *Avanti!* confuses bourgeois pacifism with revolutionary Social-Democratic internationalism, while experienced politicians like Legien and Jouhaux understand perfectly well that socialist and bourgeois pacifism are *identical*.

Why, indeed, should not Mssr. Jouhaux and his organ, the chauvinist *La Bataille*, rejoice at the 'unanimity' between Jouhaux and Merrheim when, *in fact*, the unanimously adopted resolution, which we have quoted in full above, contains nothing but bourgeois pacifist phrases; *not a shadow* of revolutionary consciousness, *not a single* socialist idea!

Is it not ridiculous to talk of the "economic liberty of all nations, big and small", and yet not say a word about the fact that, until the bourgeois governments are overthrown and the bourgeoisie expropriated, this talk of "economic liberty" is just as much a *deception* of the people as talk of the "economic liberty" of the individual *in general*, of the small peasants and rich, workers and capitalists, in modern society?

The resolution Jouhaux and Merrheim unanimously voted for is thoroughly imbued with the very ideas of "bourgeois nationalism" that Jouhaux expresses, as *Avanti!* quite rightly points out, while, strangely enough, *failing* to observe that Merrheim expresses the same ideas.

Bourgeois nationalists always and everywhere flaunt 'general' phrases about a 'federation of nations' *in general* and about 'economic liberty of all nations, big and small'. But socialists, unlike bourgeois nationalists, always said and now say: rhetoric about 'economic liberty of all nations, big and small', is disgusting hypocrisy as long as *certain* nations (for example, England and France) invest abroad, that is to say, lend at usurious interest to small and backward nations, *billions of francs*, and as long as the small and weak nations are in bondage to them.

Socialists could not have allowed a *single sentence* of the resolution, for which Jouhaux and Merrheim unanimously voted, to pass without strong protest. In direct contrast to that resolution, socialists would have declared that Wilson's pronouncement is a downright lie and sheer hypocrisy, because Wilson represents a bourgeoisie which has made billions out of the war, because he is the head of a government that has frantically armed the United States obviously in preparation for a *second* great imperialist war. Socialists would have declared that the French bourgeois government is tied hand and foot by finance capital, whose slave it is, and by the secret, imperialist, thoroughly predatory and reactionary treaties with England, Russia, etc., and therefore cannot do or say anything except utter the same lies about a democratic and a 'just' peace. Socialists would have declared that the struggle for such a peace cannot be waged by repeating general, vapid, benign, sentimental, meaningless and non-committal pacifist phrases, which merely serve to embellish the foulness of imperialism. It can be waged only by telling the people the *truth*, by telling the people that in order to obtain a democratic and just peace the bourgeois governments of all the belligerent countries must be overthrown, and that for this purpose advantage must be taken of the fact that millions of workers are armed and that the high cost of living and the horrors of the imperialist war have roused the anger of the masses.

This is what socialists should have said instead of what is said in the Jouhaux-Merrheim resolution.

The Congress of the French Socialist Party, which took place in Paris simultaneously with that of the CGT, not only refrained from saying this, but passed a resolution that is *even worse* than the one mentioned above. It was adopted by 2,838 votes against 109, with twenty abstentions, that is to say, by a bloc of the social-chauvinists (Renaudel and co., the so-called '*majoritaires*') and the *Longuetists* (supporters of Longuet, the French Kautskyites)!! Moreover, the Zimmerwaldist Bourderon and the Kienthalian Raffin-Dugens voted for this resolution!!

We shall not quote the resolution – it is inordinately long and totally uninteresting: it contains benign, sentimental phrases about peace, *immediately followed* by declarations of readiness to continue to support the so-called "national defence" of France, i.e. the imperialist war France is waging in alliance with bigger and more powerful robbers like England and Russia.

In France, unity of the social-chauvinists with pacifists (or Kautskyites) and a section of the Zimmerwaldists has become a fact, not only in the CGT, but also in the Socialist Party.

4. Zimmerwald at the crossroads

The French newspapers containing the report of the CGT Congress were received in Bern on 28 December, and on 30 December Bern and Zürich socialist newspapers published another manifesto by the Bern ISK (*Internationale Sozialistische Kommission*), the International Socialist Committee, the executive body of Zimmerwald. Dated the end of December 1916, the manifesto refers to the peace proposals advanced by Germany and by Wilson and the other neutral countries, and all these governmental pronouncements are described, and quite rightly described, of course, as a "farcical game of peace", "a game to deceive their own peoples", "hypocritical pacifist diplomatic gesticulations".

As against this farce and falsehood the manifesto declares that the "only force" capable of bringing about peace, etc., is the "firm determination" of the international proletariat to "turn their weapons, not against their brothers, but against the enemy in their own country".

The passages we have quoted clearly reveal the two fundamentally distinct policies which have lived side by side, as it were, up to now in the Zimmerwald group, but which have now finally parted company.

On the one hand, Turati quite definitely and correctly states that the proposals made by Germany, Wilson, etc., were merely a "*paraphrase*" of Italian "socialist" pacifism; the declaration of the German social-chauvinists and the voting of the French have shown that both fully appreciate the value for *their* policy of the pacifist screen.

On the other hand, the International Socialist Committee manifesto describes the pacifism of all belligerent and neutral governments as a farce and hypocrisy.

On the one hand, Jouhaux joins with Merrheim; Bourderon, Longuet and Raffin-Dugens join with Renaudel, Sembat and Thomas, while the German social-chauvinists, Südekum, David and Scheidemann, announce the forthcoming "restoration of Social-Democratic unity" with Kautsky and the Social-Democratic Labour Group.

On the other hand, the International Socialist Committee calls upon the "socialist minorities" vigorously to fight "their own governments" and "their social-patriot hirelings" (*Söldlinge*).

Either one thing, or the other.

Either expose the vapidity, stupidity and hypocrisy of bourgeois pacifism, *or* "paraphrase" it into "socialist" pacifism. Fight the Jouhaux, Renaudels, Legiens and Davids as the "hirelings" of the governments, *or* join with them in empty pacifist declamations on the French or German models.

That is now the dividing line between the Zimmerwald Right, which has always strenuously opposed a break with the social-chauvinists, and the Left, which at the Zimmerwald Conference had the foresight publicly to dissociate itself from the Right and to put forward, at the Conference and after it in the press, its own platform. It is no accident that the approach of peace, or even the intense discussion by certain bourgeois elements of the peace issue, has led to a very marked divergence between the two policies. To bourgeois pacifists and their 'socialist' imitators, or echoers, peace has always been a fundamentally distinct concept, for neither has ever understood that 'war is the continuation of the policies of peace and peace the continuation of the policies of war'. Neither the bourgeois nor the social-chauvinist wants to see that the imperialist war of 1914-17 is the continuation of the imperialist policies of 1898 – 1914, if not of an even earlier period. Neither the bourgeois pacifists nor the socialist pacifists realise that without the revolutionary overthrow of the bourgeois governments, peace *now* can only be an imperialist peace, a continuation of the imperialist war.

In appraising the present war, they use meaningless, vulgar, philistine phrases about aggression or defence in general, and use the same philistine commonplaces in appraising the peace, disregarding the concrete historical situation, the actual concrete struggle between the imperialist powers. And it was quite natural for the social-chauvinists, these agents of the governments and the bourgeoisie in the workers' parties, to seize upon the approach of peace in particular, or even upon mere peace talk, in order to *gloss over* the depth of their reformism and opportunism, exposed by the war, and restore their undermined influence over the masses. Hence, the social-chauvinists in Germany and in France, as we have seen, are making strenuous efforts to 'unite' with the flabby, unprincipled pacifist section of the 'opposition'.

Efforts to gloss over the divergence between the two irreconcilable lines of policy will certainly be made also in the Zimmerwald group. One can foresee that they will follow two lines. A 'practical business' conciliation by mechanically combining loud revolutionary phrases (like those in the International Socialist Committee manifesto) with opportunist and pacifist practice. That is what happened in the Second International. The arch-revolutionary phrases in the manifestos of Huysmans and Vandervelde and in certain congress resolutions merely served as a screen for the arch-opportunist practice of the majority of the European parties, but they did not change, disrupt or combat this practice. It is doubtful whether these tactics will again be successful in the Zimmerwald group.

The 'conciliators in principle' will try to falsify Marxism by arguing, for example, that reform does not exclude revolution, that an imperialist peace with certain 'improvements' in nationality frontiers, or in international law, or in armaments expenditure, etc., is possible side by side with the revolutionary movement, as 'one of the aspects of the development' of that movement, and so on and so forth.

This would be a falsification of Marxism. Reforms do not, of course, exclude revolution. But that is not the point at issue. The point is that revolutionaries must not exclude *themselves*, not give way to reformism, i.e. that socialists should not substitute reformist work for their revolutionary work. Europe is experiencing a revolutionary situation. The war and the high cost of living are aggravating the situation. The transition from war to peace will not necessarily eliminate the revolutionary situation, for there are no grounds whatever for believing that the millions of workers who now have excellent weapons in their hands will necessarily permit themselves to be 'peacefully disarmed' by the bourgeoisie instead of following the advice of Karl Liebknecht, i.e. turning their weapons against *their own* bourgeoisie.

The question is not, as the pacifist Kautskyites maintain: either a reformist political campaign, or else the renunciation of reforms. That is a bourgeois presentation of the question. The question is: either revolutionary struggle, the by-product of which, in the event of it not being fully successful, is reforms (the whole history of revolutions throughout the world has proved this), or nothing but talk about reforms and the promise of reforms.

The reformism of Kautsky, Turati and Bourderon, which now comes out in the form of pacifism, not only leaves aside the question of revolution (this *in itself* is a betrayal of socialism), not only abandons in practice all systematic and persistent revolutionary work, but even goes to the length of declaring that street demonstrations are adventurism (Kautsky in *Die Neue Zeit*, 26 November 1915). It goes to the length of advocating and implementing unity with the outspoken and determined opponents of revolutionary struggle, the Südekums, Legiens, Renaudels, Thomases, etc., etc.

This reformism is absolutely irreconcilable with revolutionary Marxism, the duty of which is to take the utmost possible advantage of the present revolutionary situation in Europe in order openly to urge revolution, the overthrow of the bourgeois governments, the conquest of power by the armed proletariat, while at the same time not renouncing, and not refusing to utilise, reforms in developing the revolutionary struggle and in the course of that struggle.

The immediate future will show what course events in Europe will follow, particularly the struggle between reformist pacifism and revolutionary Marxism, including the struggle between the two Zimmerwald sections.

Zürich,
1 January 1917

An Open Letter to Boris Souvarine

January 1917

Editors note:

This article was written in reply to an open letter by Boris Souvarine, the French Centrist, 'To Our Friends in Switzerland', published in *Le Populaire du Centre*, 10 December 1916.

Lenin sent the article to Souvarine who in January 1918 turned it over to the socialist *La Vérité* for publication, together with his preface. The article was to have appeared on 24 January in No. 45 of the paper, but was banned by the censor. *La Vérité* came out with a blank space, over which was the heading 'Unpublished document. A Letter from Lenin', with the signature '*Lénine*'. Three days later, on 27 January, *La Vérité* published the article, with many cuts and with its own subheadings, in No. 48. The full text was published in the magazine *Proletarskaya Revolutsia* (*Proletarian Revolution*), No. 7, in 1929 from the *La Vérité* galleys.

* * *

Citizen Souvarine says his letter is addressed also to me. I take all the greater pleasure in replying, since his article touches on vital problems of international socialism.

Souvarine believes that those who consider 'defence of the fatherland' to be incompatible with socialism are taking an 'unpatriotic' view. As for himself, he 'defends' the view of Turati, Ledebour, Brizon who, while voting against war credits, declare that they accept 'defence of the fatherland'; in other words, he defends the trend known as the 'Centre' (the 'marsh', I would say), or as Kautskyism – after its chief theoretical and literary exponent, Karl Kautsky. I might remark, in passing, that Souvarine is wrong in maintaining that

> ... they [i.e. the Russian comrades who speak of the collapse of the Second International] equate men like Kautsky, Longuet, etc... with nationalists of the Scheidemann and Renaudel type.

Neither I nor the Party to which I belong (the RSDLP Central Committee) have ever equated the social-chauvinist viewpoint with that of the 'Centre'. In our official Party statements, in the Central Committee manifesto published 1 November 1914,* and in the resolutions adopted in March 1915** (both documents are reproduced *in extenso* in our pamphlet *Socialism and War*,*** which is known to Souvarine), we have always drawn a dividing line between the social-chauvinists and the 'Centre'. The former, in our opinion, have defected to the bourgeoisie. With regard to them we demand not merely struggle, but a split. The latter hesitate, vacillate, and their efforts to unite the socialist masses with the chauvinist leaders cause the greatest damage to the proletariat.

Souvarine says he wants to "examine the facts from a Marxist viewpoint".

But from a Marxist viewpoint, such general and abstract definitions as 'unpatriotic' are of absolutely no value. The fatherland, the nation are historical categories. I am not at all opposed to wars waged in defence of democracy or against national oppression, nor do I fear such words as 'defence of the fatherland'

---

*   Lenin, 'The War and Russian Social-Democracy', in this volume, p. 17.
** Lenin, 'The Conference of the RSDLP Groups Abroad', in this volume, p. 35.
*** In this volume, p. 57.

in reference to these wars or to insurrections. Socialists always side with the oppressed and, consequently, cannot be opposed to wars whose purpose is democratic or socialist struggle against oppression. It would therefore be absurd to deny the legitimacy of the wars of 1793, of France's wars against the reactionary European monarchies, or of the Garibaldi wars, etc... And it would be just as absurd not to recognise the legitimacy of wars of oppressed nations against their oppressors, wars that might break out today – rebellion of the Irish against England, for instance, rebellion of Morocco against France, or the Ukraine against Russia, etc...

The Marxist viewpoint requires that in each individual case we define the political content of the war.

But what determines the political content of a war?

Every war is only the continuation of policy. What kind of policy is being continued in the present war? The policy of the proletariat, which from 1871 to 1914 was the sole exponent of socialism and democracy in France, England and Germany? Or imperialist policy, the policy of colonial rapine and oppression of weak nations by the reactionary, decadent and moribund bourgeoisie?

The question has only to be squarely put and we get a perfectly clear answer: the present war is an imperialist war. It is a war of slave-owners quarrelling over their chattels and eager to consolidate and perpetuate slavery. It is the "capitalist brigandage" of which Jules Guesde spoke in 1899, thereby condemning in advance his own betrayal. Guesde said at the time:

> There are other wars ... they arise every day, wars for the acquisition of markets. This kind of war does not disappear, but, on the contrary, bids fair to become continuous. It is chiefly a war between the capitalists of all countries for profits and possession of the world market, and it is fought at the price of our blood. Now, just imagine that in each of the capitalist countries of Europe, this mutual slaughter for the sake of plunder is directed by a socialist! Just imagine an English Millerand, an Italian Millerand, a German Millerand, in addition to a French Millerand, working to embroil the proletarians in this capitalist

brigandage and make them fight each other! What would remain I ask
you, comrades, of international solidarity? On the day the Millerands
became a common phenomenon, we would have to say 'farewell' to all
internationalism and become nationalists, and this neither you nor I
will ever agree to. (Jules Guesde, *En Garde!*, Paris, 1911, pp. 175-6.)

It is not true that France is waging this 1914-17 war for freedom,
national independence, democracy, and so on... She is fighting
to retain her colonies, and for England to retain hers, colonies to
which Germany would have had a much greater right – from the
standpoint of bourgeois law, of course. She is fighting to give Russia
Constantinople, etc... Consequently, this war is being waged not
by democratic and revolutionary France, not by the France of 1792,
nor the France of 1848, nor the France of the Commune. It is
being waged by bourgeois France, reactionary France, that ally and
friend of tsarism, the 'world usurer' (the expression is not mine, it
belongs to Lysis, a contributor to *l'Humanité*), who is defending his
booty, his 'sacred right' to possess colonies, his 'freedom' to exploit
the entire world with the help of the millions loaned to weaker or
poorer nations.

Do not tell me it is hard to distinguish between revolutionary
and reactionary wars. You want me to indicate a purely practical
criterion that would be understood by all, in addition to the
scientific criterion indicated above?

Here it is: Every fair-sized war is prepared beforehand. When a
revolutionary war is being prepared, democrats and socialists *are not
afraid to state in advance* that they favour 'defence of the fatherland'
in this war. When however, in contrast, a reactionary war is being
prepared, no socialist will *venture to state in advance*, before war is
declared, that is, that he will favour 'defence of the fatherland'.

Marx and Engels were not afraid to urge the German people to
fight Russia in 1848 and 1859.

*In contrast, at their Basel Congress in 1912 the socialists did not
venture to speak of 'defence of the fatherland' in the war they could see
was maturing and which broke out in 1914.*

Our Party is not afraid to declare publicly that it will sympathise with wars or uprisings which Ireland might start against England; Morocco, Algeria and Tunisia against France; Tripoli against Italy; the Ukraine, Persia, China against Russia, etc.

But what of the social-chauvinists? And the 'Centrists'? Will they have the courage openly and officially to state that they favour, or will favour, 'defence of the fatherland' in the event of war breaking out between, say, Japan and the United States, a clearly imperialist war prepared over the course of many years, and one which would imperil many hundreds of millions of people? I dare them! I am prepared to wager that they will not, for they know only too well that if they make such a statement, they will become a laughing stock in the eyes of the workers, they will be jeered at and driven out of the socialist parties. That is why the social-chauvinists and those in the 'Centre' will avoid any open statement and will continue to wriggle, lie and confuse the issue, seeking refuge in all manner of sophisms, like this one in the resolution of the last, 1915 French party congress: "An attacked country has the right to defence."

As if the question were: *Who was the first to attack*, and not: *What are the causes of the war? What are its aims? Which classes are waging it?* Could one imagine, for example, a sane-minded socialist recognising England's right to 'defence of the fatherland' in 1796, when the French revolutionary troops began to fraternise with the Irish? And yet it was the French who had attacked England and were actually preparing to land in Ireland. And could we, tomorrow, recognise the right to 'defence of the fatherland' for Russia and England, if, after they had been taught a lesson by Germany, they were attacked by Persia in alliance with India, China and other revolutionary nations of Asia performing their 1789 and 1793?

That is my reply to the really ludicrous charge that we share Tolstoy's views.* Our Party has rejected both the Tolstoy doctrine and pacifism, declaring that socialists must seek to transform the

---

* Leo Tolstoy was one of the most outstanding authors in Russian and world literature, who also developed a religious doctrine based on Christian anarchism and pacifism.

present war into a civil war of the proletariat against the bourgeoisie, for socialism.

Should you object that this is utopian, I will answer that the bourgeoisie of France, England, etc., do not, apparently, subscribe to that opinion. They would not play so vile and ridiculous a role, going to the length of jailing or conscripting 'pacifists', had they not felt and foreseen the inevitable and steady rise of revolution and its early approach.

This leads me to the question of a split, raised also by Souvarine. A split! That is the bogy with which the socialist leaders are trying to frighten others, and which they themselves fear so much!

> What useful purpose could *now* be served by the foundation of a new International? [Souvarine asks.] Its activity would be blighted by sterility, for numerically it would be very weak.

But the day-to-day facts show that, *precisely because they are afraid of a split*, the 'activity' of Pressemane and Longuet in France, Kautsky and Ledebour in Germany, is blighted by sterility! And precisely because Karl Liebknecht and Otto Rühle in Germany were not afraid of a split, openly declaring that a split was *necessary* (cf. Rühle's letter in *Vorwärts*, 12 January 1916), and did not hesitate to carry it out – their activity is of vast importance for the proletariat, *despite their numerical weakness*. Liebknecht and Rühle are only two against 108. But these two represent millions, the exploited mass, the overwhelming majority of the population, the future of mankind, the revolution that is mounting and maturing with every passing day. The 108, on the other hand, represent only the servile spirit of a handful of bourgeois flunkies within the proletariat. Brizon's activities, when he shares the weaknesses of the Centre or the marsh, are blighted by sterility. And, conversely, they cease to be sterile, help to awaken, organise and stimulate the proletariat, when Brizon really demolishes 'unity', when he courageously proclaims in parliament 'Down with the war!', or when he publicly speaks the truth, declaring that the Allies are fighting to give Russia Constantinople.

The genuine revolutionary internationalists are numerically weak? Nonsense! Take France in 1780, or Russia in 1900. The politically-conscious and determined revolutionaries, who in France represented the bourgeoisie – the revolutionary class of that era – and in Russia today's revolutionary class – the proletariat, were extremely weak numerically. They were only a few, comprising at the most only 1/10,000, or even 1/100,000, of their class. Several years later, however, these few, this allegedly negligible minority, led the masses, millions and tens of millions of people. Why? Because this minority really represented the interests of these masses, because it believed in the coming revolution, because it was prepared to serve it with supreme devotion.

Numerical weakness? But since when have revolutionaries made their policies dependent on whether they are in a majority or minority? In November 1914, when our Party called for a split with the opportunists,* declaring that the split was the only correct and fitting reply to their betrayal in August 1914, to many that seemed to be a piece of insensate sectarianism coming from men who had completely lost all contact with real life. Two years have passed, and what is happening? In England, the split is an accomplished fact. The social-chauvinist Hyndman has been forced to leave the party. In Germany, a split is developing before everyone's eyes. The Berlin, Bremen and Stuttgart organisations have even been accorded the honour of being expelled from the party... from the party of the Kaiser's lackeys, the party of the German Renaudels, Sembats, Thomases, Guesdes and co. And in France? On the one hand, the party of these gentlemen states that it remains true to 'fatherland defence'. On the other, the Zimmerwaldists state, in their pamphlet *The Zimmerwald Socialists and the War*, that 'defence of the fatherland' is un-socialist. Isn't this a split?

And how can men who, after two years of this greatest world crisis, give diametrically opposite answers to the supreme question

---

* See Lenin, 'The War and Russian Social-Democracy', in this volume, p. 17.

of modern proletarian tactics, work faithfully side by side, within one and the same party?

Look at America – apart from everything else a neutral country. Haven't we the beginnings of a split there, too: Eugene Debs, the 'American Bebel', declares in the socialist press that he recognises only one type of war, civil war for the victory of socialism, and that he would sooner be shot than vote a single cent for American war expenditure (see *Appeal to Reason* No. 1032, 11 September 1915).* On the other hand, the American Renaudels and Sembats advocate 'national defence' and 'preparedness'. The American Louguets and Pressemanes – the poor souls! – are trying to bring about a reconciliation between social-chauvinists and revolutionary internationalists.

Two Internationals already exist. One is the International of Sembat-Südekum-Hyndman-Plekhanov and co. The other is the International of Karl Liebknecht, Maclean (the Scottish schoolmaster whom the English bourgeoisie sentenced to hard labour for supporting the workers' class struggle), Höglund (the Swedish MP and one of the founders of the Zimmerwald Left sentenced to hard labour for his revolutionary propaganda against the war), the five Duma members exiled to Siberia for life for their propaganda against the war, etc. On the one hand, there is the International of those *who are helping their own governments wage the imperialist war*, and on the other, the International of those *who are waging a revolutionary fight against the imperialist war*. Neither parliamentary eloquence nor the 'diplomacy' of socialist 'statesmen' can unite these two Internationals. The Second International has outlived itself. The Third International has already been born. And if it has not yet been baptised by the high priests and Popes of the Second International but, on the contrary, has been anathemised (see Vandervelde's and Stauning's speeches), this is not preventing it from gaining strength with every passing day. The Third International will enable the proletariat to rid itself of opportunists

---

*   The title of Debs' article was 'When I Shall Fight'.

and will lead the masses to victory in the maturing and approaching social revolution.

Before concluding, I would like to say a few words in reply to Souvarine's personal polemics. He asks (the socialists now residing in Switzerland) to moderate their personal criticism of Bernstein, Kautsky, Longuet, etc... For my part, I must say that I cannot accept that. And I would point out to Souvarine, first of all, that my criticism of the 'Centre' is political, not personal. Nothing can restore the mass influence of the Südekums, Plekhanovs, etc.: their authority has been so undermined that everywhere the police have to protect them. But by their propaganda of 'unity' and 'fatherland defence', by their striving to bring about a compromise, by their efforts to draw a verbal veil over the deep-seated differences, the 'Centrists' are causing the greatest damage to the labour movement, because they are impeding the final break-down of the social-chauvinists' moral authority, and in that way are bolstering their influence on the masses and galvanising the corpse of the opportunist Second International. For all these reasons I consider it my socialist duty to fight Kautsky and other 'Centre' spokesmen.

Souvarine "appeals", among others, to:

> Guilbeaux, to Lenin, to all those who enjoy the advantage of being 'outside the battle', an advantage that often enables one to take a reasonable view of men and affairs in socialism, but one that, perhaps, is fraught also with certain inconveniences.

A transparent hint. In Zimmerwald, Ledebour expressed the same thought without any ambiguity. He accused us 'Left Zimmerwaldists' of addressing revolutionary appeals to the masses from abroad. I repeat to Citizen Souvarine what I told Ledebour in Zimmerwald. It is twenty-nine years since I was arrested in Russia. And throughout these twenty-nine years I have never ceased to address revolutionary appeals to the masses. I did so from prison, from Siberia, and later from abroad. And I frequently met in the revolutionary press 'hints' similar to those made in the speeches of tsarist prosecutors – 'hints' that I was lacking in honesty, because, while living abroad,

I addressed revolutionary appeals to the Russian people. Coming from tsarist prosecutors these 'hints' surprise no one. But I must admit that I expected arguments of another kind from Ledebour. Apparently he has forgotten that when they wrote their famous *Communist Manifesto* in 1847, Marx and Engels likewise addressed revolutionary appeals to the German workers from abroad! The revolutionary struggle is often impossible without revolutionaries emigrating abroad. That has repeatedly been the experience in France. And Citizen Souvarine would have done better not to follow the bad example of Ledebour and… the tsarist prosecutors.

Souvarine also says that Trotsky,

> … whom we [the French minority] consider one of the most extreme elements of the extreme Left in the International, is simply branded as a chauvinist by Lenin. It has to be admitted that there is a certain exaggeration here.

Yes, of course, "there is a certain exaggeration", but on Souvarine's part, not mine. For I have never branded Trotsky's position as chauvinistic. What I have reproached him with is that all too often he has represented the 'Centre' policy in Russia. Here are the facts. The split in the RSDLP has existed officially since January 1912.* Our Party (grouped around the Central Committee) accused of opportunism the other group, the Organising Committee, of which Martov and Axelrod are the most prominent leaders. Trotsky belonged to Martov's party and left it only in 1914.** By

---

*   The Prague Conference, in January 1912, marked the final parting of the ways between Bolsheviks and Mensheviks, with the latter boycotting the meeting.

**   Trotsky was invited to the Prague Conference as a representative of his *Pravda* grouping but refused to attend. He then participated in a Menshevik organised conference in Paris in March 1912, and later on he attempted to organise 'unity' between the Bolsheviks and Mensheviks at a gathering in Bern in August. The Bolsheviks refused to attend. The 'August Bloc' therefore was an unprincipled amalgam because it was made up of different tendencies with nothing in common except their hostility to Lenin, and quickly collapsed. Trotsky himself admitted he had been wrong:

> … I had not freed myself at that period, especially in the organisational sphere, from the traits of a petty-bourgeois revolutionist. I was sick with the disease of

that time the war had started. Our five Duma deputies (Muranov, Petrovsky, Shagov, Badayev and Samoilov) were exiled to Siberia. In Petrograd, our workers voted *against* participation in the war industries committees (the most important practical issue for us, just as important in Russia as the question of participation in the government in France). On the other hand, the most prominent and most influential Organising Committee writers – Potresov, Zasulich, Levitsky and others – have come out for 'defence of the fatherland' and participation in the war industries committees. Martov and Axelrod have protested and advocated non-participation in the committees. But they have not broken with their party, one faction of which has turned chauvinist and accepts participation. That is why at Kienthal we reproached Martov with having wanted to represent the Organising Committee as a whole, whereas in fact he can represent only one of its two factions. This party's Duma group (Chkheidze, Skobelev and others) is divided, with some of its members for and others against 'fatherland defence'. But all of them favour participation in the war industries committees, resorting to the ambiguous formula of 'saving the country', which, essentially, is but another wording of the Südekum and Renaudel 'fatherland defence' slogan. More, they have in no way protested against Potresov's position (which is actually identical to Plekhanov's; Martov publicly protested against Potresov and declined to contribute to his journal because Plekhanov had been invited to contribute).

And Trotsky? Having broken with Martov's party, he continues to accuse us of being splitters. Little by little he is moving to the Left, and even calls for a break with the Russian social-chauvinist

---

conciliationism toward Menshevism and with a distrustful attitude toward Leninist centralism. Immediately after the August conference the bloc began to disintegrate into its component parts. Within a few months I was not only in principle but organisationally outside the bloc. (Leon Trotsky, *In Defence of Marxism*, Wellred Books, 2019, p. 185.)

However, it was not until December 1914 – January 1915 that Trotsky made a public statement to the effect that he was not responsible for the positions of the Organising Committee (the Mensheviks).

leaders. But he has not definitely said whether he wants unity or a break with the Chkheidze faction. And that is one of the key issues. For, indeed, if peace comes tomorrow, we shall be having Duma elections the day after tomorrow, and the question will immediately arise of siding with or opposing Chkheidze. We oppose such an alliance. Martov favours it. And Trotsky? His attitude is unknown. There has been no definite indication of it in the 500 issues of the Paris Russian-language newspaper *Nashe Slovo*, of which Trotsky is one of the editors. These are the reasons why we do not agree with Trotsky.

We are not the only ones. In Zimmerwald, Trotsky refused to join the Zimmerwald Left. Together with Comrade Henriette Roland Hoist he represented the 'Centre'. And this is what Comrade Roland Hoist now writes in the Dutch socialist paper *Tribune* (No. 159, 23 August 1916):

> Those who, like Trotsky and his group, want to wage a revolutionary struggle against imperialism must overcome the consequences of émigré differences – largely of a personal nature – which disunite the extreme Left, and join the Leninists. A 'revolutionary centre' is impossible.

I must apologise for having dwelt at such length on our relations with Trotsky and Martov, but the French socialist press refers to this quite frequently and the information it gives its readers is often very inaccurate. The French comrades must be better informed of the facts concerning the Social-Democratic movement in Russia.

To the Workers Who Support the Struggle Against the War and Against the Socialists Who Have Sided With Their Governments

January 1917

The international situation is becoming increasingly clear and increasingly menacing. Both belligerent coalitions have latterly revealed the imperialist nature of the war in a very striking way. The more assiduously the capitalist governments and the bourgeois and socialist pacifists spread their empty, lying pacifist phrases – the talk of a democratic peace, a peace without annexations, etc. – the sooner are they exposed. Germany is crushing several small nations under her iron heel with the very evident determination not to give up her booty except by exchanging part of it for enormous colonial possessions, and she is using hypocritical pacifist phrases as a cover for her readiness to conclude an immediate imperialist peace.

England and her allies are clinging just as tightly to the colonies seized from Germany, part of Turkey, etc., claiming that in endlessly continuing the slaughter for possession of Constantinople, strangulation of Galicia, partition of Austria, the ruin of Germany, they are fighting for a 'just' peace.

The truth, of which only a few were theoretically convinced at the beginning of the war, is now becoming palpably evident to an increasing number of class-conscious workers, namely, that a serious struggle against the war, a struggle to abolish war and establish lasting peace, is out of the question unless there is a mass revolutionary struggle led by the proletariat against the government in every country, unless bourgeois rule is overthrown, unless a socialist revolution is brought about. And the war itself, which is imposing an unprecedented strain upon the peoples, is bringing mankind to this, the only way out of the impasse, is compelling it to take giant strides towards state capitalism,* and is demonstrating in a practical manner how planned social economy can and should be conducted, not in the interests of the capitalists, but by expropriating them, under the leadership of the revolutionary proletariat, in the interests of the masses who are now perishing from starvation and the other calamities caused by the war.

The more obvious this truth becomes, the wider becomes the gulf separating the two irreconcilable tendencies, policies, trends of socialist activity, which we indicated at Zimmerwald, where we acted as a separate Left wing, and in a manifesto to all socialist parties and to all class-conscious workers issued on behalf of the Left wing immediately after the conference.** This is the gulf that lies between the attempts to conceal the obvious bankruptcy of official socialism and its representatives' desertion to the bourgeoisie and their governments, as well as the attempts to reconcile the masses with this complete betrayal of socialism, on the one hand, and, on the other, the efforts to expose this bankruptcy in all its magnitude, to expose the bourgeois policy of the 'social-patriots', who have deserted the proletariat for the bourgeoisie, to destroy their influence over the masses and to create the possibility and the organisational basis for a genuine struggle against the war.

---

* Lenin is referring to the tendency for the state to intervene in and plan the economy in the context of the war.

** Reproduced in this volume, p. 387.

The Zimmerwald Right wing, which was in the majority at the conference, fought the idea of breaking with the social-patriots and founding the Third International tooth and nail. Since then, the split has become a definite fact in England; and in Germany the last conference of the 'opposition', on 7 January 1917, revealed to all who do not wilfully shut their eyes to the facts, that in that country too there are two irreconcilably hostile labour parties, working in opposite directions. One is a socialist party, working for the most part underground, and with Karl Liebknecht one of its leaders. The other is a thoroughly bourgeois, social-patriot party, which is trying to reconcile the workers to the war and to the government. The same division is to be observed in every country of the world.

At the Kienthal Conference the Zimmerwald Right wing did not have so large a majority as to be able to continue its own policy. It voted for the resolution against the social-patriot International Socialist Bureau, a resolution which condemned the latter in the sharpest terms, and for the resolution against social-pacifism, which warned the workers against lying pacifist phrases, regardless of socialist trimmings. Socialist pacifism, which refrains from explaining to the workers the illusory nature of hopes for peace *without* overthrowing the bourgeoisie and organising socialism, is merely an echo of bourgeois pacifism, which instils in the workers faith in the bourgeoisie, presents the imperialist governments and the deals they make with each other in a good light and distracts the masses from the maturing socialist revolution, which events have put on the order of the day.

But what transpired? After the Kienthal Conference, the Zimmerwald Right, in a number of important countries, in France, Germany and Italy, slid wholly and entirely into the very social-pacifism Kienthal had condemned and rejected! In Italy, the Socialist Party has tacitly accepted the pacifist phrases of its parliamentary group and its principal speaker, Turati, though, precisely now, when absolutely the same phrases are being used by Germany and the Entente and by representatives of the bourgeois governments of a number of neutral countries, where the bourgeoisie has accumulated and continues to accumulate enormous war profits – precisely now their utter falsehood has been exposed. In fact, pacifist phrases have proved to be a cover for the new turn in the fight for division of imperialist spoils!

In Germany, Kautsky, the leader of the Zimmerwald Right, issued a similar meaningless and non-committal pacifist manifesto, which merely instils in the workers hope in the bourgeoisie and faith in illusions. Genuine socialists, the genuine internationalists in Germany, the *Internationale* group and the International Socialists of Germany, who are applying Karl Liebknecht's tactics in practice, were obliged formally to dissociate themselves from this manifesto.

In France, Merrheim and Bourderon, who took part in the Zimmerwald Conference, and Raffin-Dugens, who took part in the Kienthal Conference, have voted *for* meaningless and, objectively, thoroughly false pacifist resolutions, which, in the present state of affairs, are so much to the *advantage* of the imperialist bourgeoisie that even Jouhaux and Renaudel, denounced as betrayers of socialism in all the Zimmerwald and Kienthal declarations, voted for them!

That Merrheim voted with Jouhaux and Bourderon and Raffin-Dugens with Renaudel is no accident, no isolated episode. It is a striking symbol of the imminent *merger* everywhere of the social-patriots and social-pacifists *against* the international socialists.

The pacifist phrases in the notes of a long list of imperialist governments, the same pacifist phrases uttered by Kautsky, Turati, Bourderon and Merrheim – Renaudel extending a friendly hand to the one and the other – all this exposes pacifism in *actual* politics as a means of *placating* the people, as a means of *helping* the governments to condition the masses to continuation of the imperialist slaughter!

This complete bankruptcy of the Zimmerwald Right has been still more strikingly revealed in Switzerland, the only European country where the Zimmerwaldists could meet freely, and which served as their base. The Socialist Party of Switzerland, which has held its congresses during the war without interference from the government and is in a better position than any other party to promote international solidarity between the German, French and Italian workers against the war, has officially affiliated to Zimmerwald.

And yet, on a decisive question affecting a proletarian party, one of this party's leaders, the chairman of the Zimmerwald and Kienthal conferences, a prominent member and representative of the Bern International Socialist Committee, National Councillor R Grimm, *deserted* to the social-patriots of *his country*. At the meeting of the Parteivorstand [Executive] of the Socialist Party of Switzerland on 7 January 1917, he secured the adoption of a decision to *postpone* indefinitely the party congress, which was to be convened for the express purpose of deciding the fatherland defence issue and the party's attitude towards the Kienthal Conference decisions condemning social-pacifism.

In a manifesto signed by the International Socialist Committee and dated December 1916, Grimm describes as hypocritical the pacifist phrases of the governments, but says not a word about the socialist pacifism that unites Merrheim and Jouhaux, Raffin-Dugens and Renaudel. In this manifesto, Grimm urges the socialist minorities to fight the governments and their social-patriot hirelings, but at the same time, jointly with the 'social-patriot hirelings' in the Swiss party, he endeavours to *bury* the party congress, thus rousing the just indignation of all the class-conscious and sincerely internationalist Swiss workers.

No excuses can conceal the fact that the Parteivorstand decision of 7 January 1917 signifies the complete victory of the Swiss social-patriots *over* the Swiss socialist workers, the victory of the Swiss opponents of Zimmerwald *over* Zimmerwald.

The *Grütlianer*, that organ of the consistent and avowed servants of the bourgeoisie in the labour movement, said what everyone knows is true when it declared that social-patriots of the Greulich and Pflüger type, to whom should be added Seidel, Huber, Lang, Schneeberger, Dürr, etc., want to prevent the congress from being

held, want to prevent the workers from deciding the fatherland
defence issue, and threaten to *resign* if the congress is held and a
decision in the spirit of Zimmerwald is adopted.

Grimm resorted to an outrageous and intolerable falsehood
at the Parteivorstand and in his newspaper, the *Berner Tagwacht*,
of 8 January 1917, when he claimed that the congress had to be
postponed because the workers were not ready, that it was necessary
to campaign against the high cost of living, that the 'Left' were
themselves in favour of postponement, etc.

In reality, it was the Left, i.e. the sincere Zimmerwaldists, who,
anxious to choose the lesser of two evils and also to expose the
real intentions of the social-patriots and their new friend, Grimm,
proposed postponing the congress until *March*, voted to postpone
it until *May*, and suggested that the meetings of the cantonal
committees be held before *July*; but *all* these proposals were voted
down by the 'fatherland defenders', led by the chairman of the
Zimmerwald and Kienthal conferences, Robert Grimm!!

In reality, the question was: shall the Bern International Socialist
Committee and Grimm's paper be allowed to hurl abuse at *foreign*
social-patriots and, at first by their silence and then by Grimm's
desertion, *shield* the *Swiss* Social patriots; or shall an honest
internationalist policy be pursued, a policy of fighting primarily the
social-patriots *at home*?

In reality, the question was: shall the domination of the
social-patriots and reformists in the Swiss party be concealed by
revolutionary phrases; or shall we oppose to them a *revolutionary*
programme and tactics on the question of combating the high cost
of living, as well as of combating the war, of putting on the order of
the day the fight for the socialist revolution?

In reality, the question was: shall the *worst* traditions of the
ignominiously bankrupt Second International be continued in
Zimmerwald; shall the workers be kept ignorant of the things the
party leaders do and say at the Parteivorstand; shall revolutionary
phrases be allowed to cover up the vileness of social-patriotism and
reformism, or shall we be internationalists *in deeds*?

In reality, the question was: shall we in Switzerland too, where the party is of primary importance for the whole of the Zimmerwald group, insist upon a clear, principled and politically honest division between the social-patriots and the internationalists, between the bourgeois reformists and the revolutionaries; between the counsellors of the proletariat, who are helping it carry out the socialist revolution, and the bourgeois agents or 'hirelings', who want to divert the workers from revolution by means of reforms or promises of reforms: between the Grütlians and the Socialist Party – *or* shall we confuse and corrupt the minds of the workers by conducting in the Socialist Party the 'Grütlian' policy of the Grütlians, i.e. the social-patriots in the ranks of the Socialist Party?

Let the Swiss social-patriots, those 'Grütlians' who want to operate their Grütlian policy, i.e. the policy of their national bourgeoisie, abuse the foreigners, let them defend the 'inviolability' of the Swiss party from criticism by other parties, let them champion the old bourgeois-reformist policy, i.e. the very policy that brought on the collapse of the German and other parties on 4 August 1914 – we, who adhere to Zimmerwald in deeds and not merely in words, interpret internationalism differently.

We are not prepared passively to regard the efforts, now definitely revealed, and sanctified by the chairman of the Zimmerwald and Kienthal conferences, to leave everything unchanged in decaying European socialism and, by means of hypocritical professions of solidarity with Karl Liebknecht, to *bypass* the real slogan of this leader of the international workers, his appeal to work for the 'regeneration' of the old parties from 'top to bottom'. We are convinced that on our side are all the class-conscious workers in all countries, who enthusiastically greeted Karl Liebknecht and his tactics.

We openly expose the Zimmerwald Right, which has deserted to bourgeois-reformist pacifism.

We openly expose Grimm's betrayal of Zimmerwald and demand convocation of a conference to remove him from his post on the International Socialist Committee.

The word 'Zimmerwald' is the slogan of international socialism and revolutionary struggle. This word must not serve to shield social-patriotism and bourgeois reformism.

Stand for true internationalism, which calls for the struggle, *first of all*, against the social-patriots in your own country! Stand for true revolutionary tactics, which are impossible if there is a compromise with the social-patriots *against* the revolutionary socialist workers!

How To Achieve Peace
(Fourth 'Letter from Afar')

12 (25) March 1917

Editors note:

As the February Revolution broke out, Lenin attempted to make sense of the situation from his exile in Switzerland. He became alarmed at the positions taken by the Party leaders in Russia, who had become infected with the carnival atmosphere which existed in the first days.

The February Revolution had overthrown the tsarist autocracy and a Provisional Government had been put in place. At the same time the workers had created their own organs of power, the Soviets (councils), which were also spreading to the countryside. Many of the Party leaders in Petrograd argued that the role of the Bolsheviks was to exercise pressure on the Provisional Government in order to push it to the left.

Lenin's position was diametrically opposed. He stated clearly that the class nature of the government was capitalist. The character of the war from Russia's point of view had not changed. The workers had illusions in the government, but the task of the Bolsheviks was not to make concessions to that mood, but rather to patiently explain that only by the workers taking power into their own hands could any of the problems posed by the revolution (peace, bread and land) be addressed.

Lenin proceeded to send a series of letters for publication in *Pravda* outlining his views. It was the beginning of a process to reorient the Party towards a clear position of no confidence in the Provisional Government and the slogan of Soviet Power.

The first four *Letters from Afar* were written between 7-12 (20-25) March 1917, the fifth, unfinished letter was written on the eve of Lenin's departure from Switzerland, on 26 March (8 April).

Such was the shock of Party leaders in Petrograd at the line defended by Lenin, which was at odds with the position they had adopted, that Lenin's letters were either published with heavy editing or suppressed.

The editorial board of *Pravda* which carried this out included LB Kamenev and JV Stalin.

* * *

I have just read in the *Neue Zürcher Zeitung* (No. 517 of 24 March) the following telegraphic dispatch from Berlin:

> It is reported from Sweden that Maxim Gorky has sent the government and the Executive Committee greetings couched in enthusiastic terms. He greets the people's victory over the lords of reaction and calls upon all Russia's sons to help erect the edifice of the new Russian state. At the same time he urges the government to crown the cause of emancipation by concluding peace. It must not, he says, be peace at any price; Russia now has less reason than ever to strive for peace at any price. It must be a peace that will enable Russia to live in honour among the other nations of the earth. Mankind has shed much blood; the new government would render not only Russia, but all mankind, the greatest service if it succeeded in concluding an early peace.

That is how Maxim Gorky's letter is reported.

It is with deep chagrin that one reads this letter, impregnated through and through with stock philistine prejudices. The author of these lines has had many occasions, in meetings with Gorky in Capri, to warn and reproach him for his political mistakes. Gorky parried these reproaches with his inimitable charming smile and with the ingenuous remark: "I know I am a bad Marxist. And besides, we artists are all somewhat irresponsible." It is not easy to argue against that.

There can be no doubt that Gorky's is an enormous artistic talent which has been, and will be, of great benefit to the world proletarian movement.

But why should Gorky meddle in politics?

In my opinion, Gorky's letter expresses prejudices that are exceedingly widespread not only among the petty bourgeoisie, but also among a section of the workers under its influence. *All* the energies of our Party, all the efforts of the class-conscious workers, must be concentrated on a persistent, persevering, all-round struggle against these prejudices.

The tsarist government began and waged the present war as an *imperialist*, predatory war to rob and strangle weak nations. The government of the Guchkovs and Milyukovs, which is a landlord and capitalist government, is forced to continue, and wants to continue, *this very same kind* of war. To urge that government to conclude a democratic peace is like preaching virtue to brothel keepers.

Let me explain what is meant.

What is imperialism?

In my *Imperialism, the Highest Stage of Capitalism*, the manuscript of which was delivered to the Parus Publishers some time before the revolution, was accepted by them and announced in the magazine *Letopis*, I answered this question as follows:

> Imperialism is capitalism at that stage of development at which the dominance of monopolies and finance capital is established; in which the export of capital has acquired pronounced importance; in which the division of the world among the international trusts has begun; in which the division of all territories of the globe among the biggest capitalist powers has been completed.*

---

* Chapter 7 of the above-mentioned book, the publication of which was announced in *Letopis*, when the censorship still existed, under the title: 'Modern Capitalism', by V Ilyin – *Lenin*

The whole thing hinges on the fact that capital has grown to huge dimensions. Associations of a small number of the biggest capitalists (cartels, syndicates, trusts) manipulate *billions* and divide the whole world among themselves. The world has been *completely* divided up. The war was brought on by the clash of the two most powerful groups of multimillionaires, Anglo-French and German, for the *redivision* of the world.

The Anglo-French group of capitalists wants first to rob Germany, deprive her of her colonies (nearly all of which have already been seized), and then to rob Turkey.

The German group of capitalists wants to seize Turkey for *itself* and to compensate itself for the loss of its colonies by seizing neighbouring small states (Belgium, Serbia, Romania).

This is the real truth; it is being concealed by all sorts of bourgeois lies about a 'liberating', 'national' war, a 'war for right and justice', and similar jingle with which the capitalists always fool the common people.

Russia is waging this war with foreign money. Russian capital is a *partner* of Anglo-French capital. Russia is waging the war in order to rob Armenia, Turkey, Galicia.

Guchkov, Lvov and Milyukov, our present ministers, are not chance comers. They are the representatives and leaders of the entire landlord and capitalist class. They are *bound* by the interests of capital. The capitalists can no more renounce their interests than a man can lift himself by his bootstraps.

Secondly, Guchkov-Milyukov and co. are *bound* by Anglo-French capital. They have waged, and are still waging, the war with foreign money. They have borrowed billions, promising to pay *hundreds of millions* in interest *every year*, and to squeeze this *tribute* out of the Russian workers and Russian peasants.

Thirdly, Guchkov-Milyukov and co. are *bound* to England, France, Italy, Japan and other groups of robber capitalists by direct *treaties* concerning the predatory aims of this war. These treaties were concluded by *Tsar Nicholas II*. Guchkov-Milyukov and co. took advantage of the workers' struggle against the tsarist monarchy to seize power, and *they have confirmed the treaties* concluded by the tsar.

This was done by the whole of the Guchkov-Milyukov government in a manifesto which the St. Petersburg Telegraph Agency circulated on 7 (20) March: "The government [of Guchkov and Milyukov] will faithfully abide by all the treaties that bind us with other powers," says the manifesto. Milyukov, the new Minister for Foreign Affairs, said the *same thing* in his telegram of 5 (18) March 1917 to all Russian representatives abroad.

These are all *secret* treaties, and Milyukov and co. *refuse* to make them public for two reasons: (1) they fear the people, who are opposed to the predatory war; (2) they are bound by Anglo-French capital which insists that the treaties remain secret. But every newspaper reader who has followed events knows that these treaties envisage the robbery of China by Japan; of Persia, Armenia, Turkey (especially Constantinople) and Galicia by Russia; of Albania by Italy; of Turkey and the German colonies by France and England, etc.

This is how things stand.

Hence, to urge the Guchkov-Milyukov government to conclude a speedy, honest, democratic and good-neighbourly peace is like the good village priest urging the landlords and the merchants to 'walk in the way of God', to love their neighbours and to turn the other cheek. The landlords and merchants listen to these sermons, continue to oppress and rob the people and praise the priest for his ability to console and pacify the 'muzhiks'.

Exactly the same role is played – consciously or unconsciously – by all those who in the present imperialist war address pious peace appeals to the bourgeois governments. The bourgeois governments either refuse to listen to such appeals and even prohibit them, or they allow them to be made and assure all and sundry that they are only fighting to conclude the speediest and 'justest' peace, and that all the blame lies with the enemy. Actually, talking peace *to bourgeois* governments turns out to be *deception of the people*.

The groups of capitalists who have drenched the world in blood for the sake of dividing territories, markets and concessions *cannot* conclude an 'honourable' peace. They can conclude only a *shameful* peace, a peace based *on the division of the spoils, on the partition of Turkey and the colonies.*

Moreover, the Guchkov-Milyukov government is in general opposed to peace at the present moment, because the '*only*' 'loot' it would get *now* would be Armenia and part of Galicia, whereas it *also* wants to get Constantinople *and* regain from the Germans Poland, which tsarism has always so inhumanly and shamelessly oppressed. Further, the Guchkov-Milyukov government is, in essence, only the agent of Anglo-French capital, which wants to retain the colonies it has wrested from Germany and, *on top of that*, compel Germany hand back Belgium and part of France. Anglo-French capital helped the Guchkovs and Milyukovs remove Nicholas II in order that they might help it to 'vanquish' Germany.

What, then, is to be done?

To achieve peace (and still more to achieve a really democratic, a really honourable peace), it is necessary that political power be in the hands of *the workers and poorest peasants*, not the landlords and capitalists. The latter represent an insignificant minority of the population, and the capitalists, as everybody knows, are making fantastic profits out of the war.

The workers and poorest peasants are the *vast* majority of the population. They are not making profit out of the war; on the contrary, they are being reduced to ruin and starvation. They are bound neither by capital nor by the treaties between the predatory groups of capitalists; they *can* and sincerely want to end the war.

If political power in Russia were in the hands of the *Soviets* of Workers', Soldiers' and Peasants' Deputies, these Soviets, and the *All-Russia Soviet* elected by them, could, and no doubt would, agree to carry out the peace programme which our Party (the Russian Social-Democratic Labour Party) outlined as early as 13 October 1915, in No. 47 of its Central Organ, *Sotsial-Demokrat* (then published in Geneva because of the Draconic tsarist censorship).*

This programme would probably be the following:

1. The All-Russia Soviet of Workers', Soldiers' and Peasants' Deputies (or the St. Petersburg Soviet temporarily acting for it) would forthwith declare that it is *not* bound by *any* treaties concluded *either* by the tsarist monarchy *or* by the bourgeois governments.

2. It would forthwith publish *all* these treaties in order to hold up to public shame the predatory aims of the tsarist monarchy and of *all* the bourgeois governments without exception.

3. It would forthwith publicly call upon *all* the belligerent powers to conclude an *immediate armistice*.

4. It would immediately bring to the knowledge of all the people our, the workers' and peasants', *peace terms*:
   – liberation of *all* colonies;
   – liberation of *all* dependent, oppressed and unequal nations.

5. It would declare that it expects nothing good from the bourgeois governments and calls upon the workers of all countries to overthrow them and to transfer all political power to Soviets of Workers' Deputies.

6. It would declare that the *capitalist gentry themselves* can repay the billions of debts contracted by the bourgeois governments to wage this criminal, predatory war, and that the workers and peasants *refuse to recognise* these debts. To pay the interest on these loans would mean paying the capitalists *tribute* for many years for having graciously allowed the workers to kill one another in order that the capitalists might divide the spoils.

Workers and peasants! – the Soviet of Workers' Deputies would say – are you willing to pay these gentry, the capitalists, *hundreds of*

---

* Lenin, 'Several Theses – Proposed by the Editors', *LCW*, Vol. 21, pp. 401-4.

millions of rubles *every year* for a war waged for the division of the African colonies, Turkey, etc.?

For *these* peace terms the Soviet of Workers' Deputies would, in my opinion, agree to *wage war* against *any* bourgeois government and against *all* the bourgeois governments of the world, because this would really be a just war, because *all* the workers and toilers in *all* countries would *work for its success.*

The German worker now sees that the bellicose monarchy in Russia is being replaced by a *bellicose* republic, a republic of capitalists who want to continue the imperialist war, and who have confirmed the predatory treaties of the tsarist monarchy.

Judge for yourselves, can the German worker trust *such* a republic?

Judge for yourselves, can the war continue, can the capitalist domination continue on earth, if the Russian people, always sustained by the living memories of the great Revolution of 1905, win complete freedom and transfer all political power to the Soviets of Workers' and Peasants' Deputies?

N Lenin,
Zürich,
12 (25) March 1917

Report at a Meeting of Bolshevik Delegates to the All-Russia Conference of Soviets of Workers' and Soldiers' Deputies

4 (17) April 1917

Editors note:

The All-Russia Conference of Party Workers (March Conference) was timed by the Russian Bureau of the RSDLP CC for the All-Russia Conference of Soviets of Workers' and Soldiers' Deputies and opened on 27 March (9 April) 1917. On its agenda were the attitude to the war, the attitude to the Provisional Government, the organisation of revolutionary forces, etc.

The meeting of 4 (17) April at which Lenin gave his report was held in the Tauride Palace. Lenin explained his *April Theses* and quoted them in part. The text of his speech is reproduced from secretarial notes containing lacunae indicated with dots, apart from some places of the notes which are not quite clear. The minutes of the March Conference were never published in the Soviet Union, but are available in Trotsky's *The Stalinist School of Falsification*, and reveal the full position of the Party leaders before the arrival of Lenin, particularly Stalin and Kamenev.

Lenin's speech was an important part of his struggle to reorient
the Party and is full of attacks on those who had a conciliatory
line towards the Provisional Government, as well as against any
idea of unification with the Mensheviks. The text of the speech
was not published in the Party press at the time. His *Theses*
were published three days later in *Pravda* (see next item in this
volume, p. 283), but were signed in Lenin's name only. The
following day, Kamenev published another article titled 'Our
Differences' in which he dissociated himself, the editors of the
paper and the Party Central Committee from Lenin's *Theses*.

* * *

I have put down a few theses on which I will make some comments.
For lack of time I was unable to present a circumstantial and
systematic report.

The basic question is the attitude to the war. The main thing
that comes to the fore, when you read about Russia and see what
goes on here, is the victory of defencism, the victory of the traitors
to socialism, the deception of the masses by the bourgeoisie.
What strikes one is that here in Russia the socialist movement is
in the same state as in other countries: defencism, 'defence of the
fatherland'. The difference is that nowhere is there such freedom
as here, and therefore we have a special responsibility to the whole
international proletariat. The new government is as imperialist as
the previous one; it is imperialist through and through, despite its
promise of a republic.

1. In our attitude towards the war, which under the new government
    of Lvov and co. unquestionably remains on Russia's part a predatory
    imperialist war owing to the capitalist nature of that government,
    not the slightest concession to 'revolutionary defencism' is
    permissible.

    The class-conscious proletariat can give its consent to a
    revolutionary war, which would really justify revolutionary
    defencism, only on condition: (a) that the power pass to the
    proletariat and the poorest sections of the peasants aligned with

the proletariat; (b) that all annexations be renounced in deed and not in word; (c) that a complete break be effected in actual fact with all capitalist interests.

In view of the undoubted honesty of those broad sections of the mass believers in revolutionary defencism who accept the war only as a necessity, and not as a means of conquest, in view of the fact that they are being deceived by the bourgeoisie, it is necessary with particular thoroughness, persistence and patience to explain their error to them, to explain the inseparable connection existing between capital and the imperialist war, and to prove that without overthrowing capital *it is impossible* to end the war by a truly democratic peace, a peace not imposed by violence.

The most widespread campaign for this view must be organised in the army at the front.

Fraternisation.

We cannot allow the slightest concession to defencism in our attitude to the war even under the new government, which remains imperialist. The masses take a practical and not a theoretical view of things. They say: "I want to defend the fatherland, not to seize other peoples' lands." When can a war be considered your own? When annexations are completely renounced.

The masses take a practical and not a theoretical approach to the question. We make the mistake of taking the theoretical approach. A class-conscious proletarian can agree to a revolutionary war, which really does justify revolutionary defencism. The practical approach is the only possible one with representatives of the mass of the soldiers. We are not pacifists in any sense. But the main question is: which class is carrying on the war? The class of capitalists, linked with the banks, cannot wage any kind of war except an imperialist one. The working class can. Steklov and Chkheidze have forgotten everything. When you read the resolution of the Soviet of Workers' Deputies, you are amazed that people calling themselves socialists could adopt such a resolution.

What is specific in Russia is the extremely rapid transition from savage violence to the most subtle deception. The main condition is *renunciation of annexations not in words*, but in deeds. *Rech* howls at *Sotsial-Demokrat's* statement that the integration of Courland with Russia is annexation. But annexation is the integration of any country with distinct national peculiarities; it is any integration of a nation against its will, irrespective of whether it differs in language, if it feels itself to be another people. This is a prejudice of the Great Russians which has been fostered for centuries.

The war can be ended only by a clean break with international capital. The war was engendered not by individuals but by international finance capital. It is no easy thing to break with international capital, but neither is it an easy thing to end the war. It is childishness and naivete to expect one side alone to end the war... Zimmerwald, Kienthal... We have a greater obligation than anyone else to safeguard the honour of international socialism. The difficulty of approach...

In view of the undoubted existence of a defencist mood among the masses, who recognise the war *only of necessity* and not for the sake of conquest, we must explain to them most circumstantially, persistently and patiently that the war cannot be ended in a non-rapacious peace unless capital is overthrown. This idea must be spread far and wide. The soldiers want a concrete answer: how to end the war. But it is political fraud to promise the people that we can end the war only by the goodwill of individual persons. The masses must be forewarned. A revolution is a difficult thing. It is impossible to avoid mistakes. Our mistake is that we (have not exposed?) revolutionary defencism to the full. Revolutionary defencism is betrayal of socialism. We cannot confine ourselves... We must admit our mistake. What is to be done? To explain. How to present... who doesn't know what socialism is... We are not charlatans. We must base ourselves only on the political consciousness of the masses. Even if we have to remain in a minority – let it be so. It is worthwhile giving up our leading position for a time; we should not be afraid of remaining in a minority. When the masses say they don't want conquest, I believe them. When Guchkov and Lvov say they don't want conquest, they are swindlers. When the worker says that he wants to defend the country, he voices the oppressed man's instinct.

2. The specific feature of the present situation in Russia is that the country is *passing* from the first stage of the revolution – which, owing to the insufficient class-consciousness and organisation of the proletariat, placed power in the hands of the bourgeoisie – to its *second* stage, which must place power in the hands of the proletariat and the poorest sections of the peasants.

   This transition is characterised, on the one hand, by a maximum of legally recognised rights (Russia is *now* the freest of all the belligerent countries in the world); on the other, by the absence of violence towards the masses, and, finally, by their unreasoning trust in the government of capitalists, those worst enemies of peace and socialism.

   This peculiar situation demands of us an ability to adapt ourselves to the *special* conditions of Party work among unprecedentedly large masses of proletarians who have just awakened to political life.

Why didn't they take power? Steklov says: for this reason and that. This is nonsense. The fact is that the proletariat is not organised and class-conscious enough. This must be admitted; material strength is in the hands of the proletariat, but the bourgeoisie turned out to be prepared and class-conscious. This is a monstrous fact, but it should be frankly and openly admitted, and the people should be told that they didn't take power because they were unorganised and not conscious enough… The ruin of millions, the death of millions. The most advanced countries are on the brink of disaster, and they will therefore be faced with the question…

The transition from the first stage to the second – the transfer of power to the proletariat and the peasantry – is characterised, on the one hand, by the maximum of legality (Russia today is the freest and most progressive country in the world) and, on the other, by an attitude of blind trust on the part of the masses in the government. Even our Bolsheviks show some trust in the government. This can be explained only by the intoxication of the revolution. It is the death of socialism. You comrades have a trusting attitude to the government. If that is so, our paths diverge. I prefer to remain in a minority. One Liebknecht is worth more than 110 defencists of the Steklov and Chkheidze type. If you sympathise with Liebknecht and stretch out even a finger (to the defencists), it will be betrayal of international socialism. If we break away from those people… everyone who is oppressed will come to us, because the war will lead him to us; he has no other way out.

The people should be spoken to without Latin words, in clear and simple terms. They have the right… – we must adapt ourselves… make the change, but it is essential. Our line will prove to be the correct one.

3.   No support for the Provisional Government; the utter falsity of all its promises should be made clear, particularly of those relating to the renunciation of annexations. Exposure in place of the impermissible, illusion-breeding 'demand' that *this* government, a government of capitalists, should *cease* to be an imperialist government.

Pravda demands of the *government* that it should renounce annexations. To demand of a government of capitalists that it should renounce annexations is nonsense, a crying mockery of…

From the scientific standpoint, this is such gross deception which all the international proletariat, all… It is time to admit our mistake. We've had enough of greetings and resolutions, it is time to act. We must get down to a sober, business-like…

4.   Recognition of the fact that in most of the Soviets of Workers' Deputies our Party is in a minority, so far a small minority, as against *a bloc of all* the petty-bourgeois opportunist elements, from the Popular Socialists and the Socialist-Revolutionaries down to the Organising Committee (Chkheidze, Tsereteli, etc.), Steklov,

etc., etc., who have yielded to the influence of the bourgeoisie and spread that influence among the proletariat.

The masses must be made to see that the Soviets of Workers' Deputies are the *only possible* form of revolutionary government, and that therefore our task is, as long as *this* government yields to the influence of the bourgeoisie, to present a patient, systematic and persistent explanation of the errors of their tactics, an *explanation* especially adapted to the practical needs of the masses.

As long as we are in the minority we carry on the work of criticising and exposing errors and at the same time we preach the necessity of transferring the entire state power to the Soviets of Workers' Deputies, so that the people may overcome their mistakes by experience.

We Bolsheviks are in the habit of taking the line of maximum revolutionism. But that is not enough. We must sort things out.

The Soviet of Workers' Deputies is the real government. To think otherwise is to fall into anarchism. It is a recognised fact that in the Soviet of Workers' Deputies our Party is in a minority. We must explain to the masses that the Soviet of Workers' Deputies is the only possible government, a government without parallel in the world, except for the Commune. What if a majority of the Soviet of Workers' Deputies takes the defencist stand? That cannot be helped. It remains for us to explain, patiently, persistently, systematically, the erroneous nature of their tactics.

So long as we are in a minority, we carry on the work of criticism, in order to open the people's eyes to the deception. We don't want the masses to take our word for it. We are not charlatans. We want the masses to overcome their mistakes through *experience*.

The manifesto of the Soviet of Workers' Deputies contains not a word imbued with class-consciousness. It's all talk! Talk, flattery of the revolutionary people, is the only thing that has ruined all revolutions. The whole of Marxism teaches us not to succumb to revolutionary phrases, particularly at a time when they have the greatest currency.

5. Not a parliamentary republic – to return to a parliamentary republic from the Soviets of Workers' Deputies would be a retrograde step – but a republic of Soviets of Workers', Agricultural Labourers' and Peasants' Deputies throughout the country, from top to bottom.

Abolition of the police, the army and the bureaucracy.*

The salaries of all officials, all of whom are elective and displaceable at any time, not to exceed the average wage of a competent worker.

This is the lesson of the French Commune, which Kautsky forgot and which the workers teach us in 1905 and 1917. The experience of these years teaches us that we must not allow the police and the old army to be restored.

The programme should be changed, it is out of date. The Soviet of Workers' and Soldiers' Deputies is a step to socialism. There must be no police, no army, no officialdom. The convocation of the Constituent Assembly – but by whom? Resolutions are written only to be shelved or sat on. I should be glad to have the Constituent Assembly convened tomorrow, but it is naive to believe that Guchkov will call it. All the chatter about forcing the Provisional Government to call the Constituent Assembly is empty talk, a pack of lies. Revolutions were made, but the police stayed on, revolutions were made, but all the officials, etc., stayed on. That was why the revolutions foundered. The Soviet of Workers' Deputies is the only government which can call that assembly. We all seized upon the Soviets of Workers' Deputies, but have failed to understand them. From this form we are dragging back to the International, which is trailing behind the bourgeoisie.

A bourgeois republic cannot solve the problem (of the war), because it can be solved only on an international scale. We don't promise liberation… but we say that it is possible only in this form (Soviet of Workers' and Soldiers' Deputies). No government except the Soviet of Workers' and Agricultural Labourers' Deputies. If you

---

* I.e. the standing army to be replaced by the arming of the whole people. – *Lenin*

talk about the Commune, they won't understand. But if you say, there is the Soviet of Workers' and Agricultural Labourers' Deputies instead of the police, learn to govern – no one can interfere with us – (that they will understand).

No books will ever teach you the art of government. Learning to govern is a matter of trial and error.

6. The weight of emphasis in the agrarian programme to be shifted to the Soviets of Agricultural Labourers' Deputies.

Confiscation of all landed estates.

Nationalisation of *all* lands in the country, the land to be disposed of by the local Soviets of Agricultural Labourers' and Peasants' Deputies. The organisation of separate Soviets of Deputies of Poor Peasants. The setting up of a model farm on each of the large estates (ranging in size from 100 to 300 dessiatins,* according to local and other conditions, and to the decisions of the local bodies) under the control of the Soviets of Agricultural Labourers' Deputies and for the public account.

What is the peasantry? We don't know, there are no statistics, but we do know that it is a force.

If they take the land, you can be sure that they won't give it back to you, they won't ask us. The pivot, the centre of gravity of the programme has shifted, and is the Soviets of Agricultural Labourers' Deputies. If the Russian peasant doesn't settle the revolution, the German worker will.

The Tambov muzhik…

The first dessiatin cost free, the second for 1 ruble, the third for 2 rubles. We shall take over the land, and the landowner will never be able to take it back.

Communal farming.

It is necessary to organise separate Soviets of Deputies from the poor peasants. There is the rich muzhik, and there is the labourer. Even if you give him land, he won't set up a farm. The large estates

_____

* 1 dessiatin = 1.09 hectare (approximately 2.7 English acres).

should be turned into model farms run on social lines, with management by the Soviets of Agricultural Labourers' Deputies.

There are large estates.

7. The immediate amalgamation of all banks in the country into a single national bank, and the institution of control over it by the Soviet of Workers' Deputies.

The bank is "a form of social book-keeping" (Marx). War teaches economy; everyone knows that the banks sap the strength of the people. The banks are the nerve, the focus of the national economy. We cannot take hold of the banks, but we advocate their amalgamation under the control of the Soviet of Workers' Deputies.

8. It is not our *immediate* task to 'introduce' socialism, but only to bring social production and the distribution of products at once under the *control* of the Soviets of Workers' Deputies.

Practice and the revolution tend to push the Constituent Assembly into the background. The important thing about laws is not that they are put down on paper, but who carries them out. The dictatorship of the proletariat is there, but people don't know how to work it. Capitalism has developed into state capitalism… Marx … only that which has matured in practice…

9. Party tasks:
    a. Immediate convocation of a Party congress;
    b. Alteration of the Party Programme, mainly:
        i.   On the question of imperialism and the imperialist war;
        ii. On our attitude towards the state and *our* demand for a 'commune state';*
        iii. Amendment of our out-of-date minimum programme;
    c. Change of the Party's name.**

---

* I.e. a state of which the Paris Commune was the prototype. – *Lenin*

** Instead of 'Social-Democracy', whose official leaders *throughout* the world have betrayed socialism and deserted to the bourgeoisie (the 'defencists' and the vacillating 'Kautskyites'), we must call ourselves the *Communist Party*. – *Lenin*

10. A new International.

We must take the initiative in creating a revolutionary International, an International against the *social-chauvinists* and against the 'Centre'.*

General conclusion.

The Soviet of Workers' Deputies has been created, it enjoys vast influence. All instinctively sympathise with it. This institution combines far more revolutionary thought than all the *revolutionary phrases*. If the Soviet of Workers' Deputies succeeds in taking government into its own hands, the cause of liberty is assured. You may write the most ideal laws, but who will put them into effect? The same officials, but they are tied up with the bourgeoisie.

It is not 'introduce socialism' that we ought to tell the masses, but put it into effect (?). Capitalism has gone ahead, war capitalism is different from that which existed before the war.

On the basis of our tactical conclusions we must go on to practical steps. A Party congress must be called at once and the Programme revised. A great deal in it is out of date. The minimum programme must be changed.

I personally propose that we change the name of our Party and call it the *Communist Party*. The people will understand the name of 'Communist'. Most of the official Social-Democrats have committed treason, they have betrayed socialism… Liebknecht is the one Social-Democrat… You are afraid of betraying old recollections. But if you want to change your underwear you must take off your dirty shirt and put on a clean one. Why throw out the experience of world-wide struggle? Most of the Social-Democrats throughout the world have betrayed socialism, and have sided with their governments (Scheidemann, Plekhanov, Guesde). What is to be done to make Scheidemann agree?… This point of view spells

---

* The 'Centre' in the international Social-Democratic movement is the trend which vacillates between the chauvinists (= 'defencists') and internationalists, i.e. Kautsky and co. in Germany, Longuet and co. in France, Chkheidze and co. in Russia, Turati and co. in Italy, MacDonald and co. in Britain, etc. – *Lenin*

ruin for socialism. It would be deception to send a radio telegram to Scheidemann about ending the war...

The term 'Social-Democracy' is inexact. Don't cling to an old word which has become rotten through and through. If you want to build a new party... and all the oppressed will come to you.

The Centre prevailed at Zimmerwald and Kienthal... *Rabochaya Gazeta*. We shall prove to you that the whole of experience has shown.... We declare that we have formed a Left wing and have broken with the Centre. Either you speak about the International, then carry out... or you...

The Left Zimmerwald trend exists in all the countries of the world. The masses must realise that socialism has split throughout the world. The defencists have renounced socialism. Liebknecht alone... The future is with him.

I have heard that there is a tendency in Russia towards unification, towards unity with the defencists. This is betrayal of socialism. I think it is better to remain alone, like Liebknecht: one against 110.

The Tasks of the Proletariat in the Present Revolution (April Theses)

4 (17) April 1917

Editors note:

Published in *Pravda* No. 26, for 7 April 1917, with the signature 'N Lenin', this article contains Lenin's famous *April Theses* read by him at two meetings held at the Tauride Palace on 4 (17) April 1917, at a meeting of Bolsheviks and at a joint meeting of Bolshevik and Menshevik delegates to the All-Russia Conference of Soviets of Workers' and Soldiers' Deputies.

The article was reprinted in the Bolshevik newspapers *Sotsial-Demokrat* (Moscow), *Proletary* (Kharkov), *Krasnoyarsky Rabochy* (Krasnoyarsk), *Vperyod* (Ufa), *Bakinsky Rabochy* (Baku), *Kavkazsky Rabochy* (Tiflis) and others.

* * *

I did not arrive in Petrograd until the night of 3 April, and therefore at the meeting on 4 April I could, of course, deliver the report on the tasks of the revolutionary proletariat only on my own behalf, and with reservations as to insufficient preparation.

The only thing I could do to make things easier for myself – and for *honest* opponents – was to prepare the theses *in writing*. I read them out, and gave the text to Comrade Tsereteli. I read them *twice* very slowly: first at a meeting of Bolsheviks and then at a meeting of both Bolsheviks and Mensheviks.

I publish these personal theses of mine with only the briefest explanatory notes, which were developed in far greater detail in the report.

Theses

1. In our attitude towards the war, which under the new government of Lvov and co. unquestionably remains on Russia's part a predatory imperialist war owing to the capitalist nature of that government, not the slightest concession to 'revolutionary defencism' is permissible.

    The class-conscious proletariat can give its consent to a revolutionary war, which would really justify revolutionary defencism, only on condition: (a) that the power pass to the proletariat and the poorest sections of the peasants aligned with the proletariat; (b) that all annexations be renounced in deed and not in word; (c) that a complete break be effected in actual fact with all capitalist interests.

    In view of the undoubted honesty of those broad sections of the mass believers in revolutionary defencism who accept the war only as a necessity, and not as a means of conquest, in view of the fact that they are being deceived by the bourgeoisie, it is necessary with particular thoroughness, persistence and patience to explain their error to them, to explain the inseparable connection existing between capital and the imperialist war, and to prove that without overthrowing capital *it is impossible* to end the war by a truly democratic peace, a peace not imposed by violence.

    The most widespread campaign for this view must be organised in the army at the front.

    Fraternisation.

2. The specific feature of the present situation in Russia is that the country is *passing* from the first stage of the revolution – which, owing to the insufficient class-consciousness and organisation of the proletariat, placed power in the hands of the bourgeoisie – to its *second* stage, which must place power in the hands of the proletariat and the poorest sections of the peasants.

    This transition is characterised, on the one hand, by a maximum of legally recognised rights (Russia is *now* the freest of all the belligerent countries in the world); on the other, by the absence of violence towards the masses, and, finally, by their unreasoning trust in the government of capitalists, those worst enemies of peace and socialism.

    This peculiar situation demands of us an ability to adapt ourselves to the *special* conditions of Party work among unprecedentedly large masses of proletarians who have just awakened to political life.

3. No support for the Provisional Government; the utter falsity of all its promises should be made clear, particularly of those relating to the renunciation of annexations. Exposure in place of the impermissible, illusion-breeding 'demand' that *this* government, a government of capitalists, should *cease* to be an imperialist government.

4. Recognition of the fact that in most of the Soviets of Workers' Deputies our Party is in a minority, so far a small minority, as against *a bloc of all* the petty-bourgeois opportunist elements, from the Popular Socialists and the Socialist-Revolutionaries down to the Organising Committee (Chkheidze, Tsereteli, etc.), Steklov, etc., etc., who have yielded to the influence of the bourgeoisie and spread that influence among the proletariat.

    The masses must be made to see that the Soviets of Workers' Deputies are the *only possible* form of revolutionary government, and that therefore our task is, as long as *this* government yields to the influence of the bourgeoisie, to present a patient, systematic and persistent explanation of the errors of their tactics, an *explanation* especially adapted to the practical needs of the masses.

As long as we are in the minority we carry on the work of criticising and exposing errors and at the same time we preach the necessity of transferring the entire state power to the Soviets of Workers' Deputies, so that the people may overcome their mistakes by experience.

5. Not a parliamentary republic – to return to a parliamentary republic from the Soviets of Workers' Deputies would be a retrograde step – but a republic of Soviets of Workers', Agricultural Labourers' and Peasants' Deputies throughout the country, from top to bottom.

    Abolition of the police, the army and the bureaucracy.*

    The salaries of all officials, all of whom are elective and displaceable at any time, not to exceed the average wage of a competent worker.

6. The weight of emphasis in the agrarian programme to be shifted to the Soviets of Agricultural Labourers' Deputies.

    Confiscation of all landed estates.

    Nationalisation of *all* lands in the country, the land to be disposed of by the local Soviets of Agricultural Labourers' and Peasants' Deputies. The organisation of separate Soviets of Deputies of Poor Peasants. The setting up of a model farm on each of the large estates (ranging in size from 100 to 300 dessiatins, according to local and other conditions, and to the decisions of the local bodies) under the control of the Soviets of Agricultural Labourers' Deputies and for the public account.

7. The immediate amalgamation of all banks in the country into a single national bank, and the institution of control over it by the Soviet of Workers' Deputies.

---

*   I.e. the standing army to be replaced by the arming of the whole people. – *Lenin*

8. It is not our *immediate* task to 'introduce' socialism, but only to bring social production and the distribution of products at once under the *control* of the Soviets of Workers' Deputies.

9. Party tasks:
   a. Immediate convocation of a Party congress;
   b. Alteration of the Party Programme, mainly:
      i. On the question of imperialism and the imperialist war;
      ii. On our attitude towards the state and *our* demand for a 'commune state';*
      iii. Amendment of our out-of-date minimum programme;
   c. Change of the Party's name.**

10. A new International.

   We must take the initiative in creating a revolutionary International, an International against the *social-chauvinists* and against the 'Centre'.***

In order that the reader may understand why I had especially to emphasise as a rare exception the 'case' of honest opponents, I invite him to compare the above theses with the following objection by Mr. Goldenberg: Lenin, he said, "has planted the banner of civil war in the midst of revolutionary democracy" (quoted in No. 5 of Mr. Plekhanov's *Yedinstvo*).

Isn't it a gem?

I write, announce and elaborately explain:

In view of the undoubted honesty of those *broad* sections of the *mass* believers in revolutionary defencism... in view of the fact that they

---

* I.e. a state of which the Paris Commune was the prototype. – *Lenin*

** Instead of 'Social-Democracy', whose official leaders *throughout* the world have betrayed socialism and deserted to the bourgeoisie (the 'defencists' and the vacillating 'Kautskyites'), we must call ourselves the *Communist Party*. – *Lenin*

*** The 'Centre' in the international Social-Democratic movement is the trend which vacillates between the chauvinists (= 'defencists') and internationalists, i.e. Kautsky and co. in Germany, Longuet and co. in France, Chkheidze and co. in Russia, Turati and co. in Italy, MacDonald and co. in Britain, etc. – *Lenin*

are being deceived by the bourgeoisie, it is necessary with *particular* thoroughness, persistence and *patience* to explain their error to them…

Yet the bourgeois gentlemen who call themselves Social-Democrats, who *do not* belong either to the *broad* sections or to the *mass* believers in defencism, with serene brow present my views thus: "The banner [!] of civil war" (of which there is not a word in the theses and not a word in my speech!) has been planted (!) "in the midst [!!] of revolutionary democracy…"

What does this mean? In what way does this differ from riot-inciting agitation, from *Russkaya Volya*?

I write, announce and elaborately explain:

> The Soviets of Workers' Deputies are the *only possible* form of revolutionary government, and therefore our task is to present a patient, systematic, and persistent *explanation* of the errors of their tactics, an explanation especially adapted to the practical needs of the masses.

Yet opponents of a certain brand present my views as a call to "civil war in the midst of revolutionary democracy"!

I attacked the Provisional Government for *not* having appointed an early date or any date at all, for the convocation of the Constituent Assembly, and for confining itself to promises. I argued that *without* the Soviets of Workers' and Soldiers' Deputies the convocation of the Constituent Assembly is not guaranteed and its success is impossible.

And the view is attributed to me that I am opposed to the speedy convocation of the Constituent Assembly!

I would call this 'raving', had not decades of political struggle taught me to regard honesty in opponents as a rare exception.

Mr. Plekhanov in his paper called my speech "raving". Very good, Mr. Plekhanov! But look how awkward, uncouth and slow-witted you are in your polemics. If I delivered a raving speech for two hours, how is it that an audience of hundreds tolerated this "raving"? Further, why does your paper devote a whole column to an account of the "raving"? Inconsistent, highly inconsistent!

It is, of course, much easier to shout, abuse and howl than to attempt to relate, to explain, to recall *what* Marx and Engels said in 1871, 1872 and 1875 about the experience of the Paris Commune and about the *kind* of state the proletariat needs.*

Ex-Marxist Mr. Plekhanov evidently does not care to recall Marxism.

I quoted the words of Rosa Luxemburg, who on 4 August 1914 called *German* Social-Democracy a "stinking corpse". And the Plekhanovs, Goldenbergs and co. feel 'offended'. On whose behalf? On behalf of the *German* chauvinists, because they were called chauvinists!

They have got themselves in a mess, these poor Russian social-chauvinists – socialists in word and chauvinists in deed.

---

* See Marx's *The Civil War in France*, and Marx and Engels' *Critique of the Gotha Programme*.

Resolution of the Central Committee of the RSDLP(B)

21 April (4 May) 1917

Having considered the situation which has arisen in Petrograd after the imperialist, annexationist and predatory Note of the Provisional Government of 18 April 1917, and after a number of meetings and demonstrations of the people held in the streets of Petrograd on 20 April, the Central Committee of the RSDLP resolves:

1. Party propagandists and speakers must refute the despicable lies of the capitalist papers and of the papers supporting the capitalists to the effect that we are holding out the threat of *civil war*. This is a despicable lie, for only at the present moment, as long as the capitalists and their government cannot and dare not use force against the masses, as long as the mass of soldiers and workers are freely expressing their will and freely electing and displacing *all* authorities – at *such a moment* any thought of civil war would be naive, senseless, preposterous; at such a moment *there must be compliance with the will of the majority of the population* and free criticism of this will by the discontented minority; should violence be resorted to, the responsibility will fall on the Provisional Government and its supporters.

2. By their outcries against civil war, the government of the capitalists and its newspapers are only trying to conceal the reluctance of the capitalists, who admittedly constitute an insignificant minority of the people, to submit to the will of the majority.

3. In order to learn the will of the majority of the population in Petrograd, where there is now an unusually large number of soldiers who are familiar with the sentiment of the peasants and correctly express it, a popular vote must at once be arranged in all the districts of Petrograd and its suburbs to ascertain what the attitude is towards the government's Note, what support the various parties enjoy, and what kind of Provisional Government is desired.

4. All Party propagandists must advocate these views and this proposal at factories, in regiments, in the streets, etc., by means of *peaceful* discussion and peaceful demonstrations, as well as meetings everywhere; we must endeavour to organise regular voting in factories and regiments, taking care that order and comradely discipline are strictly observed.

5. Party propagandists must again and again protest against the despicable slander spread by the capitalists alleging that our Party stands for a separate peace with Germany. We consider Wilhelm II as bad a crowned brigand meriting execution as Nicholas II, and the German Guchkovs, i.e. the German capitalists, just as much annexationists, robbers and imperialists as the Russian, British and all other capitalists. We *are against* negotiating with the capitalists, we are for negotiating and fraternising *with the revolutionary workers and soldiers of all countries.* We are convinced that the reason why the Guchkov-Milyukov government is trying to aggravate the situation is because it knows that the workers' revolution in Germany is beginning, and that this revolution will be a blow to the capitalists of all countries.

6. When the Provisional Government spreads rumours about utter and unavoidable economic chaos, it is not only trying to frighten the people into leaving the power in the hands of this Provisional Government, but is also vaguely, fumblingly expressing the profound and indubitable truth that *all* the nations of the world have been led into a blind alley, that the war waged in the interests of the capitalists has driven them to the brink of an abyss, and that there is really no way out except through the transfer of power to the revolutionary class, i.e. to the revolutionary proletariat, which is capable of adopting revolutionary measures.

   If there are any stocks of grain, etc., in the country, the new government of the workers and soldiers will know how to dispose of them too. But if the capitalist war has brought economic ruin to a stage where there is no bread at all, the capitalist government will only aggravate the condition of the people instead of improving it.

7. We consider the policy of the present majority of leaders of the Soviet of Workers' and Soldiers' Deputies, of the Narodnik and Menshevik parties, to be profoundly erroneous, since confidence in the Provisional Government, attempts to compromise with it, dickering over amendments, etc., would in fact mean only so many more useless scraps of paper and useless delays; and besides, this policy threatens to create a divergence between the will of the Soviet on the one hand, and that of the majority of revolutionary soldiers at the front and in Petrograd, and of the majority of workers, on the other.

8. We call upon those workers and soldiers who believe that the Soviet must change its policy and renounce the policy of confidence in and compromise with the capitalist government, to hold new elections of delegates to the Soviet of Workers' and Soldiers' Deputies and to send to that body only people who would steadfastly hold to a quite definite opinion consonant with the actual will of the majority.

Seventh (April) All-Russia Conference of the RSDLP(B)

24-29 April (7-12 May) 1917

Editors note:

The Seventh (April) All-Russia Conference of the RSDLP(B) was called by decision of the RSDLP(B) Central Committee and was held in Petrograd from 24-29 April (7-12 May) 1917. It was the Party's first conference in legal conditions.

It was attended by 131 delegates with voting rights and eighteen with speaking rights from seventy-eight Party organisations (including Petrograd and its surrounding region, Moscow and Moscow District, the Central Industrial Area, the Urals, the Donbas, the Volga area and the Caucasus), by representatives of front and rear military organisations, and also by the national organisations of Latvia, Lithuania, Poland, Finland and Estonia.

This was the conference where Lenin finally won over the party to his political positions expressed in the *April Theses* (no confidence in the Provisional Government, all power to the Soviets, no concessions to defencism, for a new International), against the opposition of many of the Party leaders.

We reproduce here Lenin's speech on the 'Resolution on the War' and the text of the resolution itself.

* * *

Speech in Favour of the Resolution on the War
27 April (10 May) 1917

Comrades, the original draft resolution on the war was read by me at the City Conference. Because of the crisis that absorbed the attention and energy of all our comrades in Petrograd, we were unable to amend the draft. Since yesterday, however, the committee working on it has made satisfactory progress: the draft has been changed, considerably shortened and, in our opinion, improved.

I wish to say a few words about the construction of this resolution. It consists of three parts. The first is devoted to a class analysis of the war; it also contains our statement of principles explaining why our Party warns against placing any trust in promises made by the Provisional Government, as well as against any support for that government. The second part of the resolution deals with the question of revolutionary defencism as an extremely broad mass movement which has now united against us the overwhelming majority of the nation. Our task is to define the class significance of this revolutionary defencism, its essence, and the real balance of forces, and find a way to fight this trend. The third part of the resolution deals with the question of how to end the war. This practical question, which is of supreme importance to our Party, required a detailed answer. We think that we have succeeded in meeting this requirement satisfactorily. The articles in *Pravda* and numerous articles on the war published in provincial newspapers (the latter reach us very irregularly because the postal service is disorganised, and we have to take every convenient opportunity of getting them for the Central Committee) reveal a negative attitude towards the war and the loan. I think that the vote against the loan settled the question as to our opposition to revolutionary defencism. I do not think it is possible to go into greater detail on this.

The present war is, on the part of both groups of the belligerent powers, an imperialist war, i.e. one waged by the capitalists for the division of the profits obtained from world domination, for markets for finance (banking) capital, for the subjugation of the weaker nationalities, etc.

The primary and basic issue is the meaning of the war, a question of a general and political character, a moot question which the capitalists and the social-chauvinists carefully evade. This is why we must put this question first, with this addition to it:

> Each day of war enriches the financial and industrial bourgeoisie and impoverishes and saps the strength of the proletariat and the peasantry of all the belligerents, as well as of the neutral countries. In Russia, moreover, prolongation of the war involves a grave danger to the revolution's gains and its further development.

> The passing of state power in Russia to the Provisional Government, a government of the landowners and capitalists, did not and could not alter the character and meaning of the war as far as Russia is concerned.

The words I have just read to you are of great importance in all our propaganda and agitation. Has the class character of the war changed now? Can it change? Our reply is based on the fact that power has passed to the landowners and capitalists, the same government that had engineered this war. We then pass on to one of the facts that reveal most clearly the character of the war. Class character as expressed by the entire policy carried on for decades by definite classes is one thing, the obvious class character of the war is another.

> This fact was most strikingly demonstrated when the new government not only failed to publish the secret treaties between Tsar Nicholas II and the capitalist governments of Britain, France, etc., but even formally and without consulting the nation confirmed these secret treaties, which promise the Russian capitalists a free hand to rob China, Persia, Turkey, Austria, etc. By concealing these treaties from the people of Russia, the latter are being deceived as to the true character of the war.

And so, I emphasise again, we are pointing out one particularly striking confirmation of the character of the war. Even if there were no treaties at all, the character of the war would be the same because groups of capitalists can very often come to an agreement without any treaties. But the treaties exist and their implications are apparent. For the purpose of co-ordinating the work of our agitators and propagandists, we think this fact should be especially emphasised, and so we have made a special point of it. The people's attention is and should be called to this fact, all the more so as the treaties were concluded by the tsar, who has been overthrown. The people ought to be made aware that the present governments are carrying on the war on the basis of treaties concluded between the old governments. This, I feel, makes the contradictions between the capitalist interests and the will of the people stand out most strikingly, and it is for the propagandists to expose these contradictions, to draw the people's attention to them, to strive to explain them to the masses by appealing to their class-consciousness. The contents of these treaties leave no room for doubt that they promise enormous profits to the capitalists to be derived from robbing other countries. That is why they are always kept secret. There is not a republic in the world whose foreign policy is conducted in the open. It is fatuous, while the capitalist system exists, to expect the capitalists to open up their ledgers. While there is private ownership of the means of production, there is bound to be private ownership of shares and financial operations. The cornerstone of contemporary diplomacy is financial operations, which amount to robbing and strangling the weak nationalities. These, we believe, are the fundamental premises upon which the evaluation of the war rests. Proceeding from these premises we conclude that:

> For this reason, no proletarian party that does not wish to break completely with internationalism, i.e. with the fraternal solidarity of the workers of all countries in their struggle against the yoke of capital, can support the present war, or the present government, or its loans.

This is our chief and basic conclusion. It determines our whole tactics and sets us apart from all the other parties, no matter how socialistic they claim to be. This proposition, which is irrefutable to all of us, predetermines our attitude towards all the other political parties.

The next point concerns the wide use which our government is making of promises. These promises are the object of a prolonged campaign by the Soviets, which have become muddled by these promises, and which are trying the people's patience. We therefore consider it necessary to add to our purely objective analysis of the class relations an analysis of those promises, promises which in themselves have, of course, no significance to a Marxist, but which mean a great deal to the people, and mean even more in politics. The Petrograd Soviet has become muddled by these promises, has given weight to them by promising its support. This is the reason why we add the following statement to this point:

> No trust can be placed in the present government's promises to renounce annexations, i.e. conquests of foreign countries or retention by force of any nationality within the confines of Russia.

'Annexation' being a foreign word, we give it an exact political definition, such as neither the Cadets nor the petty-bourgeois democratic parties (the Narodniks and Mensheviks) can give. Few words have been used so meaninglessly and slovenly.

> For, in the first place, the capitalists, bound together by the thousand threads of banking capital, cannot renounce annexations in this war without renouncing the profits from the thousands of millions invested in loans, concessions, war industries, etc. And secondly, the new government, after renouncing annexations to mislead the people, declared through Milyukov (Moscow, 9 April 1917) that it had no intention of renouncing them, and, in the Note of 18 April and its elucidation of 22 April, confirmed the expansionist character of its policy. Therefore, in warning the people against the capitalists' empty promises, the Conference declares that it is necessary to

make a clear distinction between a renunciation of annexations in word and a renunciation of annexations in deed, i.e. the immediate publication and abrogation of all the secret, predatory treaties and the immediate granting to all nationalities of the right to determine by free voting whether they wish to be independent states or to be part of another state.

We have found it necessary to mention this, because the question of peace without annexations is the basic issue in all these discussions of peace terms. All parties recognise that peace will become the alternative, and that peace with annexations will be an unheard-of catastrophe for all countries. In a country where there is political liberty, the question of peace cannot be placed before the people otherwise than in terms of peace without annexations. It is therefore necessary to declare for peace without annexations, and so the only thing to do is to lie by wrapping up the meaning of annexations or evading the question altogether. *Rech*, for instance, cries that the return of Courland means renunciation of annexations. When I was addressing the Soviet of Workers' and Soldiers' Deputies, a soldier handed me a slip of paper with the following question: "We have to fight to win back Courland. Does winning back Courland mean that you stand for annexations?" I had to reply in the affirmative. We are against Germany annexing Courland, but we are also against Russia holding Courland by force. For example, our government has issued a manifesto proclaiming the independence of Poland. This manifesto, chock-full of meaningless phrases, states that Poland must form a free military alliance with Russia. These three words contain the whole truth. A free military alliance of little Poland with huge Russia is, in point of fact, complete military subjection of Poland. Poland may be granted political freedom but her boundaries will be determined by the military alliance.

If we fight for the Russian capitalists keeping possession of the former annexed territories of Courland and Poland, then the German capitalists have the right to rob Courland. They may argue this way: we looted Poland together. At the end of the eighteenth century, when we began to tear Poland to pieces, Prussia was a very small and weak country while Russia was a giant, and therefore she grabbed more. Now we have grown and it is our intention, if you please, to snatch a larger share. You can say nothing against this capitalist logic. In 1863, Japan was a mere nothing in comparison with Russia, but in 1905 Japan thrashed Russia. From 1863 to 1873 Germany was a mere nothing in comparison with Britain, but now Germany is stronger than Britain. The Germans may argue: we were weak when Courland was taken from us, but we have now grown stronger than you, and we wish to take it back. Not to renounce annexations means to justify endless wars over the conquest of weaker nationalities. To renounce annexations means to let each nation determine freely whether it wants to live separately or together with others. Of course, for this purpose, armies must be withdrawn. To show the slightest hesitation on the question of annexations means to justify endless wars. It follows that we could allow no hesitation on this question. With regard to annexations, our answer is that nations must be free to make their own decisions. How can we secure economic freedom alongside this political freedom? To accomplish this, power must pass into the hands of the proletariat and the yoke of capital must be overthrown.

I now pass on to the second part of the resolution.

The 'revolutionary defencism', which in Russia has now permeated all the Narodnik parties (the Popular Socialists, Trudoviks and Socialist-Revolutionaries), the opportunist party of the Menshevik Social-Democrats (the Organising Committee, Chkheidze, Tsereteli, etc.), and the majority of the non-party revolutionaries, reflects, in point of class significance, the interests and point of view of the well-to-do peasants and a part of the small proprietors, who, like the capitalists, profit by oppressing weak peoples. On the other hand, 'revolutionary defencism' is a result of the deception by the capitalists of a part of the urban and rural proletariat and semi-proletariat, who, by their class position, have no interest in the profits of the capitalists and in the imperialist war.

Consequently, our task here is to determine from what sections of society this defencist tendency could emerge. Russia is the most petty-bourgeois country in the world, and the upper sections of the petty bourgeoisie are directly interested in continuing the war. The well-to-do peasants, like the capitalists, are profiting by the war. On the other hand, the mass of proletarians and semi-proletarians have no interest in annexations because they make no profit on banking capital. How, then, have these classes come to adopt the position of revolutionary defencism? Their attitude towards revolutionary defencism is due to the influence of capitalist ideology, which the resolution designates by the word 'deception'. They are unable to differentiate between the interests of the capitalists and the interests of the country. Hence we conclude:

> The Conference recognises that any concessions to 'revolutionary defencism' are absolutely impermissible and virtually signify a complete break with internationalism and socialism. As for the defencist tendencies among the broad masses, our Party will fight against these tendencies by ceaselessly explaining the truth that the attitude of unreasoning trust in the government of the capitalists, at the moment, is one of the chief obstacles to a speedy termination of the war.

The last words express the specific feature that sharply distinguishes Russia from the other Western capitalist countries and from all capitalist democratic republics. For it cannot be said of those countries that the trustfulness of the unenlightened masses there is the chief cause of the prolongation of the war. The masses there are now in the iron grip of military discipline. The more democratic the republic, the stronger discipline is, since law in a republic rests on 'the will of the people'. Owing to the revolution, there is no such discipline in Russia. The masses freely elect representatives to the Soviets, which is something that does not exist now anywhere else in the world. But the masses have unreasoning trust, and are therefore used for the purposes of the struggle. So far we can do nothing but explain. Our explanations must deal with the immediate revolutionary tasks and methods of action. When the masses are free, any attempts to act in the name of a minority, without explaining things to the masses, would be senseless Blanquism, mere adventurism. Only by winning over the masses, if they can be won, can we lay a solid foundation for the victory of the proletarian class struggle.

I now pass on to the third part of the resolution:

> In regard to the most important question of all, namely, how to end the present capitalist war as soon as possible, not by a coercive peace, but by a truly democratic peace, the Conference recognises and declares the following:
>
> This war cannot be ended by a refusal of the soldiers of one side only to continue the war, by a simple cessation of hostilities by one of the belligerents.

The idea of terminating the war in this way has been attributed to us over and over again by persons who wish to win an easy victory over their opponents by distorting the latter's views – a typical method used by the capitalists, who ascribe to us the absurd idea of wishing to end the war by a one-sided refusal to fight. They say "the war cannot be ended by sticking your bayonet in the ground", to quote a soldier, a typical revolutionary defencist. This is no argument, I say. The idea that the war can be terminated without changing the classes in power is an anarchist idea. Either this idea is anarchistic, in which case it has no meaning, no state significance, or it is a hazy pacifist idea that fails completely to appreciate the connection between politics and the oppressing class. War is an evil, peace is a blessing... Certainly this idea must be made clear to the people, must be popularised. Incidentally, all our resolutions are being written for leading Party members, for Marxists, and do not make reading matter for the masses. But they must serve as unifying and guiding political principles for every propagandist and agitator. To meet this requirement, one more paragraph was added to the resolution:

The Conference reiterates its protest against the base slander spread by the capitalists against our Party to the effect that we are in favour of a separate peace with Germany. We consider the German capitalists to be as predatory as the Russian, British, French and other capitalists, and Emperor Wilhelm as bad a crowned brigand as Nicholas II or the British, Italian, Romanian and all other monarchs.

On this point there was some disagreement in the committee, some maintaining that in this passage our language became too popular, others, that the British, Italian and Romanian monarchs did not deserve the honour of being mentioned. After a detailed discussion, however, we all agreed that, since our present aim is to refute all the slanders which *Birzhevka* has tried to spread against us rather crudely, *Rech* more subtly, *Yedinstvo* by direct implication, we must, on a question of this nature, come out with a most sharp and trenchant criticism of these ideas, having in mind the broadest masses of the people. Asked why we do not help to over throw Wilhelm if we consider him a brigand, we can say that the others, too, are brigands, that we ought to fight against them as well, that one must not forget the kings of Italy and Romania, that brigands can also be found among our Allies. These two paragraphs are intended to combat the slander, which is meant to lead to riot-mongering and squabbling. This is the reason why we must now pass on to the serious practical question of how to terminate the war.

Our Party will patiently but persistently explain to the people the truth that wars are waged by *governments*, that wars are always indissolubly bound up with the policies of definite *classes*, that this war can be terminated by a democratic peace *only* if the entire state power, in at least several of the belligerent countries, has passed to the class of the proletarians and semi-proletarians which is really capable of putting an end to the oppressive rule of capital.

To a Marxist these truths – that wars are waged by the capitalists and are bound up with the capitalists' class interests – are absolute truths. A Marxist need not dwell on that. But as far as the masses are concerned, skilful agitators and propagandists should be able to explain this truth simply, without using foreign words, for with us discussions usually degenerate into empty and futile squabbling. The explaining of this truth is what we have been trying to do in every part of the resolution. We say that in order to understand what the war is about, you must ask who gains by it; in order to understand how to put an end to the war, you must ask which classes do not gain by it. The connection here is clear, hence we conclude:

> In Russia, the revolutionary class, having taken state power, would adopt a series of measures that would undermine the economic rule of the capitalists, as well as measures that would render them completely harmless politically, and would immediately and frankly offer to all nations a democratic peace on the basis of a complete renunciation of every possible form of annexation and indemnity.

Once we speak in the name of the revolutionary class, the people have the right to ask: and what about you, what would you do in their place to end the war? This is an inevitable question. The people are electing us now as their representatives, and we must give a very precise answer. The revolutionary class, having taken power, would set out to undermine the rule of the capitalists, and would then offer to all nations well-defined peace terms, because, unless the economic rule of the capitalists is undermined, all we can have are scraps of paper. Only a victorious class can accomplish this, can bring about a change in policy.

I repeat: to bring this truth home to the uneducated mass, we need intermediate links that would help to introduce this question to them. The mistake and falsehood of popular literature on the war is the evasion of this question; it ignores this question and presents the matter as if there had been no class struggle, as if two countries had lived amicably until one attacked the other, and the attacked has been defending itself. This is vulgar reasoning in which there is not a shadow of objective truth, and which is a deliberate deception of the people by educated persons. If we approach this question properly, anyone would be able to grasp the essential point; for the interests of the ruling classes are one thing, and the interests of the oppressed classes are another.

What would happen if the revolutionary class took power?

> Such measures and such a frank offer of peace would bring about complete confidence of the workers of the belligerent countries in each other…

Such confidence is impossible now, and the words of manifestos will not create it. Where the philosopher once said that speech has been given to man to enable him to conceal his thoughts, the diplomats always say: "Conferences are held to deceive the people." Not only the capitalists, but the socialists too reason this way. This particularly applies to the conference which Borgbjerg is calling.

> … and would inevitably lead to uprisings of the proletariat against those imperialist governments as might resist the offered peace.

Nobody now believes the capitalist government when it says: "We are for peace without annexations." The masses have the instinct of oppressed classes which tells them that nothing has changed. Only if the policy were actually changed in one country, confidence would appear and attempts at uprisings would be made. We speak of "uprisings" because we are now discussing all countries. To say "a revolution has taken place in one country, so now it must take place in Germany" – is false reasoning. There is a tendency to form an order of sequence, but this cannot be done. We all went through the Revolution of 1905. We all heard or witnessed how that revolution gave birth to revolutionary ideas throughout the world, a fact which Marx constantly referred to. Revolutions cannot be made, they cannot be taken in turns. A revolution cannot be made to order – it develops. This form of charlatanism is now frequently being practised in Russia. The people are told: You in Russia have made a revolution, now it is the Germans' turn. If the objective conditions change, then an uprising is inevitable, but we do not know whose turn it will be, when it will take place, and with what degree of success. We are asked: If the revolutionary class takes power in Russia, and if no uprisings break out in other countries, what will the revolutionary party do? What will happen then? This question is answered in the last paragraph of our resolution.

> Until the revolutionary class in Russia takes the entire state power, our Party will do all it can to support those proletarian parties and groups abroad that are in fact, already during the war, conducting a revolutionary struggle against their imperialist governments and their bourgeoisie.

This is all that we can promise and must do now. The revolution is mounting in every country, but no one knows to what extent it is mounting and when it will break out. In every country there are people who are carrying on a revolutionary struggle against their governments. They are the people, the only people, we must support. This is the real thing – all else is falsehood. And so we add:

> Our Party will particularly support the mass fraternisation of the soldiers of all the belligerent countries that has already begun at the front…

This is to meet Plekhanov's argument: "What will come of it? Suppose you do fraternise, then what? Does this not suggest the possibility of a separate peace at the front?" This is jiggery-pokery, not a serious argument. We want fraternisation on all fronts, and we are taking pains to encourage it. When we worked in Switzerland, we published an appeal in two languages, with French on one side and German on the other, urging those soldiers to do the same thing we are now urging the Russian soldiers to do. We do not confine ourselves to fraternisation between German and Russian soldiers, we call upon all to fraternise. This, then, is what we mean by fraternisation:

> … endeavouring to turn this instinctive expression of solidarity of the oppressed into a politically conscious movement as well organised as possible for the transfer of all state power in all the belligerent countries to the revolutionary proletariat.

Fraternisation, so far, is instinctive, and we must not deceive ourselves on this score. We must admit this in order not to delude the people. The fraternising soldiers are actuated not by a clear-cut political idea but by the instinct of oppressed people, who are tired, exhausted and begin to lose confidence in capitalist promises. They say: "While you keep on talking about peace – we have been hearing it now for two and a half years – we shall start things moving ourselves." This is a true class instinct. Without this instinct the cause of the revolution would be hopeless. As you know, nobody would free the workers if they did not free themselves. But is instinct alone sufficient? You would not get far if you rely on instinct alone. This instinct must be transformed into political awareness.

In our 'Appeal to the Soldiers of All the Belligerent Countries' we explain into what this fraternisation should develop – into the passing of political power to the Soviets of Workers' and Soldiers' Deputies.* Naturally, the German workers will call their Soviets by a different name, but this does not matter. The point is that we undoubtedly recognise as correct that fraternisation is instinctive, that we do not simply confine ourselves to encouraging fraternisation, but set ourselves the task of turning this instinctive fraternisation of workers and peasants in soldiers' uniforms into a politically-conscious movement, whose aim is the transfer of power in all the belligerent countries into the hands of the revolutionary proletariat. This is a very difficult task, but the position in which humanity finds itself under capitalist rule is tremendously difficult, too, and leads to destruction. This is why it will call forth that explosion of discontent which is the guarantee of proletarian revolution.

This is our resolution, which we submit for consideration to the Conference.

* * *

---

* See *LCW*, Vol. 24, pp. 186-8.

Resolution on the War

24-29 April 1917

I

The present war is, on the part of both groups of the belligerent powers, an imperialist war, i.e. one waged by the capitalists for the division of the profits obtained from world domination, for markets for finance (banking) capital, for the subjugation of the weaker nationalities, etc. Each day of war enriches the financial and industrial bourgeoisie and impoverishes and saps the strength of the proletariat and the peasantry of all the belligerents, as well as of the neutral countries. In Russia, moreover, prolongation of the war involves a grave danger to the revolution's gains and its further development.

The passing of state power in Russia to the Provisional Government, a government of the landowners and capitalists, did not and could not alter the character and meaning of the war as far as Russia is concerned.

This fact was most strikingly demonstrated when the new government not only failed to publish the secret treaties between Tsar Nicholas II and the capitalist governments of Britain, France, etc., but even formally and without consulting the nation confirmed these secret treaties, which promise the Russian capitalists a free hand to rob China, Persia, Turkey, Austria, etc. By concealing these treaties from the people of Russia, the latter are being deceived as to the true character of the war.

For this reason, no proletarian party that does not wish to break completely with internationalism, i.e. with the fraternal solidarity of the workers of all countries in their struggle against the yoke of capital, can support the present war, or the present government, or its loans.

No trust can be placed in the present government's promises to renounce annexations, i.e. conquests of foreign countries or retention by force of any nationality within the confines of Russia. For, in the first place, the capitalists, bound together by the thousand threads of banking capital, cannot renounce annexations in this war without renouncing the profits from the thousands of millions invested in loans, concessions, war industries, etc. And secondly, the new government, after renouncing annexations to mislead the people, declared through Milyukov (Moscow, 9 April 1917) that it had no intention of renouncing them, and, in the Note of 18 April and its elucidation of 22 April, confirmed the expansionist character of its policy. Therefore, in warning the people against the capitalists' empty promises, the Conference declares that it is necessary to make a clear distinction between a renunciation of annexations in word and a renunciation of annexations in deed, i.e. the immediate publication and abrogation of all the secret, predatory treaties and the immediate granting to all nationalities of the right to determine by free voting whether they wish to be independent states or to be part of another state.

II

The 'revolutionary defencism', which in Russia has now permeated all the Narodnik parties (the Popular Socialists, Trudoviks and Socialist-Revolutionaries), the opportunist party of the Menshevik Social-Democrats (the Organising Committee, Chkheidze, Tsereteli, etc.), and the majority of the non-party revolutionaries, reflects, in point of class significance, the interests and point of view of the well-to-do peasants and a part of the small proprietors, who, like the capitalists, profit by oppressing weak peoples. On the other hand, 'revolutionary defencism' is a result of the deception by the capitalists of a part of the urban and rural proletariat and semi-proletariat, who, by their class position, have no interest in the profits of the capitalists and in the imperialist war.

The Conference recognises that any concessions to 'revolutionary defencism' are absolutely impermissible and virtually signify a complete break with internationalism and socialism. As for the defencist tendencies among the broad masses, our Party will fight against these tendencies by ceaselessly explaining the truth that the attitude of unreasoning trust in the government of the capitalists, at the moment, is one of the chief obstacles to a speedy termination of the war.

III

In regard to the most important question of all, namely, how to end the present capitalist war as soon as possible, not by a coercive peace, but by a truly democratic peace, the Conference recognises and declares the following:

This war cannot be ended by a refusal of the soldiers of one side only to continue the war, by a simple cessation of hostilities by one of the belligerents.

The Conference reiterates its protest against the base slander spread by the capitalists against our Party to the effect that we are in favour of a separate peace with Germany. We consider the German capitalists to be as predatory as the Russian, British, French and other capitalists, and Emperor Wilhelm as bad a crowned brigand as Nicholas II or the British, Italian, Romanian and all other monarchs.

Our Party will patiently but persistently explain to the people the truth that wars are waged by *governments*, that wars are always indissolubly bound up with the policies of definite *classes*, that this war can be terminated by a democratic peace *only* if the entire state power, in at least several of the belligerent countries, has passed to the class of the proletarians and semi-proletarians which is really capable of putting an end to the oppressive rule of capital.

In Russia, the revolutionary class, having taken state power, would adopt a series of measures that would undermine the economic rule of the capitalists, as well as measures that would render them completely harmless politically, and would immediately and frankly offer to all nations a democratic peace on the basis of a complete renunciation of every possible form of annexation and indemnity. Such measures and such a frank offer of peace would bring about complete confidence of the workers of the belligerent countries in each other and would inevitably lead to uprisings of the proletariat against those imperialist governments as might resist the offered peace.

Until the revolutionary class in Russia takes the entire state power, our Party will do all it can to support those proletarian parties and groups abroad that are in fact, already during the war, conducting a revolutionary struggle against their imperialist governments and their bourgeoisie. Our Party will particularly support the mass fraternisation of the soldiers of all the belligerent countries that has already begun at the front, endeavouring to turn this instinctive expression of solidarity of the oppressed into a politically conscious movement as well organised as possible for the transfer of all state power in all the belligerent countries to the revolutionary proletariat.

Bolshevism and 'Demoralisation' of the Army

3 (16) June 1917

Everybody is screaming for 'strong government'. The only salvation is in a dictatorship, in 'iron discipline', in silencing and reducing to obedience all the refractory members of the Right and Left. We know *whom* they wish to silence. The Rights are making no noise, they are *working*. Some of them in the government, others at the factories, all of them with threats of lockouts, orders for the disbanding of regiments, and the threat of penal servitude. The Konovalovs and the Tereshchenkos, with the help of the Kerenskys and the Skobelevs, are working in an *organised* manner for their own good. And they don't have to be silenced.

All we have is the *right of speech*.

And of this right they want to deprive us.

Pravda is barred from the front. The Kiev 'agents' have decided not to distribute *Pravda*. The Zemstvo Union is not selling *Pravda* in its newspaper stands. And now we are promised a "systematic fight against the preaching of Leninism" (*Izvestia*). On the other hand, every spontaneous protest, every excess, wherever it comes from, is *blamed on us*.

This, too, is a method for combating Bolshevism.

A well-tried method.

Unable as they are to get clear guidelines, aware instinctively how false and unsatisfactory is the position of the official leaders of democracy, the masses are compelled *to grope a way out for themselves.*

The result is that every dissatisfied, class-conscious revolutionary, every angered fighter who yearns for his village home and sees no end to the war, and sometimes simply men who are out to save their own skins, rally to the banner of Bolshevism.

Where Bolshevism has a chance to air its views openly, there we find no disorganisation.

Where there are no Bolsheviks or where they are not allowed to speak, there we find excesses, demoralisation and pseudo-Bolsheviks.

And that is just what our enemies need.

They need a pretext for saying: "*The Bolsheviks are demoralising the army*" and then shutting the Bolsheviks' mouths.

To dispose once for all of 'enemy' slander and the ridiculous distortions of Bolshevism, we quote the concluding part of a leaflet distributed in the army by one of our delegates on the eve of the All-Russia Congress.

Here it is:

Comrades, you must have your say.

Do not let us have any agreements with the bourgeoisie!

All power to the Soviet of Workers' and Soldiers' Deputies!

This does not mean that we must immediately overthrow the present government or disobey it. So long as the majority of the peoples support it and believe that five socialists can cope with all the rest, we cannot afford to fritter away our forces in desultory uprisings.

Never!

Husband your strength! Get together at meetings! Pass resolutions! Demand that all power be handed over to the Soviet of Workers' and Soldiers' Deputies! Convince those who disagree with us! Send your resolution to me at the Congress in Petrograd in the name of your regiment, so that I can quote your voice there!

But beware of those who, posing as Bolsheviks, will try to provoke you to riots and disturbances as a screen for their own cowardice! Know that though they are with you now, they will sell you out to the old regime at the first hint of danger.

The real Bolsheviks call you to conscious revolutionary struggle, and not to riots.

Comrades! The All-Russia Congress will elect representatives, to whom, pending the convocation of the Constituent Assembly, the Provisional Government will be accountable.

Comrades! At that Congress I shall demand:

First, that *all power be handed over to the Soviet of Workers' and Soldiers' Deputies.*

Second, that *a proposal for peace without annexations or indemnities* be made immediately in the name of our people *to the peoples and governments of all the belligerent nations, both our Allies and our enemies.* If any government tries to turn it down it will be *overthrown by its own people.*

Third, that the money which people have made out of the war should be converted to state needs *by way of confiscation of the capitalists' war profits.*

Comrades! Only by the transfer of power to the democracy in Russia, Germany and France, only *by the overthrow of the bourgeois governments in all countries, can the war be ended.*

Our revolution has started this, and it is our task now to give a further impetus to the world revolution by having a fully authorised popular Russian government make an order of peace to all the governments of Europe and by strengthening our alliance with the revolutionary democrats of Western Europe.

Woe betide the bourgeois government that will persist in continuing the war after this.

Together with its people we shall make revolutionary war upon that government.

It is to say all this to our government in Petrograd in your name that I have been elected to the Congress in Petrograd.

Member of the Army Committee of the 11th Army, Delegate of the Central Committee of the Russian Social-Democratic Labour Party (Bolsheviks) to the Congress of the South-Western Front, Ensign *Krylenko.*

No one who has taken the trouble to read our Party's resolutions can fail to see that the *gist* of them has been correctly expressed by Comrade Krylenko.

The Bolsheviks are calling the proletariat, the poor peasants and all the toiling and exploited people to a conscious revolutionary struggle, and not to riots and disturbances.

Only a genuine government of the people, a government belonging to the *majority* of the nation, is capable of following the *right* path leading mankind to the overthrow of the capitalist yoke, to deliverance from the horrors and misery of the imperialist war, and to a just and lasting peace.

Is There a Way to a Just Peace?

7 (20) June 1917

Is there a way to peace without an exchange of annexations, without the division of spoils among the capitalist robbers?

There is: through a workers' revolution against the capitalists of the world.

Russia today is nearer to the beginning of such a revolution than any other country.

Only in Russia can power pass to existing institutions, to the Soviets, immediately, peacefully, without an uprising, for the capitalists cannot resist the Soviets of Workers', Soldiers' and Peasants' Deputies.

With such a transfer of power it would be possible to curb the capitalists, now making thousands of millions in profits from contracts, to expose all their tricks, arrest the millionaire embezzlers of public property, break their unlimited power.

Only after the transfer of power to the oppressed classes could Russia approach the oppressed classes of other countries, not with empty words, not with mere appeals, but calling their attention to her example, and immediately and explicitly *proposing* clear-cut terms for *universal peace*.

"Comrade workers and toilers of the world", she would say in the proposal for an immediate peace.

'Enough of the bloodshed. Peace is possible. A just peace means peace without annexations, without seizures. Let the German capitalist robbers and their crowned robber Wilhelm know that we shall not come to terms with them, that we regard as robbery on their part not only what they have grabbed since the war, but also Alsace and Lorraine, and the Danish and Polish areas of Prussia.

We also consider that Poland, Finland, the Ukraine and other non-Great-Russian lands were seized by the Russian tsars and capitalists.

We consider that *all* colonies, Ireland, and so on, were seized by the British, French and other capitalists.

We Russian workers and peasants shall *not* hold *any* of the non-Great-Russian lands or colonies (such as Turkestan, Mongolia, or Persia) by force. Down with war *for the division of colonies*, for the division of annexed (seized) lands, for the division of capitalist spoils!'

The example of the Russian workers will be followed inevitably, perhaps not tomorrow (revolutions are not made to order), but inevitably all the same by the workers and all the working people of *at least two great countries*, Germany and France.

For *both are perishing*, the first of hunger, the second of depopulation. Both will conclude peace on our terms, which are just, *in defiance of their capitalist governments*.

The road to peace lies before us.

Should the capitalists of England, Japan and America try to resist *this* peace, the oppressed classes of Russia and other countries will not shrink from a revolutionary war *against the capitalists*. In *this* war they will defeat the capitalists of *the whole world*, not just those of the three countries lying far from Russia and taken up with their own rivalries.

The road to a just peace lies before us. Let us not be afraid to *take* it.

The Revolution, the Offensive and Our Party

21 June (4 July) 1917

"The Russian revolution has reached a turning-point", said Tsereteli informing the Congress of Soviets that the offensive had begun.* Yes, the whole course of the world war as well as the Russian revolution has reached a turning-point. After three months of vacillation, the Russian government has actually come to the decision demanded by the 'Allied' governments.

The offensive has been declared in the name of peace. And it is also 'in the name of peace' that the imperialists of the world send their troops into battle. Every time there is an offensive the generals in every belligerent country try to raise their troops' morale by holding out the real hope of that particular offensive leading to early peace.

The Russian 'socialist' Ministers have garnished this common imperialist method with very high-sounding phrases in which

---

* This refers to the offensive on the South-Western Front launched by the Provisional Government in June 1917, at the insistence of the Russian and Anglo-French imperialists. Kerensky, the War Minister, ordered the offensive on 16 (29) June, which was backed by the defencist Mensheviks and Socialist-Revolutionary bloc.

words about socialism, democracy and revolution sound like rattles in the hands of a clever juggler. But no high-sounding phrases can conceal the fact that the revolutionary armies of Russia have been sent into battle in the name of the imperialist designs of Britain, France, Italy, Japan and America. No arguments from Chernov, once a Zimmerwaldist and now Lloyd George's partner, can conceal the fact that while the Russian Army and the Russian proletariat do not really pursue any annexationist aims, this does not in the least change the imperialist, predatory nature of the struggle between the two world trusts. Until the secret treaties binding Russia to the imperialists of other countries are revised, and as long as Ribot, Lloyd George and Sonnino, Russia's allies, continue to talk about the annexationist aims of their foreign policy, the offensive of the Russian troops will continue to serve the imperialists.

Tsereteli and Chernov object, however, that they have repeatedly declared their renunciation of all annexations. So much the worse, we reply. That means your actions do not accord with your words, for your actions serve both Russian and foreign imperialism. And when you begin to cooperate actively with the imperialist 'Allies' you render splendid service to the Russian counter-revolution. The joy of all the Black Hundreds and all counter-revolutionaries over the decisive turn in your policy is the best evidence of that. Yes, the Russian revolution has come to a turning-point. Through its 'socialist' Ministers, the Russian Government has done something which the imperialist Ministers, Guchkov and Milyukov, could not do. It has put the Russian Army at the disposal of the general staffs and the diplomats who act in the name and on the basis of unabrogated secret treaties, in the name of designs frankly proclaimed by Ribot and Lloyd George. The government could only fulfil its task, however, because the army trusted and followed it. The army marched to death because it believed it was making sacrifices for freedom, the revolution and early peace.

But the army did so because it is only a part of the people, who at this stage of the revolution are following the Socialist-Revolutionary and the Menshevik parties. This general and basic fact, the trust of the majority in the petty-bourgeois policy of the Mensheviks and the Socialist-Revolutionaries which is dependent on the capitalists, determines our Party's stand and conduct.

We shall keep up our efforts to expose government policy, resolutely warning the workers and soldiers, as in the past, against pinning their hopes on uncoordinated and disorganised actions.

It is a question of a phase in the people's revolution. The Tseretelis and Chernovs, having become dependent on imperialism, are putting into effect a phase of petty-bourgeois illusions and petty-bourgeois phrases, which serve to disguise the same old cynical imperialism.

This phase must be brought to an end. Let us help to end it as speedily and as painlessly as possible. This will rid the people of the last petty-bourgeois illusions and bring about the transfer of power to the revolutionary class.

To the Central Committee of the RSDLP

30 August (12 September) 1917

It is possible that these lines will come too late, for events are developing with a rapidity that sometimes makes one's head spin. I am writing this on Wednesday 30 August, and the recipients will read it no earlier than Friday 2 September. Still, on chance, I consider it my duty to write the following.

The Kornilov revolt is a most unexpected (unexpected at such a moment and in such a form) and downright unbelievably sharp turn in events.[*]

Like every sharp turn, it calls for a revision and change of tactics. And as with every revision, we must be extra cautious not to become unprincipled.

It is my conviction that those who become unprincipled are people who (like Volodarsky) slide into defencism or (like other Bolsheviks) into a *bloc* with the SRs, into *supporting* the Provisional Government. Their attitude is absolutely wrong and unprincipled. We shall become defencists *only after* the transfer of power to the

---

[*] On 10-13 September, General Kornilov attempted a coup against the Provisional Government. In response, 25,000 armed workers joined the fight against Kornilov, spearheaded by the Bolsheviks.

proletariat, *after* a peace offer, *after* the secret treaties and ties with the banks have been broken – *only afterwards*. Neither the capture of Riga *nor the capture of Petrograd* will make us defencists. (I should very much like Volodarsky to read this.) Until then we stand for a proletarian revolution, we are against the war, and we are *no* defencists.

Even now we must not support Kerensky's government. This is unprincipled. We may be asked: aren't we going to fight against Kornilov? Of course we must! But this is not the same thing; there is a dividing line here, which is being stepped over by some Bolsheviks who fall into compromise and allow themselves to be *carried away* by the course of events.

We shall fight, we are fighting against Kornilov, *just as* Kerensky's *troops do*, but we do not support Kerensky. *On the contrary*, we expose his weakness. There is the difference. It is rather a subtle difference, but it is highly essential and must not be forgotten.

What, then, constitutes our change of tactics after the Kornilov revolt?

We are changing the *form* of our struggle against Kerensky. Without in the least relaxing our hostility towards him, without taking back a single word said against him, without renouncing the task of overthrowing him, we say that we must *take into account* the present situation. We shall not overthrow Kerensky right now. We shall approach the task of fighting against him *in a different way*, namely, we shall point out to the people (who are fighting against Kornilov) Kerensky's *weakness* and *vacillation*. That has been done in the past *as well*. Now, however, it has become the *all-important* thing and this constitutes the change.

The change, further, is that the *all-important* thing now has become the intensification of our campaign for some kind of 'partial demands' to be presented to Kerensky: arrest Milyukov, arm the Petrograd workers, summon the Kronstadt, Vyborg and Helsingfors troops to Petrograd, dissolve the Duma, arrest Rodzyanko, legalise the transfer of the landed estates to the peasants, introduce workers' control over grain and factories, etc., etc. We must present these demands not only to Kerensky, and *not so much* to Kerensky, as to the workers, soldiers and peasants who have been *carried away* by the course of the struggle against Kornilov. We must keep up their *enthusiasm*, encourage them to deal with the generals and officers who have declared for Kornilov, urge *them* to demand the immediate transfer of land to the peasants, suggest to *them* that it is necessary to arrest Rodzyanko and Milyukov, dissolve the Duma, close down *Rech* and other bourgeois papers, and institute investigations against them. The 'Left' SRs must be especially urged on in this direction.

It would be wrong to think that we have moved farther away from the task of the proletariat winning power. No. We have come very close to it, *not directly*, but from the side. *At the moment* we must campaign not so much directly against Kerensky, as *indirectly* against him, namely, by demanding a more and more active, truly revolutionary war against Kornilov. The development of this war alone can lead *us* to power, but we must *speak* of this as little as possible in our propaganda (remembering very well that even tomorrow events may put power into our hands, and then we shall not relinquish it). It seems to me that this should be passed on in a letter (not in the papers) to the propagandists, to groups of agitators and propagandists, and to Party members in general. We must relentlessly fight against phrases about the defence of the country, about a united front of revolutionary democrats, about supporting the Provisional Government, etc., etc., since they are just empty *phrases*. We must say: now is the time for *action*; you SR and Menshevik gentlemen have long since worn those phrases threadbare. Now is the time for *action*; the war against Kornilov must be conducted in a revolutionary way, by drawing the masses in, by arousing them, by inflaming them (Kerensky is *afraid* of the masses, *afraid* of the people). In the war against the Germans, *action* is required right now; *immediate and unconditional peace must be offered* on *precise* terms. If this is done, either a speedy peace *can* be attained or the war can be turned into a revolutionary war; if not, all the Mensheviks and Socialist-Revolutionaries remain lackeys of imperialism.

* * *

PS: Having read six issues of *Rabochy after* this was written, I must say that our views fully coincide.* I heartily welcome the splendid editorials, press review and articles by VM–n and Vol–y. As to Volodarsky's speech, I have read his letter to the editors, which likewise 'eliminates' my reproaches. Once more, best wishes and greetings!

---

* *Rabochy* (*The Worker*) was the Central Organ of the Bolshevik Party published daily from 25 August (7 September) to 2 (15) September 1917 instead of *Pravda*, which was closed down by the Provisional Government.

The Struggle Against Economic Chaos – and the War

From 'The Impending Catastrophe and How to Combat It'

10-14 (23-27) September 1917

A consideration of the measures to avert the impending catastrophe brings us to another supremely important question, namely, the connection between home and foreign policy, or, in other words, the relation between a war of conquest, an imperialist war, and a revolutionary, proletarian war, between a criminal predatory war and a just democratic war.

All the measures to avert catastrophe we have described would, as we have already stated, greatly enhance the defence potential, or, in other words, the military might of the country. That, on the one hand. On the other hand, these measures cannot be put into effect without turning the war of conquest into a just war, turning the war waged by the capitalists in the interests of the capitalists into a war waged by the proletariat in the interests of all the working and exploited people.

And, indeed, nationalisation of the banks and syndicates, taken in conjunction with the abolition of commercial secrecy and the establishment of workers' control over the capitalists, would not only imply a tremendous saving of national labour, the possibility of economising forces and means, but would also imply an improvement in the conditions of the working *masses*, of the majority of the population. As everybody knows, economic organisation is of decisive importance in modern warfare. Russia has enough grain, coal, oil and iron; in this respect, we are in a better position than any of the belligerent European countries. And given a struggle against economic chaos by the measures indicated above, enlisting popular initiative in this struggle, improving the people's conditions, and nationalising the banks and syndicates, Russia could use her revolution and her democracy to raise the whole country to an incomparably higher level of economic organisation.

If instead of the 'coalition' with the bourgeoisie, which is hampering every measure of control and sabotaging production, the Socialist-Revolutionaries and Mensheviks had in April effected the transfer of power to the Soviets and had directed their efforts not to playing at 'ministerial leapfrog', not to bureaucratically occupying, side by side with the Cadets, ministerial, deputy-ministerial and similar posts, but to guiding the workers and peasants in *their* control *over* the capitalists, in their *war against* the capitalists, Russia would now be a country completely transformed economically, with the land in the hands of the peasants, and with the banks nationalised, i.e. would *to that extent* (and these are extremely important economic bases of modern life) be *superior* to all other capitalist countries.

The defence potential, the military might, of a country whose banks have been nationalised is *superior* to that of a country whose banks remain in private hands. The military might of a peasant country whose land is in the hands of peasant committees is *superior* to that of a country whose land is in the hands of landowners.

Reference is constantly being made to the heroic patriotism and the miracles of military valour performed by the French in 1792-93. But the material, historical economic conditions which alone made such miracles possible are forgotten. The suppression of obsolete feudalism in a really revolutionary way, and the introduction throughout the country of a superior mode of production and free peasant land tenure, effected, moreover, with truly revolutionary democratic speed, determination, energy and devotion – such were the material, economic conditions which with 'miraculous' speed saved France by *regenerating* and *renovating* her economic foundation.

The example of France shows one thing, and one thing only, namely, that to render Russia capable of self-defence, to obtain in Russia, too, 'miracles' of mass heroism, all that is obsolete must be swept away with 'Jacobin' ruthlessness, and Russia renovated and regenerated *economically*. And in the twentieth century this cannot be done merely by sweeping tsarism away (France did not confine herself to this 125 years ago). It cannot be done even by the mere revolutionary abolition of the landed estates (we have not even done that, for the Socialist-Revolutionaries and Mensheviks have betrayed the peasants), by the mere transfer of the land to the peasants. For we are living in the twentieth century, and mastery over the land *without mastery over the banks* cannot regenerate and renovate the life of the people.

The material, industrial renovation of France at the end of the eighteenth century was associated with a political and spiritual renovation, with the dictatorship of revolutionary democrats and the revolutionary proletariat (from which the democrats had not dissociated themselves and with which they were still almost fused), and with a ruthless war declared on everything reactionary. The whole people, and especially the masses, i.e. the *oppressed* classes, were swept up by boundless revolutionary enthusiasm; *everybody* considered the war a just war of defence, as it *actually was*. Revolutionary France was defending herself against reactionary monarchist Europe. It was not in 1792-93, but many years later, *after* the victory of reaction within the country, that the counter-revolutionary dictatorship of Napoleon turned France's wars from defensive wars into wars of conquest.

And what about Russia? We continue to wage an imperialist war in the interests of the capitalists, in alliance with the imperialists and in accordance with the secret treaties the *tsar* concluded with the capitalists of Britain and other countries, promising the Russian capitalists in these treaties the spoliation of foreign lands, of Constantinople, Lvov, Armenia, etc.

The war will remain an unjust, reactionary and predatory war on Russia's part as long as she does not propose a just peace and does not break with imperialism. The social character of the war, its true meaning, is not determined by the position of the enemy troops (as the Socialist-Revolutionaries and Mensheviks think, stooping to the vulgarity of an ignorant yokel). What determines this character is the *policy* of which the war is a continuation ('war is the continuation of politics'), the *class* that is waging the war, and the aims for which it is waging this war.

You cannot lead the people into a predatory war in accordance with secret treaties and expect them to be enthusiastic. The foremost class in revolutionary Russia, the proletariat, is becoming increasingly aware of the criminal character of the war, and not only have the bourgeoisie been unable to shatter this popular conviction, but, on the contrary, awareness of the criminal character of the war is growing. The proletariat *of both metropolitan cities* of Russia has definitely become internationalist!

How, then, can you expect mass enthusiasm for the war!

One is inseparable from the other – home policy is inseparable from foreign policy. The country cannot be made capable of self-defence without the supreme heroism of the people in boldly and resolutely carrying out great economic transformations. And it is impossible to arouse popular heroism without breaking with imperialism, without proposing a democratic peace to all nations, and without thus turning the war from a criminal war of conquest and plunder into a just, revolutionary war of defence.

Only a thorough and consistent break with the capitalists in both home and foreign policy can save our revolution and our country, which is gripped in the iron vice of imperialism.

Marxism and Insurrection

A Letter to the Central Committee
of the RSDLP(B)

13-14 (26-27) September 1917

One of the most vicious and probably most widespread distortions of Marxism resorted to by the dominant 'socialist' parties is the opportunist lie that preparation for insurrection, and generally the treatment of insurrection as an art, is 'Blanquism'.

Bernstein, the leader of opportunism, has already earned himself unfortunate fame by accusing Marxism of Blanquism, and when our present-day opportunists cry Blanquism they do not improve on or 'enrich' the meagre 'ideas' of Bernstein one little bit.

Marxists are accused of Blanquism for treating insurrection as an art! Can there be a more flagrant perversion of the truth, when not a single Marxist will deny that it was Marx who expressed himself on this score in the most definite, precise and categorical manner, referring to insurrection specifically as an *art*, saying that it must be treated as an art, that you must *win* the first success and then proceed from success to success, never ceasing the *offensive* against the enemy, taking advantage of his confusion, etc., etc.?

To be successful, insurrection must rely not upon conspiracy and not upon a party, but upon the advanced class. That is the first point. Insurrection must rely upon a *revolutionary upsurge of the people*. That is the second point. Insurrection must rely upon that *turning-point* in the history of the growing revolution when the activity of the advanced ranks of the people is at its height, and when the *vacillations* in the ranks of the enemy and *in the ranks of the weak, half-hearted and irresolute friends of the revolution* are strongest. That is the third point. And these three conditions for raising the question of insurrection distinguish *Marxism from Blanquism*.

Once these conditions exist, however, to refuse to treat insurrection as an *art* is a betrayal of Marxism and a betrayal of the revolution.

To show that it is precisely the present moment that the Party *must* recognise as the one in which the entire course of events has objectively placed *insurrection* on the order of the day and that insurrection must be treated as an art, it will perhaps be best to use the method of comparison, and to draw a parallel between 3-4 July and the September days.

On 3-4 July it could have been argued, without violating the truth, that the correct thing to do was to take power, for our enemies would in any case have accused us of insurrection and ruthlessly treated us as rebels. However, to have decided on this account in favour of taking power at that time would have been wrong, because the objective conditions for the victory of the insurrection did not exist.

1. We still lacked the support of the class which is the vanguard of the revolution.

    We still did not have a majority among the workers and soldiers of Petrograd and Moscow. Now we have a majority in both Soviets. It was created *solely* by the history of July and August, by the experience of the 'ruthless treatment' meted out to the Bolsheviks, and by the experience of the Kornilov revolt.

2. There was no country-wide revolutionary upsurge at that time. There is now, after the Kornilov revolt; the situation in the provinces and assumption of power by the Soviets in many localities prove this.

3. At that time there was no *vacillation* on any serious political scale among our enemies and among the irresolute petty bourgeoisie. Now the vacillation is enormous. Our main enemy, Allied and world imperialism (for world imperialism is headed by the 'Allies'), *has begun to waver* between a war to a victorious finish and a separate peace directed against Russia. Our petty-bourgeois democrats, having clearly lost their majority among the people, have begun to vacillate enormously, and have rejected a bloc, i.e. a coalition, with the Cadets.

4. Therefore, an insurrection on 3-4 July would have been a mistake; we could not have retained power either physically or politically. We could not have retained it physically even though Petrograd was at times in our hands, because at that time our workers and soldiers would not have *fought and died* for Petrograd. There was not at the time that 'savageness', or fierce hatred *both of* the Kerenskys *and of* the Tseretelis and Chernovs. Our people had still not been tempered by the experience of the persecution of the Bolsheviks in which the Socialist-Revolutionaries and Mensheviks participated.

   We could not have retained power politically on 3-4 July because, *before the Kornilov* revolt, the army and the provinces could and would have marched against Petrograd.

Now the picture is entirely different.

We have the following of the majority of a *class*, the vanguard of the revolution, the vanguard of the people, which is capable of carrying the masses with it.

We have the following of the *majority* of the people, because Chernov's resignation, while by no means the only symptom, is the most striking and obvious symptom that the peasants *will not receive land* from the Socialist-Revolutionaries' bloc (or from the Socialist-Revolutionaries themselves). And that is the chief reason for the popular character of the revolution.

We are in the advantageous position of a party that knows for certain which way to go at a time when *imperialism as a whole* and the Menshevik and Socialist-Revolutionary bloc as a whole are vacillating in an incredible fashion.

Our victory is assured, for the people are close to desperation, and we are showing the entire people a sure way out; we demonstrated to the entire people during the 'Kornilov days' the value of our leadership, and then proposed to the politicians of the bloc a compromise, *which they rejected*, although there is no let-up in their vacillations.

It would be a great mistake to think that our offer of a compromise had not *yet* been rejected, and that the Democratic Conference may *still* accept it. The compromise was proposed *by a party to parties*; it could not have been proposed in any other way. It was rejected by parties. The Democratic Conference is a *conference*, and nothing more. One thing must not be forgotten, namely, that the *majority* of the revolutionary people, the poor, embittered peasants, are not represented in it. It is a conference of a *minority of the people* – this obvious truth must not be forgotten. It would be a big mistake, sheer parliamentary cretinism on our part, if we were to regard the Democratic Conference as a parliament; for even *if it were* to proclaim itself a permanent and sovereign parliament of the revolution, it would nevertheless *decide nothing*. The power of decision lies *outside it* in the working-class quarters of Petrograd and Moscow.

All the objective conditions exist for a successful insurrection. We have the exceptional advantage of a situation in which *only* our victory in the insurrection can put an end to that most painful thing on earth, vacillation, which has worn the people out; in which *only* our victory in the insurrection will give the peasants land immediately; a situation in which only *our* victory in the insurrection can *foil* the game of a separate peace directed against the revolution – foil it by publicly proposing a fuller, juster and earlier peace, a peace that will *benefit* the revolution.

Finally, our Party alone *can*, by a victorious insurrection, save Petrograd; for if our proposal for peace is rejected, if we do not secure even an armistice, then *we* shall become 'defencists', we shall place ourselves *at the head of the war parties*, we shall be the *war party par excellence*, and we shall conduct the war in a truly revolutionary manner. We shall take away all the bread and boots from the capitalists. We shall leave them only crusts and dress them in bast shoes. We shall send all the bread and footwear to the front.

And then we shall save Petrograd.

The resources, both material and spiritual, for a truly revolutionary war in Russia are still immense; the chances are a hundred to one that the Germans will grant us at least an armistice. And to secure an armistice now would in itself mean to win the *whole world*.

* * *

Having recognised the absolute necessity for an insurrection of the workers of Petrograd and Moscow in order to save the revolution and to save Russia from a 'separate' partition by the imperialists of both groups, we must first adapt our political tactics at the Conference to the conditions of the growing insurrection; secondly, we must show that it is not only in words that we accept Marx's idea that insurrection must be treated as an art.

At the Conference we must immediately cement the Bolshevik group, without striving after numbers, and without fearing to leave the waverers in the waverers' camp. They are more useful to the cause of the revolution *there* than in the camp of the resolute and devoted fighters.

We must draw up a brief declaration from the Bolsheviks, emphasising in no uncertain manner the irrelevance of long speeches and of 'speeches' in general, the necessity for immediate action to save the revolution, the absolute necessity for a complete break with the bourgeoisie, for the removal of the present government, in its entirety, for a complete rupture with the Anglo-French imperialists, who are preparing a 'separate' partition of Russia, and for the immediate transfer of all power to *revolutionary democrats, headed by the revolutionary proletariat.*

Our declaration must give the briefest and most trenchant formulation of *this* conclusion in connection with the programme proposals of peace for the peoples, land for the peasants, confiscation of scandalous profits, and a check on the scandalous sabotage of production by the capitalists.

The briefer and more trenchant the declaration, the better. Only two other highly important points must be clearly indicated in it, namely, that the people are worn out by the vacillations, that they are fed up with the irresolution of the Socialist-Revolutionaries and Mensheviks; and that we are definitely breaking with these *parties* because they have betrayed the revolution.

And another thing. By immediately proposing a peace without annexations, by immediately breaking with the Allied imperialists and with all imperialists, either we shall at once obtain an armistice, or the entire revolutionary proletariat will rally to the defence of the country, and a really just, really revolutionary war will then be waged by revolutionary democrats under the leadership of the proletariat.

Having read this declaration, and having appealed for *decisions* and not talk, for *action* and not resolution-writing, we must *dispatch* our entire group to the *factories and the barracks.* Their place is there, the pulse of life is there, there is the source of salvation for our revolution, and there is the motive force of the Democratic Conference.

There, in ardent and impassioned speeches, we must explain our programme and put the alternative: either the Conference adopts it *in its entirety*, or else insurrection. There is no middle course. Delay is impossible. The revolution is dying.

By putting the question in this way, by concentrating our entire group in the factories and barracks, *we shall be able to determine the right moment to start the insurrection.*

In order to treat insurrection in a Marxist way, i.e. as an art, we must at the same time, without losing a single moment, organise a *headquarters* of the insurgent detachments, distribute our forces, move the reliable regiments to the most important points, surround the Alexandrinsky Theatre, occupy the Peter and Paul Fortress, arrest the General Staff and the government, and move against the officer cadets and the Savage Division those detachments which would rather die than allow the enemy to approach the strategic points of the city.* We must mobilise the armed workers and call them to fight the last desperate fight, occupy the telegraph and the telephone exchange at once, move *our* insurrection headquarters to the central telephone exchange and connect it by telephone with all the factories, all the regiments, all the points of armed fighting, etc.

Of course, this is all by way of example, only to *illustrate* the fact that at the present moment it is impossible to remain loyal to Marxism, to remain loyal to the revolution *unless insurrection is treated as an art.*

---

* The Savage Division was formed during the First World War from volunteer mountaineers of the North Caucasus. General Kornilov tried to use it as a battering ram in his assault on revolutionary Petrograd.

The Tasks of the Revolution

26-27 September (9-10 October) 1917

Russia is a country of the petty bourgeoisie, by far the greater part of the population belonging to this class. Its vacillations between the bourgeoisie and the proletariat are inevitable, and only when it joins the proletariat is the victory of the revolution, of the cause of peace, freedom and land for the working people assured easily, peacefully, quickly and smoothly.

The course of our revolution shows us these vacillations in practice. Let us then not harbour any illusions about the Socialist-Revolutionary and Menshevik parties; let us stick firmly to the path of our proletarian class. The poverty of the poor peasants, the horrors of the war, the horrors of hunger – all these are showing the masses more and more clearly the correctness of the proletarian path, the need to support the proletarian revolution.

The 'peaceful' hopes of the petty bourgeoisie that there might be a 'coalition' with the bourgeoisie and agreements with them, that it will be possible to wait 'calmly' for the 'speedy' convocation of the Constituent Assembly, etc., have been mercilessly, cruelly, implacably destroyed by the course of the revolution. The Kornilov revolt was the last cruel lesson, a lesson on a grand scale, supplementing thousands upon thousands of small lessons in which workers and peasants were deceived by local capitalists and landowners, in which soldiers were deceived by the officers etc., etc.

Discontent, indignation and wrath are growing in the army, among the peasantry and among the workers. The 'coalition' of the Socialist-Revolutionaries and Mensheviks with the bourgeoisie, promising everything and fulfilling nothing, is irritating the masses, is opening their eyes, is pushing them towards insurrection.

There is a growing Left opposition among the Socialist-Revolutionaries (Spiridonova and others) and among the Mensheviks (Martov and others), and has already reached 40 per cent of the Council and Congress of those parties. And down *below*, among the proletariat and the peasantry, particularly the poorest sections, the *majority* of the Socialist-Revolutionaries and Mensheviks belong to the *Lefts*.

The Kornilov revolt is instructive and has proved a good lesson.

It is impossible to know whether the Soviets will be able to go farther than the leaders of the Socialist-Revolutionaries and Mensheviks, and thus ensure a peaceful development of the revolution, or whether they will continue to mark time, thus making a proletarian uprising inevitable.

We cannot know this.

Our business is to help get everything possible done to make sure the 'last' chance for a peaceful development of the revolution, to help by the presentation of our programme, by making clear its national character, its absolute accord with the interests and demands of a vast majority of the population.

The following lines are an essay in the presentation of such a programme.

Let us take it more to those down below, to the masses, to the office employees, to the workers, to the peasants, not only to our supporters, but particularly to those who follow the Socialist-Revolutionaries, to the non-party elements, to the ignorant. Let us lift them up so that they can pass an independent judgment, make their own decisions, send *their own* delegations to the Conference, to the Soviets, to the government, and our work will not have been in vain, *no matter what* the outcome of the Conference. This will then prove useful for the Conference, for the elections to the Constituent Assembly and for all other political activity in general.

Experience teaches us that the Bolshevik programme and tactics are correct. So little time passed, so much happened from 20 April to the Kornilov revolt.

The experience of the *masses*, the experience of *oppressed* classes taught them very, very much in that time; the leaders of the Socialist-Revolutionaries and Mensheviks have completely cut adrift from the masses. This will most certainly be revealed in the discussion of our concrete programme insofar as we are able to bring it to the notice of the masses.

Agreements with the capitalists are disastrous

1. To leave in power the representatives of the bourgeoisie, even a small number of them, to leave in power such notorious Kornilovites as Generals Alexeyev, Klembovsky, Bagration, Gagarin, and others, or such as have proved their complete powerlessness in face of the bourgeoisie, and their ability of acting Bonaparte-fashion like Kerensky, is, on the one hand, merely opening the door wide to famine and the inevitable economic catastrophe which the capitalists are purposely accelerating and intensifying; on the other hand, it will lead to a military catastrophe, since the army hates the General Staff and cannot enthusiastically participate in the imperialist war. Besides, there is no doubt that Kornilovite generals and officers remaining in power will *deliberately open the front to the Germans*, as they have done in Galicia and Riga. This can be prevented only by the formation of a new government on a new basis, as expounded below. To continue any kind of agreements with the bourgeoisie after all that we have gone through since 20 April would be, on the part of the Socialist-Revolutionaries and Mensheviks, not only an error but a direct betrayal of the people and of the revolution.

Power to the Soviets

2. All power in the country must pass exclusively to the representatives of the Soviets of Workers', Soldiers' and Peasants' Deputies on the basis of a definite programme and under the condition of the government being fully responsible to the Soviets. New elections to the Soviets must be held immediately, both to record the experience of the people during the recent weeks of the revolution, which have been particularly eventful, and to eliminate crying injustices (lack of proportional representation, unequal elections, etc.) which in some cases still remain.

   All power locally, wherever there are not yet any democratically elected institutions, and also in the army, must be taken over exclusively by the local Soviets and by commissars and other institutions elected by them, but only those that have been properly elected.

   Workers and revolutionary troops, i.e. those who have in practice shown their ability to suppress the Kornilovites, must everywhere be armed, and this must be done with the full support of the state.

Peace to the peoples

3. The Soviet Government must *straight away* offer to all the belligerent peoples (i.e. simultaneously both to their governments and to the worker and peasant masses) to conclude an immediate general peace on democratic terms, and also to conclude an immediate armistice (even if only for three months).

   The main condition for a democratic peace is the renunciation of annexations (seizures) – not in the incorrect sense that all powers get back what they have lost, but in the only correct sense that *every* nationality without any exception, both in Europe and in the colonies, shall obtain its freedom and the possibility to decide for itself whether it is to form a *separate* state or whether it is to enter into the composition of some other state.

In offering the peace terms, the Soviet Government must itself immediately take steps towards their fulfilment, i.e. it must publish and repudiate the secret treaties by which we have been bound up to the present time, those which were concluded by the tsar and which give Russian capitalists the promise of the pillaging of Turkey, Austria, etc. Then we must immediately satisfy the demands of the Ukrainians and the Finns, ensure them, as well as all other non-Russian nationalities in Russia, full freedom, including freedom of secession, applying the same *to all* Armenia, undertaking to evacuate that country as well as the Turkish lands occupied by us, etc.

Such peace terms will not meet with the approval of the capitalists, but they will meet with such tremendous sympathy on the part of all the peoples and will cause such a great world-wide outburst of enthusiasm and of general indignation against the continuation of the predatory war that it is extremely probable that we shall at once obtain a truce and a consent to open peace negotiations. For the workers' revolution against the war is irresistibly growing everywhere, and it can be spurred on, not by phrases about peace (with which the workers and peasants have been deceived by *all* the imperialist governments, including our own Kerensky government), but by a break with the capitalists and by the offer of peace.

If the least probable thing happens, i.e. if not a single belligerent state accepts even a truce, then as far as we are concerned the war becomes truly forced upon us, it becomes a truly just war of defence. If this is understood by the proletariat and the poor peasantry, Russia will become many times stronger even in the military sense, especially after a complete break with the capitalists who are robbing the people; furthermore, under such conditions it would, as far as we are concerned, be a war in league with the oppressed classes of all countries, a war in league with the oppressed peoples of the whole world, not in word, but in deed.

The people must be particularly cautioned against the capitalists' assertion which sometimes influences the petty bourgeoisie and others who are frightened, namely, that the British and other capitalists are capable of doing serious damage to the Russian revolution if we break the present predatory alliance with them. Such an assertion is false through and through, for 'Allied financial aid' enriches the bankers and 'supports' the Russian workers and peasants in exactly the same way as a rope supports a man who has been hanged. There is plenty of bread, coal, oil and iron in Russia; for these products to be properly distributed it is only necessary for us to rid ourselves of the landowners and capitalists who are robbing the people. As to the possibility of the Russian people being threatened with war by their present Allies, it is obviously absurd to assume that the French and Italians could unite their armies with those of the Germans and move them against Russia who offers a just peace. As to Britain, America and Japan, even if they were to declare war against Russia (which for them is extremely difficult, both because of the extreme unpopularity of such a war among the masses and because of the divergence of material interests of the capitalists of those countries over the partitioning of Asia, especially over the plunder of China), they could not cause Russia one-hundredth part of the damage and misery which the war with Germany, Austria and Turkey is causing her.

Land to those who till it

4. The Soviet Government must immediately declare the abolition of private landed estates without compensation and place all these estates under the management of the peasant committees pending the solution of the problem by the Constituent Assembly. These peasant committees are also to take over all the landowners' stock and implements, with the proviso that they be placed primarily at the disposal of the poor peasants for their use free of charge.

Such measures, which have long been demanded by an immense majority of the peasantry, both in the resolutions of congresses and in hundreds of mandates from local peasants (as may be seen, for instance, from a summary of 242 mandates published by *Izvestia Soveta Krestyanskikh Deputatov*), are absolutely and urgently necessary. There must be no further procrastination like that from which the peasantry suffered so much at the time of the 'coalition' government.

Any government that hesitates to introduce these measures should be regarded as a government *hostile to the people* that should be overthrown and crushed by an uprising of the workers and peasants. On the other hand, only a government that realises these measures will be a government of all the people.

Struggle against famine and economic ruin

5. The Soviet Government must immediately introduce workers' control of production and distribution on a nation-wide scale. Experience since 6 May has shown that in the absence of such control, all the promises of reforms and attempts to introduce them are powerless, and famine, accompanied by unprecedented catastrophe, is becoming a greater menace to the whole country week by week.

It is necessary to nationalise the banks and the insurance business immediately, and also the most important branches of industry (oil, coal, metallurgy, sugar, etc.), and at the same time, to abolish commercial secrets and to establish unrelaxing supervision by the workers and peasants over the negligible minority of capitalists who wax rich on government contracts and evade accounting and just taxation of their profits and property.

Such measures, which do not deprive either the middle peasants, the Cossacks or the small handicraftsmen of a single kopek, are urgently needed for the struggle against famine and are absolutely just because they distribute the burdens of the war equitably. Only after capitalist plunder has been curbed and the deliberate sabotage of production has been stopped will it be possible to work for an improvement in labour productivity, introduce universal labour conscription and the proper exchange of grain for manufactured goods, and return to the Treasury thousands of millions in paper money now being hoarded by the rich.

Without such measures, the abolition of the landed estates without compensation is also impossible, for the major part of the estates is mortgaged to the banks, so that the interests of the landowners and capitalists are inseparably linked up.

The latest resolution of the Economic Department of the All-Russia Central Executive Committee of Soviets of Workers' and Soldiers' Deputies (*Rabochaya Gazeta*, No. 152) recognises not only the "*harm*" caused by the government's measures (like the raising of grain prices for the enrichment of the landowners and kulaks), not only "the fact of the *complete inactivity* on the part of the central organs set up by the government for the regulation of economic life", but even the "*contravention of the laws*" by this government. This admission on the part of the ruling parties, the Socialist-Revolutionaries and Mensheviks, proves once more the criminal nature of the policy of conciliation with the bourgeoisie.

Struggle against the counter-revolution of the landowners and capitalists

6. The Kornilov and Kaledin revolt was supported by the entire class of the landowners and capitalists, with the party of the Cadets ('people's freedom' party) at their head. This has already been fully proved by the facts published in *Izvestia* of the Central Executive Committee.

However, nothing has been done either to suppress this counter-revolution completely or even to investigate it, and nothing serious can be done without the transfer of power to the Soviets. No commission can conduct a full investigation, or arrest the guilty, etc., unless it holds state power. Only a

Soviet government can do this, and must do it. Only a Soviet government can make Russia secure against the otherwise inevitable repetition of 'Kornilov' attempts by arresting the Kornilovite generals and the ringleaders of the bourgeois counter-revolution (Guchkov, Milyukov, Ryabushinsky, Maklakov and co.), by disbanding the counter-revolutionary associations (the State Duma, the officers' unions, etc.), by placing their members under the surveillance of the local Soviets and by disbanding counter-revolutionary armed units.

This government alone can set up a commission to make a full and public investigation of the Kornilov case and all the other cases, even those started by the bourgeoisie; and the party of the Bolsheviks, in its turn, would appeal to the workers to give full cooperation and to submit only to such a commission.

Only a Soviet government could successfully combat such a flagrant injustice as the capitalists' seizure of the largest printing presses and most of the papers with the aid of millions squeezed out of the people. It is necessary to suppress the bourgeois counter-revolutionary papers (*Rech, Russkoye Slovo*, etc.), to confiscate their printing presses, to declare private advertisements in the papers a state monopoly, to transfer them to the paper published by the Soviets, the paper that tells the peasants the truth. Only in this way can and must the bourgeoisie be deprived of its powerful weapon of lying and slandering, deceiving the people with impunity, misleading the peasantry and preparing a counter-revolution.

Peaceful development of the Revolution

7. A possibility very seldom to be met with in the history of revolutions now faces the democracy of Russia, the Soviets and the Socialist-Revolutionary and Menshevik parties – the possibility of convening the Constituent Assembly at the appointed date without further delays, of making the country secure against a military and economic catastrophe, and of ensuring the peaceful development of the revolution.

If the Soviets now take full state power exclusively into their own hands for the purpose of carrying out the programme set forth above, they will not only obtain the support of nine-tenths of the population of Russia, the working class and an overwhelming majority of the peasantry; they will also be assured of the greatest revolutionary enthusiasm on the part of the army and the majority of the people, an enthusiasm without which victory over famine and war is impossible.

There could be no question of any resistance to the Soviets if the Soviets themselves did not waver. No class will dare start an uprising against the Soviets, and the landowners and capitalists, taught a lesson by the experience of the Kornilov revolt, will give up their power peacefully and yield to the ultimatum of the Soviets. To overcome the capitalists' resistance to the programme of the Soviets, supervision over the exploiters by workers and peasants, and such measures of punishing the recalcitrants as confiscation of their entire property coupled with a short term of arrest will be sufficient.

By seizing full power, the Soviets could still today – and this is probably their last chance – ensure the peaceful development of the revolution, peaceful elections of deputies by the people, and a peaceful struggle of parties inside the Soviets; they could test the programmes of the various parties in practice and power could pass peacefully from one party to another.

The entire course of development of the revolution, from the movement of 20 April to the Kornilov revolt, shows that there is bound to be the bitterest civil war between the bourgeoisie and the proletariat if this opportunity is missed. Inevitable catastrophe will bring this war nearer. It must end, as all data and considerations accessible to human reason go to prove, in the full victory of the working class, in that class, supported by the poor peasantry, carrying out the above programme; it may, however, prove very difficult and bloody, and may cost the lives of tens of thousands of landowners, capitalists and officers who sympathise with them. The proletariat will not hesitate to make every sacrifice to save the revolution, which is possible only by implementing the programme set forth above. On the other hand, the proletariat would support the Soviets in every way if they were to make use of their last chance to secure a peaceful development of the revolution.

Second All-Russia Congress of Soviets of Workers' and Soldiers' Deputies

25-26 October (7-8 November) 1917

Editors note:

The Second All-Russian Congress of Soviets met on 25-26 October 1917, at 22:40, in the Smolny Institute. This was the meeting which legalised the taking of power by the Soviets.

Of the 649 delegates elected to the Congress of Soviets, representing 318 provincial/local soviets, 390 were Bolshevik, 160 Socialist-Revolutionaries (about 100 were Left SRs), seventy-two Mensheviks, fourteen Menshevik Internationalists, and thirteen from various other groups.

In its second session, on 26 October, the congress voted on the 'Decree on Peace' drafted by Lenin.

We publish here Lenin's report on this question, which includes the text of the decree, as well as Lenin's reply to the discussion.

* * *

Report on Peace

26 October (8 November) 1917

The question of peace is a burning question, the painful question of the day. Much has been said and written on the subject, and all of you, no doubt, have discussed it quite a lot. Permit me, therefore, to proceed to read a declaration which the government you elect should publish.

Decree on Peace

The workers' and peasants' government, created by the Revolution of 24-25 October and basing itself on the Soviet of Workers', Soldiers' and Peasants' Deputies, calls upon all the belligerent peoples and their government to start immediate negotiations for a just, democratic peace.

By a just or democratic peace, for which the overwhelming majority of the working class and other working people of all the belligerent countries, exhausted, tormented and racked by the war, are craving – a peace that has been most definitely and insistently demanded by the Russian workers and peasants ever since the overthrow of the tsarist monarchy – by such a peace the government means an immediate peace without annexations (i.e. without the seizure of foreign lands, without the forcible incorporation of foreign nations) and without indemnities.

The government of Russia proposes that this kind of peace be immediately concluded by all the belligerent nations, and expresses its readiness to take all the resolute measures now, without the least delay, pending the final ratification of all the terms of such a peace by authoritative assemblies of the people's representatives of all countries and all nations.

In accordance with the sense of justice of democrats in general, and of the working class in particular, the government conceives the annexation or seizure of foreign lands to mean every incorporation of a small or weak nation into large or powerful state without the precisely, clearly and voluntarily expressed consent and wish of that nation, irrespective of the time when such forcible incorporation took place, irrespective also of the degree of development or backwardness of the nation forcibly annexed to the given state, or forcibly retained within its borders, and irrespective, finally, of whether this nation is in Europe or in distant, overseas countries.

If any nation whatsoever is forcibly retained within the borders of a given state, if, in spite of its expressed desire – no matter whether expressed in the press, at public meetings, in the decisions of parties, or in protests and uprisings against national oppression – it is not accorded the right to decide the forms of its state existence by a free vote, taken after the complete evacuation of the troops of the incorporating or, generally, of the stronger nation, and without the least pressure being brought to bear, such incorporation is annexation, i.e. seizure and violence.

The government considers it the greatest of crimes against humanity to continue this war over the issue of how to divide among the strong and rich nations the weak nationalities they have conquered, and solemnly announces its determination immediately to sign terms of peace to stop this war on the terms indicated, which are equally just for all nationalities without exception.

At the same time, the government declares that it does not regard the above-mentioned peace terms as an ultimatum; in other words, it is prepared to consider any other peace terms, and insists only that they be advanced by any of the belligerent countries as speedily as possible, and that in the peace proposals there should be absolute clarity and the complete absence of all ambiguity and secrecy.

The government abolishes secret diplomacy, and, for its part, announces its firm intention to conduct all negotiations quite openly in full view of the whole people. It will proceed immediately with the full publication of the secret treaties endorsed or concluded by the government of land-owners and capitalists from February to 25 October 1917.* The government proclaims the unconditional

---

*   All secret treaties made by the Provisional and tsarist governments were published beginning on 10 (23) November 1917 in issues of *Pravda* and

and immediate annulment of everything contained in these secret treaties insofar as it is aimed, as is mostly the case, at securing advantages and privileges for the Russian landowners and capitalists and at the retention, or extension, of the annexations made by the Great Russians.

Proposing to the governments and peoples of all countries immediately to begin open negotiations for peace, the government, for its part, expresses its readiness to conduct these negotiations in writing, by telegraph, and by negotiations between representatives of the various countries, or at a conference of such representatives. In order to facilitate such negotiations, the government is appointing its plenipotentiary representative to neutral countries.

The government proposes an immediate armistice to the governments and people of all the belligerent countries, and, for its part, considers it desirable that this armistice should be concluded for a period of not less than three months, i.e. a period long enough to permit the completion of negotiations for peace with the participation of the representatives of all peoples or nations, without exception, involved in or compelled to take part in the war, and the summoning of authoritative assemblies of the representatives of the peoples of all countries for the final ratification of the peace terms.

While addressing this proposal for peace to the governments and peoples of all the belligerent countries, the Provisional Workers' and Peasants' Government of Russia appeals in particular also to the class-conscious workers of the three most advanced nations of mankind and the largest states participating in the present war, namely, Great Britain, France and Germany. The workers of these countries have made the greatest contributions to the cause of progress and socialism; they have furnished the great examples of the Chartist movement in England, a number of revolutions of historic importance effected by the French proletariat, and, finally,

---

Izvestia. In December, the treaties were published in a long series of books, entitled *Collection of Secret Documents from the Archives of the Former Ministry of Foreign Affairs*. Seven volumes were printed from December 1917 to February 1918.

the heroic struggle against the Anti-Socialist Law in Germany, and the prolonged, persistent and disciplined work of creating mass proletarian organisations in Germany, a work which serves as a model to the workers of the whole world. All these examples of proletarian heroism and historical creative work are a pledge that the workers of the countries mentioned will understand the duty that now faces them of saving mankind from the horrors of war and its consequences, that these workers, by comprehensive, determined and supremely vigorous action, will help us to conclude peace successfully, and at the same time emancipate the labouring and exploited masses of our population from all forms of slavery and all forms of exploitation.

* * *

The Workers' and Peasants' Government, created by the Revolution of 24-25 October and basing itself on the support of the Soviets of Workers', Soldiers' and Peasants' Deputies, must start immediate negotiations for peace. Our appeal must be addressed both to the governments and to the peoples. We cannot ignore the governments, for that would delay the possibility of concluding peace, and the people's government dare not do that; but we have no right not to appeal to the peoples at the same time. Everywhere there are differences between the governments and the peoples, and we must therefore help the peoples to intervene in questions of war and peace. We will, of course, insist upon the whole of our programme for a peace without annexations and indemnities. We shall not retreat from it; but we must not give our enemies an opportunity to say that their conditions are different from ours and that therefore it is useless to start negotiations with us. No, we must deprive them of that advantageous position and not present our terms in the form of an ultimatum. Therefore the point is included that we are willing to consider any peace terms and all proposals. We shall consider them, but that does not necessarily mean that we shall accept them. We shall submit them for consideration to the Constituent Assembly which will have the power to decide what concessions can and what cannot be made. We are combating the deception practised by governments which pay lip-service to peace and justice, but in fact wage annexationist and predatory wars. No government will say all it thinks. We, however, are opposed to secret diplomacy and will act openly in full view of the whole people. We do not close our eyes to difficulties and never have done so. War cannot be ended by refusal, it cannot be ended by one side. We are proposing an armistice for three months, but shall not reject a shorter period, so that the exhausted army may breathe freely, even if only for a little while; moreover, in all the civilised countries national assemblies must be summoned for the discussion of the terms.

In proposing an immediate armistice, we appeal to the class-conscious workers of the countries that have done so much for the development of the proletarian movement. We appeal to the workers of Britain, where there was the Chartist movement, to the workers of France, who have in repeated uprisings displayed the strength of their class-consciousness, and to the workers of Germany, who waged the fight against the Anti-Socialist Law and have created powerful organisations.

In the Manifesto of 14 March [issued by the Petrograd Soviet], we called for the overthrow of the bankers, but, far from overthrowing our own bankers, we had entered into an alliance with them. Now we have overthrown the government of the bankers.

The governments and the bourgeoisie will make every effort to unite their forces and drown the workers' and peasants' revolution in blood. But the three years of war have been a good lesson to the masses – the Soviet movement in other countries and the mutiny in the German navy, which was crushed by the officer cadets of Wilhelm the hangman. Finally, we must remember that we are not living in the depths of Africa, but in Europe, where news can spread quickly.

The workers' movement will triumph and will pave the way to peace and socialism. (*Prolonged applause*)

* * *

Concluding Speech Following the Discussion on the 'Report on Peace'

26 October (8 November) 1917

I shall not touch on the general character of the declaration. The government which your Congress sets up may amend unessential points.

I shall vigorously oppose lending our demand for peace in the form of an ultimatum. An ultimatum may prove fatal to our whole cause. We cannot demand that, since some insignificant departure from our demands on the part of the imperialist governments would give them the opportunity of saying that it was impossible to enter into negotiations for peace because of our irreconcilability.

We shall send out our appeal everywhere, it will be made known to everybody. It will be impossible to conceal the terms proposed by our workers' and peasants' government.

It will be impossible to hush up our workers' and peasants' revolution, which has overthrown the government of bankers and landowners.

The governments may not reply to an ultimatum; they will have to reply to the text as we formulate it. Let everyone know what their governments have in mind. We do not want any secrets. We want a government to be always under the supervision of the public opinion of its country.

What will the peasant of some remote province say if, owing to our insistence on ultimatums, he will not know what another government wants? He will say:

'Comrades, why did you rule out the possibility of any peace terms being proposed? I would have discussed them, I would have examined them, and would then have instructed my representatives in the Constituent Assembly how to act. I am prepared to fight by revolutionary methods for just terms if the governments do not agree, but there might be such terms for some countries that I would be prepared to recommend their governments to go on fighting by themselves. The full realisation of our ideas depends solely on the overthrow of the entire capitalist system.'

This is what the peasant might say to us, and he would accuse us of being excessively uncompromising over trifles, when for us the main thing is to expose all the vileness, all the baseness of the bourgeoisie and of its crowned and uncrowned hangmen at the head of the government.

We should not and must not give the governments an opportunity of taking refuge behind our uncompromising attitude and of concealing from the peoples the reason why they are being sent to the shambles. This is a tiny drop, but we should not and must not reject this drop, which will wear away the stone of bourgeois conquest. An ultimatum would make the position of our opponents easier. But we shall make all the terms known to the people. We shall confront all the governments with our terms, and let them give an answer to their people. We shall submit all peace proposals to the Constituent Assembly for decision.

There is still another point, comrades, to which you must pay the most careful attention. The secret treaties must be published. The clauses dealing with annexations and indemnities must be annulled. There are various clauses, comrades – the predatory governments, you know, not only made agreements between themselves on plunder, but among them they also included economic agreements and various other clauses on good-neighbourly relations.

We shall not bind ourselves by treaties. We shall not allow ourselves to be entangled by treaties. We reject all clauses on plunder and violence, but we shall welcome all clauses containing provisions for good-neighbourly relations and all economic agreements; we cannot reject these. We propose an armistice for three months; we choose a lengthy period because the peoples are exhausted, the peoples long for a respite from this bloody shambles that has lasted over three years. We must realise that the peoples should be given an opportunity to discuss the peace terms and to express their will with parliament participating, and this takes time. We demand a lengthy armistice, so that the soldiers in the trenches may enjoy a respite from this nightmare of constant slaughter; but we shall not reject proposals for a shorter armistice; we shall examine them, and it is incumbent upon us to accept them, even if we are offered an armistice of a month or a month and a half. Nor must our proposal for an armistice have the form of an ultimatum, for we shall not give our enemies an opportunity of concealing the whole truth from the peoples, using our irreconcilability as a pretext. It must not be in the form of an ultimatum, for a government is criminal that does not desire an armistice. If we do not put our proposal for an armistice in the form of an ultimatum, we shall thereby show the peoples that the governments are criminal, and the peoples will not stand on ceremony with such criminals. The objection is raised that by not resorting to an ultimatum we are displaying weakness, but it is time to cast aside all bourgeois cant when speaking of the strength of the people. According to the bourgeois conception, there is strength when the people go blindly to the slaughter in obedience to the imperialist governments. The bourgeoisie admit a state to be strong only when it can, by the power of the government apparatus, hurl the people wherever the bourgeois rulers want them hurled. Our idea of strength is different. Our idea is that a state is strong when the people are politically conscious. It is strong when the people know everything, can form an opinion of everything and do everything consciously. We need not fear to tell the truth about fatigue, for what state today is not tired, what nation does not talk about it openly? Take Italy, where, owing to this tiredness, there was a prolonged revolutionary movement demanding the termination of the slaughter. Are there not mass demonstrations of workers in Germany that put forward a demand for the termination of the war? Was it not fatigue that provoked the mutiny in the German navy that was so ruthlessly suppressed by that hangman, Wilhelm, and his hirelings? If such things are possible in so disciplined a country as Germany, where they are beginning to talk about fatigue and about putting an end to the war, we need not fear to say the same openly, because it is the truth, equally true both of our country and of all the belligerent and even non-belligerent countries.

Wireless Message of the Council of People's Commissars

30 October (12 November) 1917

Calling Everyone.

The All-Russia Congress of Soviets has set up a new Soviet Government. Kerensky's government has been overthrown and arrested. Kerensky has fled. All institutions are in the hands of the Soviet Government. A revolt of officer cadets who had been released on parole on 25 October broke out on 29 October. The revolt was suppressed that same day. Kerensky and Savinkov, together with the officer cadets and a part of the Cossacks, have made their way by deceit to Tsarskoye Selo. The Soviet Government has mustered forces for the suppression of the new Kornilov advance on Petrograd. The fleet, headed by the armoured battleship *Republic*, has been summoned to the capital. Kerensky's officer cadets and Cossacks are wavering. Prisoners arriving from Kerensky's camp assure us that the Cossacks have been deceived and that if they come to realise the true state of affairs they will refuse to shoot. The Soviet Government is making every effort to avert bloodshed. If bloodshed cannot be avoided and if Kerensky's units do begin to shoot, the Soviet Government will not hesitate to suppress the new Kerensky-Kornilov campaign ruthlessly.

We announce for your information that the Congress of Soviets which has already dispersed, adopted two important decrees: (1) on the immediate transfer of all the landed estates to the peasant committees, and (2) on the proposal of a democratic peace.

Vladimir Ulyanov (Lenin),
Chairman of the Soviet Government

For Bread And Peace

14 December 1917

Editors note:

Written on 14 (27) December 1917 at the request of the
Swedish Left-wing Social-Democrat Höglund, who had arrived
in Petrograd on an assignment from the left-wing Social-
Democratic Party of Sweden. The article was first published in
German in May 1918 in the newspaper *Jugend-Internationale*,
the organ of the International Alliance of Socialist Youth
Organisations, which was affiliated with the Zimmerwald Left
(published in Zürich from September 1915 to May 1918).

In November 1919, a facsimile of the opening paragraph was
used as an illustration to a special edition of *Det röda Ryssland*
issued by the Left-wing Socialist publishers *Fram* (*Forward*)
in Stockholm to mark the second anniversary of the October
Socialist Revolution in Russia.

* * *

Two questions now take precedence over all other political questions
– the question of bread and the question of peace. The imperialist
war, the war between the biggest and richest banking firms, Britain
and Germany, that is being waged for world domination, the
division of the spoils, for the plunder of small and weak nations;
this horrible, criminal war has ruined all countries, exhausted all

peoples, and confronted mankind with the alternative – either sacrifice all civilisation and perish or throw off the capitalist yoke in the revolutionary way, do away with the rule of the bourgeoisie and win socialism and durable peace.

If socialism is not victorious, peace between the capitalist states will be only a truce, an interlude, a time of preparation for a fresh slaughter of the peoples. Peace and bread are the basic demands of the workers and the exploited. The war has made these demands extremely urgent. The war has brought hunger to the most civilised countries, to those most culturally developed. On the other hand, the war, as a tremendous historical process, has accelerated social development to an unheard-of degree. Capitalism had developed into imperialism, i.e. into monopoly capitalism, and under the influence of the war it has become state monopoly capitalism. We have now reached the stage of world economy that is the immediate stepping stone to socialism.

The socialist revolution that has begun in Russia is, therefore, only the beginning of the world socialist revolution. Peace and bread, the overthrow of the bourgeoisie, revolutionary means for the healing of war wounds, the complete victory of socialism – such are the aims of the struggle.

Petrograd,
14 December 1917

Appendices

Resolution of the Seventh International Socialist Congress at Stuttgart

18-24 August 1907

The Congress confirms the resolutions adopted by previous international congresses against militarism and imperialism and declares once more that the struggle against militarism cannot be separated from the Socialist class struggle in general.

Wars between capitalist states are, as a rule, the outcome of their competition on the world market, for each state seeks not only to secure its existing markets, but also to conquer new ones. In this, the subjugation of foreign peoples and countries plays a prominent role. These wars result furthermore from the incessant race for armaments by militarism, one of the chief instruments of bourgeois class rule and of the economic and political subjugation of the working class.

Wars are favoured by the national prejudices which are systematically cultivated among civilized peoples in the interest of the ruling classes for the purpose of distracting the proletarian masses from their own class tasks as well as from their duties of international solidarity.

Wars, therefore, are part of the very nature of capitalism; they will cease only when the capitalist system is abolished or when the enormous sacrifices in men and money required by the advance in military technique and the indignation called forth by armaments, drive the peoples to abolish this system.

For this reason, the proletariat, which contributes most of the soldiers and makes most of the material sacrifices is a natural opponent of war which contradicts its highest goal – the creation of an economic order on a Socialist basis which will bring about the solidarity of all peoples.

The Congress, therefore, considers it as the duty of the working class and particularly of its representatives in the parliaments to combat the naval and military armaments with all their might, characterising the class nature of bourgeois society and the motive for the maintenance of national antagonisms, and to refuse the means for these armaments. It is their duty to work for the education of the working-class youth in the spirit of the brotherhood of nations and of Socialism while developing their class consciousness.

The Congress sees in the democratic organisation of the army, in the substitution of the militia for the standing army, an essential guarantee that offensive wars will be rendered impossible and the overcoming of national antagonisms facilitated.

The International is not able to determine in rigid forms the anti-militarist actions of the working class which are naturally different in different countries and for different circumstances of time and place. But it is its duty to coordinate and increase to the utmost the efforts of the working class against war.

In fact, since the International Congress at Brussels the proletariat has employed the most diverse forms of action with increasing emphasis and success in its indefatigable struggles against militarism by refusing the means for naval and military armaments and by its efforts to democratise the military organisation – all for the purpose of preventing the outbreak of wars or of putting a stop to them, as well as for utilising the convulsions of society caused by war for the emancipation of the working class.

This was evidenced especially by the agreement between the English and French trade unions following the Fashoda Affair for the maintenance of peace and for the restoration of friendly relations between England and France;* by the procedure of the Social-Democratic parties in the German and French parliaments during the Morocco crisis;** the demonstrations arranged by the French and German Socialists for the same purpose; the concerted action of the Socialists of Austria and Italy who met in Trieste in order to prevent a conflict between the two countries; furthermore, by the energetic intervention of the Socialist workers of Sweden in order to prevent an attack upon Norway; finally, the heroic, self-sacrificing struggle of the Socialist workers and peasants of Russia and Poland in order to oppose the war unleashed by tsarism, to put a stop to it, and to utilise the crisis of the country for the liberation of the working class.

All these efforts are evidence of the growing power of the proletariat and of its increasing ability to secure the maintenance of peace by resolute intervention. The action of the working class will be all the more successful the more that its spirit is prepared by a corresponding action and the labour parties of the various countries are spurred on and coordinated by the International.

The Congress is convinced that, under the pressure of the proletariat, by a serious use of arbitration in place of the miserable measures of the governments, the benefit of disarmament can be secured to all nations, making it possible to employ the enormous expenditures of money and energy, which are swallowed up by military armaments and wars, for cultural purposes.

---

*　The Fashoda Crisis was a territorial dispute between Britain and France in 1898 over control of Sudan. Both powers sought to expand their colonial influence in Africa. There was war hysteria in both countries, but the crisis was eventually resolved, with France conceding the territory to Britain.

**　The First Moroccan Crisis took place in 1905 when the German Kaiser attempted to weaken French influence in Morocco and increase German presence. The crisis brought France and Germany to the brink of war, but it was averted by a conference where Germany was supported only by Austria-Hungary and thus had to give up on its demands

If a war threatens to break out, it is the duty of the working classes and their parliamentary representatives in the countries involved, supported by the coordinating activity of the International Socialist Bureau, to exert every effort in order to prevent the outbreak of war by the means they consider most effective, which naturally vary according to the sharpening of the class struggle and the sharpening of the general political situation.

In case war should break out anyway, it is their duty to intervene in favour of its speedy termination and with all their powers to utilise the economic and political crisis created by the war to rouse the masses and thereby to hasten the downfall of capitalist class rule.

Manifesto of the Extraordinary International Socialist Congress at Basel

24-25 November 1912

At its congresses at Stuttgart and Copenhagen, the International formulated for the proletariat of all countries these guiding principles for the struggle against war:

> If a war threatens to break out, it is the duty of the working classes and their parliamentary representatives in the countries involved, supported by the coordinating activity of the International Socialist Bureau, to *exert every effort in order to prevent the outbreak of war by the means they consider most effective*, which naturally vary according to the sharpening of the class struggle and the sharpening of the general political situation.

> In case war should break out anyway, it is their duty *to intervene in favour of its speedy termination* and with all their powers to utilise *the economic and political crisis created by the war to arouse the people and thereby to hasten the downfall of capitalist class rule.**

---

* In this volume, p. 370, emphasis added by the Basel delegates.

More than ever, recent events have imposed upon the proletariat the duty of devoting the utmost force and energy to planned and concerted action. On the one hand, the universal craze for armaments has aggravated the high cost of living, thereby intensifying class antagonisms and creating in the working class an implacable spirit of revolt; the workers want to put a stop to this system of panic and waste. On the other hand, the incessantly recurring menace of war has a more and more inciting effect. The great European peoples are constantly on the point of being driven against one another; these attempts against humanity and reason cannot be justified by even the slightest pretext of being in the interest of the people.

If the Balkan crisis, which has already caused such terrible disasters, should spread further, it would become the most frightful danger to civilisation and the proletariat.* At the same time, it would be the greatest outrage in all history because of the crying discrepancy between the immensity of the catastrophe and the insignificance of the interests involved.

It is with satisfaction that the Congress records the complete unanimity of the Socialist parties and of the trade unions of all countries in the war against war.

The proletarians of all countries have risen simultaneously in a struggle against imperialism; each section of the International has opposed the resistance of the proletariat to the government of its own country, and has mobilised the public opinion of its nation against all bellicose desires. Thus, there resulted the grandiose cooperation of the workers of all countries which has already contributed a great deal toward saving the threatened peace of the world. The fear of the ruling class of a proletarian revolution

---

* A reference to the political upheavals and territorial disputes in the Balkan Peninsula, then part of the Ottoman Empire. It was to culminate in the Balkan Wars of 1912-13, where the Balkan states (Serbia, Bulgaria, Greece, and Montenegro) sought to break away from Ottoman rule and expand their territories. These conflicts destabilised the region and contributed to the outbreak of First World War.

as a result of a world war has proved to be an essential guarantee of peace.

The Congress therefore calls upon the Social-Democratic parties to continue their action by every means that seems appropriate to them. In this concerted action it assigns to each Socialist party its particular task.

The Social-Democratic parties of the Balkan peninsula have a difficult task. The Great Powers of Europe, by the systematic frustration of all reforms, have contributed to the creation of unbearable economic, national and political conditions in Turkey which necessarily had to lead to revolt and war. Against the exploitation of these conditions in the interest of the dynasties and the bourgeois classes, the Social-Democratic parties of the Balkans, with heroic courage, have raised the demand for a democratic federation. The Congress calls upon them to persevere in their admirable attitude; it expects that after the war the Social-Democracy of the Balkans will make every effort to prevent the results of the Balkan War, attained at the price of such terrible sacrifices, from being misused for their own purposes by dynasties, by militarism, and by the bourgeoisie of the Balkan states which is greedy for expansion. The Congress, however, calls upon the Socialists of the Balkans particularly to resist not only the renewal of the old enmities between Serbs, Bulgars, Romanians, and Greeks, but also every violation of the Balkan peoples now in the opposite camp, the Turks and the Albanians. It is the duty of the Socialists of the Balkans, therefore, to fight against every violation of the rights of these people and to proclaim the fraternity of all Balkans peoples, including the Albanians, the Turks and the Romanians, against the unleashed national chauvinism.

It is the duty of the Social-Democratic parties of Austria, Hungary, Croatia and Slavonia, Bosnia and Herzegovina to continue with all their power their effective action against an attack upon Serbia by the Danubian monarchy. It is their task to continue, as in the past, to oppose the plan of robbing Serbia of the results of the war by armed force, of transforming it into an

Austrian colony, and of involving the peoples of Austria-Hungary proper, and together with them all nations of Europe, in the greatest dangers for the sake of dynastic interests. In the future, the Social-Democratic parties of Austria-Hungary will also fight in order that those sections of the South-Slavic people ruled by the House of Habsburg may obtain the right to govern themselves democratically within the boundaries of the Austro-Hungarian monarchy proper.

The Social-Democratic parties of Austria-Hungary, as well as the Socialists of Italy, must pay special attention to the Albanian question. The Congress recognises the right of the Albanian people to autonomy but it protests against Albania, under the pretext of autonomy, becoming the victim of Austro-Hungarian and Italian ambitions for domination. The Congress sees in this not only a peril for Albania itself, but, in a short time, a menace to the peace between Austria-Hungary and Italy. Albania can lead a truly independent life only as an autonomous member of a democratic Balkan federation. The Congress therefore calls upon the Social-Democrats of Austria-Hungary and Italy to combat every attempt of their governments to envelop Albania in their sphere of influence and to continue their efforts to strengthen the peaceful relations between Austria-Hungary and Italy.

It is with great joy that the Congress greets the protest strikes of Russian workers as a guarantee that the proletariat of Russia and of Poland is beginning to recover from the blows dealt it by the tsarist counter-revolution. The Congress sees in this the strongest guarantee against the criminal intrigues of tsarism, which, after having drowned in blood the peoples of its own country, after having betrayed the Balkan peoples themselves innumerable times and surrendered them to their enemies, now vacillates between the fear of the consequences that a war would have upon it and the fear of the pressure of a nationalist movement which it has itself created. However, when tsarism now tries to appear as the liberator of the Balkan nations, it is only to reconquer its hegemony in the Balkans in a bloody war under this hypocritical pretext. The Congress expects that the urban and rural proletariat of Russia, Finland and Poland, which is growing in strength, will destroy this web of lies, will oppose every belligerent venture of tsarism, will combat every design of tsarism, whether upon Armenia or upon Constantinople, and will concentrate its whole force upon the renewal of the revolutionary struggle for emancipation from tsarism. For tsarism is the hope of all the reactionary powers of Europe, the most terrible enemy of the democracy of the peoples dominated by it; the achievement of its destruction must be viewed as one of the foremost tasks of the entire International.

However, the most important task within the action of the International devolves upon the working class of Germany, France and England. At this moment, it is the task of the workers of these countries to demand of their governments that they refuse any support either to Austria-Hungary or Russia, that they abstain from any intervention in the Balkan troubles and maintain absolute neutrality. A war between the three great leading civilised peoples on account of the Serbo-Austrian dispute over a port would be criminal insanity. The workers of Germany and France cannot concede that any obligation whatever to intervene in the Balkan conflict exists because of secret treaties.

However, on further development, should the military collapse of Turkey lead to the downfall of the Ottoman rule in Asia Minor, it would be the task of the Socialists of England, France and Germany to resist with all their power the policy of conquest in Asia Minor, which would inevitably lead in a straight line to war. The Congress views as the greatest danger to the peace of Europe the artificially cultivated hostility between Great Britain and the German Empire. The Congress therefore greets the efforts of the working class of both countries to bridge this hostility. It considers the best means for this purpose to be the conclusion of an accord between Germany and England concerning the limitation of naval armaments and the abolition of the right of naval booty. The Congress calls upon the Socialists of England and Germany to continue their agitation for such an accord.

The overcoming of the antagonism between Germany on the one hand, and France and England on the other, would eliminate the greatest danger to the peace of the world, shake the power of tsarism which exploits this antagonism, render an attack of Austria-Hungary upon Serbia impossible, and secure peace to the world. All the efforts of the International, therefore, are to be directed toward this goal.

The Congress records that the entire Socialist International is unanimous upon these principles of foreign policy. It calls upon the workers of all countries to oppose the power of the international solidarity of the proletariat to capitalist imperialism. It warns the ruling classes of all states not to increase by belligerent actions the misery of the masses brought on by the capitalist method of production. It emphatically demands peace. Let the governments remember that with the present condition of Europe and the mood of the working class, they cannot unleash a war without danger to themselves. Let them remember that the Franco-German War was followed by the revolutionary outbreak of the Commune, that the Russo-Japanese War set into motion the revolutionary energies of the peoples of the Russian Empire, that the competition in military and naval armaments gave the class conflicts in England and on the Continent an unheard-of sharpness, and unleashed an enormous wave of strikes. It would be insanity for the governments not to realise that the very idea of the monstrosity of a world war would inevitably call forth the indignation and the revolt of the working class. The proletarians consider it a crime to fire at each other for the profits of the capitalists, the ambitions of dynasties, or the greater glory of secret diplomatic treaties.

If the governments cut off every possibility of normal progress, and thereby drive the proletariat to desperate steps, they themselves will have to bear the entire responsibility for the consequences of the crisis brought about by them.

The International will redouble its efforts in order to prevent this crisis; it will raise its protest with increasing emphasis and make its propaganda more and more energetic and comprehensive. The

Congress therefore commissions the International Socialist Bureau to follow events with much greater attentiveness and, no matter what may happen, to maintain and strengthen the bonds uniting the proletarian parties.

The proletariat is conscious of being at this moment the bearer of the entire future of humankind. The proletariat will exert all its energy to prevent the annihilation of the flower of all peoples, threatened by all the horrors of mass murder, starvation and pestilence.

The Congress therefore appeals to you, proletarians and Socialists of all countries, to make your voices heard in this decisive hour! Proclaim your will in every form and in all places; raise your protest in the parliaments with all your force; unite in great mass demonstrations; use every means that the organisation and the strength of the proletariat place at your disposal! See to it that the governments are constantly kept aware of the vigilance and passionate will for peace on the part of the proletariat! To the capitalist world of exploitation and mass murder, oppose in this way the proletarian world of peace and fraternity of peoples!

Manifesto of the International Socialist Conference at Zimmerwald

21 September 1915

Proletarians of Europe!

The war has lasted more than a year. Millions of corpses cover the battlefields. Millions of human beings have been crippled for the rest of their lives. *Europe is like a gigantic human slaughterhouse.* All civilisation, created by the labour of many generations, is doomed to destruction. The most savage barbarism is today celebrating its triumph over all that hitherto constituted the pride of humanity.

Irrespective of the truth as to the direct responsibility for the outbreak of the war, one thing is certain. *The war which has produced this chaos is the outcome of imperialism,* of the attempt on the part of the capitalist classes of each nation, to foster their greed for profit by the exploitation of human labour and of the natural treasures of the entire globe.

Economically backward or politically weak nations are thereby subjugated by the Great Powers who, in this war, are seeking to remake the world map with blood and iron in accord with their exploiting interests. Thus entire nations and countries, like Belgium, Poland, the Balkan states and Armenia, are threatened with the fate of being torn asunder, annexed as a whole or in part as booty in the game of compensations.

In the course of the war, its driving forces are revealed in all their vileness. Shred after shred falls the veil with which the meaning of this world catastrophe was hidden from the consciousness of the peoples. The capitalists of all countries who are coining the red gold of war-profits out of the blood shed by the people, assert that the war is for defence of the fatherland, for democracy and the liberation of oppressed nations! They lie. *In actual reality, they are burying the freedom of their own people together with the independence of the other nations in the places of devastation.*

New fetters, new chains, new burdens are arising, and it is the proletariat of all countries, of the victorious as well as of the conquered countries, that will have to bear them. Improvement in welfare was proclaimed at the outbreak of the war – want and privation, unemployment and high prices, undernourishment and epidemics are the actual results. *The burdens of war will consume the best energies of the peoples for decades*, endanger the achievements of social reform, and hinder every step forward. Cultural devastation, economic decline, political reaction – these are the blessings of this horrible conflict of nations. Thus the war reveals the naked figure of modern capitalism which has become irreconcilable, not only with the interests of the labouring masses, not only with the requirements of historical development, but also with the elementary conditions of human communal existence.

The ruling powers of capitalist society who held the fate of the nations in their hands, the monarchic as well as the republican governments, the secret diplomacy, the mighty business organisations, the bourgeois parties, the capitalist press, the Church – all these bear the full weight of responsibility for this war which arose out of the social order fostering them and protected by them, and which is being waged for their interests.

Workers!

Exploited, disfranchised, scorned, they called you brothers and comrades at the outbreak of the war when you were to be led to the slaughter, to death. And now that militarism has crippled you, mutilated you, degraded and annihilated you, the rulers demand that you surrender your interests, your aims, your ideals – in a word, *servile subordination to 'civil peace'*. They rob you of the possibility of expressing your views, your feelings, your pains; they prohibit you from raising your demands and defending them. The press gagged, political rights and liberties trod upon – this is the way the *military dictatorship* rules today with an iron hand.

This situation which threatens the entire future of Europe and of humanity cannot and must not be confronted by us any longer without action. The Socialist proletariat has waged a struggle against militarism for decades. With growing concern, its representatives at their national and international congresses occupied themselves with the ever more menacing danger of war growing out of imperialism. At *Stuttgart*, at *Copenhagen*, at *Basel*, the international Socialist congresses have indicated the course which the proletariat must follow.

Since the beginning of the war, Socialist parties and labour organisations of various countries that helped to determine this course have disregarded the obligations following from this. Their representatives have called upon the working class *to give up the class struggle*, the only possible and effective method of proletarian emancipation. They have granted credits to the ruling classes for waging the war; they have placed themselves at the disposal of the governments for the most diverse services; through their press and their messengers, they have tried to win over the neutrals to the government policies of their countries; they have delivered up to their governments *Socialist Ministers* as hostages for the preservation of civil peace, and *thereby they have assumed the responsibility before the working class, before its present and its future, for this war, for its aims and its methods*. And just as the individual parties, so the highest of the appointed representative bodies of the Socialists of all countries, the *International Socialist Bureau*, has failed them.

These facts are equally responsible for the fact that the international working class, which did not succumb to the national panic of the first period of the war, or which freed itself from it, has still, in the second year of the slaughter of peoples, found no ways and means of taking up an energetic struggle for peace simultaneously in all countries.

In this unbearable situation, we, the representatives of the Socialist parties, trade unions and their minorities, we Germans, French, Italians, Russians, Poles, Letts, Romanians, Bulgarians, Swedes, Norwegians, Dutch and Swiss, we who stand, not on the ground of national solidarity with the exploiting class, but on the ground of the international solidarity of the proletariat and of the class struggle, have assembled to retie the torn threads of international relations and to call upon the working class to reorganise itself and to fight for peace.

This struggle is the struggle for freedom, for the *reconciliation* of peoples, for Socialism. It is necessary to take up this struggle for peace, for a peace without annexations or war indemnities. *Such a peace, however, is only possible if every thought of violating the rights and liberties of nations is condemned.* Neither the occupation of entire countries nor of separate parts of countries must lead to their violent annexation. No annexation, whether open or concealed, and no forcible economic attachment made still more unbearable by political disfranchisement. *The right of self-determination of nations must be the indestructible principle in the system of national relationships of peoples.*

Proletarians!

Since the outbreak of the war, you have placed your energy, your courage, your endurance at the service of the ruling classes. Now you must stand up for your own cause, for the sacred aims of Socialism, for the emancipation of the oppressed nations as well as of the enslaved classes, by means of the irreconcilable proletarian class struggle.

It is the task and the duty of the Socialists of the belligerent countries to take up this struggle with full force; it is the task and the duty of the Socialists of the neutral states to support their brothers in this struggle against bloody barbarism with every effective means. Never in world history was there a more urgent, a more sublime task, the fulfilment of which should be our common labour. No sacrifice is too great, no burden too heavy in order to achieve this goal: peace among the peoples.

Working men and working women! Mothers and fathers! Widows and orphans! Wounded and crippled! We call to all of you who are suffering from the war and because of the war: Beyond all borders, beyond the reeking battlefields, beyond the devastated cities and villages:

Proletarians of all countries, unite!

Zimmerwald,
September 1915

* * *

In the name of the International Socialist Conference:

For the German delegation: Georg Ledebour, Adolf Hoffmann
For the French delegation: A Bourderon, A Merrheim
For the Italian delegation: GE Modigliani, Constantino Lazzari
For the Russian delegation: N Lenin, Pavel Axelrod, M Bobrov
For the Polish delegation: St. Lapinski, A Warski, Cz. Hanecki
For the Inter-Balkan Socialist Federation: (for the Romanian delegation)
C Rakovsky; (for the Bulgarian delegation) Wassil Kolarov
For the Swedish and Norwegian delegation: Z Höglund, Ture Nerman
For the Dutch delegation: H Roland-Holst
For the Swiss delegation: Robert Grimm, Charles Naine

Declaration of sympathy for the war victims and the persecuted, adopted by the International Socialist Conference at Zimmerwald

September 1915

The International Socialist Conference at Zimmerwald sends its expression of profoundest sympathy to the countless victims of the war, to the Polish and Belgian people, to the persecuted Jewish and Armenian peoples, to the millions of human beings who are tormented by boundless sufferings and who have had to bear untold horrors.

The Conference honours the memory of the great Socialist Jean Jaurès, the first victim of the war who fell as a martyr and fighter in the struggle against chauvinism and for peace. It honours the memory of the Socialist fighters Tutzowicz and Catanesi, who lost their young lives on the battlefield.

The Conference sends the expression of its profound and fraternal sympathy to the Duma Deputies exiled to Siberia who are continuing the glorious revolutionary tradition of Russia, to Liebknecht and Monatte, fettered by capitalism, both of whom have taken up the struggle against the civil peace policy of the workers in their respective countries, to Comrades Luxemburg and Clara Zetkin who have been imprisoned for their Socialist convictions, and to all comrades, men and women, who have been persecuted or arrested because they have waged a struggle against war.

The Conference solemnly vows to honour the living and dead by following the example of these brave fighters and by indefatigably carrying out the task of awakening the revolutionary spirit in the masses of the international proletariat, and uniting them in the struggle against the fratricidal war and against capitalist society.

Draft Resolution and Manifesto Submitted by the Left Wing Delegates at Zimmerwald

September 1915

Editors note:

The following two documents were submitted by Lenin and Karl Radek on behalf of the Zimmerwald Left. The resolution was intended for educational use among active Socialists, and the manifesto was intended for broader agitation.

The draft resolution was signed by two representatives of the Central Committee of the Russian Social-Democratic Labour Party (Zinoviev and Lenin); a representative of the Opposition of the Polish Social-Democracy (Radek); a representative of the Latvian province (Winter); a representative each of the Left Social-Democrats of Sweden (Höglund) and Norway (Nerman); a Swiss delegate (Platten); and a German delegate. On the question of submitting the draft to the commission, twelve delegates voted for (the eight mentioned above, two Socialist-Revolutionaries, Trotsky, and Roland-Holst) and nineteen against.

* * *

Draft Resolution on the World War and the Tasks of Social-Democracy

The World War, which has been devastating Europe for the last year, is an *imperialist war* waged for the political and economic exploitation of the world, export markets, sources of raw material, spheres of capital investment, etc. It is a product of capitalist development which connects the entire world in a world economy, but at the same time permits the existence of national state capitalist groups with opposing interests.

If the bourgeoisie and the governments seek to conceal this character of the World War by asserting that it is a question of a forced struggle for *national independence,* it is only to mislead the *proletariat,* since the war is being waged for the oppression of foreign peoples and countries. Equally untruthful are the legends concerning the defence of democracy in this war, since imperialism signifies the most unscrupulous domination of big capital and political reaction.

Imperialism can only be overcome by overcoming the contradictions which produce it, that is, by the *socialist organisation of the advanced capitalist countries* for which the objective conditions are already ripe.

At the outbreak of the war, the majority of the labour leaders had not raised this only possible slogan in opposition to imperialism. Prejudiced by nationalism, rotten with opportunism, *at the beginning of the World War they betrayed the proletariat to imperialism and gave up the principles of socialism and thereby the real struggle for the everyday interests of the proletariat.*

Social-patriotism and social-imperialism, the standpoint of the openly patriotic majority of the formerly Social-Democratic leaders in Germany, as well as the opposition-mannered centre of the party around Kautsky, and to which in France and Austria the majority, in England and Russia a part of the leaders (Hyndman, the Fabians, the Trade-Unionists, Plekhanov, Rubanovich, the *Nasha Zarya* group) confess, is a more dangerous enemy to the proletariat than the bourgeois apostles of imperialism, since, misusing the banner of socialism, it can mislead the unenlightened workers. *The ruthless struggle against social-imperialism constitutes the first condition for the revolutionary mobilisation of the proletariat and the reconstruction of the International.*

It is the task of the Socialist parties, as well as of the Socialist opposition in the now social-imperialist parties, to call and lead the labouring masses to the *revolutionary struggle* against the capitalist governments for the conquest of political power for the socialist organisation of society.

Without giving up the struggle for every foot of ground within the framework of capitalism, for every reform strengthening the proletariat, without renouncing any means of organisation and agitation, the revolutionary Social-Democrats, on the contrary, must utilise all the struggles, all the reforms demanded by our minimum programme for the purpose of *sharpening this war crisis* as well as every social and political crisis of capitalism of extending them to an attack upon its very foundations. By waging this struggle *under the slogan of socialism*, it will render the labouring masses immune to the slogans of the oppression of one people by another as expressed in the maintenance of the domination of one nation over another, in the cry for new annexations; it will render them deaf to the temptations of national solidarity which has led the proletarians to the battlefields.

The signal for this struggle is the *struggle against the World War, for the speedy termination of the slaughter of nations.* This struggle demands the *refusal of war credits, quitting the cabinets*, the denunciation of the capitalist, anti-socialist character of the war from the tribunes of the parliaments, in the columns of the legal, and where necessary illegal, press, the sharpest struggle against social-patriotism, and *the utilisation of every movement of the people caused by the results of the war (misery, great losses etc.) for the organisation of street demonstrations against the governments*, propaganda of *international solidarity in the trenches*, the encouragement of *economic strikes*, the effort to transform them into *political* strikes under favourable conditions. "Civil *war*, not '*civil peace*'" – that is the slogan!*

As against all illusions that it is possible to bring about the *basis of a lasting peace*, the *beginning of disarmament*, by any decisions of diplomats and the governments, the revolutionary Social-Democrats must repeatedly tell the masses of the people that only the *social revolution* can bring about a lasting peace and the emancipation of humanity.

* * *

Draft Manifesto
Proletarians of Europe!

The war has now lasted for more than a year. The battlefields are strewn with millions of dead, millions have been crippled and doomed to remain a burden to themselves and to others for the rest of their lives. The war has caused terrific devastations, it will result in an unheard-of increase in taxes.

The *capitalists of all countries*, who at the price of proletarian blood, have been reaping enormous profits during the war, demand of the masses that they strain all their efforts and *hold out to the end*. They say: "The war is necessary for the *defence of the fatherland*, it is waged in the interests of *democracy*." *They lie!* In not a single country did the capitalists start the war because the independence of their country was threatened, or because they wanted to free an oppressed people. They have led the masses to slaughter because they want to oppress and to exploit other peoples. They were unable to agree between themselves as to how to divide the peoples of Asia and Africa that were still independent; they were lying in ambush for each other, watching for a chance to snatch from each other the spoils previously seized. It is not for their own freedom, nor for the freedom of other peoples, that the masses are bleeding in all parts

---

*   These words are taken from the letter to the Zimmerwald Conference of an
      outstanding leader of the German opposition. – *Footnote in original*
      The individual being referred to was Karl Liebknecht.

of the immense slaughterhouse called Europe. This war will bring the proletariat of Europe and the peoples of Asia and Africa new burdens and new chains.

There is, therefore, no reason why this fratricidal war should be waged to the end, to the last drop of blood; on the contrary, every effort must be strained to put an end to it.

The time for this has already come. What you must demand first is that your *Socialist Deputies*, those whom you delegated to parliament to fight against capitalism, against militarism, against the exploitation of the people, do their duty. All of them, with the exception of the Russian, Serbian and Italian comrades, and with the exception of Comrades Liebknecht and Rühle, have trampled upon that duty; they have either supported the bourgeoisie in their rapacious war, or else have vacillated and have shirked responsibility. You must demand that they either resign from their seats or that they use the platform of parliament to make clear to the people the nature of the present war, and that outside of parliament they help the working class to resume its struggle. Your first demand must be this: *refusal of all war credits, withdrawal from the cabinets in France, Belgium, and England.*

But that is not all! The Deputies cannot save you from that rabid beast, the World War, that subsists on your blood. *You must act yourselves.* You must make use of all your organisations, of your entire press, to rouse the broadest masses groaning under the burden of the war to revolt against it. You must go out *into the streets* and throw into the face of the ruling classes your rallying cry: '*Enough of slaughters!*' Let the ruling classes remain deaf to it, the discontented masses will hear it and they will join you and take a part in the struggle.

The demand must immediately and energetically be made that the war be stopped, a *loud protest* must be raised against the exploitation of one people by another, against the division of any people among several states. All this will take place if any capitalist government comes out victorious and is able to dictate the terms of peace to the others. If we allow the capitalists to conclude peace in the same manner as they started the war, without the participation of the masses, the *new conquests* will not only strengthen *reaction* and arbitrary police rule in the victorious country, but they will *sow the seeds of new wars even more horrible.*

The overthrow of the capitalist governments – this is the object which the working class in all belligerent countries must set themselves, because only then will an end be put to the exploitation of one people by another, an end put to wars, when capital has been deprived of the power of disposing of the life and death of peoples. Only peoples who shall be freed of want and misery, of the rule of capital, will be in a position to settle their mutual relations, not by war, but by friendly agreement.

Great is the goal we set ourselves, great are the efforts that will be required to attain it, great will be the sacrifices before it is attained. Long will be the road to victory. Methods of peaceful pressure will be insufficient to overcome the enemy. But it is only when you are ready to make for your own liberation, in the struggle against capital, part of those innumerable sacrifices that you have been making on the battlefield for the interests of capital, only then will you be able to put an end to the war, to lay a firm foundation for a lasting peace, which will transform you from slaves of capital into free people.

But if the deceitful phrases of the bourgeoisie and of the Socialist parties that support it succeed in restraining you from energetic struggle, and if you confine yourselves to pious wishes because you are unwilling to proceed to an attack and to sacrifice your bodies and souls for the great cause, then capital will go on shedding your blood and wasting your belongings at its own discretion.

In all countries, the number of those who think as we do grows daily. It is by their order that we have assembled representatives of various countries to address to you this call to battle. We shall carry on this struggle with mutual support as there are no interests to divide us. It is essential that the revolutionary workers of each country deem it their duty and honourable distinction to serve as a model for others, a model of energy and self-sacrifice. Not timid expectation as to whither the struggle of others will lead, but struggle in the first ranks – that is the road that leads to the formation of a powerful International which will put an end to war and capitalism.

* * *

The draft resolution and manifesto is signed by the delegations of the Central Committee of the Social Democratic Labour Party of Russia; the Regional Committee of the Social Democracy of Russian Poland and Lithuania; the Central Committee of the Social Democracy of Latvia; the Swedish and Norwegian Social Democratic Youth League; a representative of the revolutionary Social Democrats of Germany; and a Swiss delegate.

Two Declarations of the Zimmerwald Left

September 1915

1

The undersigned declare as follows:

The manifesto adopted by the Conference does not give us complete satisfaction. It contains no pronouncement on either open opportunism or opportunism that is hiding under radical phraseology – the opportunism which is not only the chief cause of the collapse of the International, but which strives to perpetuate that collapse. The manifesto contains no clear pronouncement as to the methods of fighting against the war.

We shall continue, as we have done heretofore, to advocate in the Socialist press and at the meetings of the International, a clear-cut Marxist position in regard to the tasks with which the epoch of imperialism has confronted the proletariat.

We vote for the manifesto because we regard it as a call to struggle and in this struggle we are anxious to march side by side with the other sections of the International.

We request that our present declaration be included in the official proceedings.

N Lenin, G Zinoviev, Radek, Nerman, Höglund, Winter

2

The other declaration, which was signed, in addition to the group that had introduced the resolution of the Left, by Roland-Holst and Trotsky, read as follows:

Inasmuch as the adoption of our amendment (to the manifesto) demanding the vote against war appropriations might in a way endanger the success of the Conference, we do, under protest, withdraw our amendment and accept Ledebour's statement in the commission to the effect that the manifesto contains all that is implied in our proposition.

It may be added that Ledebour, as an ultimatum, demanded the rejection of the amendment, refusing to sign the manifesto otherwise.

Kienthal Manifesto

April 1916

Editors note:

The Kienthal Manifesto was drafted by a committee of Giuseppe Modigliani, Ernst Meyer and Karl Radek, representing respectively the conference's Right, Center and Left currents. It was adopted on 30 April 1916.

* * *

Proletarians of all countries, unite!

Two years of world war! Two years of devastation! Two years of victims' blood and reaction's fury!

Who is to blame? Who stands behind those who threw the burning torch into the keg of gunpowder? Who had long desired this war and prepared for it?

The ruling classes!

In September 1915, we met as socialists from warring and neutral countries alike in Zimmerwald, joining hands across the bloody chaos. Amid the horrors unleashed by war, we united to declare in our manifesto:

> The ruling powers of capitalist society who held the fate of the nations in their hands, the monarchic as well as the republican governments,

the secret diplomacy, the mighty business organisations, the bourgeois parties, the capitalist press, the Church – all these bear the full weight of responsibility for this war which arose out of the social order fostering them and protected by them, and which is being waged for their interests.

As Jaurès said a few days before his death: "Every nation rushed through the streets of Europe brandishing burning torches."

* * *

Millions of men have fallen into their graves. Millions of families are obliged to mourn. Millions of women and children have been turned into widows and orphans. Ruins have been piled on top of ruins, while irreplaceable cultural monuments have been destroyed. And after all this, the war has reached a dead end.

Despite the untold masses of victims on all battlefronts, nothing decisive has been achieved. The governments sacrifice millions upon millions of soldiers merely to shift the battle lines ever so slightly.

Neither victors nor vanquished! Or rather, all sides are defeated – all are bled white, all are ruined, all are exhausted: that will be the outcome of this gruesome war. All this to show the ruling classes that their fantasies of imperialist world domination have not been achieved.

Once again it has been made clear that the only socialists to have served the interests of their peoples are those who, despite persecution and slander, have stood firm against nationalist hysteria and demanded an immediate peace without annexations.

So join with us in crying out across the battlefields: Down with the war! Long live peace!

Workers of city and countryside:

The governments and imperialist cliques, together with their press, tell you to hold out to the end, in order to liberate oppressed nations. This is the crudest method of deception of all those that have been utilised in this war. The true goal of this generalised slaughter is, for some, to secure lands that they have assembled and conquered through centuries of war. Others want to divide the world anew in order to expand their holdings. They aim to annex additional lands, to cut apart and tear apart entire peoples, in order to reduce them to the status of common serfs and chattels.

Your governments and your press tell you that the war must be continued in order to destroy militarism.

Do not be deceived! Militarism in a nation can only be eliminated by this nation itself, and the task of bringing it down is posed in every country.

Your governments and your press also tell you that the war must be continued so that it can be the last war. This too is a deception. Never has a war put an end to war. On the contrary, each war awakens the lust for revenge. Violence begets violence.

Thus after each sacrifice, your tormentors will demand new ones. Nor do the bourgeois pacifist zealots offer an escape from this vicious circle.

There is only one way to prevent future wars, namely for the working classes to conquer political power and abolish capitalist property.

Enduring peace can only be achieved by victorious socialism.

Proletarians! Who are those who urge you to 'hold out to the end' until 'victory'?

They are the ones who were truly responsible for causing the war. Among them: the venal press, the war contractors, the war profiteers, and also the social patriots who ape the bourgeois war slogans. Among them are the reactionaries, who are secretly pleased by the death on the battlefields of those who only yesterday were threatening the rulers' privileges – socialists, trade unionists, and all those who sowed the seeds of socialism in town and countryside.

That is the party of the politicians who insist that we hold out!

They control state power; they rule over the mendacious press that poisons the people; they enjoy freedom to agitate for continuing the war and increasing death and devastation.

And you are the victims. You have only the right to go hungry, to be silent, to suffer the chains of the state of siege, the censorship, and the musty air of the dungeon.

* * *

You, the people, the working masses, are made victims of a war that is not your own.

You, the workers from city and countryside, stand in the trenches, in the front lines, while behind the lines you see many of the rich and their accomplices – shirkers living in safety. For them war means the death of others.

And even as they wage their class struggle against you even more fiercely than before, they preach to you of 'civil peace'. Mercilessly they draw profit from your poverty, your suffering, while inciting you to betray your class and drive from your heart your greatest strength – your hopes in socialism.

Social injustice and class rule are even more apparent in war than in peacetime.

In peace, the capitalist system robs workers of the joys of life; in war it robs them of everything, including life itself.

* * *

And let us be done with devastation. It is you, working people, who will bear the burden of these heaps of ruins today and in the future.

The hundreds of billions in cash thrown into the maw of the god of war are unavailable for maintaining the people's well-being, for cultural purposes, and for social reform that could ease your lot, promote popular education and alleviate poverty.

And tomorrow new and heavy taxes will be laid on your stooped shoulders.

So let us end the squandering of your labour, your money, and your life's energy. Rise up in struggle for an immediate peace with no annexations!

* * *

In every warring country, working women and men are turning against the war and its consequences, against poverty and want, against joblessness and inflation. Let them raise their voices for restoration of the civil rights taken from them, for social legislation presenting the demands of the working classes in city and countryside.

Let proletarians of the neutral countries stand by socialists in the warring countries in their difficult struggle and resist with all their strength any further expansion of the war.

Let socialists of every country act on the decisions of international congresses, which made it the duty of the working class to make every effort to bring the war to a rapid conclusion.

Put all the pressure that you can on your deputies, parliaments and governments.

Demand that parliamentary representatives of parliamentary parties immediately reject any form of support for the governments' war policies. Demand that from now on they vote against all budgetary credits for the war.

Use every means possible to bring a rapid end to the human slaughter!

Take up the slogan: For an immediate armistice! Peoples suffering ruin and murder, rise up in struggle!

Take courage! Bear in mind that you are the majority and, when you so desire, you can assume power.

Let the governments know that hate against the war is growing in every country and, with it, the desire for social retribution. This is bringing closer the hour of peace among the peoples.

Down with the war!

Long live peace, immediate peace, without annexations!

Long live international socialism!

The Second International Socialist
Zimmerwald Conference

Timeline

1907

18-24 August   Stuttgart Congress of the Second International; Lenin and Luxemburg amendment on the attitude towards war passed

1910

28 August –
3 September   Copenhagen Conference of the Second International; resolution on the International's position on war and struggle, firming up the proposals made by Lenin and Rosa Luxemburg at the congress in Stuttgart

1912

October   Outbreak of the First Balkan War

24-25 November   Basel Congress of the Second International; reinforced the International's firm stance of "war on war" which had been declared in Stuttgart and Copenhagen, and a call to socialists to "exert every effort in order to prevent the outbreak of war" and to use the conditions created by the war to "hasten the downfall of capitalist class rule"

1913

June Outbreak of the Second Balkan War

1914

28 July First World War begins

4 August German SPD votes for war credits triggering the collapse of the Second International

5 September Lenin is forced to leave Austria-Hungary for neutral Switzerland

1915

5-8 September Zimmerwald Conference of anti-war Socialists

1916

24-30 April Kienthal Conference of anti-war Socialists (Second Zimmerwald Conference)

1917

8-12 March February Revolution in Russia; the tsar is forced to abdicate; Soviets are organised; Provisional Government formed

16 April Lenin returns to Russia and presents the *April Theses*

10-13 September Kornilov's attempted coup against the Provisional Government is defeated

7 November October Revolution in Russia; the Soviets take power; Lenin drafts Decree on Peace

Glossary

Names

Adler, Victor (1852-1918) – Austrian politician, a leader of the labour movement and founder of the Social Democratic Workers' Party (SDAP).

Aladin, Aleksei (1873-1927) – Founder and leader of the Trudoviks, a breakaway of the Socialist-Revolutionary Party. He was elected to the First Duma in 1906.

Alekseyev, Mikhail Vasilyevich (1857-1918) – Imperial Russian Army general during the First World War and the Russian Civil War.

Alexinsky, Grigory Alexeyevich (1879-1967) – Early member of the Bolsheviks in Moscow. He was a Social-Democratic member of the Second Duma of 1907. He became an 'Otzovist' after the 1905 Revolution and social-chauvinist in the war. During the revolution Alexinsky joined Plekhanov's Yedinstvo Group. After July, he became a counter-revolutionary and an author of forgeries against Lenin in his role as a German agent.

Axelrod, Pavel Borisovich (1850-1928) – A leading Menshevik.

Badayev, Alexei (1883-1951) – One of the five Bolshevik deputies in the Duma exiled to Siberia.

Bakunin, Mikhail (1814-76) – Russian anarchist and the leader of the split from the forces of Marxism in First International.

Bauer, Otto (1881-1938) – Leader of the so-called 'Austro-Marxists', he played a leading role in the Social Democratic Party of Austria.

Bebel, August (1840-1913) – Leading figure of the social democratic movement in Germany. He served as chairman of the Social Democratic Party of Germany from 1892 until his death.

Bernstein, Eduard (1850-1932) – German Social-Democrat who tried to revise Marx's revolutionary theory on the lines of bourgeois liberalism. Bernsteinism, the opportunist trend in German and International Social-Democracy, hostile to Marxism, derives its name from his ideas. Among his supporters in Russia were the legal Marxists, the Economists, the Bund, and the Mensheviks.

Bismarck, Otto Eduard Leopold von (1815-1898) – Chancellor of the German Empire from its foundation in 1871 until 1890.

Bissolati, Leonida (1857-1920) – Italian socialist and member of parliament. He took a social-chauvinist position to the war.

Blanc, Alexandre (1874-1924) – French socialist and pacifist who attended the Kienthal Conference.

Bonomi, Ivanoe (1873-1951) – Italian socialist who held reformist views, and was a social-chauvinist in the war.

Borgbjerg, Frederik (1866-1936) – Danish social-democrat.

Bourderon, Albert (1858-1930) – French syndicalist who adopted a pacifist position in the war.

Branting, Hjalmar (1860 - 1925) – Reformist leader of the Swedish Social Democratic Party.

Briand, Aristide (1862-1932) – French Prime Minister from 1909-11 and in 1913, and also Minister of Justice during the war.

Brizon, Pierre (1878-1923) – French Socialist deputy, initially accepting the 'social truce', then taking a pacifist position. He attended the Kienthal Conference, where he opposed the proposal to form the Third International.

Brouckère, Louis de (1870-1951) – Belgian socialist and academic who joined the army during the First World War as a social patriot.

Burtsev, Vladimir Lyovich (1862-1942) – Active in the revolutionary student movement from the early 1880s, Burtsev was arrested and exiled to Siberia in 1885. He escaped in 1888 and went into exile, publishing anti-tsarist magazines, growing close to the SRs during the 1905 Revolution. After the outbreak of the war, Burtsev began his tirades against the Bolsheviks, accusing Lenin of being a German agent. Arrested by Trotsky, Burtsev was released and left Soviet Russia in 1918, where he became a leader of White counter-revolutionaries in exile.

Chelnokov, Mikhail (1863-1936) – One of the leading figures in the Cadets.

Chernov, Victor (1873-1952) – Socialist-Revolutionary who became a minister in Kerensky's Provisional Government.

Chernyshevsky, Nikolay (1828-1889) – Russian author and the leading theoretician of the Narodniks.

Chkheidze, Nikolai Semyonovich (1864-1926) – Georgian Menshevik who was a member of the Third and Fourth Dumas. He was the first Chairman of the Petrograd Soviet in 1917. He became Chairman of the Central Committee of All-Russian Soviets, as well as Chairman of the Constituent Assembly of Georgia in 1918.

Chkhenkeli, Akaki (1874-1959) – Leading Menshevik from Georgia who was elected to the Fourth Duma.

David, Eduard (1863-1930) – Reichstag member for the SPD after 1903, leading the social-chauvinist majority.

Debs, Eugene Victor (1855-1926) – American socialist, political activist, trade unionist and one of the founding members of the Industrial Workers of the World.

Dobrolyubov, Nikolay (1836-1861) – Radical Russian literary critic and poet.

Gorky, Maxim (1868-1936) – Russian novelist, Bolshevik supporter and financial backer during the struggle against tsarism.

Grimm, Robert (1881-1958) – Leader of the Swiss Social-Democratic Party. In 1909-18 he was secretary of the party and editor-in-chief of the newspaper *Berner Tagwacht*. He was elected as a Member of Parliament from 1911. Grimm was in attendance at the Zimmerwald and Kienthal conferences. He was Chairman of the International Socialist Commission.

Guchkov, Alexander Ivanovich (1862-1936) – Moscow landowner and industrialist. He was the founder and leader of the 'Octobrists', a tendency formed in 1905. Guchkov was President of the Third Duma, and then Minister of War and Navy in the Provisional Government from March – May 1917. He resigned on 31 May 1917.

Guesde, Jules (1845-1922) – French socialist who was included in the national unity government of René Viviani during the war as a Minister without Portfolio until 1916.

Haase, Hugo (1863-1919) – SPD member of the Reichstag in 1897 and co-chair of the SPD from 1911-16. Haase opposed voting for the war credits in 1914, but voted for them to observe the discipline of the parliamentary group in the SPD. He later voted against the war credits in 1916. Haase was later the co-chair of the Independent Social-Democratic Party (USPD) in 1917.

Henderson, Arthur (1863-1935) – Right-wing Labour MP and a member of the National Executive of the party until his death. In 1914 he supported Britain's part in the war and army recruitment. He was later a Minister in Lloyd George's wartime cabinet.

Hervé, Gustav (1871-1944) – French socialist, initially taking a pacifist position before becoming an ultra-nationalist.

Hindenburg, Paul von (1847-1934) – German field marshal who led the Imperial German Army during the First World War.

Hoffmann, Carl (1869-1927) – German military strategist. At the end of 1917, he negotiated with Russia to sign the Treaty of Brest-Litovsk.

Höglund, Zeth (1884-1956) – Leading Swedish socialist, and a leading member of the Zimmerwald Left.

Huysmans, Jean Joseph Camille (1871-1968) – Belgian socialist.

Hyndman, Henry (1842-1921) – Leading member of the British Socialist Party.

Jaurès, Jean (1859-1914) – French socialist and pacifist who represented the reformist wing of the French section of the Second International, the SFIO. He took an anti-war position, which lead to his assassination in July 1914.

Joffre, Joseph (1852-1931) – Commander-in-Chief of French forces on the Western Front from until the end of 1916.

Zhordania, Noe (1868-1953) – Menshevik, who took a social-chauvinist position in the war.

Jouhaux, Léon (1879-1954) – Leader of the French General Confederation of Labour.

Junius – Pseudonym used by Rosa Luxemburg for her 1915 pamphlet 'The Crisis of German Social Democracy', known as the *Junius Pamphlet*.

Kaledin, Alexel Maximovich (1861-1918) – Tsarist General.

Kautsky, Karl (1854-1938) – One of the leading theoreticians of the Social Democratic Party of Germany and the Second International. By the outbreak of the First World War, he had abandoned revolutionary Marxism and took up an indecisive position between revolutionary opposition to the war and patriotic support for the German bourgeoisie. As such, he became the theoretician of this 'centrism' in the socialist movement, and a bitter opponent of the Russian Revolution.

Kerensky, Alexander Fyodorovich (1881-1970) – Lawyer and a member of the Social-Revolutionary party. He was elected as a deputy to the Fourth Duma in 1912. After the February Revolution of 1917 which overthrew the Tsar, he became the outstanding representative of petty-bourgeois conciliationism: first as Minister of Justice, then as War Minister. Kerensky headed the Provisional Government from July to October 1917, at which point he fled the country.

Khvostov, Alexei (1872-1918) – Leader of the Russian Assembly and member of the Black Hundreds.

Kievsky – Pseudonym of Georgy Pyatakov.

Kitchener, Herbert (1850-1916) – British Army Field Marshal.

Kluck, Alexander von (1846-1934) – German general during the First World War.

Kolb, Wilhelm (1870-1918) – SPD Reichstag member and opportunist.

Kol, Henri van (1852-1925) – Dutch politician, engineer, and part owner of a coffee plantation in the East Indies. Having been introduced to Marxism at university, he sought out socialist ideas which were pro-colonialism. He fought for the Communards during the Paris Commune, before joining the First International in 1876. He later co-founded the Dutch

Social Democratic Workers Party, before being elected to parliament.

Konovalov, Aleksandr (1875-1949) – Cadet and one of Russia's biggest textile manufacturers.

Kornilov, Lavr Georgevich (1870-1918) – Siberian Cossack and Commander on the South Western Front in 1917. He replaced Brussilov as Commander-in-Chief under the Provisional Government in July 1917. Kornilov was arrested on 14 September after an attempted counter-revolutionary uprising on 7-12 September which was repelled by the workers, headed by the Bolsheviks. He later escaped and led the White Volunteer Army.

Krichevsky, Boris (1866-1919) – Russian socialist, editor of *Rabocheye Dyelo*.

Kropotkin, Pyotr (1842-1921) – Leading Russian anarchist, who sided with England and France in the war.

Larin, Yuri Aleksandrovich (1882 – 1932) – Born in Simferopol as Mikhail Aleksandrovich Lurie. Joined the RSDLP in 1900. He was arrested in 1903 for his revolutionary activity and sentenced to exile in the Russian Far East, before escaping in 1904. Larin wrote 'A Broad Labour Party and a Labour Congress' in 1906, which Lenin replied to in depth. He joined the Bolsheviks in 1917.

Ledebour, Georg (1850-1947) – Reichstag deputy for the SPD, having been on the left before the war. After its outbreak he took up a centrist position. Lebedour was hostile to the Bolsheviks and the Spartacists.

Legien, Carl (1861-1920) – SPD Reichstag member 1893-98 and 1903-20. Leader of the right wing of the SPD and a virulent social-chauvinist.

Lensch, Paul (1873-1926) – SPD Reichstag member elected in 1912. He took social-chauvinist positions which he dubbed "war socialism".

Liebknecht, Karl (1871-1919) – Founder of the German Communist Party (KPD). In 1914, together with Luxemburg, Mehring and Zetkin, he publicly opposed the Social Democratic Party's support for the war. He co-organised the Spartacus League from 1915 and was expelled from the SPD parliamentary group the following year. Liebknecht was imprisoned for anti-war agitation. On the day of his trial, 50,000 munitions workers downed tools, as demonstrations and strikes spread across the country. He was murdered during the Spartacist Uprising in January 1919

Liebknecht, Wilhelm (1826-1900) – One of the principal founders of the German SPD and the father of Karl Liebknecht.

Litvinov, Maxim (1876-1951) – Founding member of the Bolshevik faction at the Second Congress of the RSDLP.

Lloyd George, David (1863-1945) – Welsh Member of Parliament for the Liberal Party from 1890-1945. He was Chancellor of the Exchequer from 1908-1915, Minister of Munitions from 1915-1916, Secretary of State for War in 1916 and Prime Minister from 1916-1922. Lloyd-George was a co-author of the Treaty of Versailles and an active anti-Soviet interventionist.

Lunacharsky, Anatolii Vasilevich (1875-1933) – Joined the Social Democratic movement in 1890s, becoming a Bolshevik after the split with the Mensheviks. Lunacharsky carried out journalistic work in the Party press. He split with Lenin in 1908, but after the February Revolution returned to Russia and rejoined the Bolsheviks as a member of the Mezhraiontsy (Inter-District Organisation).

Luxemburg, Rosa (1871-1919) – Joined the SPD in Germany in 1898 and was on the bureau of the Second International from 1903. Luxemburg was the leader of the Left wing against the revisionist Right and, after 1910, against the Kautskyist group. She was a leading revolutionary opponent of the war and a founder of Spartacus group. In prison for most of the war, she was murdered during the Spartacist Uprising in January 1919.

Lvov, Prince Georgy Yevgenyevich (1861-1925) – Cadet and first Prime Minister of the Russian Republic from March to July 1917.

MacDonald, James Ramsay (1886-1938) – Scottish Labour politician and member of ILP who adopted a pacifist position during the First World War.

Mackensen, Anton August (1899-1945) – German field marshal during the war.

Maclean, John (1879-1923) – Scottish schoolteacher and revolutionary socialist. He was arrested for his opposition to the First World War. In 1918, he was arrested for sedition. Maclean formed the Scottish Workers Republican Party.

Maklakov, Vasily Alekseyevich (1869-1970) – Moscow landowner, leading lawyer and right-wing Cadet. He was a member of the Second, Third and Fourth Dumas.

Martov, Yuri Osipovich (Julius) (1873-1913) – The ideological leader of the Mensheviks and a close friend of Lenin.

Martynov, Alexandr (1865-1935) – Leading Menshevik.

Maslov, Petr (1867-1946) – Menshevik liquidationist and a social-chauvinist in the war.

Merrheim, Alphonse (1871-1923) – French syndicalist who took a left-wing position in the war; Zimmerwald delegate.

Meyer, Ernst (1887-1930) – SPD member who took a left-wing position in the war, delegate to the Zimmerwald and Kienthal conferences.

Millerand, Alexandre (1859-1943) – French socialist who joined the bourgeois government of Waldeck-Rousseau. Lends his name to the opportunist tactic Millerandism (or 'ministerial socialism', or else Ministerialism), referring to socialists' participation in reactionary bourgeois governments.

Milyukov, Pavel Nikolayevich (1859-1943) – Leader of the Cadet Party, ideologue of the imperialist bourgeoisie and deputy to the Third and Fourth Dumas. In 1917, he became Foreign Minister in the first cabinet of the bourgeois Provisional Government.

Monatte, Pierre (1881-1960) – Entered politics as an anarchist, founding the revolutionary syndicalist publication *La Vie Ouvrière*, and editing *l'Humanité*. He was the French delegate to the Zimmerwald Conference.

Morgari, Oddino (1865-1944) – Italian socialist, involved in the preparations for the Zimmerwald Conference.

Muranov, Matvei (1873-1959) – One of the five Bolshevik deputies in the Duma to be exiled to Siberia.

Mussolini, Benito (1883-1945) – Mussolini was initially a prominent socialist, and an editor of the Italian Socialist Party's (PSI) Central Organ, *Avanti!*. He began to express an increasingly confused position after 1912, and took a social-chauvinist position soon after the start of the war. For this, he was expelled by the PSI. He began his own paper, campaigning for the war and 'revolutionary nationalism'. He went on to enlist in the army, before being wounded in action, returning to Italy and founding the Fascist movement in 1919.

Tsar Nicholas II, Nikolai Romanov (1868-1918) – Last Emperor of Russia, King of Poland and Grand Duke of Finland, ruling from 1 November 1894 until his abdication on 15 March 1917.

Pannekoek, Anton (1873-1960) – Dutch Socialist and astronomer. Formed a Marxist party in the Netherlands. He was active in the German Social Democratic Party while living in Germany 1906-14 where he contributed to *Die Neue Zeit*. In 1914 he took a firm internationalist position and was an early advocate of the need for a new International. After the founding of the Communist International he became an ultra-left advocate of 'council communism'.

Petrovsky, Grigory (1878-1958) – One of the five Bolshevik deputies in the Duma exiled to Siberia.

Plekhanov, George Valentinovich (1856-1918) – The founder of Russian Marxism. He was an émigré from 1883 until the February Revolution in Russia. During this time he edited *Iskra* and *Zarya*. He broke with the Bolsheviks, becoming an opponent of the October Revolution.

Potresov, Alexander Nikolayevich (Starover) (1869-1934) – Aligned with the Marxists in the 1890s, Potresov took part in founding *Iskra* and *Zarya*. After the Second Congress of the RSDLP he became a leader of the Mensheviks.

Pressemane, Adrien (1879-1929) – Member of the French Workers' Party; pacifist and centrist in the war.

Purishkevich, Vladimir (1870-1920) – Extreme reactionary and Russian monarchist Duma member who organised the Black Hundreds in the 1905 Revolution. He took part in the assassination of Rasputin in 1916.

Radek, Karl (1885-1939) – Joined the revolutionary movement in Austrian Poland before 1905, where he became a leader of the left wing of the Polish and German workers' movements. Radek was an internationalist during the war, a collaborator of Lenin and a supporter of the Zimmerwald Left. He joined the Bolsheviks in 1917 and was elected a member of the Bolshevik Central Committee from 1917-24.

Raffin-Dugens, Jean (1861-1946) – French socialist who took a pacifist position in the war.

Rakovsky, Christian Georgievich (1873-1941) – Prominent in the social-democratic movement in Bulgaria, Switzerland, Germany,

France and Romania from 1885. He was one of the Zimmerwald Left and took an internationalist stand in the First World War, for which he was imprisoned.

Renaudel, Pierre (1871-1935) – Leading French right-wing social-democrat; editor of *l'Humanité*.

Renner, Karl (1870-1950) – Austrian social-democrat.

Riazanov, David (1870-1938) – Russian socialist who shared the internationalist views of the Bolsheviks on the question of the war but disagreed with them on organisational matters, seeking unity with revolutionary elements in the Menshevik camp.

Ribot, Alexandre (1842-1923) – Minister of Finance in the French wartime government.

Rodzyanko, Mikhail Vladimirovich (1859-1924) – Russian reactionary politician. He was a major landowner and one of the leaders of the Octobrist party. Rodzyanko served as the chairman for the Third and Fourth Dumas. In 1917, he supported the Kornilov coup.

Roland-Holst, Henriette (1869-1952) – Dutch poet and writer who joined the Dutch socialist movement in 1897. She belonged to the left wing of the Social Democratic Workers Party (SDAP). She then joined left-wing SDP in 1916 and was a member of the Zimmerwald Left during the war.

Rubanovich, Ilya (1859-1920) – Russian Socialist-Revolutionary and social-chauvinist.

Rühle, Otto (1874-1943) – SPD member in the Reichstag who took an internationalist position in the war, and a member of the *Internationale* group.

Samoilov, Fedor Nikitich (1882-1952) – One of the five Bolshevik deputies in the Duma exiled to Siberia.

Savinkov, Boris Viktorovich (1879-1925) – A leader of the Russian Socialist-Revolutionary Party. A minister in the Provisional Government he led armed actions against the Soviet government during the civil war.

Scheidemann, Philipp (1865-1939) – SPD Minister of the Weimar Republic, who alongside Ebert and Noske led the charge in destroying the gains of the November Revolution. He joined the SPD in 1883, was a member of the SPD executive from 1911 and a social chauvinist during the war.

Savinkov, Boris (1879-1925) – French social-democrat and minister in the wartime governments.

Semkovsky, Semen (1882-1937) – Ukrainian Menshevik.

Shagov, Nikolay R (1882-1918) – One of the five Bolshevik deputies in the Duma exiled to Siberia.

Skobelev, Matvey Ivanovich (1885-1937) – Social-democrat from 1903, siding with the Mensheviks. Elected to the Fourth Duma in 1912. Minister of Labour in the Provisional Government from May to September 1917. In June 1917 he was elected deputy chairman of the All-Russian Soviet Executive Committee.

Sonnino, Sidney Constantino (1847-1922) – Italian minister of Foreign Affairs during the war.

Souvarine, Boris (1895-1984) – Joined the French Section of the Workers' International (SFIO) in 1916. A founding member of the French Communist Party.

Spiridonova, Maria Alexandrovna (1884-1941) – Joined the SRs in 1906. She was arrested after assassinating a security official. Freed from prison in 1917 after the February Revolution, she joined the Left SRs after October and sided with Lenin and the Bolsheviks.

Steklov, Yuri Mikhailovich (1873- 1941) – Joined the RSDLP in 1893. He sided with the Bolsheviks after the Second Congress of the RSDLP (1903). Wrote for *Sotsial-Demokrat*, *Zvezda* and *Pravda* from 1907-14. Editor of *Izvestia* after the October Revolution.

Stolypin, Pyotr Arkadyevich (1862-1911) – One of the largest feudal landowners and Russian Minister of the Interior, later Prime Minister in the period of counter-revolutionary terror after the 1905 Revolution. He initiated agrarian reforms of private land ownership to the rich peasants. Stolypin was assassinated in 1911.

Ströbel, Heinrich (1869-1944) – SPD member; Editor-in-chief of *Vorwärts* during the war, and member of the *Internationale* group.

Struve, Peter Berngardovich (1870-1944) – Russian political economist, philosopher, historian and editor. He started his career as a Marxist, later became a liberal and after the Bolshevik Revolution joined the White movement.

Südekum, Albert (1871-1944) – SPD Reichstag member and social-chauvinist.

Tereshchenko, Mykhailo Ivanovych (1886-1956) – Cadet who was a major Ukrainian landowner, proprietor of several sugar factories, and financier. Minister of Foreign Affairs in the reconstructed Provisional Government following Milyukov's resignation.

Thalheimer, August (1884-1948) – SPD member and Chief Editor in Göppingen in 1909. He was a member of the *Internationale* group and was active in the Spartacus League during the war. Thalheimer was conscripted during 1916-18, and played an important role in the 1918 November Revolution in Stuttgart.

Thiers, Adolphe (1797-1877) – French politician, journalist, and revisionist historian. First president of the Third Republic (1871-73). Thiers was noted for his brutality in crushing all popular rebellions against the monarchy, particularly at Duchesse de Berry in 1832 and of the Republicans in 1834. He later assisted Louis Napoleon Bonaparte in 1848 to attain the throne, and became a deputy under his government in the Second Empire. In May 1871, Thiers sent French soldiers, with the support of the Germans, into Paris to brutally destroy the Paris Commune.

Thomas, Albert (1878-1932) – Joined the French Socialist Party in 1902 and became leader of its right wing. A deputy in parliament from 1910, he supported the French war effort and became the Minister for Munitions from 1916-17.

Tolstoy, Leo (1828-1910) – Russian author who developed a religious doctrine based on Christian anarchism and pacifism.

Treves, Claudio (1869-1933) – Founding member of the Italian Socialist Party in 1892 and a colleague of Turati. He was editor of *Avanti!* in 1910-12 and a parliamentary deputy 1906-26. In 1917, Treves became a supporter of Italy's national defence through to the end of the war.

Troelstra, Pieter (1860-1930) – Leader of the Dutch Socialist Party from 1894-1924. He made an unsuccessful bid for power during a mass workers' uprising in November 1918.

Trotsky, Leon (Lev Davidovich Bronstein) (1879-1940) – Ukrainian-born revolutionary who joined the socialist movement in 1897. Growing close to Lenin in his youth, he ended up supporting the Mensheviks at the RSDLP Congress in 1903, upset at Lenin's sharp approach. He vacillated amongst the various groups during the period of reaction after 1905, but consistently took an internationalist position. Edited the daily internationalist paper *Nashe Slovo* in Paris during the war. A supporter of the Zimmerwald Left. Trotsky in 1917 recognised the impossibility of unity with the left-wing of the Mensheviks and formally joined the Bolsheviks, where he was very quickly elected to the Central Committee. Together with Lenin, he was one of the main leaders of the Russian revolution and went on to organise the Red Army.

Tsereteli, Irakli (1881-1959) – Menshevik who became a minister in Kerensky's Provisional Government.

Turati, Filippo (1857-1932) – One of the founders and leaders of the Italian Socialist Party. As the party started radicalising to the left in 1912, he emerged as the leading figure of the reformist minority, advocating a collaboration with the liberals and opposing the idea of proletarian revolution.

Vaillant-Couturier, Paul (1892-1937) – Lawyer who joined the French Socialist Party as a soldier in 1916. He was jailed for anti-war articles in 1918. Editor for *l'Humanité* and later editor-in-chief.

Vandervelde, Émile (1866-1938) – Leader of the Belgian Workers' Party and chairman of the Brussels office of the Second International from 1900-14. Member of Belgian Council of Ministers 1916-21.

Volodarsky, V (1891-1918) – Joined the Bund in 1905, before joining the Mensheviks. Exiled in 1911, he lived in Archangel and then Philadelphia. Volodarsky returned to Russia in May 1917 and joined the Mezhraiontsy. This group joined the Bolsheviks in July and he quickly became one of the best agitators in the party, focusing his work around the Putilov Ironworks. He was assassinated by a member of the SRs in June 1918.

Webb, Sidney (1859-1947) and Beatrice (1858-1943) – Founders of the Fabian Society and the major British exponents of reformism.

Kaiser Willhelm II, Friedrich Albert (1859-1941) – Emperor of Germany 1888-1918. He fled to the Netherlands following the November 1918 revolution.

Wurm, Emanuel (1857-1930) – SPD Reichstag member and editor of *Die Neue Zeit* alongside Kaustky.

Zasulich, Vera (1851-1919) – Russian socialist who joined the Narodniks as a young student. She was a member of the editorial board of Iskra alongside Lenin and Plekhanov. After the split in the Russian Social-Democratic Party she soon went over to the Mensheviks. During the war she was a social chauvinist and later held a hostile attitude to the Soviet Government.

Zetkin, Clara (1857-1933) – Joined the German socialist movement in 1878 and was a co-founder of Second International in 1889. A leader of its Marxist wing and close associate of Rosa Luxemburg in the SPD left wing she organised the internationalist conference of socialist women in 1915 before joining the German Communist Party (KPD) in 1919.

Zinoviev, Grigorii Evseyevich (1883-1936) – Founding member of the Bolshevik Party, Lenin's closest collaborator in exile before and during the war.

Groups, periodicals and other terms

Appeal to Reason – Newspaper published by the American socialists, founded in Girard, Kansas, in 1895. It had no official connections with the Socialist Party of America, but it propagated socialist ideas and enjoyed wide popularity among the workers. The paper took up an internationalist position in the First World War.

Avanti! – Central Organ of the Socialist Party of Italy.

Basel Conference – The Basel Congress of the Second International was held on 24-25 November 1912. It was the extraordinary congress called in connection with the Balkan War and the imminent European war. The Congress adopted a manifesto emphasising the imperialist nature of the approaching world war, and called on the socialists of all countries to wage a vigorous struggle against war (reproduced in this volume on p. 371).

Berner Tagwacht (*Berne Reveille*) – Organ of the Social-Democratic Party of Switzerland, published in Berne from 1893.

Bernsteinism – An opportunist trend in German and International Social-Democracy hostile to Marxism. It emerged in Germany at the end of the nineteenth century, and got its name from Eduard Bernstein, a German Social-Democrat, who tried to revise Marx's revolutionary theory on the lines of bourgeois liberalism. Among his supporters in Russia were the legal Marxists, the Economists, the Bund and the Mensheviks.

Birzheviye Vedomosti (*Stock-Exchange Recorder*) – Daily published in St. Petersburg from 1880. Its abbreviated name *Birzhevka*' became a generic term for the unscrupulous and venal bourgeois press.

Bolsheviks – The revolutionary faction in the RSDLP. The word Bolshevik means 'majority' in Russian, a reference to the fact that the Bolsheviks made up a majority at the 1903 Congress. They defended the class independence of the working class in relation to bourgeois parties, implacable firmness in questions of theory, as well as tactical and organisational flexibility.

Brentanoism – A bourgeois reformist theory which "recognised the 'school of capitalism', but rejected the school of the revolutionary class struggle", as Lenin explained. Lujo Brentano, a German bourgeois economist and advocate of so-called 'State Socialism', tried to prove that it was possible to achieve social equality within the capitalist system by means of reforms and the conciliation of the interests of the capitalists and the workers. Under the cloak of Marxist phraseology, Brentano and his followers tried to subordinate the working-class movement to the interests of the bourgeoisie.

British Socialist Party (BSP) – Formed in 1911, the British Socialist Party conducted Marxist propaganda and agitation and was described by Lenin as "not opportunist," and as "really independent of the Liberals." Its small membership and isolation from the masses lent the party a somewhat sectarian character.

Bund – The General Union of Jewish Workers in Lithuania, Poland and Russia, or the Bund, was a secular Jewish socialist party formed in Tsarist Russia aiming to organise Jewish workers. It affiliated to the RSDLP from 1898-1903 and sided with the Mensheviks from 1906.

Cadets – A bourgeois liberal party in tsarist Russia, founded 1905. They advocated for constitutional monarchy, opposed the October Revolution and supported the Whites in the Civil War.

CGT – See General Confederation of Labour.

Copenhagen Congress – The Copenhagen Congress of the Second International was held between 28 August and 3 September 1910, the RSDLP being represented by Lenin, Plekhanov, Lunacharsky and others. The Congress' resolution 'The Struggle Against Militarism and War' confirmed the Stuttgart Congress' resolution on 'Militarism and International Conflicts', which included amendments by Lenin and Rosa Luxemburg calling on the socialists of all countries to use the crisis the war would bring to overthrow their own bourgeoisie.

Die Neue Zeit (*New Times*) – Theoretical organ of the German Social-Democratic Party (SPD), published in Stuttgart from 1883 to 1923.

De Tribune – Organ of the Left wing of the Social-Democratic Labour Party of Holland.

Duma – During the reign of Nicholas II the State Duma was the name given to the national parliament, which only had an advisory role. There were also local dumas, the equivalent of local councils.

Economists, Economism – A tendency that theoretically limited the aspirations of the working class to an economic struggle for higher wages and better working conditions, asserting that further political struggle was the business of the liberal bourgeoisie. They denied the vanguard role of a party with the working class, considering that the party should merely observe the spontaneous process of the movement and register events. Lenin thoroughly tackles this tendency in his classic text *What is to be Done?*

Fabians – Members of the Fabian Society, a British reformist organisation founded in 1884.

French Socialist Party – Founded in 1905 by the merger of the Socialist Party of France led by Guesde and the French Socialist Party led by Jaurès. Dominated by reformists, the party adopted a chauvinist position from the very start of the imperialist war. Its leaders openly supported the war and justified participation in the bourgeois government.

General Confederation of Labour (*Confédération Générale du Travail*) (CGT) (French) – Founded in 1895, strongly influenced by anarcho-syndicalists and reformists. Its leaders recognised only economic struggle, opposed the proletarian party's leadership of the trade union movement, sided with the imperialist bourgeoisie in the First World War and advocated class collaboration and 'defence of the fatherland'.

Gleichheit, Die (*Equality*) – A Social-Democratic fortnightly journal, organ of the German women's movement (it later became the organ of the international women's movement), published in Stuttgart from 1890 to 1925 and edited by Clara Zetkin from 1892 to 1917.

Grütlianer – A newspaper published for Swiss émigrés.

Independent Labour Party (ILP) – Formed in 1893 under such leaders as Keir Hardie and Ramsay MacDonald. At the beginning of the imperialist world war (1914-18) the Independent Labour Party issued a manifesto against the war on 13 August 1914, but later, at the London Conference of Entente Socialists in February 1915, its representatives supported the social-chauvinist resolution adopted by that conference. From that time onward the ILP leaders, under cover of pacifist phrases, continued their social-chauvinist position.

International Socialist Bureau (ISB) – The executive body of the Second International, established by decision of the Paris Congress of 1900. Lenin was the RSDLP representative on the ISB from 1905 until June 1914, after which Litvinov represented the RSDLP, on Lenin's proposal. When the First World War broke out, the ISB became a pliable tool in the hands of the social-chauvinists.

Internationale, Die (The International) – The *Internationale* group, who produced the organ *Die Internationale*, was an internationalist sub-group within the German SPD, formed by Karl Liebknecht, Rosa Luxemburg, Franz Mehring, Clara Zetkin and others at the beginning of the First World War. Soon after, the group denounced the SPD, and formed the Spartacus League (the Spartacists).

Internationale Korrespondenz – A weekly newspaper run by German social-chauvinists which dealt with problems of international politics and the working-class movement. Published in Berlin from 1914 to 1917.

Iskra (The Spark) – The first all-Russian illegal Marxist newspaper, founded by Lenin in 1900. It played a decisive part in the establishment of the revolutionary Marxist party of the working class. Soon after the Second Congress of the RSDLP, the Mensheviks, helped by Plekhanov, gained control of *Iskra* from issue No. 52 onwards.

Izvestia (News) – A daily of the Petrograd Soviet of Workers' and Soldiers' Deputies which first appeared on 28 February (13 March), 1917. The newspaper was controlled by the Mensheviks and Socialist-Revolutionaries for many months, and it often attacked the Bolshevik Party. From 27 October (9 November), 1917, after the Second All-Russia Congress of Soviets, *Izvestia* became the official organ of the Soviet Government.

Izvestia Vserossiiskogo Soveta Krestyanskikh Deputatov (News of the All-Russia Soviet of Peasants' Deputies) – A daily newspaper, the official organ of the All-Russia Soviet of Peasants' Deputies, published in Petrograd from May to December 1917. It expressed the views of the Right wing of the Socialist-Revolutionary Party.

Jugend-Internationale – Organ of the International League of Socialist Youth Organisations.

Kienthal Conference – Held between 24-30 April 1916, this conference was an international meeting of socialists against the war, continuing on the process of clarification and organisation from the Zimmerwald Conference.

l'Humanité – Daily French socialist newspaper founded in 1904 by Jean Jaurès. It was controlled by the socialist right wing during the First World War and followed a chauvinist policy.

La Bataille (*The Battle*) – Organ of the French anarcho-syndicalists who also adopted a social-chauvinist position in the First World War.

Labour Leader – A weekly newspaper founded in 1891. Organ of the ILP from 1893.

Leipziger Volkszeitung (*The Leipzig People's Paper*) – Organ of the Left wing of the German Social-Democratic Party. Published daily from 1894 to 1933. Franz Mehring and Rosa Luxemburg were members of its editorial board. From 1917 to 1922 the *Leipziger Volkszeitung* was the organ of the USPD. In 1922 it became the organ of the Right-wing Social-Democrats.

Liquidationists, liquidators – A set of tendencies within the RSDLP after the 1905 Revolution, where the question of the combining of legal and illegal work came under contention. The Liquidators were split between the 'lefts', who fetishised illegal work, and the 'right', chiefly the Mensheviks, who insisted on solely using legal methods of struggle. These tendencies expressed the mood of impatience caused by the period of reaction. Lenin for some considerable time waged a ruthless struggle against both of these tendencies.

The London Conference of Socialists of the 'allied countries' of the Triple Entente – A conference that met on 14 February 1915. Its delegates represented the social-chauvinists and the pacifist groups of the Socialist parties of Britain, France, Belgium, as well as the Russian Mensheviks and Socialist-Revolutionaries.

Luch (*The Ray*) – The daily newspaper of the liquidator-Mensheviks, published legally in St. Petersburg from September 1912 to July 1913. As Lenin pointed out, it was maintained "by funds provided by rich friends among the bourgeoisie".

Mensheviks – The opposition faction in the Russian Social-Democratic Labour Party (RSDLP). The word Menshevik means 'minority' in Russian. They pursued a policy of class collaboration with the bourgeoisie.

Millerandism (or 'ministerial socialism', or else Ministerialism) – The opportunist tactic of socialists' participation in reactionary bourgeois governments, named after the French Socialist Millerand who joined the bourgeois French government of Waldeck-Rousseau in 1899.

Mysl, Rabochaya (*Worker's Thought*) – Organ of the Economist tendency, published from 1897-1902.

Narodniks – A revolutionary movement active in the 1860s and '70s, led by students and the intelligentsia. Believing the peasantry was the revolutionary class that would overthrow the monarchy, they regarded the village commune as the embryo of socialism. This tactic eventually proved to be a dead end, which provoked the movement to enter into crisis. Out of this movement emerged the *Narodnaya Volya* (*People's Will*) group, which advocated the methods of individual terror. However, Lenin recognised the revolutionary dedication of the early Narodniks and it was out of this movement and through the struggles against it that the early Russian Marxists were formed.

Nasha Zarya (*Our Dawn*) – Legal monthly paper of the Menshevik liquidators.

Nashe Slovo (*Our Word*) – A Russian language socialist internationalist paper published daily in Paris from January 1915 to September 1916, after the military authorities banned *Golos*. One of the main editors of the paper was Trotsky, who attended the Zimmerwald conference as its representative. Other editors were Martov (who broke with it in 1915), Manuilsky, Lozovski, Uritski, Chicherin and Antonov-Ovseyenko. The Bulgarian Christian Rakovsky helped finance the paper.

Neues Leben (*New Life*) – Monthly journal of the Swiss Social-Democratic Party, published in Berne from January 1915 to December 1917. It expressed the views of the Zimmerwald Right and early in 1917 took up a social-chauvinist position.

Novosti – Daily Socialist-Revolutionary Party newspaper published in Paris from August 1914 to May 1915.

Octobrists – The League of October Seventeenth was a counter-revolutionary party of the big merchants, industrialists and big landowners who ran their estates on capitalist lines.

Organising Committee (OC) – The Mensheviks' governing centre, formed at the August conference of Menshevik liquidators and all anti-Party groups and trends in 1912.

Otzovists – A tendency which demanded the recall of the Social-Democratic deputies from the Third Duma (1906-12) and the cessation of activities in legal organisations such as the trade unions, the cooperatives, etc.

Pravda – Legal Bolshevik daily published in St. Petersburg, founded in April 1912. *Pravda* was a popular working-class newspaper, published with money collected by the workers themselves. Lenin directed *Pravda* from exile abroad, writing for the paper almost daily. He gave instructions to the editorial board, and rallied the Party's best literary forces around the newspaper.

Preussische Jahrbücher (Prussian Yearbook) – A conservative monthly of the German capitalists and landowners published in Berlin from 1858 to 1935.

Proletarsky Golos (Proletarian Voice) – Organ of the St. Petersburg Committee of the RSDLP, published underground from February 1915 to December 1916. Four issues appeared. Its first issue published the manifesto of the Central Committee of the RSDLP, entitled 'The War and Russian Social-Democracy'.

Provisional Government – The Russian government established after the February Revolution of 1917, which lasted until the October Revolution of 1917.

Rabochy (The Worker) – The Central Organ of the Bolshevik Party published daily from 25 August (7 September) to 2 (15) September 1917 instead of *Pravda*, which was closed down by the Provisional Government.

Rech (Speech) – Central Organ of the Cadet Party. Published from 1906 until it was shut down by the Petrograd Soviet on 8 November 1917.

Russian Social-Democratic Labour Party (RSDLP) – The Russian Marxist party formed in 1898 in Minsk. It united the various isolated revolutionary groups in Russia into a single, unified party based on the principles of Marxism. At its Second Congress, the party was divided into the Bolshevik and Menshevik factions. Until 1917, the Bolshevik Party went under the name, Russian Social-Democratic Labour Party (Bolsheviks), abbreviated as RSDLP(B).

Russkaya Volya (Russian Freedom) – A daily paper funded by the big banks in Moscow. It was printed from December 1916 until shortly after the November Revolution.

Shiroki (Broad) Socialists – An opportunist trend within the Bulgarian Social-Democratic Party.

Second International (or Socialist International) – Founded in 1889 as the successor to the First International that had been founded by Marx and Engels in 1864. In 1914, almost all national sections of the International supported 'their own' imperialist governments in the First World War, and the International collapsed.

Social-Democracy – All the revolutionary Marxists were called Social Democrats before the outbreak of the First World War in 1914. The name Social-Democracy was sullied by the fact the majority of the old leaders supported the war. It was in 1919, with the creation of the Communist Third International that the genuine Marxists began to call themselves Communists.

Social-Democratic Labour Group (Germany) – An organisation of German Centrists founded in March 1916 by Reichstag members who had broken with the Social-Democratic Reichstag group. It had the support of the majority of the Berlin organisation and became the backbone of the Independent Social-Democratic Party of Germany (USPD), founded in April 1917. The new party sought to justify avowed social-chauvinists and advocated preservation of unity with them.

Socialist-Revolutionary Party (SRs) – A petty-bourgeois party founded in Russia in late 1901 and early 1902 as a result of the amalgamation of various Narodnik groups and circles. Their views were an eclectic hodgepodge of Narodnik and revisionist ideas.

Sotsial-Demokrat – Central organ of the RSDLP, published as an underground newspaper from February 1908 to January 1917. It featured more than eighty articles and other items by Lenin, who became its editor in December 1911.

Sovremenny Mir (*The Contemporary World*) – A literary, scientific and political monthly published in St. Petersburg from 1906 to 1918. The Mensheviks, including Plekhanov, were frequent contributors. Bolsheviks also contributed to the magazine during the period of the bloc with Plekhanov's group of pro-Party Mensheviks. During the war, it became the organ of the social-chauvinists.

Sozialistische Monatshefte (*Socialist Monthly*) – Chief organ of the German Social-Democratic opportunists and an organ of international opportunism. During the First World War it took a social-chauvinist stand.

Tesnyaki ('Narrow') – The revolutionary tendency of the Social-Democratic Labour Party of Bulgaria, formed in 1903 after a breakaway from the Social-Democratic Party. Dimitr Blagoyev, founder and leader of the Tesnyaki, was succeeded by his followers Georgi Dimitrov and Vasil Kolarov. During 1914-18, the Tesnyaki opposed the imperialist war. In 1919 it affiliated to the Communist International and formed the Communist Party of Bulgaria.

Tribunists – Left group in the Social-Democratic Labour Party of Holland which in 1907 published the newspaper *De Tribune*. In 1909, the Tribunists were expelled from the Social-Democratic Labour Party of Holland and organised an independent party (the Social-Democratic Party of Holland). The Tribunists were not a consistently revolutionary party, but they represented the Left wing of the working-class movement of Holland. In 1918 the Tribunists formed the Communist Party of Holland.

Trudoviks – A revolutionary group of peasants and intellectuals supporting a revolutionary agrarian program for the peasantry, to fully integrate them into a capitalist Russia. Most Trudoviks took a social-chauvinist position to the war.

Ultimatumists – A variant of Otzovism.

Volksrecht (*People's Right*) – Daily organ of the Swiss Social-Democratic Party founded in Zürich.

Vorwärts (*Forwards*) – Central Organ of the German Social-Democratic Party, published daily in Berlin from 1891 to 1933. Engels wrote for *Vorwärts*. In Russia, it backed the Economists and then, after the split in the Party, the Mensheviks. During the First World War, *Vorwärts* took a social-chauvinist stand, its later articles were against the October Revolution.

Yedinstvo – A small group of extreme right Menshevik defencists. It was organised in March 1917, headed by Plekhanov and others. The Yedinstvo group denied the possibility of a victorious socialist revolution in Russia and supported the Provisional Government. It stood for the war being carried on to 'complete victory' and often hounded the Bolsheviks for their internationalist stand.

Zimmerwald Conference – The first conference of internationalist socialists, held in Zimmerwald, Switzerland, on 5-8 September 1915. A struggle flared up at the conference between the Kautskyite centrist majority and the revolutionary internationalists headed by Lenin. At the conference, Lenin organised the internationalists into the Zimmerwald Left group.

Zimmerwald Left – Formed by Lenin at the first socialist conference of internationalists at Zimmerwald, Switzerland, in early September 1915. It was, Lenin said, the first step in the development of the internationalist movement against the war. The group also included a number of inconsistent internationalists.

Titles by Wellred Books

Wellred Books is a publishing house specialising in works of Marxist theory. Among the titles we publish are:

Anti-Dühring, Friedrich Engels

Bolshevism: The Road to Revolution, Alan Woods

Chartist Revolution, Rob Sewell

China: From Permanent Revolution to Counter-Revolution, John Peter Roberts

The Civil War in France, Karl Marx

Class Struggle in the Roman Republic, Alan Woods

The Class Struggles in France, 1848-1850, Karl Marx

The Classics of Marxism: Volumes One & Two, Various authors

Dialectics of Nature, Friedrich Engels

The Eighteenth Brumaire of Louis Bonaparte, Karl Marx

The First Five Years of the Communist International, Leon Trotsky

The First World War: A Marxist Analysis of the Great Slaughter, Alan Woods

Germany: From Revolution to Counter-Revolution, Rob Sewell

Germany 1918-1933: Socialism or Barbarism, Rob Sewell

History of British Trotskyism, Ted Grant

Stalin, Leon Trotsky

The State and Revolution, VI Lenin

Ted Grant: The Permanent Revolutionary, Alan Woods

Ted Grant Writings: Volumes One and Two, Ted Grant

Thawra hatta'l nasr! - Revolution until Victory!, Alan Woods & others

What Is Marxism?, Rob Sewell & Alan Woods

What Is to Be Done?, VI Lenin

Women, Family and the Russian Revolution,
   John Roberts & Fred Weston

Writings on Britain, Leon Trotsky

To make an order or for more information, visit wellred-books.com, email books@wellred-books.com or write to Wellred Books, 124 City Road, London, EC1V 2NX, United Kingdom.